Computer Technology Encyclopedia: Quick Reference for Students and Professionals

Michael Graves

⁂ DELMAR
CENGAGE Learning™

Australia • Brazil • Japan • Korea • Mexico • Singapore • Spain • United Kingdom • Ur

DELMAR
CENGAGE Learning™

Computer Technology Encyclopedia: Quick Reference for Students and Professionals

Michael Graves

Vice President, Career and Professional Editorial: Dave Garza

Director of Learning Solutions: Matthew Kane

Acquisitions Editor: Nick Lombardi

Managing Editor: Marah Bellegarde

Senior Product Manager: Michelle Ruelos Cannistraci

Editorial Assistant: Sarah Pickering

Vice President, Career and Professional Marketing: Jennifer McAvey

Marketing Director: Deborah Yarnell

Marketing Manager: Erin Coffin

Marketing Coordinator: Shanna Gibbs

Production Director: Carolyn Miller

Production Manager: Andrew Crouth

Content Project Manager: Andrea Majot

Art Director: Kun-Tee Chang / Benj Gleeksman

For product information and technology assistance, contact us at **Professional & Career Group Customer Support, 1-800-648-7450**
For permission to use material from this text or product, submit all requests online at **cengage.com/permissions**.
Further permissions questions can be e-mailed to **permissionrequest@cengage.com**.

Microsoft ® is a registered trademark of the Microsoft Corporation.
Library of Congress Control Number: 2008934855
ISBN-13: 978-1-4283-2236-3
ISBN-10: 1-4283-2236-1

Delmar
5 Maxwell Drive
Clifton Park, NY 12065-2919
USA

Cengage Learning products are represented in Canada by Nelson Education, Ltd.

For your lifelong learning solutions, visit **delmar.cengage.com**
Visit our corporate website at **cengage.com**.

Notice to the Reader
Publisher does not warrant or guarantee any of the products described herein or perform any independent analysis in connection with any of the product information contained herein. Publisher does not assume, and expressly disclaims, any obligation to obtain and include information other than that provided to it by the manufacturer. The reader is expressly warned to consider and adopt all safety precautions that might be indicated by the activities described herein and to avoid all potential hazards. By following the instructions contained herein, the reader willingly assumes all risks in connection with such instructions. The publisher makes no representations or warranties of any kind, including but not limited to, the warranties of fitness for particular purpose or merchantability, nor are any such representations implied with respect to the material set forth herein, and the publisher takes no responsibility with respect to such material. The publisher shall not be liable for any special, consequential, or exemplary damages resulting, in whole or part, from the readers' use of, or reliance upon, this material.

Printed in Canada
2 3 4 5 6 7 12 11 10 09 08

Contents

Introduction

These days, any attempt to write a full-blown encyclopedia or dictionary of computer terminology would be an exercise in futility. New terms and buzzwords appear every day, and information technology fields overlap with so many other fields it can be hard to determine if a word is IT, telecommunications, or graphics arts, and so on. It's hard to specialize in a field that has absorbed so many other techonologies.

This book is intended to be a portable guide, not a full-blown dictionary. The intent of the author was to provide a tool that the average PC hardware technician or network specialist could use to look up the occasional word or acronym that temporarily vacated the brain cells. It is a cross between a dictionary and an encyclopedia. Some terms get full treatment with mini-articles written. Others are used so commonly that a simple one- or two-line description seemed sufficient.

Because the idea was for a compact book and not one that required a dedicated shelf in the library, a great deal of selectivity was employed. Common words and acronyms, protocols, and a few significant company names are included. With very few exceptions, people are not.

Organization

This encyclopedia is divided into three sections. In the first section, the author defines a number of terms that are entirely numeric. In the computer industry, two profession- als can have an entire conversation consisting of acronyms and numbers. The number section defines some of the more commonly encountered numeric terms. The second consists of a collection of approximately 3,800 terms that are frequently encountered by professionals in the field. Along with the technically correct definitions for each term, where appropriate; alternate slang usage is also included. While accurate knowledge of your vocabulary is essential, if you intend to communicate with your peers, you need to know the inside "definitions" as well.

Section three consists of around 750 commonly used acronyms. This is a scaled-down acronym listing. To include every acronym known in the computer industry would result in a volume that could bring the average desk crashing down. Here, I tried to limit the listings to only those that were likely to be encountered by an average hardware technician or network engineer.

Target Audience

Anyone who works in the computer industry encounters words, acronyms, and slang that are new to them on a daily basis. Hardware technicians, network engineers, and most especially students just getting started in the computer industry will benefit by having an adequate collection of definitions they can reference. This book is intended for those people.

Teachers who present classes in PC Hardware, Networking Basics, Server Management, and Basic Programming will do their students a great favor by including this book along with the standard textbook for the class.

Acknowledgments

The author and Delmar Cengage Learning would like to thank the following reviewers for their input and suggestions during the development of this book.

David E. Yeary
North Lawrence Career Center
Bedford, IN

Kim Doane
Mott Community College
Flint, MI

Ronald E. Koci
Madison Area Technical College
Madison, WI 53704

NUMERIC ENTRIES

10-gigabit Ethernet   Known as 10GbE for short, this is a version of Ethernet that supports up to 10,000 Mb/s, based on the 802.3ae specifications. A key technology switch from older forms of Ethernet and GbE is that GbE, by default, is full duplex. It cannot switch to half duplex or simplex modes. Also, GbE no longer makes use of carrier sense multiple access/collision detection (CSMA/CD) as a method for gaining access to the wire. GbE Fibre Channel is a fiber optics protocol that is capable of distances surpassing 40 km. By the time you read this, it is likely that devices capable of transmitting a signal in excess of 80 km will be on the market.

10/100   A device that is able to automatically switch communications speeds between 10 Mb/s and 100 Mb/s. Examples are 10/100 hubs, 10/100 switches, and 10/100 network adapter cards. Speeds are negotiated during a handshaking process. During the handshake, each device transmits its capabilities to the other. The faster device clocks itself down to the speed of the slower one.

100   One of the status codes for Hypertext Transfer Protocol (HTTP). It lets the client know that it can continue with its request. The server has received the request, acknowledged it, and approved the client for further processing. If the initial request was not completely contained within the client's initial transmission, it should immediately transmit the remainder of the request.

1000BaseCX   Gigabit Ethernet over copper wiring. This is now an obsolete standard, having been replaced by 1000BaseT. Its biggest limitation was that it could only run over 25 m or shorter segments.

1000BaseLX   Gigabit Ethernet over single-mode fiber. Using high-power laser diodes, this medium can be run up to 70 km. Table 1 lists four different modes of 1000BaseLX.

TABLE 1
The modes of 1000BaseLX

FIBER DIAMETER	BANDWIDTH (MHz)	DISTANCE (Meters)
62.5 µ multimode	500	550
50 µ multimode	400	500
50 µ multimode	500	550
9 µ single mode	N/A	5000

1000BaseSX   Gigabit Ethernet over multimode fiber. Using high-power laser diodes, this medium can be run up to 2 km. Table 2 lists four different modes of 1000BaseSX.

TABLE 2
The modes of 1000BaseSX

FIBER DIAMETER	BANDWIDTH (MHz)	DISTANCE (Meters)
62.5 μ multimode	160	220
62.5 μ multimode	200	275
50 μ multimode	400	500
50 μ multimode	500	550

1000BaseT   Gigabit Ethernet over twisted pair cable. Wiring for 1000BaseT must be category (Cat) 5e at a minimum. Cat 6 is preferred. This standard is very popular for local area networks, but without a repeater, an individual segment is limited to 100 m. 1000BaseT is a ratified standard of the Institute of Electrical and Electronic Engineers (IEEE).

1000BaseTX   Gigabit Ethernet over two pairs of data-grade twisted pair cabling. The reasoning behind this proposed protocol was to provide a less expensive interface for using Cat 6 cable. It never really got off the ground and never received the blessing of IEEE. The accepted gigabit protocol for twisted pair is 1000BaseT.

100BaseT   100-Mb Ethernet over twisted pair cable. Limited to 100-m segments without a repeater. For a number of years, this has been the most popular networking architecture for the local area network (LAN). Recently, 1000BaseT has started chipping away at its popularity.

100BaseT4   100-Mb Ethernet over four pairs of telephone-grade twisted pair wiring. Useful for running 100-Mb Ethernet in places where a higher quality cable cannot be run.

100BaseTX   100-Mb Ethernet over two pairs of data-grade twisted pair cabling. Without a repeater, a segment is limited to 100 m. This protocol saw very little implementation and was not officially ratified by IEEE.

100BaseFX   100-Mb Ethernet over a pair of fiber optic cables. Although the speed certainly does not take advantage of the capabilities of fiber, its main reason for existence is that it makes it possible to have a 2-km link between two different 100-Mb networks.

100VG-AnyLAN   A now-discontinued form of Fast Ethernet that used an intelligent hub to manage traffic on the network.

10Base2   10-Mb Ethernet over thinnet coaxial cable. Cable runs up to 180 m are possible.

10Base5   10-Mb Ethernet over thicknet coaxial cable. Cable runs up to 500 m are possible. A device called a *vampire clamp* is used to tap into the wire.

10BaseT   10-Mb Ethernet over twisted pair cable. Without a repeater, a segment is limited to 100 m.

101   An HTTP status code that notifies the server that the client is about to switch protocols. The HTTP protocol includes an upgrade field in the header of each packet. If it is advantageous to change to a protocol and both devices have indicated that they support the intended protocol, the server initiates the change by issuing a 101 message. Even if a newer protocol is available to both devices, the switch will not happen if no advantage will be gained. The latency of changing protocols is more costly in terms of performance than is the use of an older protocol in many cases.

101 keyboard   The once-standard layout for a computer keyboard consisting of a cluster of character keys, twelve function keys at the top, another cluster of navigation keys, and a numeric keypad on the right. Although you would not think of keyboards as something requiring standards, there are some specific tolerances to the keys. Spacing between keys is .75″ from center to center. With the exception of the space between the A-row and the Q-row, key rows are separated by a distance of .375″. The A- and Q-rows are separated by a distance of .188″. Today's keyboards have so many variations that the old 101-key model shown in Figure 1 is becoming obsolete. After all, how can we live without our Internet shortcut keys?

FIGURE 1   The Standard 101-key keyboard.

1394   The IEEE specification for Firewire. *See* **Firewire** for more specific details.

16-bit   A device, operating system, or piece of software that is designed to process code 16 bits at a time. This evolved from the fact that the original central processing unit (CPU) used on IBM-compatible computers made use of 16-bit registers. For many years after 32-bit and then 64-bit systems were common, legacy applications required that everything be compatible with 16-bit registers.

16-bit color   A graphics adapter setting that allocates a total of 16 bits to all three of the colors. Two different methods have been used for dividing the bits three ways. One method allocates 5 bits per color and drops the 16th bit. This leaves a total of 32,768 possible colors. The second method allocates 5 bits each to red and blue and 6 bits to green. This method provides up to 65,536 possible colors. 16-bit color was frequently referred to as *High Color*.

16450 An earlier version of the universal asynchronous receiver transmitter (UART) chip that was capable of a maximum speed of 9,600 bits per second. It was a real speed demon.

16550 A version of UART chip that was capable of a maximum speed of 115,200 bits per second. This is often the UART of choice for many 56K modems.

16650 A version of UART chip that was capable of a maximum speed of 430,800 bits per second. Frequently used in proprietary serial devices.

16750 A version of UART chip that was capable of a maximum speed of 961,600 bits per second. Used almost exclusively in proprietary serial devices, but also shows up as the integrated UART on some motherboards.

16850 A version of UART chip that was capable of a maximum speed of 1.5 Mb/s. Used on some high-speed serial devices and some motherboard designs.

1GL First-generation language, where the number indicates the generation. In general, the higher the generation number, the more closely the programming language approximates human communication.

    1GL Machine language (the code of the hardware)

    2GL Assembly languages

    3GL Programming languages

    4GL Statements on the level of human language

    5GL Visually augmented languages, such as Microsoft's Visual Basic

200 An HTTP code that indicates the successful transmission of a client's request. The server's response will include any one of a variety of pieces of information, depending on the type of request originally made by the client. For example, if the client issued a GET request; the server will respond with a 200 response code; if there is sufficient room in the response packet's payload, it may include the data requested by the client.

201 An HTTP code that indicates that a request has been successfully fulfilled and that the device has been reset for a new session. This generally occurs when a new resource must be called or created by the server to fulfill the client's request. In general, the 201 response packet will include at a minimum the location of the new resource and a listing of that resource's characteristics relevant to the communications session. Before responding with a 201 packet, the server must create the resource or the pointer to the resource and include that information in the response packet. If it cannot accomplish this in a timely manner before responding, the server will respond with a 202 response packet instead.

202 An HTTP code that indicates that a request has been accepted, but not yet processed by the receiving device. At this point, once the 202 packet has been transmitted, the server still has the option of denying the request, based on the results of further processing of the request. This number is also the area code for Washington, DC.

204 An HTTP code that indicates that there was no content with which to respond from the target device. It is possible that the 204 response packet might contain new and/or updated information relevant to the client's request. It will never include user data; therefore, it is rarely seen by the user and requires no user response.

205 An HTTP code that instructs the client machine that the client's request has been received and processed. It tells the client to reset the page view to include the content contained in the transmission. The primary purpose for this response code is to allow for user input on a page and then refresh the page to reflect the input provided by the user. It may also respond by clearing the form to accommodate additional user input.

206   An HTTP code that indicates that a device is responding with a portion, but not all, of the content requested by the client. This response is only possible when the original request included a RANGE field in the header that specified a desired array of information. The 206 response will include a header that tells the client what part of the requested range is being fulfilled, the date of transmission, location-specific data indicating the source of the information provided, and an "expiration date" for the request. If the remaining data cannot be provided by this time, the request will be abandoned.

24-bit   The use of 24 bits to represent a single iteration or value. A 24-bit string can represent any one of 16,777,216 values. In the CPU industry, a 24-bit memory register was used with the 80386 and 80486 microprocessors. Therefore, those processors could address up to 16,777,216 bytes of address space. 24-bit color (also known as *True Color*) is capable of registering up to 16,777,216 colors.

24-bit color   A configuration for display adapters that allocates 8 bits per color. This setting allows for the maximum display setting of 16,777,216 colors. This is also the setting referred to as *True Color* in Windows. The colors are derived by assigning 8 bits to each of the three primary colors. This allows for up to 256 variations on each color. When blended together, the combined value is 256 raised to the power of three, resulting in the value previously given. Realistically speaking, the human eye can see less than 15,000 individual hues.

24/7   Indicates that a device or resource must be available twenty-four hours a day, seven days a week.

2600   A signal originally transmitted over a telephone line (at 2,600 Hz) to indicate that a line is free. This is not seen by the end user, but lets the device know that it is able to dial. When unethical people started transmitting a 2,600-Hz signal down a line in order to get free telephone service, the telephone companies moved on to other methods.

286   A shortened term for the Intel 80286 microprocessor used in IBM AT and AT-compatible computers. *See* **80286** for a more detailed description.

287   A shortened term for the Intel 80287 math coprocessor, designed to accompany the 80286 microprocessor.

2GL   Second-generation programming language. This is generally accepted as the assembly language, or the language recognized by the processor's *decode unit* to initiate and execute low-level commands. The assembly language commands are in plain text so that programmers understand them. *See* **1GL** for a list of all language generations.

3.5" floppy   A form of removable storage that was able to store 720 KB, 1.44 MB, or 2.88 MB of data (depending on the device and medium used). A 3.5" floppy drive needed to be installed into a computer in order to make use of a 3.5" diskette. Figure 2 shows a 3.5" floppy disk drive and Figure 3 is a photo of a 3.5" floppy diskette. Floppy disks had a long and fruitful life and served well as emergency boot devices. They still appear on new computers as of this writing but are rapidly giving way to flash drives as a removable storage mechanism. Floppy diskettes were very susceptible to damage and even a small amount of electromagnetic radiation was capable of corrupting the data store on them.

300 An HTTP code that indicates there were multiple possible responses to the user's request. Each response requires redirection to a different location. Sufficient information is provided to allow the user to select the appropriate alternative and respond to the server's alert. HTTP programming allows for automated response to this code; however, there is no uniform standard by which an automated response is generated. Therefore, the general preference is toward manual response.

301 An HTTP code that indicates the requested resource has been permanently moved. This code is used by redirecting software to forward the request to the appropriate address. In general, the 301 response packet will contain the forwarding uniform resource locator (URL), when available. This information is in the form of a forwarding hyperlink.

302 An HTTP code that indicates that the requested information was found but is in a different location. The 302 code differs from the 301 code in that 302 indicates a temporary relocation of the resource. Therefore, the user or client software should not permanently alter any hyperlinks or bookmarks pointing to the originally requested URL. The response packet generally includes a hyperlink to the current location and automatically redirects the client.

303 An HTTP code indicating that the response to the client request is actually found under a different URL. This is a user-transparent response to a request that automatically redirects the client to a different location. This information will not be cached; however, the resulting URL opened by the client is cacheable.

304 An HTTP code that indicates that a local copy of the requested material is present in cache. This prevents the client software from tying up bandwidth downloading-redundant material. The message is transparent to the user and simply redirects the client to the local cache.

305 An HTTP code that indicates that the requested resource can only be accessed to an approved proxy. A LOCATION field in the response packet may provide the proxy address. The client software will automatically repeat the request through

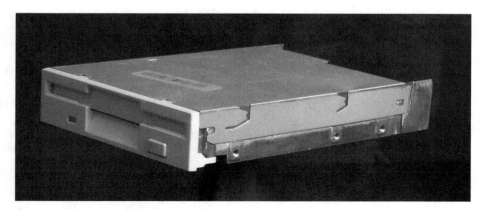

FIGURE 2   A 3.5" floppy disk drive.

FIGURE 3   A 3.5" floppy diskette.

this proxy. If the appropriate permissions are present, the user will be allowed access to the resource.

306   A currently unused HTTP code. Although used by the original version of HTTP as a switch proxy, current versions do not use it. The code is reserved for future use.

307   An HTTP code that temporarily redirects the client to a different URL. The temporary URL may or may not be cacheable, depending on the contents of a cache-control field. The header will contain a hypertext field with a hyperlink to the temporary URL and the user will be transparently redirected to the new site.

32-bit   Any device or software designed specifically to run four bytes of code at a time. IBM's OS2 was the first true 32-bit operating system (OS) designed to run on a personal computer (PC). Some hybrid operating systems, such as Windows 9x, made use of some 32-bit code and some 16-bit code. The 80386 microprocessor was Intel's first 32-bit CPU. A 32-bit value is capable of representing up to 4,294,967,296 values. The 32-bit memory address of the Intel CPU could address up to 4,294,967,296 bytes of data, or 4 gigabytes.

32-bit color   A display adapter setting that provides 8 bits per color plus an 8-bit alpha channel. This allows the same 16,777,216 colors provided by 24-bit color, and the alpha channel provides additional color effects such as transparency, haziness, or texture to be added. The 32-bit color is also called *True Color* (32-bit). The use of 32-bit display settings on a computer system that does not use a coprocessed graphics adapter can noticeably slow down performance.

32-bit disk access   A Windows 3.x disk driver that bypassed all DOS drivers and accessed disks directly using a 32-bit driver. You might also see the term *FastDisk* used with this driver setting. It was the source of frequent headaches for administrators attempting to support legacy DOS applications in the WIN3x environment. All modern operating systems use 32-bit disk access, but since that is the default and not an "advanced" setting, it has no effect on the system.

33.3   A modem setting that provided maximum data throughput of 33,400 bits per second, which was why it was called *33.3*. It was the speed supported by the V.94 protocol.

386   A shortened term for Intel's 80386 microprocessor. This was one of Intel's first chips to come with several different variations in design. *See* **80386** for a more detailed description.

386 Enhanced Mode   An operating mode of Windows 3.x that took full advantage of the "advanced" features of the 80386 microprocessor. Enhanced Mode was required by these early versions of the Windows OS in order to provide virtual memory services. In theory, this operating mode allowed for older MS-DOS applications to be multitasked. In reality, all it allowed was task switching. When configured to run in enhanced mode, Windows would load an extended memory driver (HIMEM.SYS), an enhanced kernel file (WIN386.EXE), and the three files of the 386 kernel. These files were KRNL386.EXE, USER.EXE, and GDI.EXE. Where there were choices available, the system would also load 32-bit drivers in place of 16-bit options. In order to provide multitasking of Windows applications, virtual machines were created that separated Windows applications from DOS applications.

386DX   A full-blown 80386 with 32-bit internal and external data busses (EDBs) and a 32-bit address bus.

386SX   An 80386 designed to run on 16-bit platforms. It had a 32-bit internal data bus and a 32-bit memory address, but the EDB was limited to 16 bits, so older platforms could use the chip.

386SL   A lower-voltage 80386SX that was designed for portable computers.

387   A shortened name for the 80387 math coprocessor designed to run alongside the 80386 microprocessor.

3D   Three-dimensional. The term refers to any graphics device or application that is capable of rendering an image to appear to possess all three dimensions of the "real world," which, by the way, counting time, actually has four.

3D accelerator   An auxiliary card that installs in a computer that runs alongside a video card that greatly enhances the speed of 3D rendition. For the most part, modern graphics cards have 3D acceleration built into their chipset, making a secondary device unnecessary.

3gp   A file compression format used for audio and video data transmitted over a cell phone. In was introduced in the MPEG4 file compression protocol. In order to play back a 3gp file, you must have a media player that supports the format. The 3gp files are of considerably poorer quality than other audio or graphics file formats because of the extreme degree of compression used. This loss of quality is considered acceptable since the device on which the file is intended for use isn't capable of rendering much better quality.

400   An HTTP code indicating a bad request.

401   An HTTP code telling you that you are not authorized for access. This can come from a Web site that allows only authorized users, or it can come from a configured firewall if a site contains content blocked by the firewall.

402   An HTTP code indicating that payment is required to gain access. The server was unable to access a properly authorized charging source to validate your request.

403   An HTTP code that means access is forbidden. Similar to code 401.

404   An HTTP code that means the resource you requested was not found. It may mean the Web page you are looking for has moved or been deleted. But it might also simply mean that the site is in the process of being updated. If you try again later, it might be there.

405   An HTTP code that means the method your client used to make a request was not recognized or is not allowed. Not much you can do about this one.

407   An HTTP code that means proxy authorization is required before you will be allowed in. It means direct access by your computer is not allowed.

408   An HTTP code that means there has been a request timeout. Too much time elapsed between the time you made the request and the current time. It could mean the server is down. You might have different results if you try again later.

416   An HTTP code that means "Request Range Not Satisfiable." The server cannot process partial responses and the full range of information you requested is no longer available.

486   A shortened term for the Intel 80486 microprocessor. This was little more than a 386 on steroids. There was no increase in bus speed or address bus size, but Intel added a math coprocessor and some Level 1 (L1) cache.

487   A shortened name for the 80487 math coprocessor designed to run alongside the 80486SX microprocessor. The 80486DX, DX2, and DX4 processors didn't need one because the circuitry was built into the chip on those three designs.

486DX2   A later generation of 80486 microprocessor on which the internal data bus was capable of running at twice the speed of the EDB.

486DX4   A later generation of 80486 microprocessor on which the internal data bus was capable of running at three times the speed of the EDB. With a name like DX4 you would expect it to run three times faster, would you not?

486SX   This is a scaled-down Intel 80486 microprocessor that is missing the math coprocessor. An interesting side note is that the circuitry for the math coprocessor existed on all 486 chips. Intel simply took an extra step in processing to disable the feature in the SX and SL series of chips.

486SX2   A scaled down 486DX2 that was missing the math coprocessor.

486SL   The SL was a low-voltage 486SX microprocessor designed for use in portable computers.

50/50/90 rule   Many times in life we encounter situations in which there are only two choices, one of which is the correct choice. The 50/50/90 rule states that if you should be able to expect a 50 percent chance of making the correct choice, there is a 90 percent chance you will get it wrong. This is a simplification of nature. In reality, the chances of correctly selecting a 50/50 shot are inversely proportional to the negative impact of making the wrong choice.

500   An HTTP code that means there has been an internal server error.

501   An HTTP code that means "not implemented." You may get this error message when you attempt to access a server on which a specific service required is either not installed or not working properly.

505   An HTTP code that means your version of HTTP is not supported. This error is most likely to occur when your client is running a new version of HTTP and attempts to access a very old Web server that has not been upgraded.

5.25″ floppy   A form of removable storage that was able to store 360 kB or 1.2 MB of data (depending on the device and medium used). A 5.25″ floppy drive needed to

FIGURE 4   A 5.25" floppy diskette.

be installed into a computer in order to make use of a 5.25" diskette. Figure 4 is a photo of a 5.25" floppy diskette. The 5.25" floppy disappeared from the computing scene by the early 1990s. Floppy diskettes were very susceptible to damage and even a small amount of *electromagnetic radiation* was capable of corrupting the data stored on them. In addition, 5.25" diskettes were very flexible and not very resistant to physical damage.

56K   A modem speed that supports up to 53.3K downloads and 33.6K uploads, which is why it was called *56K*. This is the speed supported by both the V.90 and V.92 protocols.

568A   A wiring standard that defines the pattern of termination for eight-conductor RJ-48 terminals on twisted pair cable. Of the 568A and 568B patterns, the 568A is the least commonly used. Figure 5 illustrates the 568A wiring scheme.

568B   A wiring standard that defines the pattern of termination for eight-conductor RJ-48 terminals on twisted pair cable. Of the 568A and 568B patterns, the 568B is the most commonly used. Figure 6 illustrates the 568B wiring scheme.

586   What the Pentium chip would have been called if the courts had not decided that Intel could not trademark a number. So the 586 became the Pentium.

5x86   A term used by Cyrix for a Pentium-compatible CPU.

64-bit   Computer software or hardware that is capable of processing data in 64-bit (or 8-byte) chunks. From a hardware standpoint, a 64-bit system would have a 64-bit microprocessor and a 64-bit expansion bus, along with 64-bit memory. A 64-bit value is capable of 18,446,744,073,709,551,616 iterations. A 64-bit memory bus is therefore theoretically capable of addressing up to 18 *exabytes* of memory. However current hardware and software limitations impose a far more modest ceiling on our capabilities. A 64-bit expansion bus can move 8 bytes of data with each transfer. Since this is double that of a 32-bit bus, the bandwidth is doubled without increasing *clock speed*. From a software standpoint, the ability to use

64-bit registers on a 64-bit CPU and 64-bit pointers in the OS reduces the number of processing cycles required to perform most operations. In addition, a 64-bit instruction set is capable of far more complex instructions, in addition to a much greater potential number of instructions.

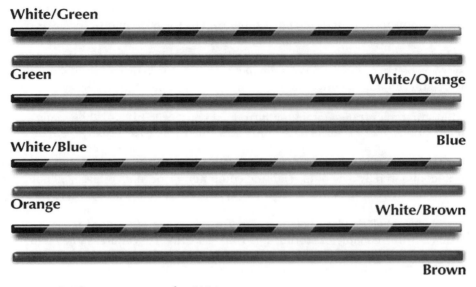

FIGURE 5   The wiring pattern for 568A.

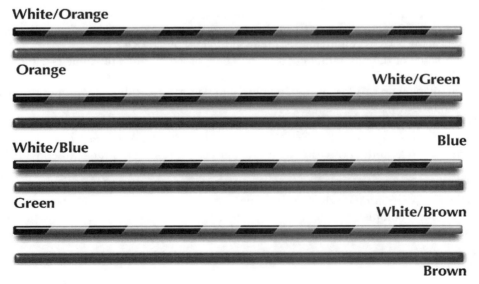

FIGURE 6   The wiring pattern for 568B.

640K   The original MS-DOS limitation for memory that could be used for applications or user data. This area of memory is also called *conventional memory*. This was based on the *20-bit* memory address of the 8088 microprocessor used on the original IBM PC. The 20-bit address space was capable of addressing up to 1 MB of total memory. 384K of that memory was allocated to *high memory* to be used by system hardware, which left 640K.

640K barrier   A memory limitation imposed on MS-DOS that allowed it to access only the 640K of *conventional memory* supported by the 8088 microprocessor. This is also the memory limitation of *real mode* processing. An MS-DOS program could only run in conventional memory. Therefore, when Windows and other operating systems began to make use of *extended memory*, these programs had to think they were still running in conventional memory. *Virtual machines* were used to keep each DOS program running in its own environment.

701   IBM's first mainframe computer, introduced on April 7, 1953. While many publications give a release date of April 29, 1952, this was actually the date on which the project was announced only. It would take another year to get the first model out the door. Among its various claims to fame was the fact that it was the first commercially available scientific computer. Prior to its release, all computers were handmade giants that were the property of either the government or a research organization. Another first for the 701 was that it was the first device to use electronically addressable memory, a predecessor of random access memory (RAM). It was capable of storing 2,048 36-bit words. This addressable memory consisted of 72 vacuum tubes. It could perform 16,000 single integer operations per second. The machine consisted of eleven individual devices that hooked together to make a single computer and took up enough space to fill a small office. It also generated enough heat to keep that office warm in the winter. You were on your own in the summer. However, if you could afford the $16,000 per month that it cost to lease one, you could afford the electric bill to keep yourself cool in the summer.

8.3 naming convention   A file-naming scheme used by earlier *16-bit* file systems that permitted file names of up to eight characters, plus an extension of up to three characters. An example of an 8.3 named file is NOVEL.DOC.

8-bit   A value or data path that consists of 8 bits, or a *byte*. An 8-bit value is capable of 256 iterations. Therefore, an 8-bit character set can have 256 characters; 8-bit color can display up to 256 values of a color; and so forth. The standard computer byte is an 8-bit string.

8-bit color   A graphics adapter setting that allocates a total of 8 bits between all three colors, allowing for a total of 256 colors. This was *not* the standard Video Graphics Array (VGA) setting of yesteryear. The old VGA cards used three 6-bit converters that provided a total of 262,144 colors, 256 of which could be used at any given time.

80/20 rule   A variation on the law of diminishing returns. The 80/20 rule basically says that, for a complex problem in computing, 80 percent of the problem can be solved using 20 percent of the code you will need to solve 100 percent of the problem.

802 standards   In February 1980, the Institute of Electrical and Electronic Engineers created a series of committees whose responsibility it would be to review new technologies in different areas of computer networking. Because the committees were formed in the second month of 1980, they became named the 802 committees. The standards ratified by these committees are known as the 802 standards.

- **802.1** LAN/MAN Bridging and Management. Covers different Internet working standards as well as the Spanning Tree Algorithm.
- **802.2** Logic Link Control (LLC). As its name suggests, this committee oversees the standards used by the LLC sublayer of the Data Link Layer.
- **802.3** CSMA/CD Access Method. Sometimes simply called *Ethernet*. This committee keeps up with the different advances in Ethernet technology.
- **802.4** Token-Passing Bus Access Method. A bus network that used a token-passing method of media access. This committee is no longer active.
- **802.5** Token Ring Access Method. A ring network that uses a token-passing method of media access.
- **802.6** DQDB Access Method. *Distributed Queue Dual Bus* access to media.
- **802.7** Broadband LAN. A method for building LANs using broadband technology instead of baseband technology.
- **802.8** The Fiber Optics Technical Advisory Group. Oversees development of fiber optics solutions.
- **802.9** Isochronous LANs. Frequently referred to as *Integrated Voice/Data Communications*.
- **802.10** Integrated Services. Also known as *Security*. Administers development of methods by which access to the network and the transmission of data can be made secure.
- **802.11** Wireless Networking. Defines various methods of moving data without wires. Table 3 offers more detail on the different 802.11 standards.

TABLE 3

802.11 iterations

IEEE 802.11	The initial release of the standard capable of transmissions of 1 to 2 Mb/s and operates in the 2.4 GHz band
IEEE 802.11a	Capable of transmissions of up to 54 Mb/s and operates in the 5 GHz band
IEEE 802.11b	Improves the 2.4 GHz band signal rate to 11 Mb/s
IEEE 802.11c	Defines wireless bridge operations
IEEE 802.11d	Introduces standards for companies developing wireless products in different countries

TABLE 3
(*Continued*)

IEEE 802.11e	Defines Quality of Service (QoS) standards for wireless networking
IEEE 802.11f	Defines Inter Access Point Protocol (IAPP)
IEEE 802.11g	Defines transmission rates of between 20 Mb/s to 54 Mb/s and operates in the 2.4 GHz band
IEEE 802.11i	Introduces Wi-Fi Protected Access (WPA) encryption
IEEE 802.11j	802.11 extension used in Japan
IEEE 802.11n	A 2005 implementation of wireless networking that supports up to 100 Mb/s

- **802.12** Demand Priority Access. Allows access to network media based on message priority.
- **802.14** Standard Protocol for CableTV-based broadband communications.
- **802.15** Working Group for Personal Area Networks. Very short-range wireless networks.
- **802.16** Broadband Wireless Access Standards.
- **802.17** Resilient Packet Ring Working Group. Uses fiber optic ring networks and packet data transmission.

8042 The designation of the keyboard controller chip used on the early incarnations of the IBM PC and AT computers. This chip accepted the incoming signals from the keyboard, processed the data and instructions, and converted them into information the CPU could use. This chip was one of the first dedicated chips to be incorporated into early *chipset* designs.

8086 An Intel microprocessor released in 1978. It was used as the template for the chip used by IBM on their first line of personal computers (the 8088). The 8086 featured 16-bit registers, EDB, and a 16-bit memory address bus.

8088 The first microprocessor used on an IBM personal computer. The 8088, released in 1979, was simply a modification of the 8086, already in production, but differed in that it offered an 8-bit EDB and a 20-bit memory address bus.

8087 An Intel math coprocessor designed to accompany the 8088 microprocessor.

80186 An Intel microprocessor released in 1982 that was used primarily as an embedded processor for computerized gadgets. It did not see much use in the PC world, although Tandy Corporation used it on their Tandy 2000 desktop computer. It was basically an enhanced 8086.

80286 The first 16-bit microprocessor by Intel (released in 1982), to be used extensively in personal computers. The 80286 featured a 16-bit EDB, dual 16-bit registers, and a 24-bit address bus.

80287 The Intel math coprocessor designed to accompany the 80286 microprocessor.

80386 A 32-bit microprocessor released by Intel in 1986. This chip featured 32-bit internal and external data busses and a 32-bit address bus as well. In addition to the wider bit width, the 80386 featured an enhanced instruction set, commonly known as the *i386 instruction set,* and was able to perform advanced (at the time, anyway) tricks, such as virtual memory addressing and the ability to switch from the older style of 16-bit *segmented addressing* to 32-bit *flat addressing.* An interesting historical note surrounding the 80386 is that this was the first chip Intel released to the PC world that it did not first provide to IBM. With the 80386, Intel worked with Compaq Computer Corporation and Microsoft, making Compaq the first computer to run the "new" Windows 3.0 operating system on a 386.

80386DX   The code name given the full-featured version of the 80386 microprocessor.

80386SX   This is a 386 processor that was scaled down to make it compatible with the then-existing world of 16-bit motherboards and devices. The 80386SX featured the 32-bit internal data bus and address bus of the 80386DX, but a 16-bit EDB was shipped with it to make it easier to adapt to 16-bit technology.

80386SL   A version of the 80386SX that ran at a lower 3.3V (compared with the 5V core voltage of the then-current lineup of Intel microprocessors). This made it an ideal candidate for use in portable computers because the chip would draw less power from the batteries.

80387   A math coprocessor designed to accompany the 80386 microprocessors.

8042   The keyboard controller chip used on early PCs. Later on, this chip and several others would be incorporated into the BIOS chip and become an historical artifact.

80486   The 80486 (or 486 for short) was really nothing more than a feature upgrade to the 80386. There were no new technological marvels added. Although there were a few minor additions to the i386 instruction set, none of them were groundbreaking moments in computing history. What it did add was an integrated math coprocessor, and it became the first Intel chip to feature L1 cache—a whopping 8K of it.

80486DX   This is the code for the standard 80486 CPU.

80486SX   The 80486SX was nothing more than a standard 80486 with the math coprocessor disabled. All of the circuitry for the chip was identical in every aspect.

80486SL   This is a 3.3V version of the 80486SX used for portable computers.

80486-DX2   The 80486-DX2 was the first Intel chip to feature *clock-doubling* technology. Clock-doubling was a feature that allowed the chip to process data internally at twice the clock speed of the EDB. As long as the data could be fed to the CPU in a timely fashion, this technology allowed the processor to work faster.

80486-DX4   If you were expecting clock-quadrupling technology because of the 4 in the DX, I hate to be the one to disappoint you. The DX4 chips featured clock-tripling technology that allowed them to process data internally at three times the speed of the EDB. Hence, the DX4 designation.

80487   The math coprocessor that Intel shipped that allowed users to upgrade their 80486SX chips to the capabilities of the 80486DX at only twice the price.

8237   The original Intel chip used as a *direct memory access (DMA)* controller on the IBM PC and PC-AT. The original PC possessed a single 8237 and could manage four DMA channels. On the PC-AT, a second 8237 was cascaded onto the first one, allowing the system to access up to seven channels (one being lost to the cascade function). As with the 8042 and so many other chips, the 8237 was absorbed by the chipset.

8259   This is the original *Interrupt ReQuest* (*IRQ*) controller chip used on the early IBM PCs. The original IBM PC featured a single 8259 and could manage up to eight IRQ channels. The PC-AT added a second 8259, cascaded through IRQ2, to increase the total number of supported IRQs to 15 (one of the channels being lost to the cascade).

A

A+ A certificate issued by the Computing Technology Industry Association that indicates an individual's competence in working with computer hardware and operating systems. The A+ certification has gone through several evolutionary stages over the years. The current curriculum consists of passing two exams. The A+ Essentials Exam covers the basic material that any computer technician should be expected to know. Then the candidate selects from one of three different secondary exams, based on their goals. The 220-602 exam targets individuals who expect to work in a mobile or corporate environment. This would include desktop support technicians and field technicians. The 220-603 exam is the one that a potential help desk person, call center operator, or other remotely based technician should take. People who do not expect to have a lot of interaction with the end user can take the 220-604 exam.

A cable A standard 50-pin cable used for narrow small computer system interface (SCSI) devices. A standard A cable has latches similar to the ones on a parallel printer cable to hold it in place on the connector. There were several variations of the A cable, including ribbon cables and rounded cable clusters. One variety used 25 twisted pairs terminating in a 25-pin D-shell connector. A cables used for hard disks were 50-pin D-shell connectors like the one shown in Figure A.1.

FIGURE A.1   A fifty-pin A cable used to connect older internal SCSI devices.

A20   On a PC-compatible computer, the A20 is an address line that points to all memory above 1 MB. It got its name from the fact that the original 8088 CPU had a 20-bit address line. When the 80286 came out with its 24-bit address, backward compatibility required that the address barrier be switched off. IBM took it upon themselves to use a spare pin on the 8042 controller—the keyboard controller of the day, if you will—to carry the current that disabled the memory address that acted at the gate. Therefore, the switch was called A20. As a result of the keyboard controller carrying the signal, now when you get a keyboard failure, the BIOS often reports it as an *A20 failure*, which these days, has nothing to do with extended memory.

A/B switch   A switching box that allows two peripherals to be connected to a single computer port. In order to select which peripheral is used, the user selects either the A position or the B position. A problem that sometimes rears its ugly head with A/B switches is when the voltage of the devices exceeds the capacity of the switch, or when the capacitance of the switch itself causes issues. The former situation causes the switch to burn out, whereas the latter results in one or both of the devices not appearing to the OS.

A/D converter   Analog to digital converter. This is a chip or device that takes a standard electrical waveform and processes it in such a way that it becomes digital information. Sound cards, modems, and Video Graphics Array (VGA) adapters all require some form of A/D converter. On the flip side, in order to send digital information back out to the analog world, a D/A converter, which works in the opposite direction, is needed.

A drive   This references the primary floppy disk drive on a PC. Two drive letters were reserved for floppy disk drives, the A and B drive. The A drive is always the bootable drive by default, although this could be changed in the system BIOS of most computers. For those computers with two floppy disk drives, there were two ways to designate which drive was the A drive and which was the B drive. Floppy disk cables that supported two devices featured a twist in the cable between the first and second device connectors. This twist occurs between conductors 10 through 16 on the 34-conductor cable. The drive on the far end was drive A by default. However, the user could go into the BIOS and select a setting called *Swap Floppy* and the drive attached to the middle connector would become drive A. At this point, drive B became the bootable device because, when set to boot from the floppy disk, the system always boots from the device attached to the end connector.

A record   Address record. The A record is an entry used by the domain name system (DNS) to resolve a domain name to an *IP address*. The first thing that DNS does when asked to locate a domain name is look up the A record. The A record hands DNS the IP address and the search continues from there.

abacus   An old calculating device that used beads on strings as counters. The abacus predates the Roman Empire in terms of its time frame. The oldest surviving relic is the Salamis Tablet, from approximately 300 BC, although written references to the tool predate this by many centuries. The abacus consists of several rows of beads divided into two decks. Beads in the upper deck have a value of 5 and those in the lower deck have a value of 1. The rows represent the decimal values. The row to the far right represents 1s, the next row to the left 10s, and so on. It is interesting to note that in the early days of electronic calculators, some expert abacus users took on some people proficient with electronic calculators, and won.

abandonware   Software that is no longer sold, supported, or actively protected by the original publisher. Many old MS-DOS programs fall under this category. There are a number of sites that promote abandonware, but a little caution is in order here. Even though a program may no longer be sold or supported, this does not necessarily mean that the publisher has abandoned the copyright. Were a program to become resurgent in popularity, or should the publisher suddenly decide to issue a new version of a program, a site hosting that program—as well as any users who downloaded it—might find themselves in violation of copyright.

abend   A term derived from two words: abnormal end. It is a fancy name for a system crash. Abends usually occur when faulty code asks the system to do something impossible, like divide by zero or calculate Bill Gates' bank balance at any given moment. Other sources for abends are driver errors or faulty hardware.

abort   To terminate a process or program during operation. Generally when an application begins a process, it is expected to run from beginning to end without interruption. However, under certain circumstances, it might be necessary to stop the process. For example, if a process hangs or stops responding to the system, an abort would be necessary. In the old days of MS-DOS, about the only way to accomplish this objective was to reset the system. This could be done by pressing <Ctrl>+<Alt>+<Delete> or by pressing the reset button on the computer. Multitasking operating systems offer some form of utility to accomplish this. For example, when Windows users press <Ctrl>+<Alt>+<Delete>, the *Task Manager* or *Windows Security*, which offers a task manager shortcut, opens. Task manager allows you to select applications or individual processes and then stop them. You will probably have to tell Windows several times before it responds, but eventually you can kill a nonresponding process or application.

Abort, Ignore, Retry, Fail   Users of MS-DOS or Windows users working from a command prompt would see this message when reading from a floppy disk drive. When a *sector* on a floppy disk could not be read by the drive, this was the most common message that resulted. By pressing the key representing the first letter of the desired option, the user could abort (stop trying to read the diskette), ignore (skip the bad sector and return whatever information the drive could read), retry (try reading the bad sector again), or fail (about the same result as abort). Often when this message was displayed, the diskette was good; it simply was not properly seated in the drive. An unformatted diskette would also return this message.

absolute   This term refers to any calculation that will always return a positive result. Programmers use the absolute (ABS) command to force positive values. By inputting the line ABS(75 − 100), the system would return 25 and not −25.

absolute address   Any address that points to a very specific and identifiable location in the computer system. Examples of an absolute address would be IDE0, Head 2, Sector 14,820. When Windows returns an error that reads *Memory could not be read at address (0x80070006)*, it is giving an absolute address in memory.

It's also V&S Absolut Spirits, Årstaängsvägen 19a, 117 97 Stockholm, Sweden where the vodka is made. Only once again, they misspelled it.

absolute cell reference In a *spreadsheet*, a *cell* is the intersection point between a specific row and a column. Most spreadsheet applications allow the user to insert rows and columns as they see fit. However, since the majority of calculations the spreadsheet uses to perform its magic are based on data found in other cells, when a row or column is inserted, the program looks for references to the rows or columns displaced and then automatically changes the formulae to point to the new position. Sometimes this is not desirable. An absolute reference points to a specific place in a worksheet. Column A, Row 22 is always Column A, Row 22. If you insert a new column that becomes Column A, all formulae that use absolute cell references will point to the new column.

absolute value A reference to any numerical value, with regard to whether it is a positive value or a negative value. For example, both 2 and –2 each have an absolute value of 2.

abstract A generalized representation of data in which finer details are either concealed or ignored. A data abstraction allows programmers or systems analysts to find commonalities between two or more data types. Protocols use data abstraction in order to eliminate platform-specific information from the information being transmitted. This allows two disparate machines to communicate with one another.

abstract syntax The type of data that is to be moved or stored. One form of abstract syntax is the form that any data takes as it moves over a LAN or WAN connection. The networking protocols render the data in a form independent of any specific hardware or OS platform for transmission and then, on the receiving end, translate it back into the form that platform uses. While on the wire, the data assumes its abstract syntax. Another form of abstract syntax is the form that specific types of data assumes while stored in a file. For example, a music or video clip is one form of abstract syntax, and a text document is another. Programmers use the term in yet another way. A compiler sees the commands written by the programmer in categories, such as statements or identifiers. In this case, abstract syntax refers to representation of a program as a collection of command types.

abstraction layer An abstraction layer is any method that a program or operating system uses to hide specific functionality of one layer from another and yet still make sure the services of the layers are available. An example of this is the hardware abstraction layer (HAL). HAL consists of a collection of files in an operating system that provides an interface between applications running on the system and the OS kernel or between different programs running on the system. The individual applications are never allowed to directly communicate with the hardware. If two applications were to directly access the same device at the same time this would result in a system crash. Figure A.2 shows a breakdown of the layers of a typical operating system, including the hardware abstraction layer. On a software level, it is an abstraction layer that makes it easy for multiple instances of the same program to run at the same time on a computer without driving the CPU nuts.

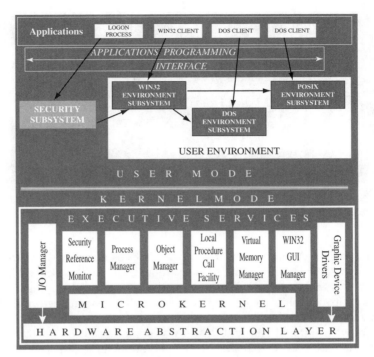

FIGURE A.2   The hardware abstraction layer, seen at the bottom of this image, is one of many abstraction layers used by a typical operating system.

accelerator   Any device or program that is designed to increase the relative speed of another device or program. Internet browsers use utilities that compress data before transmission in order to speed up the Internet experience. This is an example of a software accelerator. Almost all graphics cards made today have dedicated microprocessors that handle complex graphics calculations. High-end workstations may employ accelerator cards, which allow the video card to offload some of its own work.

AC adapter   A small electrical converter that takes alternating current (AC) from the wall and turns it into direct current that a device is able to use. These are typically the black boxes that take up all the space on your power strip so you cannot use all the AC sockets available. Figure A.3 shows a pair of typical AC adapters hogging a power strip.

Accelerated Graphics Port   Also called simply *AGP*, this is a 66-MHz bus that is used exclusively for video cards. AGP comes in different varieties from AGP to AGP 8x. Sometimes you see terms such as *133 MHz* or *266 MHz AGP* in place of the more accurate AGP 2x or AGP 4x. This is technically inaccurate because the bus is still operating only at a clock speed of 66 MHz. The 2x AGP moves 2 bits per cycle and the 4x moves 4 bits per cycle. This gives an *effective* rate of 133 MHz or 266 MHz,

FIGURE A.3   Many devices used alongside the computer require AC adapters to provide their current.

but not a true rate. Another note is that AGP 8x does not provide a true doubling of speed over AGP 4x, and in fact most systems cannot detect the difference. But since some systems are unstable when an 8x card is used, dropping the card down to 4x can improve stability without a noticeable decrease in performance. Figure A.4 shows an AGP video card.

accelerator board   In the old days of PCs, it was sometimes possible to purchase an expansion card onto which a faster CPU could be mounted. This effectively increased the speed of the computer. Note that these older systems could not make use of multiprocessing. Therefore, the addition of another process was a replacement process and not a doubling of power. Accelerator boards are a thing of the past as the speed of CPUs long ago surpassed the speed of the expansion bus.

acceptable use policy   Rules and regulations governing how the resources on a network or Internet site may be used, and by whom they may be used. Unlike a network policy, administrators and users must physically monitor acceptable use policies. Most companies that provide Internet services of any sort publish an

FIGURE A.4   For many years AGP video cards dominated the market. PCI-X and PCI Express have since moved in on their territory.

acceptable use policy. Judging by the content on the Internet, it would appear that dismally few of them enforce it.

acceptance testing   A defined series of procedures that a client or end user will put a system through in order to ascertain whether or not it fully meets the design specifications. These procedures will obviously vary with the type of equipment being analyzed. For example, a system server might be checked for hard disk and input/output (I/O) performance. An array of servers might be tested for interoperability. If the equipment passes the tests to a sufficient degree, the customer will then sign a form acknowledging that the equipment meets specifications, thereby accepting delivery.

access   (v) To gain entry to a channel or network or to interface with a device attached to a computer or network. For example, when you send a print job to a printer, you are accessing the printer. When you type in your user name and password when you log onto your computer at work, you are accessing the network. (n) Your permission to enter a channel or network or to interface with a device. When you are assigned a user name and password to a network, you are given access.

access control entry (ACE)   A single descriptive entry in the Windows *access control list.*

access control list   A collection of information housed by a network server that identifies what users have what rights and permissions to the various resources on the network. Each resource is treated as a system object and owns an entry in the ACL. Each user account is also treated as a system object and is tagged with a list of attributes assigning permissions and privileges. Each time a logged-on user attempts to access a resource, such as a file or a printer, the server checks the access control list and compares it with the user's permissions to see if that user is allowed to use that resource.

access light   Also called an *activity light* or an *indicator light,* an access light is a small light-emitting diode (LED) on a disk drive or on the front of a computer that links to an internal disk drive that flashes whenever that device is being used to read or write data. Access lights are also good troubleshooting devices. If the access light on a floppy drive is constantly on, even when there is no disk in the drive or when the drive is not in use, it indicates that the floppy disk cable is plugged in backwards. A hard drive access light that is always active, even when the computer is idle, indicates problems with the file system. Also, if your computer is connected to a network or to the Internet, flashing lights can suggest that someone or something is accessing your computer remotely. The drives shown in Figure A.5 possess access lights.

access list   A collection of statements mapped to a router or switch interface that defines conditions under which packets will be permitted to pass, or will be denied access. Access lists must be very specific in what activity they are allowing or denying. Allow statements should precede deny statements, and all access lists must end in a deny statement.

access log   A file on a Web server that compiles a list of all the different files stored on that server that are opened by users during a specific time frame. The access log can record a wide variety of information, depending on the server software in

FIGURE A.5 The drives on the front of this computer enclosure feature activity lights to indicate when the drives are busy.

use. Typically, the IP address and the type of browser that the visiting computer uses are recorded. Also recorded are the date and time that computer paid its visit. Optionally, an access log might record the operating system and its version used by the system paying the visit. The access log is a raw data file that looks like little more than gibberish to the average user. Utilities running on a computer can extract that data and convert it into charts and reports that then make sense to the average user.

access method The process by which a networking device places data onto the transmission medium. For example, Gigabit Ethernet encodes data into electrical signals that are transmitted over a wire. In order to make sure that it does not send data at the same time as another device, it uses a technology called *CSMA/CD* (carrier sense multiple access/collision detection) to listen to the carrier signal on the wire. When it senses that the carrier is free of data, it transmits its own data. Wireless networking methods incorporate either pulses of light or radio waves to carry the data, and therefore must use a more specialized access method.

access network A local network that is available to the individual end users. Generally, access networks are any networks that gain entry to a larger network over a *backbone*. Each individual access network maintains its own security, and users on the access network can only make use of resources on the outside networks for which they have permissions. By definition, any network that has access to the Internet is an access network.

access point The base station in a typical wireless network. It takes the place of a standard hub and frequently doubles as a router and/or the interface for Internet access. The access point consists of a device with a wireless transmitter, a receiver, and an antenna. Although it is true that simple peer-to-peer networks can function without a dedicated access point, the additional security of client-server networking requires a bit more sophisticated infrastructure. One limitation of currently available hardware is that most models support a maximum of 255 users. In addition, Federal Communications Commission regulations severely limit transmission distances for these devices. However, with some protocols and hardware, access points can be daisy-chained, effectively increasing the physical size of the network.

access time   A performance specification for memory or disk drives that measures how long it takes from the moment a request is made to retrieve data, to the instant it is able to lock onto the location of that data on the media. With memory, access time is measured in nanoseconds, and with disk drives it is measured in milliseconds. Memory access time is measured as a function of how long it takes for the *row access strobe* to locate the correct row of memory cells and for the *column access strobe* to lock onto the column. Disk drives are not so scientific in their approach. Average access time for a disk drive is the amount of time it takes for the *actuator arm* to travel one third of the distance across the platter.

access validation   The process of access validation is what makes Windows security work the way that it does. When the user attempts to access an object for the first time, an NT function called the *Security Reference Monitor* (SRM) examines the user's access token and compares it to the object's ACL. Each access control entry (ACE) in the ACL is read in the order it is listed. No access entries are listed first. This reduces system overhead for processing requests that will not be honored anyway. Once any ACEs in the ACL specific to the user's token indicate that the user should be allowed access, SRM opens the object to the user.

accessory   Any device or component that is added onto a computer or network that was not originally part of the design. If an accessory fails or is removed from the system, the rest of the system is not affected. There are a wide variety of accessories available for the computer user, ranging from scanners to printers to digital capture devices. An externally attached accessory is generally called a peripheral.

account   In the real world, an account is any listing or group of listings that records quantities of just about any value that is specific to a certain entity. A person's bank account is a listing of all transactions related to a specific repository of money. In the computer world, the term refers to a group of settings on a computer or network server that provides information relevant to a specific user. In general, in order to access an account the user must prove his *credentials*, which consist of a user name and password. On a secured network, a user's permissions are associated with the account and not the credentials.

accumulator   A set of registers in a microprocessor where intermediate results of data processing are stored while waiting for the next step. This is the equivalent of jotting down the sum of a series of numbers and then making a note of how many numbers there were so you remember those values when you are ready to calculate an average. The general registers of the CPU act as an accumulator for a standard microprocessor; therefore you do not usually see this term used in relation to modern CPUs.

achromatic   A lens that does not focus one bandwidth of light waves at the same point as the other colors. In general, the aberrant color is red. Oddly enough, it is this very attribute of red light that makes it so easy to see over other colors at night. While this sounds like a bad thing, most lenses made are achromatic because it is very difficult to get red light to focus on the same point as other colors. Generally, in average photographic conditions, the human eye cannot detect the minimal difference in focus shift. However, many digital photographers have discovered that some digital cameras and/or scanners benefit greatly from applying additional sharpening to the red layer in photo-editing programs such as Photoshop.

acknowledgment number (ACK)   In the transmission control protocol/Internet protocol (TCP/IP), each packet contains a field for a value called the *acknowledgment number*. This is a 32-bit value that works in conjunction with the *sequence number* to manage flow control and assure error-free transmissions. The acknowledgment number identifies the last packet that it successfully received. This informs the transmitting computer that the receiving computer is ready to accept the next packet in the sequence. A key point here is that TCP/IP acknowledges only data up to the first missing packet. As such, if an application accepts out-of-order packets, a chunk of data might show up missing in the middle of a transmission. Programmers must decide how to deal with this situation.

acoustic coupler   A device that allows a computer to interface with a standard telephone. It works by placing the handset of the telephone into a saddle. The saddle interfaces with a serial port on the computer. The acoustic coupler generates audible tones, which it sends over the telephone wire to the receiving computer. These rather primitive devices are not often used these days, but might still come in handy if you need to transmit data over a pay phone. The last time I saw one in use was in a spy movie, where the villain transmitted the contents of a compact disc (CD) in about 6 seconds. I wish my DSL connection could do that.

acronym   A shortened term derived by combining the first letter (or letters) of the words in a multiword term. For example, PCI represents *Peripheral Components Interconnect* and PCMCIA represents *People Cannot Memorize Computer Industry Acronyms*. Officially it means Personal Computer Memory Card International Association.

action statement   A command in any programming language that initiates another event to occur. An action statement is used to send a file to a printer. Separate action statements are used for opening and closing files.

active   The device or application that is currently in use by the system. In a graphical operating system such as Windows or OS X, the active window is the one that is receiving user input and displaying the results of processing data. An active printer is the one that fires up by default when a print job is sent to paper.

Active Desktop   A method of configuring the Windows desktop to behave as if it is a Web page, allowing single-click activation of icons and other Web-like features. It works by incorporating HTML code into the desktop interface. It got its start in 1997 as a method of allowing users to incorporate features such as a stock ticker, weather monitor, or news headlines that were constantly changing into the desktop without forcing the user to log onto the Internet every time he wanted to check these items.

Active Directory   Directory services provided by Microsoft's Windows 2000 and later operating systems. Similar to Novell's Directory Services, Active Directory is based on the Lightweight Directory Access Protocol (LDAP). It treats each resource on the network, including users, as an object. Characteristics such as permissions and privileges are applied as attributes. Users can search objects on the network in a manner similar to looking for files on a local hard drive.

active hub   A device that interconnects several devices on a network. When it receives the signal from one device, it cleans up any noise the signal might have picked up along the way, amplifies it back to its original strength, and then sends it along its way. An active hub acts like a *repeater* in this respect. This is different from a traditional hub, which does nothing to clean up or amplify the signal. Most modern networks make use of *switches* wherever possible because a switch provides each connection with uncontested bandwidth in its own *collision domain.*

active matrix   A type of liquid crystal display (LCD) monitor found on many laptop computers. The active matrix display, also called the *thin film transistor* (TFT), makes use of four different transistors for each pixel displayed on the screen. Presence or absence of voltage on a given transistor dictates the color and intensity that the pixel will glow. A slower alternative to the active matrix display is (you guessed it) the *passive matrix display.* Active matrix displays are sharper, brighter, and exhibit better color saturation than passive matrix. A key point is that all LCD displays offer the highest quality when used at their *native resolution.*

active monitor   In a *Token Ring* network, the active monitor is the device that generates the token and makes sure it stays on the network. If the token is lost for any reason, it is the job of the active monitor to generate a new token and throw it out onto the network. A computer earns the dubious honor of being the active monitor by being the first machine turned on when the network goes active. If the active monitor is shut down gracefully, then an election will determine which computer on the network will assume the role of active monitor. If it simply crashes or if the user powers it down without shutting down, then Token Ring will begin the process of *beaconing* to figure out what happened and then start the election when it discovers that the active monitor is missing.

active object   When a program is running on the computer, there are generally several different *threads* or *processes* that will be running, seemingly at once. At any given nanosecond, only one of these strings of code can be running within the CPU *pipeline* (although most modern CPUs have multiple pipelines). The threads and processes are generically referred to as *objects* and the active object is the one currently running through the pipeline.

active partition   A primary partition on a hard disk drive that has been identified in the master boot record (MBR) as being the bootable partition. If a partition is not marked as active in the partition tables, it cannot host a usable operating system. Many earlier operating systems could not boot from any partition that was not marked active, and the system can only have one active partition on any given disk. In order to configure a multiboot system, the active partition will contain some file that defines different *system partitions.* On modern operating systems the system files can reside on different partitions than the MBR.

Active Reconfiguring Message   Also known as *ARM*, this technology allows the hardware in an ARM-compatible device to be reconfigured on the fly, based on the data that is being received for processing or being transmitted. Information in the message header provides configuration data in compressed format. The header information is extracted, read, and used to perform the reconfiguration of the device. The data is then processed and the next incoming message may or may not reconfigure the device for its needs.

active window   In a graphical operating system such as Windows or OS X, the active window is the one that is currently open and accepting user input. Keep in mind that in a tiled screen several windows may be open and visible, but only the one in which numbers and letters show up when you type is the active window. The OS maintains a very complex user interface that keeps track of all open windows and which one is currently active. User I/O is limited to the active window, while system I/O can be active in any open window. Figure A.6 shows a desktop with two windows open; the active window is identified. The first reader to contact Delmar Cengage Learning with the time, day, and year that the image was created will win a signed and matted print from the author's portfolio of fine art photography.

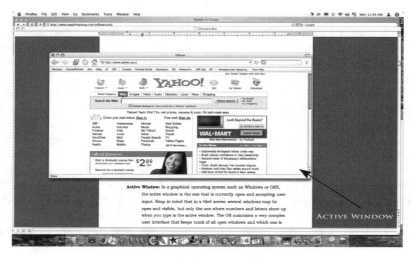

FIGURE A.6   *The active window on a user's desktop is the one accepting user input at the moment.*

ActiveX   A type of programming module or component that is capable of registering itself with the host operating system. ActiveX objects generally have some form of user interface (although not always) and are able to embed themselves into other modules. ActiveX is an evolutionary product of an older technology that is still in use called *Object Embedded Linking* that allowed data from one application to be incorporated into that of another. For example, a series of cells from a spreadsheet might be embedded in a word processing document. When the spreadsheet is updated, the document automatically updates. ActiveX controls follow the same philosophy, but are much smaller and use much more efficient code so they can be incorporated into Web pages without drastically slowing Internet performance. ActiveX controls that are designed to be incorporated into an existing program are called *plug-ins*. Most Internet browsers support plug-ins, as do many image processing applications. An example of an ActiveX plug-in would be a file decompression tool that automatically unzips a file as it is downloaded without requiring any user intervention.

activity   The most basic transfer of information that occurs in the course of a communications session. A single activity might be the transfer of an acknowledgment packet to a server, or a clock signal to resynchronize a session.

activity light An LED on a device such as a hard disk enclosure or a network interface that flickers when there is traffic or electrical current present in the circuit. With some activity lights, the color of the light can be an indication the present condition of the device. Green is good, amber is usually a warning, and red indicates either failure or an error condition. *See* **access light**.

actual cell rate In the *asynchronous transfer mode* (ATM) protocol, this is the maximum transfer rate in cells per second that the transmitting device is allowed to send data.

actuator arm A device inside of a hard drive on which the read/write (R/W) heads are mounted. A motor of some sort (generally voice coil-activated) moves the arm back and forth across the disk platters to position the R/W heads over the correct track in order to record or access data. When the disk is powered off when the system shuts down, it moves the heads to a safe "parking" zone. Figure A.7 shows the actuator arm over the platter of a hard disk.

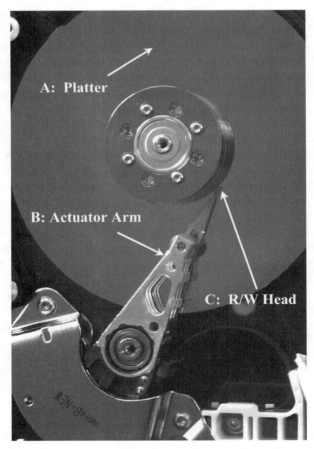

FIGURE A.7   *Actuator arms (B) move the disk read/write heads (C) across the disk platter (A) in the search for data.*

acute   On the keyboard, the acute is the backwards apostrophe (`). It is found on the same key as the *tilde* (~), just above the <Tab> key. It is also a term that means pronounced or exaggerated.

ad banner   These are those annoying (and usually animated) frames on a Web page that try to get you to purchase some product you have never needed, will never need, and probably have never heard of (and never wanted to). The most annoying ones are the ones that follow you down the page as you scroll down. And the really infuriating ones are the ones that invite you to punch some big-name celebrity or politician in the nose to win a prize that does not exist.

Adaptable User Interface (AUI)   A set of utilities provided by Oracle that allows developers to create applications that are portable between multiple window applications. Using AUI, a developer can have a single interface, resource manager, and workflow for the application regardless of whether the application is being ported to Windows, OS X, or the X Window system for Linux.

Adaptec   A manufacturer of computer components that specializes in controllers for storage systems. Their line of *SCSI* adapters, RAID controllers, and other devices has long been a standard for server and high-end workstation integrators. Their Web site is at http://www.adaptec.com.

adapter   Any device that allows two dissimilar interfaces or signals to coexist peacefully. An *AC adapter* converts AC current to DC current. A PS2/USB adapter allows a PS2 mouse or keyboard to be used in a USB port. Frequently you see the term *adapter* used to describe an expansion card. This may or may not be accurate usage of the term. Unless it actually acts as an interface, it is more likely that an expansion card is actually a controller. For example, a VGA card is a controller not an adapter.

adapter load balancing   With adapter load balancing (ALB), two different NICs are statically configured with the same IP address. Now, as you might imagine, TCP/IP's simplistic approach to addressing is going to take exception to this process unless you do something to let the protocol know that everything is all right. Even if the presence of identical IP addresses did not cause a conflict, replies from a networking protocol such as the Dynamic Host Configuration Protocol (DHCP) have a tendency to respond to the server with the lowest MAC address. A MAC address is hard coded into an NIC at the factory and cannot be changed by a user. Therefore, one adapter would still attract all DHCP requests until it ran out of addresses in its pool.

To make the process work, a third-party application, such as NSI Software Balance, juggles the traffic between the two adapters. As workstations log on to the network, they will be bound to one of the NICs and that is the interface through which they will communicate with the server for the rest of that session. The software makes sure that each adapter carries its share of the load.

ALB also provides a good measure of fault tolerance. Should one adapter fail, the other adapter will carry on as if nothing happened. A server with only a single NIC would be dead in the water if the NIC failed.

adapter teaming   Adapter teaming allows the server to "lie" to the rest of the network and tell everybody out there that both of the adapters installed are really only one. It is easy enough to configure two NICs to the same IP address. You need specific software to make the network think there is only one MAC address between them.

When teaming is configured on a server, a single MAC address is selected from the pair (usually the one with the lower physical number). This becomes the primary NIC. The secondary NIC responds to that MAC even though that is not its actual address. When any device sends a packet to the server asking for its address, either NIC will respond with the set of addresses (IP and MAC) assigned to the pair. As a result, inbound traffic is easily divided between the two adapters, and the network moves blithely on. Network load is more efficiently balanced and there is still only one address as far as the rest of the network is concerned.

adaptive answering   This feature is what allows combination fax/modem devices to analyze an incoming call and determine if it is a data- or a fax-driven call. Adaptive answering is capable of distinguishing between voice and fax or between data and fax. It cannot tell voice and data calls apart, however. In order for adaptive answering to work, it must be enabled. Adaptive answering is available on Windows 2000 and later versions of Microsoft operating systems.

adaptive routing   See **dynamic routing**.

additive colors   The primary colors of red, green, and blue. Additive colors are used by a wide variety of devices to create the different *hues* the human eye perceives. For example, when red and green are mixed, the resultant hue is purple. Blue and yellow make green. The relative intensity of each additive color in the mix contributes to the final hue. Additive colors are the reverse values of *subtractive colors*. Color monitors, scanners, and many digital cameras use additive colors. Most printers use subtractive colors.

address   (n) A description of the physical location of a resource on a computer or network. A memory address points to the specific location on the address bus corresponding to the row and column on the individual memory chip on which a particular bit of information resides. (v) The ability of a device to locate and then communicate with another device and exchange information.

address bar   In an Internet browser application, such as Netscape Navigator, Firefox, or Internet Explorer, it is the field in which you can type a specific web address. The arrow in Figure A.8 points to the address bar in Firefox. This is different from the search bar, in which you type keywords to help you find what you are looking for. The address bar assumes you know exactly where you want to go. The search bar tells you where to go and gives you a road map.

address book   A small database file that interfaces with certain applications running on the computer that provides name and address data on demand. Programs such as a word processing program can access the address book to fill in information for envelopes, mailing labels, and so forth.

address bus   A bank of wires running throughout the system and into the CPU that specifies specific locations. The total addressable space is calculated as 2^x, where x represents the total number of wires in the bus. The address bus dictates the theoretical limit to the amount of memory a system supports. The old 8088 CPU used on the first IBM PC sported a 20-bit address bus. $2^{20} = 1,048,576$, which is the actual value of a *megabyte*. A 32-bit address bus, typical of Intel Pentium 4 CPUs, can address up to 4,294,967,296 bytes of memory (4 GB). The newer 64-bit processors are theoretically capable of addressing up to 16 *exabytes* of RAM. However, because of limitations in both the operating

FIGURE A.8 The address bar is where a user can manually type in a URL to navigate to a specific Web site.

system and in chipsets, the actual address space is much smaller than that. The Mac OS X can support up to 16 GB of RAM, while the Linux 2.6.16 kernel comes in at a whopping 64 GB.

address phase   The portion of an I/O operation in which the controller accesses the *address bus*, locates, and locks onto the location of the data being sought in a transaction that is about to occur. Nearly every *I/O operation* needs to enter an address phase during its cycle.

address register   A reserved portion of memory in which a table is stored that details what information is stored in all areas of system memory, and at what address in memory each item of information is stored. There are basically three forms of address register. The general memory address register (MAR) stores the address in memory that is to be accessed on the upcoming cycle. Outgoing addresses are stored in the destination memory address register (DMAR). Addresses in memory where the incoming data is stored are in the source memory address register (SMAR).

Address Resolution Protocol (ARP)   One of the many supplemental protocols of the *TCP/IP* stack of protocols. The ARP maps physical hardware addresses to IP addresses. As such, ARP can discover the *MAC address* of a device on the network by sending a packet to that device's *IP address*. The resultant *acknowledgment packet* will contain the information the protocol is looking for. Most operating systems have some sort of utility that allows the user to make use of this utility. Windows users can open a command line and type ARP, followed by the *trigger* that elicits the response he desires. ARP triggers include:

-a	Displays the current ARP cache, listing both MAC and IP addresses of all devices contained in the cache
-d Inet Addr	Deletes the Internet address listed. If * is used in place of an Internet address, all ARP entries are deleted
eth_addr	Ethernet address. Specifies a particular MAC address

-g	Identical to –a
if_addr	Interface address
inet_addr	Internet address
-N Interface	Shows ARP entries for the specific interface defined
-s *Ipaddress macaddress*	Where ipaddress is replaced by the actual IP address and macaddress is replaced by the actual MAC address of the desired interface. Adds a static entry to the ARP tables

MAC users can do the same thing by opening a terminal session and typing in the same commands.

address strobe   An input signal used by a memory module to indicate that the address range provided by the controller is a valid address. Once the address strobe signal is received, the requested memory I/O operation can commence.

adjacency   The ability of two network devices, such as a router or switch, that are interconnected by the same segment of medium to exchange data without the need for routing through another device. For example, consider two switches on a network that are both connected to the same router. If the two switches can exchange packets without needing the services of the router, they exhibit adjacency. If the router must process the information before passing it between routers, it does not.

administrative distance   A numerical rating used by Cisco routers that is assigned to a routing path that defines the relative reliability of a specific path between two interfaces. When multiple paths are available between the source and the destination, the administrative distance will determine the shortest route. Administrative distance is based on the reliability of the protocol used and not the number of hops or other factors the administrator deems relevant to selecting between different paths for data to travel on the network. There are certain default values that Cisco uses for common protocols. Table A.1 lists these values.

administrative domain   Any part of the network, including servers, routers, host computers, users, media, and so forth that is under the management of a singular authority. Note that a larger network can consist of multiple administrative domains, each one managed by a separate administrator. Multiple domains on a single network are interconnected through *trusts*. Users on a trusting domain can access those resources for which they have permission, but nothing else. Administrators from the trusting domain cannot manage resources on the trusted domain and vice versa.

administrator   (1) In terms of computer usage, the administrator is the user and/or account or group that has full and complete privileges to do anything and everything on the network. The account is also called *Admin* on some networks. By default, the administrator account or group has unlimited power. Therefore, many top administrators limit the powers of subordinate administrators by doing two things. First, they rename the administrator account from *administrator* or *admin* to something a little less obvious to hackers or disgruntled employees. Only a select few users are privy to the real administrator account. Then, all administrators who require fewer privileges are added to the administrator group, and this group is edited to include only the permissions and privileges that the powers that be want them to have. (2) A person who is responsible for managing all aspects or certain aspects of an organization.

TABLE A. 1

Administrative distances of varying interfaces

ROUTE SOURCE	DEFAULT DISTANCE VALUES
Direct Connection	0
Static Route	1
Enhanced Interior Gateway Routing Protocol	5
External Border Gateway Protocol	20
Internal EIGRP	90
IGRP	100
OSPF	110
Intermediate System-to-Intermediate System	115
Routing Information Protocol	120
Exterior Gateway Protocol	140
On Demand Routing	160
External EIGRP	170
Internal BGP	200
Unknown (will not be added to routing tables)	255

Adobe Systems A software developer that specializes in graphics editing and page layout programs. Adobe Photoshop is the industry standard for working with digital photographic images. In addition, Adobe was the developer of Postscript. Their Web site is at http://www.adobe.com.

Advanced Configuration and Power Interface (ACPI) This is a complicated hardware interface, developed in cooperation by Hewlett Packard, Intel, Microsoft, Phoenix, and Toshiba, that extends the power management features of the system BIOS to the majority of devices on the system. The specification is written in such a manner that new power management technology can be developed separately from operating systems and hardware. ACPI can interface with other pieces of hardware connected to the *expansion bus;* it communicates with applications running on the system and it interfaces with the system OS. Modern operating systems even allow interfacing with noncomputer peripherals, such as a telephone system or an alarm system in a house, allowing the computer to manage power throughout a building.

Advanced Programmable Interrupt Controller (APIC) A circuit built into all recent Intel (and most compatible) CPUs that handles system interrupts. While all CPUs throughout history have had some form of interrupt controller, the APIC offers several advantages. It is essential for any system using *symmetric multiprocessing* (SMP) because the APIC prevents system lockups resulting from two processors hitting the same piece of hardware on the same clock cycle. The APIC provides three basic functions: (1) It generates interrupts in order to initiate communication between the CPU and any device. (2) It accepts interrupt generated by a device. (3) It incorporates a timer mechanism that prevents any one device from hogging the CPU.

affiliate program   An arrangement between a business and the owner of a Web site that pays the Web site owner a commission for each sale referred to the business by that Web site. A successful Web site that operates a number of different affiliate programs can generate cash while its owner basks in the sun in Fiji.

advisory   A document or e-mail notice that is posted or sent out whenever there is a required update to a program or operating system, or when there is a potential security risk. Many antivirus software manufacturers send out advisory e-mails when a new virus is launched that is a potential hazard to their customers. Most operating system manufacturers do not e-mail their customers, but rather post notices about critical upgrades or patches on their Web site. If an advisory is sufficiently critical, a company may issue a press release.

Aero   Both a name and an acronym. It is the name for Microsoft's new graphical interface used on Windows Vista. It stands for *A*uthentic, *E*nergetic, *E*ffective, and *O*pen. (I wonder how long it took for somebody to come up with *that* one.) The Aero interface has several new looks, including making certain parts of windows transparent, displaying all open applications in a 3D array, and allowing a user to flip through applications using the scroll wheel on a mouse.

agent   In computer terminology, this is an application or utility that fulfills requests by gathering the information requested by a manager application. Generally an agent sits in the background, running RAM-resident, and only becomes active when the specific event it is programmed to watch for occurs. By definition, an agent should exhibit certain characteristics. It should be autonomous. In other words, the agent needs to be able to decide when to engage without interaction from the management software or from a human user. It should also be persistent. It runs in the background and has its own method of deciding when to activate any one of its functions. An agent should also be reactive. It knows the function it has been programmed to perform and can recognize conditions within the system that should initiate that function. Lastly, it should exhibit interactivity. An agent needs to be able to activate other software components on the system in order to either perform a specific function or to communicate results. Agents are frequently used by system management software to measure performance, watch for anomalies, and/or collect data for system reporting. They are also used by the operating system for similar purposes and for the purpose of auditing.

aggregator   (1) A piece of software that automatically retrieves specific types of Web content (usually syndicated) and feeds it to a specific application running on your computer. An example of an aggregator is a stock ticker. It might collect data from multiple sources in order to track your stock portfolio, but all of the information appears in a single feed. Other software services that use aggregators include music services, news feeds, and interactive Webcasts. (2) A device that takes a large number of incoming analog telephone or DSL signals or ISDN signals and combines them all into a single unified signal that is transmitted over a high-speed backbone. Internet service providers use aggregators to provide Internet access to multiple subscribers. Larger organizations use aggregators to provide remote access to multiple off-site users.

AGP aperture size   This is a setting in computer BIOS that allows the user to configure how much system memory can be used to store preconfigured textures that the video card can use when assembling images. This memory works in conjunction with the memory incorporated on the video card. When the video card's memory fills up, system memory can be used. This can help video cards with a limited amount of memory, but it is no substitute for having sufficient memory on the video card. Extracting textures from system RAM always incurs extra clock cycles.

alarm   Any audible or visible signal used to alert a user that some sort of event (generally an error condition) has occurred. Alarms can be used by server applications to notify the administrator of an anomaly, or a scheduling program can use it to let a user know an appointment time is nearing.

alarm filtering   A process by which multiple alarms on a system that may have been precipitated by a single event can be sorted out, narrowing all the information down until the cause of the alarm is isolated. A single failure of a device or application can create a cascade effect, causing numerous other devices or applications to fail. If no alarm filtering is employed, it can be very difficult to isolate the original cause of the problem.

alert   An audible or visual signal that occurs on a user's system that indicates one of two things. Either an error condition exists or an event that was defined into an *agent* has occurred. An alert is very similar to an *alarm*.

ALGOL   A programming language from the early 1960s targeted toward scientific calculations. It was one of the first programming languages to allow commands to be executed in blocks. Data was structured into an array format. It was the first programming language to introduce the *if-then-else* statement.

algorithm   A collection of precisely defined procedures that will either lead to the solution of a problem or provide the desired results in a query. In an algorithm, there will be a detailed listing of the steps involved in getting from QUESTION to ANSWER.

alias   Any substitute name for any resource on a computer or network. For example, you might map a network drive and name the mapped drive "Music." The real path to a network drive might be //servermain/documents/music, but the alias will always be Music, and that is what you know it by. The *domain name services* (DNS) protocol makes use of aliases when it renders its services. It generates a *canonical name record* (CNAME) for every entry in the DNS tables. The CNAME assigns an alias that is used in place of the true name of the server in the CNAME record.

aliasing   A stairstep effect in computer graphics or typography that occurs on diagonal lines. This is caused by the fact that the pixels that make up an image are rectangular and you cannot cut the corners off of pixel to smooth out a font or image. Figure A.9 is an example of aliasing at work.

allocate   To reserve system resources for a device or application. Allocation is performed by the system during POST and is constantly being managed by the operating system the whole time the system is on. During POST, Plug and Play must allocate IRQs and I/O addresses to devices on the system. This information is collected and stored in a file called the *Extended System Configuration Data* file (ESCD). On subsequent posts, if no changes are detected, ESCD already has the information needed. Once the OS has control of the system, it also takes control of allocation. Each time an application launches, the OS must allocate memory and CPU time for that application. As data is called by the user or programs, memory space must be allocated.

FIGURE A.9   *This enlarged snippet from a digital photograph shows aliasing at work. Aliasing in an image is the result of trying to make a diagonal line out of square blocks.*

allocation scan   A BIOS routine that reassigns resources to Plug and Play devices installed on a computer system. Resource allocation is managed in two steps. Before anything else can happen, *static resource allocation* must be completed. This involves mapping all resources (where known) that are manually configured on the system and cannot be reconfigured. This includes legacy system resources (which are generally known) and older legacy devices such as ISA cards (which may not be known). For the devices that cannot be detected by the system, an external configuration utility must be used to identify these devices. *Dynamic resource allocation* is when the BIOS can configure those devices, such as PCI, AGP, and others that allow external software-managed configuration. During the *recognition scan*, Plug and Play collected information about all the devices on the system, along with the resources they used. This information is now used to configure the devices.

alpha blending   A function of a computer graphics API that allows it to combine the *alpha channel* of a file with other layers in the image to create effects of translucency. Since the alpha channel is 8 bits wide, this provides up to 256 different levels of translucency. With many applications it is possible to have multiple image layers, and each image layer can incorporate its own alpha channel. Working with this technique can result in a much wider *gamut* of effects, although it will also place a much larger load on the video card's memory and processor. Because alpha blending is a primary effect used in creating 3D effects, overall performance is greatly enhanced if it is one of the integrated functions of the video card's chipset.

alpha channel   Eight bits used by graphics files that 32-bit True Color can use to apply effects such as translucency and fogging. Since there are 8 bits available, a total of 256 different levels of effect can be generated. How an alpha channel is used is a function of the graphics program used to manipulate the file. Simple graphics viewers can only display the effects and cannot edit them in any way. Other programs, such as Adobe Photoshop, make extensive use of the alpha channel. Photoshop can incorporate separate alpha channels onto as many as twenty-four different layers. TIF, PNG, and JPEG2000 are all file formats that support alpha rendering. GIF89a supports a 1-bit alpha channel that allows one level of translucency on one of the primary colors.

alpha release   Also called alpha version, the very first compiled version of a software application that is ready for in-house testing. As you might expect, this is going to be a less-than-perfect version of the software. After extensive testing and the bugs are shaken out, a revision of that program is written that eliminates the problems that were detected in alpha testing. The next release is referred to as the *beta version,* or in the parlance of at least one OS publisher, Service Pack 4. This is when actual users beat the program into submission to shake out even more bugs.

alphanumeric   Any series of characters that contains both alphabetic characters and numerals. Alphabetic characters can be represented as either upper case or lower case, and the computer or software sees each form as a different character altogether. While people see significant differences between letters and numbers, the computer sees them as the same thing. Therefore, the use of both types of characters in a computer program or operating system offers a significantly greater range of options. Alphanumeric characters differ from *punctuation* characters in both form and function, and computer software treats them differently as well. *A24Bravo* is an alphanumeric term.

Altair 8800   This was one of the first personal computers released that used the Intel 8088 microprocessor. It was available only in kit form and had to be assembled by the end user. It was the Altair 8800 that launched the careers of Bill Gates and Paul Allen when they notified the manufacturer that they could provide a version of the BASIC programming language to run on the Altair. There was no such thing as an operating system for the Altair. Data and commands were input into the computer via a binary front panel. Devices such as paper tape readers made the process of entering data faster and more efficient.

alternate routing   The built-in ability to send data over a backup transmission line should the primary line fail or be occupied. Routing tables frequently contain multiple paths between the source and various target destinations. The routing tables include a value known as a *metric* that defines the relative speed of each path. By default, the fastest path between source and destination, taking into account the number of *hops* and the relative speed of each hop, is the primary path. If that path is down or busy, a router or protocol that is capable of alternate routing can select the next path down the list and send the data along on its way.

alternating current (AC)   An electrical current that reverses the direction of current flow many times each second. This is the typical electrical current that comes from a standard wall outlet (Figure A.10). AC outlets may be polarized to make sure that current direction between the line voltage and the device are consistent and to provide grounding. Polarized outlets have one prong socket slightly larger than the other as well as a rounded socket for the grounding prong. The narrow slot is the "hot" lead, providing power from the electric company. The larger slot provides return current to the power company. In the United States, direction is reversed 60 times per second. In Europe it is reversed 50 times per second. Most devices are very picky about cycle frequency. Therefore, when traveling, you will find it necessary to have some form of *adapter* to convert the local electricity supply to that which your device requires. The counterpart to AC is *direct current.*

ambient   A term that refers to surrounding conditions. Ambient temperature is how warm or cold is the air surrounding you. Ambient temperature can affect computer equipment because it affects how easily the equipment dissipates heat. Ambient sound is the noise level in a room. While ambient sound has little or no effect on

FIGURE A.10   A typical AC
outlet is polarized for safety
reasons.

computer equipment, the equipment contributes to ambient sound with its cooling
fans.

Amiga   A small personal computer released by Commodore in 1985. This was an
early 16-bit computer with a memory space of 64 KB and a unique user interface
called *GEM*. This was a graphical interface that competed squarely with the
Apple Macintosh. The original idea was that the system would be entirely mouse-
driven. Unfortunately, development problems prevented this from happening
until a subsequent release. The Amiga was intended to be a gamer's computer
with business acumen. As such, the design called for superior graphics but with
the ability to run word processing programs and spreadsheets. Unfortunately for
Commodore, many executives in the company were satisfied to bask in the glory
of past accomplishments and paid little or no attention to some up-and-coming
company with delusions of grandeur that called itself Microsoft. The release of
Windows on a 32-bit system proved to be the death knell for Commodore. Amiga
refused to die, however. Amiga, Inc. continues to release products, including their
own Amiga operating system.

amorphous   Completely lacking in organized structure or so vague that the structure
is difficult, if not impossible, to define. This term is frequently used in reference
to graphic forms. For example, a cloud is an amorphous form. The term can also
be used in other respects as well. A spot on a CD-RW that will not reflect the
laser beam of the recorder is considered to be an amorphous state. Its reverse
counterpart that will reflect the beam is called the *crystalline state*. The majority
of politicians I've come in contact with are in an amorphous state.

ampere   A measurement of the actual flow of an electrical current. Also called *amp*
for short. An ampere is precisely 6.28×10^{18} electrons passing a single point in

1 second. That is a lot of electrons. In an electrical current, measurement of amperage is like measuring the electrical pressure.

ampersand The "and" sign (&) on a standard keyboard. In code or formatting, the ampersand is used to precede characters that should be underlined. Programmers use it as a *Boolean* AND function. In addition, HTML programmers place an ampersand followed by a colon prior to a *less than* or *more than* character to render HTML code as text rather than have the enclosed code perform its actual HTML function.

amplifier An electrical circuit that takes a smaller signal and turns it into a bigger one. An amplified signal has only its relative intensity altered. Amplifiers are used to boost audio, optical, and electrical signals. Frequency of the waveform is not changed in any way. Any change made to the frequency during amplification represents a form of *distortion*. There is often a certain degree of distortion associated with amplification; therefore, it should be used judiciously. Higher quality amplifier circuits minimize the amount of distortion induced. Amplifier circuits are broken down into various classes. Each class of amplifier affects the native signal slightly differently because each one works in a different way. The descriptions listed here cover some of the more conventional amplifier types. Figure A.11 is a graphical representation of the sine wave of a signal and how each amplifier type affects the signal.

- **Class A** All current is conducted (and amplified) throughout the entire 360-degree range of the wave cycle. This type of amplifier is very inefficient in that a lot of heat is generated for a minimal amount of amplification. However, distortion levels are minimal. This form of amplifier is used either for low-power applications or in very high-end audio equipment in which performance is a more critical factor than cost.

- **Class B** The amplifier circuit conducts and amplifies only 180 degrees of the electrical waveform. To amplify the other half of the wave cycle, a separate circuit is used. This induces a form of switching distortion created when the circuit moves from one amplifier to the other. This is used in low-end audio products.

- **Class AB** As the name implies, this is a hybrid of the Class A and Class B types of amplifier. Both types of circuit are used, but the *BIAS* current on the B circuit is set low enough to render the switching distortion virtually inaudible.

- **Class C** The current is conducted and amplified for less than a complete half of a wave cycle. A Class C amplifier is extremely efficient but produces excessive distortion.

- **Class G** A modification of the AB amplifier that uses different power "rails" for different amplification factors. Each rail is basically a circuit with a different voltage level.

- **Class H** Another modification of AB in which the power supply voltage is modulated along with the signal, but always remains higher than the level of the signal voltage.

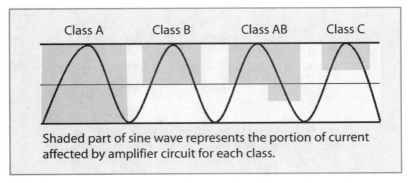

Class A   Class B   Class AB   Class C

Shaded part of sine wave represents the portion of current affected by amplifier circuit for each class.

FIGURE A.11   Various amplifier classes affect the original signal in different ways.

amplitude   The relative strength of an electrical signal. When referencing an audio signal, the term refers to the overall volume of the sound. Amplitude is measured in *decibels* and represents the relative energy of any given signal. On a standard *sine wave*, amplitude is represented by the distance above and below the center line that a wave for any given pulse projects.

analog   Any attempt to recreate a naturally occurring phenomenon using a similar natural effect. It literally means "something that is the same as." An analog device will track a natural phenomenon, such as sound, temperature, or motion, and convert it to an electronic, mechanical, or electromechanical form that is its equivalent. For example, the vibrating paper cone of a speaker creates natural sound waves that simulate the real sound of music or a creature in the wild. A speaker can reproduce a sound similar to a cricket as long as the electromechanical stimuli create similar vibration patterns.

anamorphic   An optical lens or a software application that takes a wide object and squeezes it onto a narrower medium for storage. Then when it is ready for presentation, it stretches it back out to its original format. The original use of anamorphic lenses was to fit wide-screen films onto standard 35-mm or 70-mm film, but during projection be able to project the film in wide-screen format again. Figure A.12 shows a wide-field view of an image alongside its anamorphic counterpart. Notice that the image is compressed horizontally, making everything look taller and broader.

animated   Moving images in a film or on a Web site that are composed of a series of still images shown together in sequence. Each static image is known as a *frame*. How smoothly the perceived motion appears to the human eye is a function of how many frames are displayed each second.

animated GIF   A small moving picture stored in the graphics interchange format (GIF) that is frequently used to annoy people visiting a Web page. The animated GIF consists of a short series of frames compressed into a single file that display in sequence when opened. Typically, an animated GIF recycles and starts the sequence all over again when completed, resulting in a never-ending cycle.

FIGURE A.12 *Anamorphic lenses allow wide-field images to be stored on conventional film formats.*

animation   A moving picture that is made up of a long sequence of artist-rendered images. *See* **animated**. Analog animation requires that an artist paint each picture in the sequence. Computer animation uses computer-generated graphics.

anisotropic   Any property, such as speed or amplitude, that varies in accordance to the direction of the signal. Many communications protocols are anisotropic. For example, a 56K modem can receive at 53.3K, but it can only transmit at 33.6K. Conventional DSL, sometimes known as *asymmetric DSL*, is another anisotropic communications link. The opposite of anisotropic is *isotropic*.

anomaly   Any unexplained event or output. A software conflict between two similar applications might be considered an anomaly. A hardware device that works on one system, but not on another identically configured system, is another example. A classic example of an anomaly is an operating system that continuously crashes, has more holes in its security than a mohair sweater under attack by a litter of kittens, but for some reason is the best-selling product in the entire industry.

anomaly detection   This is a procedure used by network security professionals to monitor systems for unusual behavior from both users and applications on the network. Software that uses this technique works by having an administrator set a baseline value for specific types of behavior or events. Events that are monitored might include failed logon attempts, intrusion attempts, or attempts to access secured resources. Whenever baseline values are exceeded, the software issues an alert. Optionally, the user might be locked out of the network.

anonymous FTP   Any file storage site on the Internet that uses the File Transport Protocol (FTP) and does not require authentication by the user. The term also refers to the process of logging on to such a site to access information without supplying credentials. Because of the lack of security, anonymous FTP sites are almost always isolated from the rest of the networks on which they reside. In addition, unless specifically designed as a public forum for the storage of files, they do not accept uploads from the general population.

anonymous logon　The ability of a user to access a server or network without having to provide a user ID or password. Many networks feature an anonymous account to accommodate guests on the network. In general, this account is given only minimal access and a limited set of permissions.

answer modem　When two computers are in communication over a telephone line, the answer modem is the device that is being called. Most modems on the market are configured by default to be autoanswer. In other words, the user can set a specific number of rings, after which the modem will pick up any call. The answer modem notifies the calling modem that it is indeed another modem by issuing an audible frequency that initiates the *handshake* routine.

antialiasing　A process through which diagonal lines in an image are redrawn to smooth out the jaggies. This is accomplished by filling in adjacent pixels with intermediate colors or shades of gray. For more information, *see* **aliasing**.

antidisestablishmentarianism　Organized opposition to the disestablishment of the Church of England. Yes, I realize the term has nothing to do with computer technology, but I was not about to have a dictionary that did not include this marvelous word.

antistatic　Any material or device that either prevents the buildup of, or dissipates static electricity from, a surface or component. Antistatic protection can be either active or passive in nature. An active antistatic protection device absorbs static electricity through a surface and uses a conductive element to drain the unwanted electrons to ground. These devices include antistatic wrist straps and mats. Mats can be either floor mats that the operator stands on, or bench mats where sensitive equipment is placed. Manufacturing with certain materials provides passive antistatic protection. Carbon fiber is good for draining away static electricity. Copper oxide impregnated into polycarbonate makes a good antistatic container material. Antistatic bags should be used for storing components. Figure A.13 shows an antistatic wrist strap sitting on top of an antistatic bag.

antivirus　Any form of protection against malignant software (*malware*) such as viruses, worms, and Trojan horses from a computer system. Antivirus software works by scanning your file system and looking for certain strings of code associated with known malware components. The file that contains the comparison code is known as the *signature file*. Because new viruses are popping up all the time, signature files must be constantly updated. Most antivirus packages ship with a signature file that was current when the version you are installing was current. However, by the time the product is packaged, shipped, sold, and delivered, that file will already be out of date. When you install the product, it is necessary to allow the software to update the signature files. Once that process is completed, it needs to be repeated on a regular basis. Your basic package will contain a *subscription* to new signature files for a certain period. Once the included subscription has elapsed, you will be forced to pay for new signature files. Fortunately, not all antivirus software is expensive. ALWIL Software offers noncommercial users a personal copy of their Avast! program

FIGURE A.13   *Antistatic protection is necessary both while you are working and when you store parts.*

and free subscriptions to their signature files. The Avast! program is available in both Windows and Linux versions at http://www.avast.com. Another equally fine product is AVG Technologies (formerly Grisoft) software AVG personal edition. AVG is also available for Windows and Linux users at no charge for either the product or the subscription. AVG personal editions are available at http://www.freegrisoft.com.

any key   A nonexistent key on your keyboard that the tech support people always insist that you press in order to continue. It is located right between the forward-space key and Away key.

apochromatic   A lens that is able to focus all wavelengths of light onto the same point in space. Apochromatic lenses are virtually free of *chromatic aberration*. Regular lenses focus light waves in the red spectrum on a different plane than the other two primary colors. An apochromatic lens focuses all three colors on the same point. Most lenses that claim to be apochromatic are actually achromatic in that they minimize focus shift in the red spectrum, but do not completely eliminate it. Generally speaking, a true apochromatic lens is significantly more expensive than a standard lens.

append   To tack on at the end. When a file is appended, instead of overwriting the file with a completely new copy, additional data is merely glued onto the end of the existing file. A database record can have new fields appended. To append is different than to *insert*. Data that is inserted into a file can be placed into the infrastructure and not necessarily tacked onto the end.

applet   A small but important program that performs a specific task. Generally speaking, an applet is executed from within another application, but runs independently of the application that invoked it. Ideally, an applet should be accessible by many applications. The applications that run from the Windows control panel are examples of applets. Also, Web-based devices such as online dictionaries, calculators, and unit conversion programs are excellent examples of applets.

AppleTalk   A suite of networking protocols developed by Apple, Inc. for their Macintosh computers. The protocol suite is very similar in many respects to *IPX/SPX*. It consists of a collection of different protocols with varying functions, including:

- AppleTalk Address Resolution Protocol (AARP)
- AppleTalk Data Stream Protocol (ADSP)
- AppleTalk Echo Protocol (AEP)
- AppleTalk Filing Protocol (AFP)
- AppleTalk Session Protocol (ASP)
- AppleTalk Transaction Protocol (ATP)
- Datagram Delivery Protocol (DDP)
- Name-Binding Protocol (NBP)
- Printer Access Protocol (PAP)
- Routing Table Maintenance Protocol (RTMP)
- Zone Information Protocol (ZIP)

AppleTalk Address Resolution Protocol (AARP)   Appletalk's implementation of TCP/IP's *Address Resolution Protocol*. It calls on the services of the *Datagram Delivery Protocol* for its functionality and provides the same services as ARP.

Appletalk Data Stream Protocol (ADSP)   A protocol from Appletalk that allows for a *connection-oriented transfer* of data between hosts. By using ADSP, data transfer is assured of error-free transmissions and that the information will arrive in the proper sequence. ADSP provides flow control and error correction.

Appletalk Echo Protocol (AEP)   An Appletalk protocol that provides an echoing service similar to TCP/IP's *PING*. AEP allows for the user to specify a packet size up to 585 bytes. There are two types of AEP packet. An *echo request* packet includes the data to be echoed and prompts the receiving computer to respond. The *echo reply* packet copies the data from the echo request packet, along with pertinent information about the echoing computer and sends it back to the original host.

Appletalk Filing Protocol (AFP)   AFP is a file-sharing protocol from the Appletalk suite. It provides a user-friendly interface to Apple file system objects. AFP can extract information such as the file's original creator, the create date, date that the file was last accessed, the length of the file, and many other attributes as well. Users of OS X see this protocol in action when they right-click on a file in *Finder* and select the *Get Info* option.

Appletalk Session Protocol (ASP)   ASP is an Appletalk protocol that manages session activity for upper-layer protocols. Each time a logical connection is initiated, ASP generates a unique session identifier. As long as that session remains open, ASP monitors the session and keeps it alive by exchanging status packets with the companion host. Once data transfer is completed and the session is no longer needed, ASP shuts down the link and cleans up any temporary files created.

Appletalk Transaction Protocol (ATP)   ATP is an Appletalk protocol designed to handle *transaction-oriented* data transfer operations. When such an operation is initiated, ATP issues a token that both computers will use throughout the transaction. This assures that only data relevant to a specific transaction will be included. ATP differs from a standard file transfer protocol in that if a transaction is not successfully completed, all traces of the attempted transaction will be eliminated. ATP is useful for such data transfers as an automatic teller cash withdrawal that is terminated before cash is issued.

application   A complete set of files that makes up one of the programs that run on your computer. The term is derived from the fact than an application performs one or more applied functions required by the user to perform a specific task. This includes all the *executables*, *binary support files*, *dynamic link libraries*, and *virtual device drivers*. WordPerfect and Netscape Navigator are examples of applications. Applications differ from system software in that system software performs functions for the operating system. System software includes operating systems, programming language compilers, and certain types of utility.

application layer   The layer of the Open Standards Interconnect (OSI) networking model that provides a gateway to the network for all applications running on a networked computer. The application layer confirms the availability of a connection, provides authentication services, verifies the presence of all necessary resources to complete a virtual connection (including hardware and mutually acceptable protocols), and negotiates flow control and error correction methods (although it provides neither of these services). Note that although there are applications specific to the application layer, the application layer is not so named because it runs applications.

application server   A computer running on a network whose job it is to run individual programs for the users and process data on their behalf. Application servers come in three basic flavors. A dedicated application server is a single machine that provides access to one or more applications to all users on the network. A distributed application server is actually more than one machine. Several different servers host applications and share the load of providing services to all users. Finally, there are peer-to-peer application servers. These are not really servers as much as they are other machines on the network that share applications.

application sharing   A specialized ability of certain programs that allows multiple users to interface with the same application at the same time. Only one machine runs the program files associated with the application, but the I/O from all other connected users is recorded and the computer responds to all users connected to the program. This allows multiple users to work as a team on the same project. Data conferencing is one of the most common implementations of application sharing.

archive   A location, site, or file that acts as a repository for information or data. For example, a database application can be an archive for information that you collect about specific subjects. A backup tape drive can archive all of your important files. A museum can act as an archive for valuable paintings. The term can also refer to a single file on a computer system that collects multiple files and compresses them to save space and file table entries.

archive bit   This term refers to a single bit in the file table for each file that indicates whether or not that file has been backed up since the last time it was modified. When set to 0, the file is marked as having been backed up. Any time a file is created or modified, the archive bit is set to 1. Any time a file is saved after changes have been made, the archive bit is reset to 1. The next time the file is backed up, it will be set to 0 once again.

argument   Any variable or modifier that is added to a command or instruction to modify or define its behavior. If you just type the word TYPE at the command prompt, nothing of value happens. If you add the argument NOVEL.DOC after the TYPE command, the entire NOVEL.DOC file will spill onto your screen so fast you cannot possibly attempt to read it. Arguments can be used in conjunction with *triggers* to further modify behavior. Typing the command TYPE NOVEL.DOC /P at the command prompt will show one screen of the file at a time.

areal density   This is another term for *bit density*. It defines the total amount of storage capacity for a specific unit of area on the surface of the drive platter. You might see this value represented as gigabytes per square inch (GBpsi; the most common) or in gigabytes per platter. Older media was measured in megabytes per square inch, but modern technology has pushed that up into gigabytes per square inch. As of this writing, there were drives on the market that boast 80 GBpsi, with announced plans for even greater densities. Increasing areal density has two effects on a drive system. First, there is the obvious effect of increasing total storage capacity. Secondly, because file *allocation units* are packed closer together, more of them pass beneath the read/write heads in any given nanosecond. This essentially increases the *data transfer rate*. In general, the two methods of increasing areal density were (1) decrease particle size and (2) decrease the number of particles required to record a single bit of data electronically. A technology known as *perpendicular recording* increases areal density without decreasing particle size or the number of particles used to record a single bit.

arithmetic logic unit (ALU)   The ALU is one of the subcomponents of the *CPU's* execution unit. The ALU is responsible for executing simple mathematical calculations such as add, subtract, multiply, and divide. It cannot perform floating-point calculations. In the early days of microprocessing, the ALU was capable only of add and subtract functions. However, it could also perform certain logic functions, such as AND, NOT, and XOR. In order to perform multiply and divide functions, these early processors depended on software emulation that used a series of cascaded add or subtract functions. Multiply and divide functions were added as independent functions in later incarnations.

ARPANET   The Advanced Research Projects Agency Network. This was the first collection of computers ever networked. The project saw success in 1969 when two different campuses of the University of California joined their Honeywell DDP-516 mainframe computers to those of The University of Utah and the Stanford Research Institute. The connection was made over conventional telephone *modems* at an amazing speed of 50 Kbps.

array   A collection of different components configured to work together as a single unit. For example, all of the individual data cells in a memory chip work together in an array. Several hard disks can be configured in such a way that the computer system sees them as a single disk. This is an example of an array. Any *RAID* configuration consists of an array of two or more hard disks. A number of *supercomputers* have been built by configuring an array of individual computers to work together as one.

arrow keys   On the computer keyboard these are the keys with arrows on them. They are for navigating the cursor from right to left or up and down on the page. More critically, they allow you to navigate your character through the mazes of destruction as you seek out and destroy aliens invading the earth.

artifact   Any stray digit created when an analog object such as an image or a piece of music is converted into digital form. Ideally, all digits in the file would represent an integral part of the original piece. Unfortunately, during the analog-to-digital conversion process, there is often a lot of stray "information" created. These artifacts are what lead to *digital noise*. Artifacts can be the result of several things. Hardware limitations are common causes. A video game might be designed specifically to make use of specific *APIs* for optimum performance, but also work on a more limited basis with some other, more primitive API. This would result in the generation of artifacts in the image. Software limitations, such as those of file conversions utilities, will result in artifacts as well. The owners of large-screen LCD or plasma televisions see two very common artifacts of imaging every day. One of these is caused when the thick scan lines of the larger screen are forced to reproduce thin objects. The second is caused when the motion of the object is faster than the frame rate of the digital reproduction.

artificial intelligence   In the world of computers, this term refers to any device or application that has been programmed so intricately that it can simulate human intelligence in many ways. A device that exhibits artificial intelligence will "learn" which procedures work and which ones fail and will adapt its future behavior patterns accordingly.

ascending sort   In a database or spreadsheet application, this refers to the process of sorting data starting with elements of the lowest value and working up to the elements of higher value. Sorting from 1 to 10 is an ascending sort, as is sorting from A to Z.

ASCII   The American Standard Code for Information Interchange (ASCII) was the first set of characters that translated binary into something mere mortals could understand. However, ASCII was not exclusively a character set. The 8 bits of the byte were used to generate 256 values.

   In the original ASCII, that one set of characters had to deal with both the human interface and also be used to send commands to graphics devices, such as printers. In the original ASCII, there were actually only 128 printable characters; the remainder of the set was used as commands. The Extended ASCII character set removed the control characters and provided 256 printable characters.

associate   To define how a specific type of file will be recognized and treated by the operating system or applications running on the system. For example, when properly associated, a file with a .DOC extension will automatically launch MS Word when you double-click on that file in Windows Explorer. File associations can be managed by the user in Explorer by clicking on Tools>Folder Options>File Types. Figure A.14 shows how to associate a JPEG file in this way.

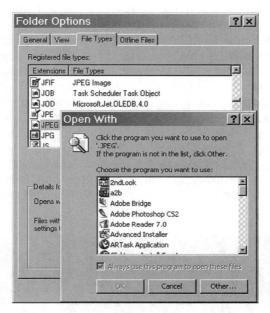

FIGURE A.14   Associating a file in Windows Explorer.

asterisk   The star-shaped character on the keyboard above the number 8. This character represents the *wild card* in general searches and is used by many publishers as a separator to indicate a transition in scenes in a manuscript.

asymmetric multiprocessing   A method by which an operating system makes use of more than one processor, loading OS code onto one processor and application code and user data onto all others. This is as opposed to *symmetric multiprocessing*, in which all processors share the load equally. Asymmetric multiprocessing is no longer used by modern operating systems.

asynchronous communication   A form of serial communication that transmits data a byte at a time over a single conductor. With asynchronous communication, either device may start or stop transmitting at any time. Data is transmitted in clusters of 9 to 11 bits per byte, with either 7 or 8 bits used for user data, a *start bit* to indicate the beginning of the frame, a *stop bit* to indicate the end, and an optional parity bit to be used for *error detection*. With asynchronous communication there is no true error correction, nor is *flow control* an issue. If a packet is lost or corrupted, that is just tough luck. This form of data transfer is generally used when very small pieces of data are being moved, or where it really does not matter that much if the data arrives intact.

asynchronous timing   This is a technique used when two devices are incapable of negotiating a mutually acceptable data transfer speed. The transmitting device delivers its data at any speed it sees fit to a reserved area of memory called a *buffer*. Data is then fed to the target device at a rate optimal to that device. This gets around the different speeds of the two devices. It should go without saying that for this technique to work, both devices must support it.

AT bus   Another term for the 16-bit *ISA bus* that was first introduced on the IBM PC-AT computer. This bus was extremely common on all PC-compatible computers up to and including the Pentium II. The AT bus was merely an extension of the 8-bit *PC bus* (sometimes mistakenly called 8-bit ISA), introduced on the original IBM PC. In addition, with increased bit width, the bus also allowed for a 24-bit address bus and increased the number of available IRQs from 8 to 15. All additional connectors necessary for the additional bit width, extra IRQs, and wider memory bus fit into a slot behind the 8-bit slot. This made the slot backwardly compatible to the PC bus. An 8-bit device fit perfectly into the front slot and a 16-bit device straddled the separator key, making use of both slots. After the year 2000, the 16-bit bus began struggling toward its inevitable death. Figure A.15 shows one of the 16-bit slots used on the AT bus.

FIGURE A.15   A 16-bit AT or ISA slot.

attachment   (1) A device that hooks up to a computer through an interface. Another more commonly used term for an attachment is *peripheral*. A key difference is that peripherals are generally external devices. An attachment can also include hard disks, optical disks, tape drives, and other devices that are installed within the enclosure. (2) Any file that is inserted into an e-mail transmission that can be opened by the intended recipient. Attachments from unknown senders should be opened with caution as attachments are common vehicles for transmitting viruses, worms, and Trojan horses into your system. It is not uncommon for e-mail service providers to limit the size of attachment that you are allowed to transmit, insomuch as attachments can really eat up available *bandwidth*. Also, on a secured network, attachments might be blocked. Inbound attachments present a threat for the reasons already mentioned. Outbound attachments can easily contain confidential or classified information that is not supposed to leave the organization.

attenuation   A measurable loss of power or signal strength of any transmission as it travels over a length of wire or through space. All signals exhibit attenuation to some extent. In copper-based systems, attenuation can be caused by *resistance* and by picking up external noise from the background. Wireless systems are not immune to attenuation. *Free space loss* attenuation is the result of the signal dissipating as it travels through space. In indoor systems, there are environmental variables such as the type and color of walls. *Amplifiers* or *repeaters* can be used in a circuit in order to return a signal to its original strength and send it along its way.

attribute   Any characteristic that defines a specific object. In the computer world, the term has three different applications. Information included with each file on the system that tells the OS and the applications what kind of file it is and how they are supposed to interact with that file. Attributes can also define specific properties of the file. A file's attributes are stored in a specific field in the file system's file table. In the various versions of FAT, these tables are the *file allocation tables;* hence, the name. NTFS stores the information in the *master file table* (MFT). The number of attributes possible in any file system is directly dependent on the number of bits available for the field. In FAT, it was an 8-bit field. Only 6 bits were used to create six different attributes, shown in Table A.2. Attribute bits can be combined, allowing multiple attributes to be applied to a single file. For example, a hidden, read-only file would be marked 00000011. NFTS stored file information into larger structures called *metadata files.* Therefore, any given file could have a large number of different attributes applied to it. Those attributes vary between the different versions of NTFS. Because those attributes do not use bit code, they will simply be listed in Table A.2.

audit   (1) A process by which certain activities on a system or network are monitored and recorded. Auditing can be done for security reasons, to see who is logging onto the system and when they are doing it. It is possible to monitor either successful or unsuccessful logon attempts. Auditing can also be performed in order to track system performance. When you create a baseline performance report for a server, you employ a form of auditing in order to collect the data you use. (2) A detailed analysis of a computer system or network's configuration, specifically targeting the implementation of security measures. A good audit will identify any potential leaks, allowing administrators to apply the appropriate patches to seal those leaks.

audit trail   A record of transactions that lead from the beginning of a process to its end and reports every step that occurs in between. An audit trail can begin when a user requests a service. As each technician performs a particular task, that person records what he did and adds it to the collection of documents. Later on, if there are ever any questions, the series of transactions are all recorded. Anyone who has ever been visited by the IRS is quite familiar with the importance of a good audit trail.

authentication   A process used by computers and applications to properly identify a user and confirm whether or not that user has the correct permissions to perform a task, access a file, or log on to a system. Authentication can take any one of several forms, but almost always involves forcing the user to provide a user name (ID) and a password. Other forms of network user authentication include *biometrics* and *smart cards*. Different forms of biometric authentication include fingerprints and retinal scans. Device drivers and other files can be authenticated by way of *digital certificates*, providing that both parties involved trust the origin of the certificates.

authentication server   A network server with the specific responsibility of checking the logon credentials of all users attempting to log on to the network. An authentication server maintains a collection of information called the *security database* that identifies the rights and privileges of each user on the network. It also maintains an *access control list* that associates permissions to resources. Even after the user is successfully logged on, the authentication server will constantly check each user's permissions as he attempts to access various resources on the network.

authenticity   Proof of origin of any given object. Software manufacturers will use such devices as serial numbers, holographic logos, and electronic activation to verify the *authenticity* of the software you attempt to install. On a simpler level, sometimes you need to verify that a file is the same one you originally saved to your hard disk or that the e-mail you received is really from someone you know. When you do this, you are checking the authenticity of these items.

authorize   This term can be used in reference to a user; it indicates that the user has been granted permission to access a system or file. It can also be used in reference

TABLE A.2
FAT attributes

ATTRIBUTE	DESCRIPTION	BIT CODE
Read-Only	Prevents the user from modifying or deleting the file.	00000001
Hidden	Prevents the user from seeing the file in a standard directory listing.	00000010
System	Similar to Read-Only, but also marks the file as critical to system operation.	00000100
Volume Label	Actually not a file attribute, but a descriptive attribute stored in the root directory that identifies a particular disk or partition.	00001000
Directory	Indicates a FAT entry as a directory node rather than a file node.	00010000
Archive	Indicates whether or not a file or directory has been added or modified since the last time it was backed up.	00100000

NTFS attributes

ATTRIBUTE	DESCRIPTION
Attribute List	Literally, this is an attribute that defines other attributes. Attributes external to the metafile system are considered to be nonresident. This attribute resides in the original MFT record as a pointer to the non-resident attribute.
Bitmap	Provides the information that points to the file location on the hard disk
Data	Defines the actual file. By default, all the data in any single file is defined by a single data attribute. Realistically speaking, a larger file is very likely to occupy a number of different physical locations. As far as the MFT is concerned, it is still a single attribute.
Extended Attribute (EA) and Extended Attribute Information	Both of these attributes are historical artifacts from the days when NFTS was attempting to be compatible with OS2. No longer used in Windows.
File Name (FN)	Self-explanatory. Note that a single file might have more than one file name. Long file names will have an 8.3 alias. Also, NTFS supports the POSIX naming conventions and may host Unix-compatible names as well.
Index Root Attribute	Contains an actual index of files contained within a specific directory. A small entry can house all of the necessary information within the MFT attribute. If the directory is too large for this, a pointer will direct the file system to the Index Allocation Attribute.
Index Allocation Attribute	This is where the file system learns where to find additional indexing information for large directories.
Security Descriptor (SD)	Contains the Access Control Lists (ACLs) and other data related to file security. Any information regarding file ownership and all auditing configuration also resides here.
Standard Information (SI)	Basic properties such as date/time-stamps for when the file was created, modified, and accessed, along with the NTFS equivalents of the "standard" FAT attributes listed in top section.
Volume Name	Self-explanatory. It is the name of the disk or partition.
Volume Information	Miscellaneous information defining the volume, such as the location of start and stop sectors, total volume size, and so forth.
Volume Version	Identifies the version of NTFS in use.

to a server, granting it the authority to perform some particular function on the network. For example, a *DHCP server* must be authorized before it can hand out IP addresses.

AUTOEXEC.BAT   A file in the root directory of a hard disk that contains specific instructions as to what environmental variables to load, what utilities (and in some cases, device drivers) to load, and certain other user settings. For the most part, modern operating systems do not make much use of the AUTOEXEC.BAT any more, relying on far more sophisticated configuration routines.

autofill   A feature of some applications by which commonly used words and phrases, such as your name and address, are filled into forms automatically after only a few letters are typed. In Web browsers and on some Web sites, autofill works by scanning a Web form for data fields with common names. The information that autofill uses to fill in the blanks is stored in a file on the computer. Some applications encrypt this information so that the casual user cannot easily access it. Although autofill greatly speeds up production, it can also be somewhat of a security risk. I am not anxious to have my Social Security number in the autofill box of the browser on a public library system. Other applications, such as Microsoft Excel, make use of the autofill function as well.

automount   The process of making the files on a remote directory or removable disk immediately available when the presence of the network resource or when a disk is detected in the drive. While this is something Windows users take for granted, there was a time when drives and network locations had to be mounted each time they were accessed.

autonomous   Any network or infrastructure that is completely under management control of local authority. It is derived from two Greek terms, *auto*, which means self, and *nomos*, which means law. Therefore, an autonomous system is a self-governing system.

autoresponder   A feature of some e-mail clients that automatically sends a reply to incoming messages whenever the feature is turned on. Such a feature allows a user to receive some sort of response even when the person they are attempting to contact is on vacation, providing some assurance that the sender is not being intentionally ignored. After 3 or 4 weeks elapse, it is safe to assume you are being ignored.

autosave   Some applications have a feature built in that automatically saves the file you are working on to a temporary file every so many minutes. Generally, the interval between saves is something the user can configure based on personal needs and work habits. The actual file opened by the user is not saved until the user intentionally saves it. Therefore, if the user does not want to overwrite the original file with new information, autosave will not force the issue. If the system or application crashes, it is possible to recover all new data that was entered up until the last autosave. Sometimes, it is possible to recover a file even if the application does not offer you the option once you restart. If you can locate the temporary file, it could be possible to extract the unsaved data from the autosave file. The following is a list of commonly used extensions for autosave files.

- .abk   Corel Draw
- .asd   Word for Windows
- .asv   DataCAD
- .bak   Used by a large number of programs
- .bk   Used by a large number of programs
- .bk!   Used by a large number of programs
- .bk$ Used by a large number of programs
- .bks   MS Works Spreadsheet
- .boe   Outlook Express
- .bud   Quicken
- .bzi   WinTotal
- .fwb   FileWrangler data file
- .idif   Netscape saved address book
- .mbf   Microsoft Money
- .med   WordPerfect macro
- .mtt   Microsoft Messenger saved contact
- .oeb   Outlook Express
- .ptb   Peachtree Accounting
- .qbb   Quickbooks
- .qdb   Quicken
- .sv$ Autocad
- .svd   WordPerfect for Windows
- .svg   Glossary, MS Word
- .svs   Style sheet, MS Word and WordPerfect for Windows
- .vbk   Visual Cad
- .wbk   WordPerfect Workbook
- .xlk   Excel

average access time   Frequently, manufacturers will advertise their average seek time. This is all fine and good, and it is a wonderful thing to know. However, average seek time is only half the equation that yields average access time. Average access time is the time that elapses between a request for data and the instant that the first bit in information is picked up by the R/W head. The other half of the equation is the drive's latency.

Latency is how long it takes for the R/W heads to lock onto the sector once the track has been located. This specification is calculated by taking rotational speed and calculating how much time one half of a complete rotation will take. Therefore, a hard drive with a rotational speed of 10,000 rpm will have a published latency of 3 milliseconds.

average seek time   Average seek time is a guess at how long it will take to move the R/W heads into position to lock onto the correct track. When the manufacturers make these measurements, they are based on moving the heads a distance equal to one third the diameter of the platter. Obviously, if the actuator arm has to move from the first track to the last, this time will be longer. Conversely, if it is only moving from track one to track five, it will be much shorter. Still, it provides a good comparison between two competing drives.

B

Babbage, Charles   (1791–1871) Born in Teignmouth, United Kingdom, Charles Babbage was an inventor, mathematician, and professor. His invention of the analytical engine, which formed the basis for modern computing, actually overshadowed the fact that he was the inventor of the cowcatcher located on the front of railroad engines. While it was never assembled because of the lack of funding, the analytical engine was a device that was to have been powered by a steam engine. Data input would be provided by punch cards and the machine would then perform a series of calculations on the data and return the results on other punch cards.

baby AT   A motherboard form factor based on the IBM PC-AT computer, but smaller. The baby AT motherboards were 8.5" wide, compared to the 12" width of the standard AT motherboard. While the specifications allowed baby AT motherboards to be up to 13" long, most boards that sported this form factor were between 9 and 11" long. All other features of the form factor, including component positioning, location of screw holes, and other physical characteristics were the same as the standard AT form factor. All AT form factors are now obsolete.

back door   This term refers to a secret account or password left on a system by a person who configured a server so that even if the administrator passwords she configured are changed, they still have a way into the system. Another term used for this same practice is *trap door*.

back link   A *hyperlink* that takes a visitor to a Web page back to the last page she was visiting. You can incorporate a back link into your page by inputting the code <input type=button value="Back" onClick="history.go(–1)">.

backbone   A high-speed connection between two network or subnets on a network that provides data communication between the networks. A large backbone might have a number of smaller networks called *access networks* that tap into it. The Internet is made possible by a network of backbone circuits interconnecting different access networks around the country.

background processing   Work that a computer does that does not involve interaction with the user. This would include activities such as processing hardware interrupts, system calls, and other OS-dependent activity. Background processes come in several types, but two main categories affect the user. A *daemon* is a background process that performs a specific service. For example, if you connect to a network printer, a small applet might be running in the background that automatically locates the printer on the network and sends the job when you have something to print. This is a printer daemon.

The other type of background process is the job that the CPU put on the back shelf to wait while it processes some other job in the queue. Newer operating systems, such as Microsoft Vista, can schedule certain types of background tasks to run only when a primary task is not using computer resources. This gives the foreground task priority. Earlier versions time-shared resources so that all processes got a share of time, even if it did not matter if a particular process was critical.

backoff timer   A logical mechanism used by Appletalk that tells a device how long it must wait to retransmit after a collision occurs. Appletalk uses a collision avoidance mechanism that works by sensing traffic on the wire. If activity is sensed, the backoff timer randomly selects a number of time slots that the transceiver must wait before attempting to transmit again.

backplane   A circuit board on a system that allows peripheral or internal devices, such as expansion cards or even hot-swappable hard disks to be plugged in. Some backplanes, such as the back panel of any computer system, are externally accessible. Others, such as the interface that connects to hot swap hard disks, are internal. Backplanes may be passive, meaning that they do no processing of data on their own. They merely act as a conduit for data and some other device does all the brainwork. An active backplane, such as a Fibre Channel Arbitrated Loop (FCAL) backplane, may contain a rudimentary processor, some firmware, and local memory, and the system might offload a lot of the processing directly related to the devices the backplane supports to the backplane.

backside bus   A portion of the CPU's data bus that connects to Level 2 cache. It is the path that data takes as it moves from cache loaded on the CPU's die into the CPU's registers. This circuitry was first introduced in the Intel Pentium Pro CPU and is incorporated directly onto the CPU die. The backside bus on early CPUs that featured this component ran at the same speed as the internal clock speed of the CPU. Later improvements allow the backside bus to run at a multiple of the CPU bus speed.

backside cache   This is another term for the *Level 2 cache* built onto a CPU die that directly couples to the CPU and runs at (or above) the speed of the internal CPU clock speed.

backslash   A keyboard character located next to the left <Shift> key, on the same key as the question mark. This character is used in programming to indicate that the following character is a quote and not part of the statement. It is also used to separate levels in a URL.

backspace   A key (Figure B.1) on the keyboard that backtracks a single space in a document for each time you press the key, deleting any character in its

FIGURE B.1   The backspace key on my keyboard is one of the most heavily used.

path. That way when you *tipe* a word wrong, you can backspace and *type* it correctly.

backup   One or more copies of a file or files that are available to the users in the event some catastrophe causes the original copies of the files to be lost. A good backup/recovery scheme is part of any network administrator's arsenal of tools. Backup can be performed as copies, *incremental backups*, *differential backups*, or *daily backups*. See each of these terms for more specific details on each backup type.

backup strategy   A complete plan of action detailing the hardware and software configuration used as well as the backup method and frequency that will be used. A good backup strategy takes a number of factors into consideration. Among these factors are:

- What is the hardware and software that will be used for making backups?
- Who will do the backup?
- How frequently will the backup be performed?
- What backup type will you use?
- What kind of backup rotation will you use?
- When will practice recovery runs be performed?
- Where will backup media be stored?

The backup strategy should be documented, and that documentation should be stored in a location where anyone who needs it can find it in time of need. During a major crisis, precious time should not be lost looking for paperwork.

backward compatibility   A feature of any piece of hardware or software that makes it work with previous versions of the same device or program. Generally, in order to make sure that something is backwardly compatible, some form of sacrifice must be made. For example, when Microsoft entered the 32-bit world with its operating systems, it was determined to maintain backward compatibility with all of the 16-bit applications and devices on the market. In order to do that, the engineers created a 16-bit kernel and a 32-bit kernel. Data moving from one kernel to the other had to undergo additional processing steps in order to make the move. This degraded OS performance to a significant degree.

bad sector   Any sector on a hard disk that cannot be read. While seeing a lot of bad sectors on a hard drive might give you a sinking feeling, take heart. Every drive in the world has a few bad sectors here and there. Hard disk manufacturers plan for this and provide several extra tracks that provide replacement sectors for the bad ones found by disk utilities. Disk utilities can detect and mark a sector bad before it gets to the point where the data cannot be read. The utility then moves the data to another sector and marks the weak one as bad. Then it moves the end of disk sector up by the number of sectors marked bad and the user never knows the difference.

ball grid array (BGA)   A type of mounting interface for microprocessors that uses a matrix of tiny conductive spheres on the base that integrate with associated indentations in the socket when the chip is mounted. For many implementations, this is a superior design in that there is no chance of bending fragile pins during installation. The chip is easier to install because it simply snaps into place. BGA chips and sockets are able to pack a high density of connectors into a smaller area and they dissipate heat more readily than pin-based packages. Design engineers like BGA because the shorter conductors suffer from a much lower degree of *inductance* and are less susceptible to electrical interference.

ballast   The power supply that provides current to a fluorescent light fixture. Ballasts are notorious for emitting extreme levels of *RFI*, which can interfere with network signals or, in extreme cases, can even cause data loss in computers. Since ballasts are typically located in the *plenum* between the ceiling and the floor above, if you absolutely MUST run your network cables through this area, it is a good idea to run it through shielded *conduit*.

balloon   A short explanation or tip that appears in the window of an operating system or application with text when a user hovers the mouse cursor over an object. The balloon might contain a short description of the object or a tip on what to do to make use of the object.

bandpass filter   A circuit that allows all frequencies within a certain range to pass, and filters out any signal above or beyond that range of frequencies. A byproduct of using bandpass filters that some engineers consider to be a negative feature is the fact that the frequencies that are allowed to pass exhibit a degree of *attenuation* at the extreme limits of the allowed frequencies. In a perfect world, a circuit with a high pass filter knocking out the high frequencies and a low pass filter blocking low frequencies would return a square waveform, with all blocked frequencies being 100% attenuated and allowed frequencies showing no attenuation. In the real world you get somewhat of a bell curve effect of the frequencies that pass.

band printer   A type of impact printer that uses a metal strip rolled around in a loop with the characters imprinted on the strip. Several different print columns can be imprinting type on the paper at one time. For each band of print, a separate impact driver pushes paper against an inked ribbon. The advantage of a band printer is that it can print multipart forms at up to 2,000 characters per second. In addition, it is capable of working in harsher environmental conditions than those of typical *line printers* or *dot matrix* printers. By the way, they are very noisy.

bandwidth   The transmission capacity of any medium. Bandwidth is generally measured in kilobytes, megabytes, or gigabytes per second. Obviously, more is better. Your overall bandwidth defines the limitation of your transmission speed when sending or receiving data over any network or Internet connection.

bank   In general, this term refers to any *array* of identical hardware components. The most common usage is with memory, where banking is a key issue in memory configuration. A bank of memory is a chip or combination of chips that must work together in tandem in a single I/O operation. With conventional configurations, all that is required is that the *bit width* of the memory equals that of the CPU. A CPU with a 64-bit external data bus must be able to see 64 bits of memory at a time. However, other factors can also influence the requirements of the memory bank. *Dual channel* memory requires that there are two 64-bit slices for a 64-bit CPU. Therefore, twice the number of chips is required for each bank. Figure B.2 is a photograph of a motherboard that has the memory set up in dual channel banks.

FIGURE B.2   The Apple Power Macintosh computer is equipped with four banks of dual channel memory.

barcode   A series of lines of varying thickness in which data is encoded. When a barcode reader is passed over, an LED or laser beam bounces off the lines and reflects back into a photosensitive receiver. The light and dark areas of the bars against the lighter substrate cause a flickering effect, which the receiver converts into an oscillating electrical current. This current is subsequently converted into digital information. Figure B.3 shows the barcode from the new keyboard on which I typed these very words.

barebones   This term refers to any type of system that contains only the minimum essential elements of the overall system it represents. For example, a barebones computer contains only an enclosure, a motherboard, and a CPU. It is up to you to provide memory, a hard disk, any removable disks you may need, and any and all input/output devices such as a mouse, keyboard, and monitor. Other than all that, the system is complete.

FIGURE B.3 *Nearly every product sold today has a barcode to enable computerized tracking of the product from manufacture to final sale.*

base A very versatile term, one with several meanings. (1) In mathematics, it represents the multiplier in a counting system. For example, with base 10, you count from 0 to 9 before you need a second set of digits to carry on. With base 16, you go from 0 to 9, then A through E, and then you need a new column of digits. (2) In electronics, the base is the switch on a transistor. (3) In general terms, the base is any starting point or reference point. (4) The term also refers to a solid stand on which an object rests. (5) It is also where the runner stands in order to be safe. If a base runner wanders off base, an opposing player can tag her with the ball and she will be out.

base address Most data occupies a range of memory addresses. The only exception is a single bit, which would rarely be accessed individually. The base address is the physical address of the first bit in that address range. This method of addressing points a large file to an absolute address that can be used to locate the data contained within. This comes into play particularly with I/O addresses. The CPU must be able to address each and every one of the devices on the system. The only method it has for doing so is the address register. In order to turn a device into a memory address, a pool of memory is assigned to the device, which acts as a dumping ground for the data moving back and forth between device and CPU. Knowing the base address of the device you are working with is critical if you ever need to manually configure the device. Table B.1 lists some common I/O base addresses.

baseband Any signal that can include frequencies approaching zero. In reality, the signal will consist of a range of frequencies. Only one signal can occupy that range. Baseband signals must be *modulated* in some fashion in order to encode data. *Amplitude modulation* and *frequency modulation* are the two most commonly used forms. Ethernet is a form of baseband technology.

baseline The level of performance that a device or system is capable of achieving with a minimal load imposed. For example, a server baseline is a measurement of that server's performance with a minimal OS configuration, the basic applications, and services that server is expected to run, and a minimal set of device drivers loaded. No users are added. The baseline measurement allows an administrator to accurately track the performance impact of additions to the system, including users, additional services, and applications. A baseline measurement of a system should be

TABLE B.1

Common base addresses

BASE ADDRESS	DEVICE
00 – 1f	Primary DMA Controller
20 – 3f	Primary Interrupt Controller
40 – 5f	System Timer
60 – 6f	Keyboard Controller
70 – 7f	Real Time Clock
8f	Refresh
a0 – bf	Secondary Interrupt Controller
c0 – df	Secondary DMA Controller
170 – 177	Secondary IDE Controller
1f0 – 1f7	Primary IDE Controller
200 – 20f	Game Controller
278 – 27f	Secondary Parallel Port
2e8 – 2ef	COM4
2f8 – 2ff	COM2
320 – 32f	XT Hard Disk Interface (Legacy)
378 – 37f	Primary Parallel Port
3e8 – 3ef	COM3
3f0 – 3f7	Floppy Disk Controller
3f8 – 3ff	COM1

performed when it is first brought online. Periodic measurements of performance should be made from time to time using the same parameters of performance and measurement techniques that were used to create the baseline. Whenever major changes to the system are made, a new baseline should be performed.

BASIC   Originally, an acronym that meant *Beginners All-Purpose Symbolic Instruction Code*, the term eventually evolved into a standard term. It began back in the 1960s as a simplified programming language for mainframe computers. With the development of personal computers, it was not long before people were modifying the language to work with these devices. A certain young college student by the name of Bill Gates got his start by modifying BASIC to run on an Altair computer.

basic disk   A disk that has been configured to conform to the legacy partition-oriented approach to file systems. Until the release of Windows 2000, all computers running Microsoft operating systems made use of basic disks. A basic disk can contain four *primary partitions* or three primary partitions plus one *extended partition* with numerous *logical volumes*. The partitions of a basic disk are defined within the *partition table* stored in the master boot record. This contrasts with a *dynamic disk* as supported by Win2K or later.

basic rate interface   A service package that is part of *ISDN* that offers two 64 Kbps channels for user data and one 16 Kbps channel for control data. *See* ISDN for a description of the channels used and their purposes.

batch file   A single text file that contains a series of commands, each of which launches an independent executable program. Batch files typically end in a .BAT extension to identify them as a batch file. The most commonly seen batch file in the days of MS-DOS was AUTOEXEC.BAT. An important characteristic of a batch file is that once a command is launched, it is in memory. If one program is dependent on the presence of another, the order in which they appear in the batch file is critical.

batch processing   Grouping a number of different procedures and processing them as a group can save time and be more efficient in terms of memory and CPU utilization. For example, you might have a number of different images on which you want to run the same group of filters. By lining them up and batch processing them, you can go have a cup of tea while they are running.

battery memory   A phenomenon exhibited by certain types of rechargeable batteries where the pattern of recent charge cycles affects the maximum charge the battery will accept. Nickel-cadmium batteries are particularly susceptible to this effect. A battery that is not completely discharged from time to time will subsequently not accept a full charge. The end result is that the battery no longer lasts as long as when it was new. This can be held off by occasionally *dump-charging* the battery.

baud   A method of measuring the signal bandwidth of a wire based only on the number of voltage transitions that occur each second. Since most modern technologies transfer far more than a single bit of data on each transition, as was the case in the early eons of computing, baud was used interchangeably with transmission speed. You will also see the term *baud rate*, but since the term *baud* refers to a rate, baud rate is somewhat repetitiously redundant.

bay   In a computer enclosure, a bay is a housing for a disk drive of some sort. External drive bays are the ones that hold the disks you can actually reach out and touch, such as a CD-ROM drive or a floppy disk drive. Most enclosures also have from one to a dozen internal drive bays that are used almost exclusively to house hard disk drives. Figure B.4 illustrates a case with several internal and external drive bays.

bayonet connector   A mounting base and socket combination that involves a simple push-and-twist motion in order to mount a device into a socket. A bayonet connecter is one that twists on and locks. It gets its name from the rather grisly weapon that soldiers lock onto the front of a rifle for close-range combat. Bayonet connectors are used with light bulbs and as a method of attaching cables to devices. *Coaxial* cable and some forms of *fiber optic* cable are types of cabling that use bayonet mounts. A positive aspect of the bayonet mount is that it is a fast and simple way to mount something. Conversely, it is not exactly the strongest mount available. The weak link in a bayonet mount is the pins that are used on the male end of the assembly. All too often, these consist of nothing more than a pair of rounded knobs. A bayonet mount is not the best choice for a connection that will be exposed to a lot of stress. Figure B.5 shows a bayonet connector.

B-channel   A carrier channel used by ISDN for transmitting user data at 64 Kbps. ISDN sends user data and control data over totally separate channels. A minimum of

FIGURE B.4   This computer enclosure supports up to six internal drives as well as four external ones.

FIGURE B.5   The BNC connector on this T-connector is a form of bayonet connector.

two B-channels provide up to 128 Mb/s of bandwidth. Up to 23 B-channels can be combined for higher transmission rates, if you are willing to pay the bill. *DSL* is cheaper and nearly as fast.

beaconing (1) In general, beaconing is any continuously repeating transmission of packets advertising an error condition. More specifically, beaconing is a process that the Token Ring protocol uses to find out what station has dropped from the network. Each device sends a beacon frame to both its upstream neighbor and its downstream neighbor. Once the culprit has been found, the MAU can bypass that station internally. (2) On a similar, but less negative note, the *access point* of a wireless network is constantly sending out advertisement packets announcing its presence. This process is also called beaconing.

bead A metal cylinder (usually ferrite) placed on the end of a conductor that is used to suppress external noise that might interfere with the signal. The device derives its name from its design. The bead is a cylindrical piece of metal in which a hole is bored to allow the cable to run through it. Since this is how beads are strung on a necklace, the name is descriptive. Many monitor manufacturers install a bead on the end of the cable to reduce interference. It also appears on many forms of communications or interface cable.

bearer channel One of the channels used by ISDN to carry user data. This is the same as the B-channel.

beep codes A series of audible sounds emitted by a PC speaker during POST that indicate an error condition. By knowing the correct sequence of sounds for the specific brand of BIOS installed on the computer, the beep codes will tell you what failed as the system was trying to boot.

bells and whistles This is a slang term for lots of extra goodies that you probably do not really need that are piled onto a system. Or a car. Or your house. Or anything else, for that matter.

benchmark A measurement of raw performance of a device or system. When comparing benchmarks, it is critical that you know how data was collected for assessing performance. In order to properly benchmark a system, you are not merely measuring the performance of a specific component, but rather that of the system. If two manufacturers of components use two different methods of measuring performance, with each one emphasizing the performance of their product, then the numbers can be pretty meaningless. Benchmarking software packages frequently used to measure performance include Dhrystone, MIPS, Whetstone, and PassMark.

Beowolfe A system in interconnecting computers using different processors and hardware platforms in order to create a single parallel computing system. Essentially by taking advantage of idle processor time, many computers can be called upon to work on a singular problem, such as searching for UFOs or weather modeling. Beowolfe is an offshoot of the Linux operating system and requires that the participating systems run Linux, along with Beowolfe software.

benign virus A computer virus or worm that, while it might be annoying, does no real harm. Its only purpose is to amuse the moron who wrote and distributed it.

beta release Once an application in development has reached the point where the publisher thinks it is almost ready for release, it will generally be sent out in a limited distribution to members of the public who are willing to be guinea pigs and test the software for bugs the alpha testers missed (or thought were funny enough to watch users deal with). Beta software is generally still riddled with bugs, albeit minor ones. In some cases, beta releases have been known to lock up machines. An advantage of being a beta tester for a software developer is that beta testers frequently get deep discounts on the final release when it is available. Those who do beta testing regularly will frequently maintain a separate computer for running beta software so that their computer does not lock up in the middle of typing a....

bezel   The plastic frame that masks off the unusable part of a monitor's image or conceals the workings of an external disk drive. The only real function of the bezel is to improve the appearance of the device. On a CRT display, it also covers up a portion of the image that is of insufficient quality to be used. On disk drives, the bezel will usually provide support for one or more indicator lights. The CD-ROM drive shown in Figure B.6 has the disk tray, a drive indicator light, and an eject button neatly framed by the drive's bezel.

FIGURE B.6   *The bezel on this CDR covers the internal mechanisms and provides support for the eject key and a status light.*

bias   A controlled DC current applied to a wire whose sole purpose is to stabilize the circuit. Bias can be either forward or reverse. Forward bias voltage is sent down the wire in the same direction as current flow. Reverse bias sends the stabilizing current against the stream in the opposite direction. Bipolar transistors feature a pin called the *bias pin* that acts as the front door for current arriving from the battery or power supply.

bidirectional   A conductor or circuit that allows current to flow either upstream or downstream (although not in both directions at once). Some types of cable, such as a fiber optics connection, do not allow for movement in both directions on the same strand of medium. Therefore, a separate strand carries the signal for each direction. Copper media carrying electronic signals may be designed to move data in both directions on the same strand. However, some form of control needs to be in place in order to prevent signals from colliding. A variety of protocols are available that permit this.

bifurcate   A term used when a path splits off and goes in two different directions. The word is derived from the Latin *bifurcus,* which means two-pronged.

big-endian   Binary code generally streams through a CPU in one of two directions. It either moves *most significant bit first* or *least significant bit first.* Most CPUs require that the code move one way or the other. A big-endian system processes the most significant bit first. In terms of data storage, in a big-endian system the most significant byte will occupy the lowest numbered memory address. Many mainframe computers, including models of IBM, are big-endian. Intel-based PCs are little-endian. Some CPUs, such as the PowerPC, can read code either direction as long as something in the software tells it which way to swing. These processors are *bi-endian.*

bilevel display   A monitor or other display that uses only two hues. Text and rudimentary graphics are displayed either as darker pixels against a lighter background, or vice versa. The early Hercules displays were bilevel and came in three varieties. All had a dark gray (approaching black) background. Text was amber, green, or a very light gray, depending on model. While we have definitely entered a full-color generation of electronic devices, the bilevel display is still alive and well. Many LCD watches and monochromatic electronic devices, such as PDAs and cell phones, use this type of display.

bilinear filtering   A 3D graphics texturing method that takes the average of four surrounding *pixels* and interpolates a value for a pixel whose value is otherwise unknown. The term is derived from the fact that the pixels used for interpretation are the two directly above and below, and the two directly to the right and left. Since interpretation is coming from two dimensions, it is bilinear. Bilinear filtering is great for reducing obvious pixelization in an image. However, this is done at the sacrifice of sharpness.

binary   A base 2 counting system that consists of the two characters 0 and 1. Binary code is the basis for all computer code. 0 is off, closed, or no; 1 is on, open, or yes. Because all computer data is binary, it is not uncommon to see raw data files or executable code referred to as *binary files.* Although George Boole is frequently credited with inventing binary mathematics, it actually dates back much farther. An Indian mathematician named Pingala first described a base 2 numbering system as far back as circa 800 BC. Francis Bacon described a system for encoding text using a base 2 format. Early in the development of computers, engineers used the on/off function of basic switches as the basis for converting an electrical signal into binary code. This became the basis for computing as we know it today. Some terms that come into play when discussing binary include:

- *Bit:* a single zero or one
- *Byte:* any combination of eight zeros or ones
- *Nibble:* Four bits
- *Word:* Two to four bytes
- *Page:* One to twenty kilobytes
- *Kilobyte:* Two to the tenth power bytes, or 1,024 bytes
- *Megabyte:* Two to the twentieth power bytes, or 1,048,576 bytes

The values in binary all include nothing but 1s and 0s. For example, the decimal number 173 in binary is 1010 1101. 10 represents the number 2.

The order of bits in a byte is significant as well. Programmers refer to this order by way of least significant bit and most significant bit. The most significant bit of a single byte has a mathematical value of 256, whereas the least significant bit has a value of zero. With all of this to remember, it is easy to see why there are only 10 types of people in the world…those who understand binary and those who do not.

There are a number of different values used in binary that indicate the number of bits or bytes. Table B.2 is based on bytes, but can also be used to calculate bits. Substitute a lower-case b in the abbreviation to indicate bits.

TABLE B.2

Binary values and their nomenclature

VALUE	NAME	ABBREVIATION
$1,000^1 = 10^3$	Kilobyte	KB
$1,000^2 = 10^6$	Megabyte	MB
$1,000^3 = 10^9$	Gigabyte	GB
$1,000^4 = 10^{12}$	Terabyte	TB
$1,000^5 = 10^{15}$	Petabyte	PB
$1,000^6 = 10^{18}$	Exabyte	EB
$1,000^7 = 10^{21}$	Zettabyte	ZB
$1,000^8 = 10^{24}$	Yottabyte	YB

bind   To link. In programming the term is used in reference to the process of linking different subroutines together in order to allow them to be called as needed. It is also necessary to link the code from an operating system to the system BIOS and code stored in the chipset. This process is also called *binding*. When a network interface card is configured with a specific protocol, the firmware of the NIC must bind to the code of the protocol before the two will work together.

biometric authentication   A form of security that uses information specific to biological attributes of the person being authorized. Biological attributes can either be measurable physical characteristics that are unique to an individual, or behavioral characteristics such as handwriting analysis. Physical biometrics can include fingerprints, retinal scans, voiceprint analysis, or DNA samples. Behavioral characteristics include signature recognition and voice recognition. Ongoing research is studying the possibility of using the way someone walks as a method of digitally identifying someone from a distance. In order to perform biometric authentication, a sample of the biological imprint must be converted to a digital file that the computer can recognize. For example, a fingerprint is collected and then scanned. The resultant image is then converted to a mathematical key. Later, when a person submits to authentication, the fingerprint is collected and run through the same process. A mathematical model tells the system how much variance between the sample taken and the stored key is allowed before authentication is passed.

An identical match would not be possible since varying pressure may cause compression of the ridges on the fingertips and subsequently generate minimal differences in the number code generated.

BIOS extension   A string of code that interfaces the operating system to the BIOS interrupts. Standard BIOS code loaded on the EEPROM cannot solve every problem the OS has with hardware interfacing. Many specific problems are resolved by installing a BIOS extension. When the computer boots, this code is loaded along with the conventional BIOS. Some issues that have been solved via BIOS extensions include hard disk interfacing, VESA graphics, the Y2K problem that was not, and even antivirus technology.

bipolar   Any circuit with a distinct positive direction and a distinct negative direction. A magnet is considered bipolar because it has one end that repels another magnet, and the other end attracts. Some types of transistors are bipolar. My boss is definitely bipolar.

birefringent   Light waves can be either horizontal or vertical. Sunlight is a random mixture of light waves moving at all angles. Polarized light is light in which all light waves except for those at a certain angle have been filtered out. Birefringent light is light that is filtered to horizontal and vertical waves only, and one set of waves is traveling at a slightly slower speed. In addition, one set of light waves refracts into a slightly different angle than the other. As a result, a birefringent image will actually show two overlapping versions of the same object. A calcite crystal is a birefringent object substance.

bit   Short for *binary digit*. This is the most basic data unit recognized by a computer. A single bit can reference one of two values. That value may be represented as 0 and 1, on and off, or yes and no. By collecting multiple bits together into blocks, larger data sets are made possible. Eight bits make up a *byte*. Although it might be easy to question the value of a single bit, there are many cases where a single bit is very powerful. The file descriptor in a file allocation table uses a single bit to determine certain critical file attributes. Certain forms of serial communication use a *start bit* and a *stop bit* to determine the beginning and end of a byte of data being transmitted. Also, the unintentional inversion of the value of any bit changes the value of the block of data for which it is a member.

bit cell   The collection of magnetized particles that host a single bit of data on magnetic media. Null areas where data will not be recorded surround the bit cells on most media surfaces. This prevents magnetic charges from one bit overlapping those of another. A key focus of design engineers trying to cram more data onto each square inch of medium has been to reduce the size of the bit cell along with the null area required to isolate each cell.

bit density   This is a measurement of the total number of bits that can be stored on the surface of any physical medium. Bit density is directly correlated to the size of each *bit cell*. *See* **areal density**.

bit depth   The number of bits used by a display driver to calculate the color values of a single pixel. Different bit depths are given more user-friendly names such as *True Color* and *High Color*.

   4-bit color   Standard VGA
   8-bit color   Super VGA

15-bit color A variation of 16-bit color that dropped the odd bit
16-bit color High Color
24-bit color True Color
32-bit color True Color with an *alpha channel*

Early operating systems, such as DOS and Windows 3.x, only supported up to 16-bit color. As the world of computing has evolved, we have gone in the opposite direction. In Windows XP and Vista, there is only support for 24- and 32-bit color.

bit error ratio Also sometimes seen as *bit error rate*. This is a calculation of the number of bits per unit of time that are inverted or lost during transmission. You will generally see this value represented in scientific notation. For example, if a memory chip averages one error per billion bits passed, its bit error ratio is 1×10^9. This may be displayed in a document as 1e-09. With some types of data, such as music or images, a moderate error rate is acceptable. With other forms, most especially executable code, even a very low rate is unacceptable.

bit flipping Switching a 1 to a 0 or a 0 to a 1. Bit flipping is a form of memory error that occurs in nature, although it is extremely rare. On a base level, a NOT operation incorporates bit flipping to invert the value of 1 to 0 or vice versa. Hackers may engage in a bit flipping attack in which they alter the bit patterns of enciphered data in an attempt to learn the encryption model used.

bit rate The speed at which data travels over the wire, usually expressed in bits per second (bps) or kilobits per second (Kbps). Do not confuse this with bytes per second, and do not confuse it with baud rate, which is the frequency of the carrier signal in hertz. Since the data moving across the medium is a mixture of user data and control data, the bit rate is only peripherally related to actual data transfer rate.

bit stream The actual binary data that is moving across any communications medium at any moment in time. While a user may be interested only in the data being transmitted, information being transmitted will also include additional data. A data packet contains a *header* and a *footer* (or trailer, as it may also be called), which contain addressing information, protocol data, and error correction code as well as a number of other bits of data required by the system in order to successfully transmit data. When analyzing traffic or troubleshooting a networking issue, a technician can capture a snippet of the bit stream and break it down using network analyzers.

bit striping A technique of distributing data across multiple drives or partitions on a bit-by-bit basis. Unlike other data striping methods, bit striping breaks individual bytes of data across multiple drives. Two levels of RAID incorporate bit striping. Neither one sees much (if any) use. RAID 2 uses bit striping with Hamming code. In this scenario, each bit of a block of data is written to separate drives, and for each block of data (called a *data word*) an error correction algorithm creates a data check block called the *Hamming code*. This technique did not gain much favor because of the extremely high number of disks required, nearly half of which were used for error correction. RAID 3 uses bit striping with parity. Like RAID 2, it stripes data across disks as individual disks. Unlike RAID 2, the RAID 3 parity blocks require but a single disk drive added to the array for parity information.

bit stuffing Adding nondata information to a frame in order to bring it up to a minimum size. Some protocols require that all data frames be of a minimum size and will drop "runt" frames. In order to send smaller data sets that do not meet the frame size requirements, noninformational data bits will be used to fill the remainder of the frame. In order to make sure that the data is properly transferred, both the transmitting computer and the receiving device need to know where the data ends and the stuffing begins.

bit timing A method used by transceivers to accurately extract encoded data from an analog signal using clock cycles as a basis for determining the beginning and end of a data structure. Serial communication is inherently dependent on bit timing techniques in order to assure that the receiving device interprets the data in the same way the transmitting device sent it. To make sure bit timing is kept accurate, each device periodically sends out a synchronization signal. A parcel of data, which can be read by individual protocols as individual bits, bytes, or packets of data, is a function of the timing signal. All data that falls between a designated start point and stop point is considered a parcel.

black box A term used for any handmade or custom-made device that is not generally available to the public. Many of the devices that you walk into the store and buy for a few bucks today started out life as exorbitantly expensive black boxes. There is also a company called Black Box that manufactures a variety of high-quality specialty devices.

blackout A complete loss of power to an entire area. Blackouts can be particularly damaging to computer equipment. When the power is suddenly lost, a system shuts down abruptly if it is not hooked up to a *UPS* or a *standby power supply*. Temporary files are not cleaned up, data in cache or in virtual memory is not written to the hard disk, and any new data in RAM but not previously saved is totally lost. When the power is suddenly returned, the voltage surge can damage or even destroy *integrated chips*.

blade One of several components, such as a server or storage unit, in which multiple units are housed in a single cabinet. A blade system consists of an enclosure and the servers/storage units. Typical servers, such as tower servers or rack-mount servers, are self-contained units that can act as stand-alone computers. Blade servers offload certain components to the blade enclosure. A rack-mount server requires a minimum of 1U of rack space (1.75" × 19"), while most servers are 2U or 4U devices. As an example of a blade system, an Intel blade chassis fits up to 14 servers into a 7U rack space. The enclosure contains a pair of dual-redundant power supplies that provides power to all devices in the enclosure. A single 1.44" floppy diskette drive and a single DVD-ROM drive interface with all servers, along with a USB connection. Since the enclosure features hot-swappable blade bays, servers can be added or removed on the fly without affecting the performance of the other systems in the enclosure. Using a blade system of this nature, a large network operations center could house up to 84 servers in a single 42U rack. Because the servers and other modules interface with the enclosure, a vast number of cables required by other systems are eliminated. Blade modules that can be mounted onto the rear of a blade enclosure include hub and switch assemblies, management modules, and additional blowers for cooling.

blanket   To cover completely. When you blanket a network you are hitting every device with the same signal.

bleed   (1) To print an image to the very edge of the paper. Most printers are not capable of a full bleed. In order to accomplish this, you must print the document or image onto a sheet of paper the next size larger and then trim the sheet to size. (2) The amount of free space left on the edge of the paper to allow for inconsistencies in the printing process. The intent is that this area will be trimmed off before presenting the image for display. Typically, a 3-mm bleed is considered safe in the printing industry.

blinky lights   Slang for the status lights you seen on the various devices on a network or computer desk. These status lights are there to indicate power on/power off and different error conditions.

block   A group of data bytes that are stored or transmitted as a single unit, whether they are related bytes or not. Storing data in blocks requires that the file system be bypassed and data integrity be restored before transmitting or recopying that data. Many enterprise level database applications support block mode for storing the data. Certain forms of RAID copy data in blocks as well. The advantage of storing data in block format is that *disk slack* is all but eliminated. The disadvantage is that additional overhead is added to the system as data is converted to a format that other applications can read and write.

block cipher   A technique for *encrypting* data that works on data strings that are of a fixed length (blocks). An example of a block cipher is 128-bit DES encryption. With this method, a string of data 128 bits long is run through an algorithm that scrambles the order of the bits in that block. An electronic key is provided to an authorized user that indicates the correct order for the bits to be reassembled.

block mode   (1) The data transfer setting that allows multiple commands to be moved over an interface from the OS to the hard disk controller on a single interrupt cycle. (2) A data transfer mode used by IDE devices that allows multiple clusters of data to be read from the disk surface and transferred to memory in a single interrupt. Early incarnations of IDE allowed only a single cluster to be copied on a single I/O operation. Depending on the file system used, this could be anywhere from 1,024 bytes to 64 KB. If a 64-KB file was requested from a hard disk formatted with 1,024-byte clusters, a total of 64 I/O operations (and interrupts) would be required before the data was transferred. Block mode allows up to 64 KB to move across the bus in each I/O operation.

block striping   A technique of distributing data across multiple drives or partitions in chunks of a specific size, regardless of whether or not the data in a single block belongs to the same file. Block sizes can typically be selected from several sizes, ranging from 8 K to 64 K. Unlike the clusters supported by the file system, data blocks can contain information from more than one file. Therefore, disk slack is not an issue. The choice of block size should be based on the relative size of files typically used by the system. A system with many small files should use a smaller block because if a 64-K block is selected and there are many 32-K files on the system, some files may not be striped across multiple drives.

block transfer   The movement of multiple commands over an interface on a single interrupt cycle. *See* **block mode**.

blog   A slang term for a *Web log*. Blogs are basically online diaries that are input in chronological order. Generally, the most recent entries are on top and you read down the page, going back in time. Usually blogs contain links to other blogs or Web pages of interest to the author, and may or may not include useful information.

blooming   A form of electronic distortion experienced by *CCD* devices when the light that hits them is more intense than they are designed to record. The excess intensity results in a voltage higher than the image processor can handle and the image flares out around the affected area. Nearly all modern CCDs incorporate a secondary circuit whose sole job is to counteract blooming. Conveniently enough, this is called the *antiblooming circuit*. *CMOS*-based devices do not experience this problem to a big enough extent to worry about.

Bluetooth   A wireless networking technology that makes use of packet-based transmissions over short range radio signals. Bluetooth is used to interface peripherals with computers, to link earpieces with cell phones and a wide variety of other applications.

bonding protocol   One of several protocols that provide the services that allow data to be transmitted over several different channels simultaneously. Also known as *channel aggregation protocols*.

Boolean   An algebraic mathematical model that is based on Base2 (or binary) mathematics. The name was derived from George Boole, the mathematician who described the model. Boolean mathematics is the base for all binary operations used by computers today.

boot   This is the general term for the process that a computer or other digital device goes through from the instant that it is turned on until the operating system is finally loaded and ready to go. The process of booting the computer is fairly complicated and involves invoking code from different programs on the *BIOS* chip, code stored in a hidden partition called the *master boot record*, and finally the complex process of starting the operating system. The term is derived from an old-fashioned phrase, "to bring it up by the bootstraps." I did not think my computer had boots until one day I looked closer, and sure enough, there was a *boot sector*.

boot block   A feature present on most modern system boards that allows the system to boot to a minimal configuration, including floppy drive support, in the event that the BIOS is corrupted or destroyed by a virus. A secondary chip on a motherboard contains sufficient BIOS code to bring the machine up to its most rudimentary bootable device. If, during POST, the *system block* of the BIOS cannot be read (missing or corrupted), a restore routine is invoked that searches the floppy disk drive (or other bootable removable device) for a file that can be used to restore the BIOS. For example, AMI BIOS looks for a file called AMIBOOT.ROM. This file should contain the most up-to-date version of the system BIOS for your motherboard. Award BIOS routines look for AUTOEXEC.BAT so the user can boot to floppy and manually flash the BIOS using a flash upgrade routine. Boot block will be available only on systems with Flash BIOS (which is practically every motherboard sold today).

boot sector   The sector or sectors on a hard drive that contains either the *master boot record* or the *volume boot record*, depending on whether the disk is bootable or not. This holds information that defines the file system used by the OS, the layout of partitions on the drive, and a pointer to the OS. A disk formatted with only a single partition will contain a volume boot record. This contains all the information required to locate and load the OS. A disk with multiple partitions will contain a master boot record. Like the volume boot record, it contains a pointer to the OS. However, the OS might be located on a different partition or even a different drive. In addition to OS pointers, the master boot record contains partition tables mapping up to four primary partitions that can be configured on the disk. Because of the critical importance of the boot sector, it is frequently the target of malicious viruses attempting to cripple the computer system. Boot sector viruses can erase or modify OS pointers and partition tables or wipe the boot record altogether.

boot sequence   The process that a computing device goes through from the moment that the power is turned on to the point that it is available to the user. In general, the process goes as follows. The bootstrap loader in the system BIOS reads the setup configuration to find what storage devices are listed as being bootable. These devices are listed in a specific order (also referred to as *boot sequence*, which can get a little confusing). Bootstrap loader checks each of these devices in turn, looking for a *volume boot record* or a *master boot record* that will assume the remainder of the boot sequence. The boot record identifies the file system used by the storage device and loads it into system memory. From this point forward, the drive is now a readable device. Another string of code in the boot record is a pointer to the OS that directs the boot process to the first line of code for the OS identified by the boot record. From here, the boot sequence is operating system-specific and can vary between brands and version of operating system as to what the boot sequence will be.

boot virus   Malignant code that gets written to the boot sector of a disk. In the old days this was a pretty common approach because a large number of machines booted to floppy disk drives. Also, there was no BIOS-level protection against the attack. These days, you are warned every time something tries to alter the boot record, so it is much more difficult to affect the boot sector.

bootable   Any device that contains information needed to define the file system; any partitions that exist on the drive and a pointer to the OS. This information is called a *boot sector*. In the early days of computing, the only bootable devices were hard disks and floppy disks. Now virtually any form of storage can become a boot device. As the system boots, several different devices can be called on to provide a boot sector. The order in which devices are queried for a boot sector is called the *boot sequence*.

bootleg   Another term for counterfeit or pirated software. Bootleg software is any commercial program that has been illegally copied or has been made available for download on the Internet. Another form of bootlegging that does not involve illegal copying, but that is just as illegal, is the process of selling *OEM* software without following the guidelines prescribed by the manufacturer. For example, many disreputable companies have been known to strip out of the package the accompanying CDs for the software that ships bundled with a computer system and then sell them separately. This practice, sometimes known as *double dipping*, allows a vendor to realize revenues twice from the same package. The problem is that with newer registration technologies, such as *product activation*, the second user to attempt to register the product may be denied activation. This is particularly annoying when you think you purchased legal software. It serves you right when you know you didn't.

BootP   Short for Boot Protocol, this is a protocol that allows a computer to boot from a remotely installed operating system. A Bootp enabled computer will send out a broadcast over the network looking for a Bootp server, which will respond with an IP configuration and path to the necessary boot files.

bootstrap loader   A program that resides on the BIOS chip or other nonvolatile device that is responsible for locating and initializing the *master boot record*. The bootstrap loader is the last program that the BIOS runs. Once a boot record is located, the BIOS turns the boot process over to the boot device and it takes over until the point that the OS loads. This program has been replaced recently on some systems by the *Extensible Firmware Interface*, which generates a working environment for the system without requiring any external support.

boss screen   A screen that is purely graphical that looks, feels, and smells like a legitimate business application. This screen can be invoked with a simple keystroke or set of keystrokes. Its only real function is to hide what the user was really doing, such as playing Redneck Rampage, when the boss suddenly walked in. Explaining the insipid "HEE HAW!!" coming from the speakers is the employee's problem.

bot   Short for *robot*, this is a small application that interfaces with the Internet and performs a specific automated function or a series of automated functions. Bots are used to monitor Internet usage by individual users; they provide tracking data on what sites are visited the most. If you manage a Web site, your ranking on search engines depends rather heavily on the services provided by bots. If you block them, you will never increase your rankings.

bottleneck   This is the slowest conduit for data on the system, or to use an old cliché, the weak link in the chain. No matter how fast data moves through the rest of the system, the overall system can be no faster than its slowest point. Bottlenecks exist in computers and on networks. In a computer, the bottleneck is represented by the slowest component. You have a fast CPU and lots of memory, but you are using an old and slow PCI VGA card. The system can process data quickly, but the results are displayed so slowly you will never know that. The video card is the bottleneck. On a network, it might not be so much the speed of the component of medium that ties up traffic, so much as the amount of traffic trying to pass over or through the bottleneck. If 16-gigabit segments all spill into a single 100-megabit connection to the server, that last connection is the bottleneck.

bounce   (1) To return unexpectedly. An e-mail that does not get delivered is said to bounce when the reply that arrives in your mailbox indicates that it was undeliverable. (2) To restart. A common slang term for rebooting a server is to *bounce* it. Please remember that when your boss asks you to bounce the server, she is speaking in a figurative sense. That person is likely to get upset if you try to literally bounce the machine off the floor.

boundary error   An application error that occurs when data exceeds a set of limitations that has been put on the value it represents. For example, if you have a database field that requires a minimum of six characters and you only put in four, this will return an error. It may not call itself a boundary error, but it is. Another form of boundary error occurs when an OS or application is looking for values that fall within a specific range, and a value outside of that range is returned. Hackers have been able to exploit known boundary error conditions in software in order to break into systems remotely. Both Windows 2000 and some versions of Internet Explorer possessed documented boundary errors that, if not corrected by a patch, allowed a hacker to take over a system.

boundary router   An external *router* that connects an autonomous network to the Internet or a wide area network. The boundary router is the last device on the network directly under the administrative control of an organization as data makes its way to the outside world. Boundary routers contrast with *core routers*, which direct data traffic within the organization's autonomous network. Boundary routers can be configured to set up a protected area called a *demilitarized zone*. This router acts to disguise the organization's IP addresses from potential hackers.

bounded media   Any medium that physically connects a device to the network by way of a tangible cable. Because of this, data travels over a specifically defined pathway. Certain limitations for setting up a network using bounded media are created by the distance limits imposed by the media selected. Copper-based media is limited to as little as 100 meters per segment. Fiber optics offers a much greater range, but can still be limited, depending on the choice of fiber and the protocol used. Routers, bridges, and switches are devices that allow networks to be expanded. Bounded media includes all copper-based and fiber optic media.

branch prediction   In the course of processing data, there are a lot of forks in the road ahead. If the user inputs "Y" to a particular prompt, one set of instructions will be called, and if "N" was inserted, then an entirely different set would be needed. In early days, until the end user input the selections, the CPU sat twiddling its thumbs. Branch prediction processing is a process by which the processor will use one of several algorithms to "look into the future" and load the first few lines of code that will be used whichever way the user decides to go. Branch prediction is an essential element for any processor that provides multiple processing pipelines because these processors expect to have the next line of code waiting in the halls before the instruction in process is completed. This frequently requires that a little code prophecy be used.

break   Any stop in the process of running code, whether induced by a user or not. It is possible to induce a break in some batch files and in the POST routine by pressing down on the Pause key. Which is, oddly enough, how that key got its name.

break code   A signal generated by a keyswitch when the key is released. On each key of the keyboard, a unique string of code is generated when the key is pressed and another is generated when the key is released. The break code is the release code. Having a separate release code allows for printing or displaying repeat characters or determining how long you want your hero to keep strafing the enemy. Without the use of separate make and break codes, you could only fire one shot at the alien slime before it nailed you with a plasma bolt. Unless you have really fast fingers.

break/fix   This is a slang name for a service call that involves repairing downed hardware. It is a shortened alliteration of "you break it, we fix it."

BREW   (1) Binary Runtime Environment for Wireless. This is an application development language developed by Qualcomm that is used to create applications small enough to run on cell phones. The applications encoded on the device are there to provide enhanced services. It is this type of application that allows a cell phone user to transmit text messages and photos. (2) The strong black beverage you drink in the morning to get you going. (3) The cold amber (or nearly black) beverage you drink in the evening to wind you down.

brick and click   A business with an established physical location as well as an Internet presence. That would be most businesses in place today.

brick and mortar   A slang term for a conventional business that resided at a fixed address with a permanent physical location. The term came about as a way to distinguish between businesses that exist solely on the Internet from physically located businesses. The old dry goods store in Figure B.7 is a classic example of a store that is better off on the ground than on the Internet.

FIGURE B.7   *The old way of doing business was to set up in a building. Brick and mortar, as they say.*

bridge   (1) A circuit that transfers data from one channel or bus to another. (2) A specialized circuit that moves data between two disparate devices or busses in such a manner that both devices become compatible. Bridges work at the *data link* layer of the OSI model, and are therefore dependent on the *MAC address* of the transmitting and receiving devices for directing traffic. Bridges are intelligent devices insomuch as they can dynamically build and maintain an address table that identifies what devices reside downstream from any port. Bridging can be done in one of two methods. A *transparent bridge* maintains a local database of MAC addresses. When a packet is received, the device scans its database to discover which port is the correct tunnel for transmitting the data. If the packet contains an unrecognized address, the bridge broadcasts the frame through all ports. All of the devices that receive this broadcast message will respond, but only one will transmit a positive reply. The bridge can then update its address tables, adding that MAC address to the corresponding port. *Source route* bridges add the ability to calculate the best route from source to destination. On a busy network, multiple source route bridges can ease congestion by providing a degree of load balancing to the network. If multiple routes exist, and one is clearly busier than the other, the route with the least congestion will be selected.

bridge router   A hybrid device that combines the functions of both a router and a bridge. It functions as a bridge in that it supports multiple protocols and each port can be configured with a different protocol. It functions as a router in that each port can be configured with a different network address.

broadband   A telecommunications medium that allows multiple signals to be transmitted on the same conductor by assigning each signal to a channel. Channels are defined by a strict frequency bandwidth. No two signals may overlap in frequency. Most broadband services are relatively fast. As a result, the term has also started to become (incorrectly) synonymous with high speed. Another advantage of broadband communications is that nearly all the broadband services offered are of the "always-on" nature. Users do not have to initiate a new connection every time they want to use the network. DSL and cable are forms of broadband.

broadcast   A data transmission directed at all hosts on the network. For this to happen, the networking protocol uses one of a fairly narrow range of addresses that targets the entire network. Every device that is part of a *broadcast domain* will receive the data included in a broadcast. Many protocols make use of broadcast messages for a number of reasons. Routers and switches will broadcast out of all ports and then analyze the return packets to build address tables. When a computer that acquires its IP configuration from a *DHCP server* first boots up, it sends out a broadcast message asking all servers for an address. Some protocols make heavy use of broadcasts for many functions. While this is a "quick and dirty" way of discovering a specific host, it also adds to network traffic. An efficient network protocol uses broadcasting as a last resort.

broadcast domain   All of the devices on a network that will receive a message that is sent to all users. Specifically, if only *data link* addressing is used, the broadcast domain consists of any device reachable by a layer 2 broadcast. Broadcasts are usually blocked by routers, but not by switches and bridges. The exception to that is a device called a *layer 3 switch*, which can filter logical addresses at the network layer as well as data link information. Therefore, the outside perimeter of a broadcast domain is defined by a router address or a layer 3 switch.

broadcast storm   An unexpected and uncontrolled release of excessively large numbers of broadcast packets from a device interface. Broadcast storms can quickly bring a network to its knees for a couple of reasons. First of all, the broadcasts themselves are tying up excessive bandwidth. Secondly, those broadcast packets are likely to result in *ACK* packets from each device that receives them. The final result of propagating a broadcast storm is that new clients cannot log on to the network and those that were already logged on might get dropped.

broken link   Any hyperlink on a Web page that leads to nowhere. Either you click on it and nothing happens or you click on it and get a DNS error. Broken links can result from several things. The Web address it points to no longer exists, it may have been changed, or the person who created the link types 126 mistakes per minute. If you are a Web page programmer, you can avoid the embarrassment of broken links by running a utility designed to detect them. Most Web page authoring programs, such as Adobe GoLive, have this facility built in.

brouter   A shortened term for a bridge router.

brownout   A drop in voltage that lasts a noticeable period of time. With a brownout, you do not lose power completely. You do, however, see lights flicker and/or go dim. Generally, brownouts are unintentional and are the result of unexpected high demand on the circuits or perhaps the failure of a critical piece of hardware. However, from time to time, the electric company may intentionally limit power to certain areas in response to excessive demand or as an economy measure. Brownouts can cause a computer to reboot, data to be lost, and network connections to be dropped. A computer hooked up to a UPS is immune to the effects of brownouts as long as the UPS has battery power.

browse To view or skim the contents of a directory or other grouping of files. Jumping from one text document to another in search of the most recent revision of your *Encyclopedia of Computer Terminology* is one form of browsing. Bouncing from site to site on the Internet while telling your wife you are only reading the articles is another form. Every current operating system offers two forms of software called a *browser*. One of these is designed to search the contents of your local drives or network and the other is an Internet browser. In most cases, the local browser may be used to locate Internet content; however, it is not as convenient or fast as a dedicated Internet browser.

browser A piece of software that allows you to sift through a large collection of data easily and efficiently. An Internet browser, such as Netscape or Firefox (Figure B.8) makes it easy to surf the Net. Microsoft Explorer (Figure B.9) is a form of local system browser.

brute force When a hacker uses every possible means at her disposal to break into a secured system, this is known as *brute force*. One example of this is attempting to break a cryptographic key by trying every possible combination. Two problems

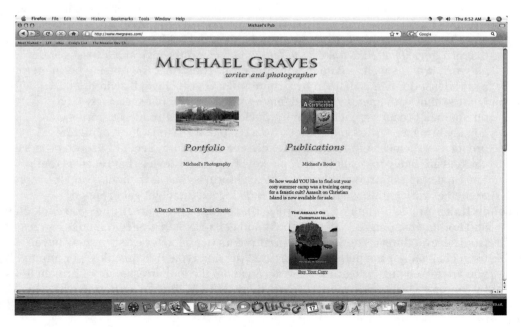

FIGURE B.8   *Firefox is a popular version of Internet browser.*

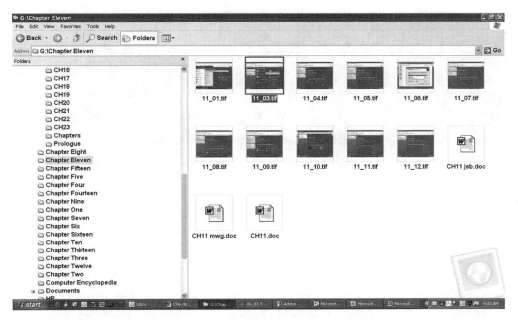

FIGURE B.9   *Windows Explorer is a graphical file browser provided with Microsoft operating systems.*

exist for the hacker using brute force. First of all is the sheer magnitude of breaking code in this way. The law of averages says that you will try around half the possible combinations before you land on the right one. If you are trying to crack a 128-bit key, this means that (on the average) it will take you 2^{127} tries to get it right. The second problem is that, since the hacker is undoubtedly using some form of automated method of trying several trillion keys, there needs to be some accurate algorithm that detects when the key has been found. Unless the data being mined is plain text or some predefined data string, a successful hack might go unnoticed. A brute force attack is in contrast to a single-method approach, such as executing a *dictionary attack*.

bubblejet printer   *See* **thermal printer**.

buffer   A reserved block of memory that used to temporarily store data for a device until it was needed. In general, separate memory regions are maintained for each device for input and output. Any time two computer devices communicate at different rates of speed, they will incorporate some form of buffer. It is also particularly important to devices such as hard disks, which need to stream large amounts of data as quickly as possible. While the definition of buffer may sound similar to that of *cache*, the two concepts are quite different. A buffer holds actual data or commands being moved, while cache holds data or commands that are anticipated.

buffered memory   Memory that contains additional electrical circuits that act as a cushion against the effects of electrical loading. When large numbers of memory modules are installed, excessive load can cause the system to become unstable.

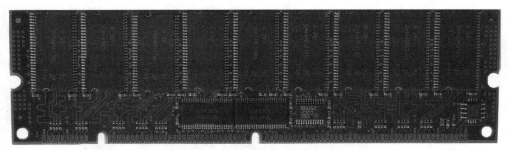

FIGURE B.10 Buffered memory has additional chips for storing the buffer data.

Buffered memory puts an additional register between the DRAM modules and the memory controller to reduce electrical load. Figure B.10 shows an example of buffered memory.

buffer overflow   An error situation develops with most devices when its reserve of *buffer memory* completely fills up, but the data is still streaming in faster than the device can process it. This situation is a *buffer overflow*. Because the data does not stop streaming in, if there is additional memory available beyond the allocated buffer zone, that data is stored in what amounts to unmapped memory. When the device goes to fetch that data, it cannot find it. Buffer overflows are a common source of aggravation when working with recording optical devices such as CD-RWs or DVD-Rs. Also, in networking situations, buffer memory can be exploited by hackers who stitch malicious code into known buffer addresses.

bug   A flaw in programming that leads to unpredictable behavior, holes in security, erratic performance, and/or frequent system crashes. And no, I am not describing your operating system. Those are not bugs; they are undocumented features.

bug fix   A program file released by a software developer that contains code that corrects a bug. Microsoft calls them *patches* or *service packs*.

build   Between official publicized releases of software programs, developers frequently quietly slip a minor revision onto the market. These revisions between revisions are referred to as a *build*. For example, when booting NT 4.0, you might see a screen at the very beginning that says Build Number 1087. For the most part, the average user neither knows nor cares what build number their OS happens to be. However, when calling technical support it is likely that you will be asked to identify your build.

bunny suit   A special uniform that anyone who enters a *clean room* is required to wear. Bunny suits go over the worker or visitor's outer clothing, essentially encasing any contaminating particles of dust. The fabric of the uniform is specially sanitized and vacuumed to remove even the smallest particles of dust.

burn   (1) To record onto an optical medium such as a CDR or DVD-R. Since the process involves heating pits into a pliable medium using a laser beam, the process became known as *burning*. (2) To run a newly configured system constantly for an extended period to see if any components will fail.

burn-in   (1) The tendency for a CRT or plasma monitor to permanently etch an image onto the inner surface of the tube if the image stays on the screen for too long a period. This happens because the phosphorous compound that generates the image is prone to lose its electroluminescent capacity over time. If all of the molecules of the coating were exposed to the same general degree of electrical stimulation, the monitor would simply fade gradually over time. When the same image is left on the screen for excessive periods, the brightest areas are going to fade fastest. In severe cases, the molecular structure is altered to the point where an image is faintly visible on the screen even when the monitor is off. (2) To run a newly configured system constantly for an extended period to see if any components will fail. Ideally, for a burn-in to be effective, the components of a system should be subjected to a relatively stressful barrage of tasks that resemble a real-life working environment. In order to accomplish this, a number of companies have written software specifically for the purpose of burning in computer components.

burst mode   The ability of a device to transfer a large chunk of data in a single data phase. In many I/O operations, the device controller must issue a set of commands, wait for data to move, issue more commands, wait, and so on. Burst mode allows a single set of commands to move larger blocks of data. A certain amount of compromise is in order with most devices. Otherwise it would be possible for a device such as a DVD-ROM drive to completely take over the computer system while it was burning a new DVD. Burst mode is also known as *internal host transfer rate* when discussing hard disk performance parameters.

bus   A path or channel that data follows as it moves from device to device. In the computer industry the term is used in many ways. The registers that hold data as it moves through the CPU is the CPU's *internal data bus*. Data enters and leaves the CPU through the *external data bus*. The *expansion bus* consists of the plugs and slots where you plug new toys you bought for your computer. A bus is defined both by its speed (in *megahertz*) and by its *width* (in bits). A 64-bit, 33-MHz bus will transfer 64 bits of data 33 million times per second. If you do the math, you will see that leaves a maximum theoretical limit of 264,000,000 bytes per second. In order to increase this limit, manufacturers have incorporated technologies such as dual data rate transfer and quad pumping.

bus mastering   A technology that allows two compatible devices to exchange data directly without requiring arbitration or processing of that data by the CPU. In the early days of computing, the only "master of the bus" was the CPU. Emerging technologies rendered this philosophy obsolete as the amount of data being moved across the bus increased in logarithmic proportions. In a bus-mastering scheme, one device becomes the master. This device controls the address bus and the clock crystal that manages timing. The other device marches to the master device's beat.

bus network   *See* **bus topology**.

bus snooping   A process by which individual processors in an SMP system mark their own dedicated memory address spaces. Each processor has its own cache controller. Each cache controller keeps a close eye on the system bus and watches for any condition that might affect its own integrity and/or data line. When cache controller executes a "read miss," all other cache controllers detect this state. They all examine their own cache contents, and if the data being sought by one controller resides in the contents of another, it sends a copy of that data to the requesting controller.

bus topology   A network structure in which all devices are attached end-to-end in a long chain. Several limitations of the bus network prevent it from being popular in the real world of local area networks. For one thing, the network must be terminated at both ends. Also, the entire network depends on direct *continuity* between each and every device on the network. If one device is physically removed without reconnecting the cable in some fashion, the entire network goes down.

byte   Currently, the byte is defined as any combination of eight zeros or ones. In early character sets, a byte may also have been defined as a 6- or 7-bit chunk of data. With the advent of the Intel 8088 chip as the official processor of the IBM PC, the 8-bit internal bus of the CPU set the tone for future computer development and the byte would forever be 8 bits.

byte mode   A parallel communications method that provides bidirectional communication between a device and the computer. Byte mode transmits 8 bits on each cycle, and each bit of the byte is transferred over a separate data line. In byte mode, the longest parallel cable supported is 2 meters. It has a maximum data transmission rate of 1.2 Mb/s.

C

C   A procedural programming language used to build high-level applications. A procedural language is one that specifies each individual step that a program must take to get from point A to point B. Such languages depend heavily on commands called *procedure calls* that reach out to other parts of the program when specific functions are needed. This prevents the programmer from having to insert the code for that function in every point where it is needed. Dennis Ritchie developed the original version of C in 1972 while he was an employee of Bell Laboratories. C has been the language of choice for the development of a number of operating systems as well as a huge number of applications. Over the years, subsequent generations, including C+ and C++ have emerged. C++ added object-oriented capabilities to its mix of talents.

C drive   On a PC running most Microsoft operating systems, the C drive is the primary partition of the primary system drive. In the early days of MS-DOS, all drives on the system carried letters for names. There could only be as many logical drives as there are letters to the English alphabet. Letters A and B continue to be reserved for floppy disk drives, even though relatively few computers feature the drives. Therefore, the first available drive letter for a hard disk was C.

CAB file   *See* **cabinet file**.

cabinet file   A compressed file that holds a large number of smaller files that can be uncompressed and installed as needed. These are routinely known as *cab files*. A key difference between cab files and other compressed files is that the cab file uses a compression algorithm native to the Microsoft operating system. The compression process used within includes support for LZX and Quantum compression/decompression methods as well. Unlike some of the open-source compression technologies, the cab file supports digital signing. This allows a file to have a digital token embedded in the file header that assures that the file that the user unzips is the same as the one the creator originally compressed. Because of this, the risk of malicious tampering is kept to a minimum. Many third-party file compression utilities include support for the cab file. However, there are also utilities that use the .CAB extension on files that are not of the same format.

cable   A flexible conductor that carries any form of signal. Cables can be metal and carry an electrical signal or they can be glass or optical plastic and carry a signal over light waves. A cable is not limited to having a single conductor. Cables can be constructed from a significant number of individual strands of wire or glass, each of which carries a single signal. Cables can be braided, twisted, or coaxial in nature.

cable harness   A cluster of individual wires and their associated connectors that is preconfigured for a specific wiring design. Cable harnesses are assembled as a bundle and fit the geometric and electronic specifications of the device for which they are designed. Because the wires are bound together as a group, they are easier to install. They are already the correct length and have the proper connectors attached to the wires. Cable harnesses are commonly used in the automotive industry. In the computer industry, you frequently see cable harnesses used with *KVM switches* to minimize the clutter of multiple cables. Many computer enclosures feature cable harnesses for the electrical connections between the case electronics and the motherboard. Figure C.1 shows an example of a cable harness used in a computer enclosure. The cables are completely concealed behind the harness.

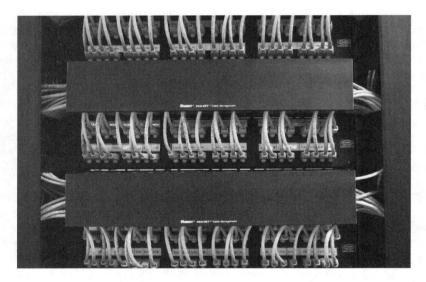

FIGURE C.1   *Cable harnesses prevent excessive tangling by keeping associated wires bundled together.*

cable management arm   A component on a server rack that allows the wiring of the system to be routed along specific paths. Properly managed, a cable arm allows the server manager to effectively manage the web of cables that can take over an installation of multiple servers. Cable arms can be installed horizontally from front to back along the sides of a rack, or they can be mounted horizontally or vertically on the back. A common objection to cable arms is that they block effective air flow in the rack and that when a server needs to be removed for service, they make easy access almost impossible.

cable modem   A device that captures and *demultiplexes* a broadband signal from the incoming cable TV signal. Many cable TV providers also provide Internet services.

Since a number of different subscribers access the same cable, each user gets a small range of frequencies, which becomes his specific channel. The cable modem separates that user's channel from all the others and from the cable television services that are resident on the same wire. Technically speaking, a cable modem is not actually a modem. It does no modulation or demodulation of a signal. Rather, it moves data across disparate hardware and software platforms, effectively making it a bridge. In some cases, an Internet service provider may provide a cable router that directly interfaces with the network.

cable tie   A plastic strip used for managing the wiring of a larger installation. A cable tie has one serrated side and one smooth side. The tip of the cable loops around to a slot on the other end with a plastic ridge that grips the teeth on the serrated side. When the cable is pulled tight, it cannot slip backward.

cache   A dedicated area of memory or disk space that is used as temporary storage for data that is expected to be needed in the very near future. Memory cache can be defined in several different levels. Level 1 (L1) cache is extremely high-speed memory that resides on the CPU circuit and operates at the same internal bus speed as the CPU. Level 2 cache resides on the CPU die, but is not part of the actual CPU circuitry. It may or may not run at actual CPU speeds, depending on the make and model of CPU. Level 3 cache may reside on the CPU die in a select few models of CPU, but is more likely to be memory on the system board. The *swap file* or the *paging file* are forms of disk cache used by the operating system to store data on the hard disk that programs think is stored in memory.

cache block   This is the smallest unit of data that can be transferred from system memory to cache. Most cache entries do not consist of a single byte, but rather strings of code or instructions. Since the cache controller will move additional lines of code or instructions along with the actual request, this additional data adds to the overall collection of data that is to be moved. This data is then broken down into a series of *words*. The number of words that make up a block depends on the size of the external data bus of the processor in use.

cache coherency   A computer system makes use of a number of different types of cache. Many times, data from the same memory location will exist at multiple cache locations. It is possible that data may have been updated at one location, but not at the other locations or written to memory. Cache coherency is the synchronization of data at multiple cache locations so that the CPU is always receiving the most up-to-date version of the data it seeks. This is a particular issue with a computer using multiple CPUs, in that each CPU might be maintaining a separate cache yet all of them are working on the same problem.

cache conflict   An error situation that arises when a sequence of consecutive memory I/O operations attempts to overwrite the same cache entry. Cache conflicts can occur from several conditions, but the most common are these. First of all, if data is being accessed repeatedly because of a programming loop, but each consecutive read involves a different data set, a conflict can occur. Secondly, if two blocks of data reside within a single cache block, but are simultaneously requested, a conflict will occur. (*See* **cache block**.)

cache hit   The CPU went looking for data or instructions in *cache* and voila! There it was.

cache line   *See* **cache block**.

cache miss   The CPU went looking for data or instructions in *cache* and bummer! It was not there.

caddy   On a CD-ROM (or similar) drive, caddy is a form of loading mechanism that consists of a plastic CD holder that supports the CD while it is in the drive. This is similar to the jewel box used to protect a CD during storage, but is designed for a specific drive to hold the disk while it is in the computer. While caddies have lost popularity for single-disk drives, they still remain a popular option for audio players with multiple-disk capability (Figure C.2).

FIGURE C.2   *This six-disk caddy is used in an audio CD player.*

calculated field   Any field in a database that is dynamically written as the result of a mathematical expression that is performed on one or more other fields in the same database. Data located in calculated fields is not entered by users, and in most cases the fields are locked from editing.

calibrate   To perform one or more adjustments on a device in order to fine-tune its performance. In order to properly calibrate a device, there must be a specific standard against which performance is measured. For example, when calibrating an imaging device, a 21-level gray scale of tones from black to white, with graduated shades of gray in between, allows the user to compare an image created by the device with the gray scale. The user can then make adjustments in contrast, density, or exposure to make the image match the scale. Many devices such as scanners, monitors, and even some software applications, such as Photoshop, work better if certain user calibrations are performed.

Callback Control Protocol   A protocol that provides additional security to a *remote access* connection by calling a client back to a specific number after an attempted connection.

canonical   A standard format for writing mathematical formulae. Students of mathematics will learn a long list of rules for making sure the formulae they write are canonical. The purpose of using canonical formulae is to make it easier to compare different equations to find differences and similarities with less confusion. In programming, a canonical code is one that is written strictly to a predefined set of procedures. The canonical name of a host on the Internet is the first name listed for that host after the IP address in the official host name database maintained by Network Information Services.

capacitance   The property of certain substances that cause them to hold an electrical charge. Capacitance is measured in *farads*. All electrical devices exhibit capacitance to some degree. In some cases this is an issue that must be considered when making upgrades. For example, two different brands of memory might have the same storage capacity, but a different electrical capacitance. While the system might boot quite nicely with both installed, the system might experience increased memory errors. On some older systems differences in capacitance caused some of the installed modules to not be recognized by the computer.

capacitor   An electrical component that stores electrical current in an *electrostatic field* and provides it to the circuit as needed. The device consists of two layers of a conductive metallic alloy separated by a substance called a *dielectric*. One metallic layer generates a positive charge and the other a negative charge. The degree of capacitance is a function of two factors. Stored charge is directly proportional to the surface area of the conductive layers and inversely proportional to the distance of separation between the conductive layers. Capacitors can hold an electrical charge for a long period of time. Because of this, great care should be taken when working on devices with large capacitors, such as computer monitors and power supplies. A capacitor in a device that is unplugged can deliver a dangerous shock even after sitting unused for extended periods. Figure C.3 illustrates a small capacitor.

capacity   (1) The maximum amount of substance, data, or electrical charge that an object can store. The term is used in reference to computers most often in terms of data storage. When you read about a 500-GB hard disk drive, the capacity of that hard disk is 500 billion bytes. The term can also refer to the overall ability of a system to process data. (2) The role or function of a person or device. A network administrator creates user accounts in his administrative capacity.

capstan   A cylinder attached to a motorized spindle in a tape drive that traps tape against a free-moving cylinder. The capstan presses against a rubber (or other high-friction substance) roller called a *pinch roller*. The purpose of the capstan is to

FIGURE C.3 A capacitor is a device much like a storage battery that holds an electrical charge until such time as the circuit on which it is installed requires the energy.

create tension in the tape as it passes over the recording heads and make sure that the tape moves through the drive at a constant rate of speed. In order to function properly, a capstan must have a very smooth surface. It must rotate at a constant and very precise speed, and it should be located in a position that allows easy cleaning. Most high-quality tape drives made today use dual capstans, with one being positioned on either side of the heads. If a single capstan is used, it must be placed downstream of the heads.

capture   To acquire and retain. In a computer sense, the term is used to describe methods of taking data from one source and/or format and transferring or converting it to another source or format. For example, when a digital camera takes the light waves generated by the lens and converts them into a digital file, it is capturing an image. A video capture card reads the incoming stream of images from a video camera and converts it into a digital video file for use or processing on the computer.

card   A generic term for any expansion device that is manufactured on a *printed circuit board* and plugs into a standard expansion slot. The term also refers to one of several forms of *flash memory* that is used in devices such as digital cameras or personal digital assistants.

card reader   A device that can take the data from a flash memory card and transfer it to a computer system, or conversely, transfer data from the computer to the flash memory card. Card readers are fairly popular with digital camera enthusiasts because they are capable of transferring data to the computer much more quickly than can most digital cameras. Card readers are frequently incorporated into other devices, such as printers or USB hubs.

card services   The portion of a PC card driver that interprets the command set for a specific device. It is through card services that functions such as hot-swapping and automatic configuration occur. All system resources, such as I/O address, IRQ, and DMA, are under the control of card services. Card services provides support to another layer of the PC card driver called *socket services*.

CardBus   An earlier 33-MHz, 32-bit implementation of the *PCMCIA* bus. It was released in 1995 and used on a variety of laptop computers. CardBus defines several different voltages that manufacturers can use in designing their products. Maximum theoretical throughput of the CardBus was 132 MB/s. CardBus devices supported *bus mastering* and advanced power management.

caret   The "arrowhead" (^) on the keyboard, also called a *circumflex*. On most keyboards it is produced by pressing <Shift> + 6.

Careware   A method of distributing software that suggests that voluntary payments for the program be in the form of a donation to a specific charity.

carpal tunnel syndrome   A disorder that results from prolonged repetitive motions that causes severe discomfort and/or numbness in the joint involved in making those motions. Other symptoms of the disorder include numbness of the joints or extremities, swelling or stiffness in the joints, or a tingling sensation. Computer keyboards and mice are notorious for causing carpal tunnel syndrome. There are steps a person can take to prevent this syndrome. These include ergonomically designed wrist pads and a chair that forces correct posture. Some of the methods suggested by manufacturers are not always the best choice. For example, changing from a mouse to a trackball simply moves the CTS from your wrist to your finger joints. You can always tell people who write computer books for a living by the fact that those few times they're seen in daylight, they walk around flexing their wrists and fingers all the time.

carriage   (1) A mechanism on a printer that moves the print head back and forth across the paper. Generally, the carriage is a belt-fed mechanism. Sometimes paper fiber or other debris gets down into the carriage and blocks it from moving. (2) A mechanism that holds the *platen* on impact printers that moves the paper through the printer.

carrier   (1) An electrical current that travels over a conductor that acts as the envelope in which a data signal is moved over the wire. Generally, the carrier signal is a fixed-frequency signal that does not vary in *amplitude*. Data is encoded using any one of several data-encoding mechanisms. The data signal might use frequency modulation, amplitude modulation, or a combination of these techniques to modify a secondary frequency that is different from the carrier frequency. The two signals are then blended and transmitted over the wire. On the receiving end, the carrier signal is filtered out and what remains is the data signal. (2) Any organization or business that provides the infrastructure necessary for providing telecommunications services. The larger carriers include AT&T, Verizon, and Sprint.

carrier detect This is a signal that is transmitted by a modem to confirm that the device has successfully detected a *carrier* signal and is now ready to transmit or receive data. The carrier detect signal will remain present on the line as long as two devices are connected. If a phone system includes call waiting services, the carrier detect signal can be interrupted, dropping the data connection and allowing the voice phone to ring.

cartridge Any self-contained device for holding tape, ink, toner, or ribbon. Virtually all tape machines used today make use of magnetic tape housed in a cartridge. All ink-jet printers employ cartridges as well.

CAS latency CAS stands for column access strobe (See CAS). CAS latency refers to the number of computer clock cycles that elapse from the instant the memory controller issues a request for data to the instant the data is transmitted through the output pins of the memory module. Also known as *RAS/CAS delay*. CAS latency is measured in clock cycles and is a standard performance rating for modern memory. It shows up with numbers such as CL2, CL2.5, or CL3. CAS latency is a parameter than can be configured in many versions of system *BIOS*. When tweaking the performance of a system, this is one thing to look at closely. If you are running CL2 memory and your system is set for CL3, everything is working quite nicely. However, for every memory I/O operation that ever occurs, one full clock cycle is spent waiting that could be spent transferring data. Conversely, if you set your memory to a higher speed than at which it can respond, then your system will refuse to boot.

cascade A process by which multiple circuits are linked together in such a way that they appear to the system as a single device. The PCI bus has a limit to the number of PCI slots that can exist on a single bus. To get around this, PCI uses a cascade design in order to allow multiple PCI busses to exist in a single system, yet still appear to the computer as a single bus. Another place where the cascade principle is used is in extending the geographic distribution of a network. Multiple hubs or switches are interconnected across the network, acting as repeaters for the networking media.

case-sensitive Alphabetic characters can be either capital or lower case. Some computer functions do not pay attention to capitalization of letters. In other cases, the software reads each condition of the letter as a separate character. This is case-sensitive software. In most situations, the password assigned to a user is case-sensitive. As a result, if the <Caps Lock> key is on, a password will be incorrectly interpreted.

category Twisted pair cable is manufactured in a variety of fashions. Some use different types of copper in the strands of wire, some use more twists per inch, and some add shielding to the exterior jacket while others do not. To make it easier to identify each type of twisted pair the term category, along with a number, is used. Table C.1 lists the various twisted pair categories along with a short description of each.

TABLE C.1
Twisted-Pair Categories

CATEGORY	FREQUENCY SUPPORTED	USAGE
1	Voice only, no data	Telephone only
2	4Mhz	Localtalk/ISDN
3	16Mhz	Ethernet
4	20Mhz	Token Ring
5	100Mhz	Fast Ethernet
5e	400Mhz	Gigabit Ethernet/ATM to 622MB/sec
6	550Mhz	Gigabit Ethernet/ATM to 2.4GB/sec

cathode   A negatively charged device that emits a stream of electrons when heated.

CD burner   Another term for a recordable CD-ROM drive. While technically a CD burner would be one that records disks that are not rewritable, these days, the term is used interchangeably. CD burners have appeared in two incarnations. The simple CD-Recordable (CD-R, now nearly obsolete) can only record a disk once. It cannot erase and record over a disk. The CD-Rewritable (CD-RW) can do that last trick.

Recordable CDs are all based on some form of phase-change technology. Phase change is a fancy way of saying that a substance is changed from one form to another. A spiral track on the CD-R blank is imprinted onto the blank at the factory at the time of manufacture. This is known as the *pregroove*, and it is the target area for the pits that will be eventually burned by the CD-R drive. The dye is poured over the grooved base in a very thin layer. To simulate the reflectance of the aluminum layer of standard CDs, a microscopically thin layer of metal is placed over the dye.

CD-R drives are equipped with a dual-powered laser. The lowest power is similar to that of a conventional CD. However, when the user wants to record data to a CD-R, the write power of the laser is sufficiently powerful to burn a hole in the dye layer. The burned area becomes opaque, effectively duplicating the function of a pit in the read process.

The first dye used in CD-Rs was cyanine dye. More recent disks make use of phthalocyanine dye. Phthalocyanine is better than cyanine in two respects. First of all, it lasts longer. Cyanine dye is not archival in that it has a life expectancy of 20 years or less. Certain light frequencies, including UV and other frequencies found in normal sunlight, can degrade the dye. Leaving the CD-R that contained the overheads for a critical presentation on the dashboard of your car in the middle of July could result in unemployment. Phthalocyanine is not nearly as susceptible to photosensitivity and can be expected to last in excess of a century.

CD-Rs became very popular, very fast. Still, there was something missing. If you are working on a large project that takes a long time to complete, say this book, for example, the data changes on a constant basis. CD-Rs allowed for archiving data, but not modifying it. The CD-RW solved this problem.

In place of dyes on which to record data, the CD-RW blank has a layer of a rather exotic material made out of silver, antimony, tellurium, and indium. This compound reacts to different intensities of heat in different ways. Like all metals, it has a melting point. Unlike most metals, however, this compound also has a crystallization point. Melting point occurs at a moderately low temperature. Intense heat crystallizes it.

Therefore, in order to do its job, the CD-RW drive has a laser beam capable of three different intensities. The lowest is for reading back data. This is known as *read power. Erase power* is the next setting because it actually requires less power to melt the material than it does to crystallize it. *Write power* is the setting that generates sufficient heat to crystallize the material. When data is written to the medium, the laser burns a crystalline pit.

The Orange Book had allowed for multisession recording, but it had not provided for rewriting the table of contents to allow for changes in the location of data on the disk. This was added with the release of the Orange Book III.

Celeron   A line of lower-end CPUs manufactured by Intel, starting with the Pentium II microprocessors and continuing to the present. Celeron processors generally have identical clock speeds as their upper echelon companions, but feature smaller L1 and L2 cache. Some of the earler models of Celeron had no L2 cache at all, and in some models, the Celeron required a different CPU socket.

cell   (1) The square on a spreadsheet where a row and a column intersect. In this respect, the cell can hold any amount of data that the spreadsheet allows in a single field. (2) On a memory chip, a cell is the grouping of a transistor or transistors and the associated microcapacitors that can store a single bit of data. As with the spreadsheet, a memory cell is located where a row and column meet. However, on a memory chip, a cell will hold but a single bit. (3) The 53-byte fragment of data transmitted over an *ATM* connection. Frames generated by upper level protocols will be broken down into multiple ATM cells.

cell phone   A wireless telephone that takes advantage of *cellular* communications technology. By owning a cell phone you can take your work with you wherever you go. Even when you are on vacation or on the golf course, your boss can find you. With a cell phone, you can turn from a safe and reasonable driver into a deadly menace.

cell relay   A transmission technology (also known as *cell switching*) that moves data using blocks of data of a specific size. Keeping all data blocks similarly sized enhances their ability to be switched at high speed as it is easier to build a switch that processes fixed-length packets than one that must deal with ones of variable size. *ATM* is a form of cell relay technology.

cell switching   *See* **cell relay**.

cellular   A communications system that limits the number of frequencies required for millions of users by breaking the geographic area covered into smaller regions, or cells. On a global level, tens of thousands of telephones are all working off of the same frequency range. However, frequency assignments distribute these across a wide range so they do not overlap. The size of any given cell can be controlled by the transmission power of the towers covering that area. The population density of any given region will determine the size and number of cells included. Each user talks over a single channel assigned to a small radio transceiver that receives its signal from a transmission tower. The signal from the tower is limited in power in order to contain that signal within the designated region. As a user moves from the coverage area of one tower to another, he transitions to a new signal. Areas between coverage areas are known as *dead zones.*

centimeter   1/100 of a meter. In inches that works out to a little less than 4/10 of one inch.

Central Arbitration Point (CAP)   A circuit that offloads the responsibility for refereeing and processing the transfer of data between two bus-mastering devices or between two load-balanced devices. PCI is a bus that makes use of arbitration. The central arbitration point allows multiple devices to simultaneously occupy the bus without one of the devices taking control. If only a single device is using the bus, then that device receives 100% of the bandwidth available. When two or more devices require access, the CAP will regulate traffic to make sure that all devices have a turn at the bus. In a load-balancing circuit, the CAP monitors incoming traffic and directs requests to the least busy circuit.

central processing unit (CPU)   The primary processor of a computer system. In reality, a computer relies on far more than one chip to do its job. The BIOS chip holds the information necessary to allow the system to communicate with basic hardware. The *chipset* is the central *firmware* for the computer system, holding the primary command set for the hardware supported by the system. The CPU is the data cruncher. It executes user and program commands and processes the data that passes through the system. A CPU is a collection of microcircuits that can be broken down into a variety of subcomponents. Modern CPUs include a floating point unit for performing mathematical calculations and a decode unit for breaking down complex instructions into simpler commands the CPU can understand. Cache memory installed on the CPU holds commands or data until the processor is ready to use them.

CPUs come in a variety of form factors, but the two most common are the Single Edge Cartridge and the Staggered Pin Grid Array. These two types of CPU are shown together in Figure C.4.

A microphotograph of a CPU looks a little like an aerial view of a city, complete with buildings and streets. This miniature city is laid out in blocks, and each of these blocks represents a subcomponent of the processor. These consist of:

- **The Control Unit** The "commander in chief," if you will. This is the unit in charge of keeping track of the task at hand, determining what needs to be done next, and which of the other subcomponents needs to do it.
- **The Prefetch Unit** When the CPU needs additional data or instructions, it sends the prefetch out looking for that data.
- **The Data and Instruction Cache** Once the prefetch has located and retrieved the data or instructions, it needs a place to store it until the control unit is ready to direct it to the correct set of registers.
- **The Decode Unit** Most instructions that come into the CPU are far too complex for the control unit to be able to handle. The decode unit breaks these instructions down into the simple binary commands that the CPU understands.
- **The Arithmetic Logic Unit (ALU)** This is the basic calculator of the CPU. It handles simple integer calculations.
- **The Floating Point Unit (FPU)** The "scientific" calculator of the CPU. It does the more advanced math functions.

FIGURE C.4   It's pretty easy to tell the difference between a PGA chip and a SEC
processor.

- **The General Registers** In the course of processing, it is likely that the same set of data is going to be massaged by a number of different instructions. The general registers are the locations where data is being stored as it is processed.

One of the most overstated features of the CPU, in terms of performance, is its raw clock speed. Sure, it is wonderful to have a chip that can execute instructions a few billion times a second. However, if you want to take full advantage of that speed, you have to make sure the CPU always has something to do. Performance is not greatly enhanced if you have a 2.8-Ghz CPU that spends 1.8 billion of those clock cycles waiting for something to do. Also, if the instruction set is so limited that programmers are using complex commands to accomplish things that could be directed by the CPU, this will introduce another kind of bottleneck. A single line of code written by a programmer might have to be broken down into a dozen or more CPU instructions.

Therefore, a faster frontside bus and a powerful instruction set will have a much greater influence on overall system performance than simple clock speed. The amount of installed cache is also a powerful influence on performance. The CPU will always ask for the next few lines of code beyond the one it actually needs and store those lines in cache. The more cache that is available, the more anticipatory code it can store.

certificate authority   An organization whose primary responsibility is to issue *digital certificates*. This organization also makes sure that these certificates are updated and renewed on a regular basis to ensure the integrity of the certification process. Once a certificate has been issued, a *public key* gets issued to anyone who needs to make use of the certificate. The public key, in conjunction with the certificate, ensures that only people with the correct authorization are seeing data, or that people who are receiving information or files can be assured that the data is authentic. Two main certificate authorities are VeriSign and Thawte.

certification   The issuance of a document that confirms some form of authenticity. A professional in a particular field might be issued a certification to prove that he is truly qualified to perform a specific function. Many hardware manufacturers and software distributors issue certifications for their products. Hardware might receive certification from an operating system's manufacturer, verifying that specific devices run properly with their software. In order to receive certification, the person or device must undergo one or more tests to measure the relative ability to perform.

chad   The piece of paper that is dislodged when a hole-punch is used to mark a computer-read card. Several different types of medium rely on hole-punches to encode data. Punch cards, such as the ones used at voting booths, are a prime example. A *chadded* form is one where the hole is supposed to be punched through all the way. A *chadless* form leaves the paper attached to the hole. A *hanging chad* is found on a ballot from a Miami/Dade voting machine. Since punched holes have proven to be inaccurate methods of collecting data, most machines using this method have been replaced by fully electronic methods of collecting votes.

challenge/response   A method that many forms of software use to authenticate a user. When logging onto the system, the system asks the user to provide his *credentials* (usually consisting of a user ID and password). This is the challenge. In response, the user types in the requested information. Challenge response can also occur on the software level. The *authentication server* issues a challenge to the workstation where the user is logging in. The client software running on the user's machine processes that challenge and responds to the server with a token it received when it was added to the network. More sophisticated forms of challenge response include security tokens, which change the response code at predefined intervals. The user carries this token, and when logging onto the network, types in whatever number is displayed on the token at that moment.

channel   (1) A dedicated pathway that data uses to travel from source to destination. A system with multiple channels can work with as many independent streams of data as it has channels to support those streams. (2) An assigned range of frequencies that carries a single signal over a *broadband* carrier. For example, cable TV sends 244 separate channels of total garbage over a single wire. A *demultiplexor* filters out all but the selected channel, leaving the user blissfully unaware that the others exist. (3) The distribution path that products follow from the manufacturing plant to the end user. Typically, the customer buys a product from a retail outlet, who purchases from a wholesaler, who gets their products from a distributor, who buys from the manufacturer. Each one adds a certain percentage of profit onto each transaction, assuring you that by the time you receive your shiny new toy, you have paid far more than you really should have.

channel aggregation protocol   A generic term for any protocol that binds two or more signals of lower bandwidth into a single signal of higher bandwidth. Channel aggregation protocols include BONDING, Multilink PPP, H.Multilink, and others. *ISDN* is a telecommunications service that uses this technology. Anywhere from 2 to

23 64 Kb/s channels are bound together to form a single high-speed link of 128 Kb/s to 1.48 Mb/s. The end user has no idea that multiple channels are carrying the data.

channel bank   *See* **demultiplexing** and **multiplexing**.

channel bonding   A technique by which transmission speed can be increased severalfold by splitting the signal up into several different streams and sending each stream across a separate carrier. An example of a communications technology that makes use of channel bonding is *ISDN*. ISDN uses between 2 and 23 64 Kb/s channels to transmit data. The more channels you have contracted for, the faster your throughput. Another form of channel bonding occurs when a server contains multiple network interface cards that are configured to communicate over the same network address. Data can move across both interfaces at the same time, effectively doubling throughput. Because two devices cannot actually exist on the network with the same address, a software overlay translates real addresses assigned to the interfaces to the virtual addresses seen on the network.

channelized   Any communications architecture that transmits data across multiple communications lines in order to increase overall bandwidth. A *channel aggregation protocol* binds the multiple channels into what is effectively seen by the system as a single channel. Multiple message threads are then sewn back together on the receiving end. ISDN is a channelized system. All *T-lines* are channelized as well.

character   (1) Any single alphabetic, numeric, punctuation, or other symbol that can be used to display concepts, ideas, or information in such a way that the average human can understand it. Digital information must be transcribed into characters before it can be understood. With most encoding mechanisms, a single character consists of eight or sixteen characters. (2) In a computer game, a character is one of the animated objects that the player pushes around the game's virtual universe. In a *first-person shooter* the character represents the player. In third-person action adventure games, the character is controlled by the player, but does not represent the player.

character map   A utility that displays graphically each and every symbol used by a specific *character set*. Figure C.5 shows the character map used by Microsoft Windows to display characters.

character recognition   Some computerized devices have the ability to read printed symbols and convert them into binary code. This is character recognition. Two commonly used forms of character recognition are *optical character recognition* (OCR) and *magnetic ink character recognition* (MICR). OCR analyzes the shapes of graphical elements on a scanned page and compares those elements to symbols in its database. The symbol with the closest proximity to the scanned image is inserted at that point in a text document, which can be manipulated by any word processing program. MICR performs a similar trick, except that it only reads characters printed with magnetic ink, which is, coincidently, how the technology got its name.

character set   The mapping of computer code to the symbols used to generate letters and numbers that human users can understand out of binary code generated by a computer. Most of the early character sets were based on 8-bit code and contained 256 characters per set. *Unicode* is a 16-bit character set that holds

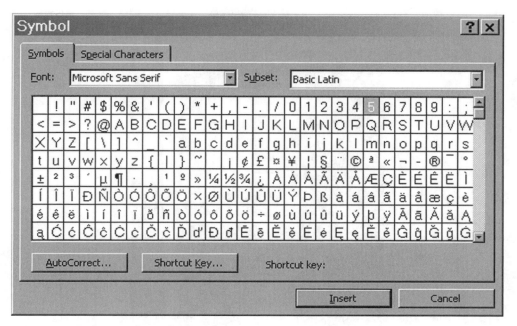

FIGURE C.5   The Windows character map.

65,536 characters. Since this is a bit too much for the average person to keep track of in a single set of letters and numbers, it is broken down into font sets as well as symbol sets.

charge coupled device (CCD)   A small chip consisting of an array of thousands or even millions of microscopic light-sensitive photocells. The CCD is an integral part of digital cameras and scanners. It is the component that collects reflected light from the subject, analyzes the light for color and intensity, and then converts it into digital form. A CCD requires that it receives a *precharge* prior to exposure that assures that all the photocells are active.

chassis   The "skeleton" or frame of any multicomponent system that holds everything together. The chassis of a car basically consists of the frame and body structure. On a computer system, the enclosure is often referred to as the *chassis*, even though more accurately it would be the enclosure's frame. The enclosure includes other artifacts, including removable drive bays and bezels. Figure C.6 clearly shows the chassis of a computer enclosure.

chat   A process by which people can exchange messages in real time over an Internet connection. Chatting consists of the exchange of text messages back and forth. Generally, the process is facilitated by a protocol such as *Internet Relay Chat* (IRC). Chat servers can isolate people who wish to chat in private in their own private chat rooms. These consist of dedicated channels set up and managed by a dedicated server. Once the chat room is established, certain parameters dictate who can and cannot join the group.

FIGURE C.6   The chassis of your enclosure is
the skeleton that provides structural support.

cheat code   Virtually every computer game has certain functions built in that allow
the player to circumvent certain rules of the game. For example, in a *first-person
shooter* there might be a set of keystrokes that, when pressed, makes the player's
character impervious to damage from the computerized opponents. Another set of
keystrokes allows the character to pass through solid objects. For every obstacle,
there is a way to cheat. And is that not what winning is all about?

check bit   One or more bits of data that are used to check the integrity of data as it is
transmitted through a system. Several forms of check bit schema include *parity*,
checksum, and *cyclical redundancy check*. In most cases the check bits are the
result of mathematical calisthenics performed on the package of data and adding
the result to the end of the data stream. The transmitting computer performs the
operation on the data prior to shipping it out. The receiving device performs the

same calculations on the data and compares the results with the value stored in the check bits. If the values match, the data is accepted. If not, it is discarded and the transmitting computer retransmits.

check box A small box on a Web page or in a database or other program that, when clicked, inserts a check. Internally, the check box is the equivalent of a yes or no, on or off, or a 1 or 0. The program uses the value that the presence of a check represents to perform other calculations or to set up the next series of actions. For instance, checking the box next to the statement "Send me more information" will fill your e-mail client's inbox with thousands of junk mail messages from all the spammers that bought your private information from the owners of the Web site.

checkpoint A small piece of data embedded in a data transmission that acts as a bookmark. Checkpoints are generally added at specific intervals. Some protocols are able to use these checkpoints to determine the point where a failure in communications occurred. During transmission, the data transmitted is stored in a temporary file on a hard disk or other form of permanent storage medium, with the embedded checkpoints in place. In the event that transmission is interrupted, once a connection has been re-established, the receiving device sends the last successful checkpoint it received. The transmitting computer starts sending data at that point, alleviating the necessity of transmitting all of the data all over again.

checksum A method of error detection that simply keeps track of the number of 1s in the packet. If the receiving device calculates a different checksum than that stored in the trailer, the packet will be rejected and a *NACK* returned to the sender. Checksum is a method used by certain antivirus software packages to see if a particular file has changed since the last time it was scanned.

child In a *hierarchical* system, a child is any object that is subordinate to an object in the next higher level of authority. For example, in a file system, a file is a child to a subdirectory, which is a child to a directory.

child menu A secondary menu (Figure C.7) that pops up when an object in a primary menu is clicked. Most Windows and Macintosh OS X applications make heavy use of child menus to prevent the main menus from being too cluttered. It is not uncommon for a child menu to spawn additional child menus.

child process In computing, this is any process that is spawned by another process rather than requested by a user or directly by the CPU. A child process will be dependent on all system parameters imposed by the system on the originating (or parent) process and will inherit any attributes of the parent process. Permissions to resources that belonged to the parent process will pass on to the child process.

chip (1) A collection of miniaturized electronic circuits housed on a single wafer. Chips come in a wide variety of packages and perform vast numbers of functions. The most widely known chip is the *central processing unit* of a computer system. But other chips are used to convert analog audio signals to digital form, and vice versa. Some hold the instruction set that controls a hardware device. A single chip the size of your thumbnail can house tens of millions of individual transistors. (2) The fundamental snack that goes along with watching *football*. For this type of chip to be effective, it must be accompanied by an appropriate *dip*, and preferably a cold *brew*.

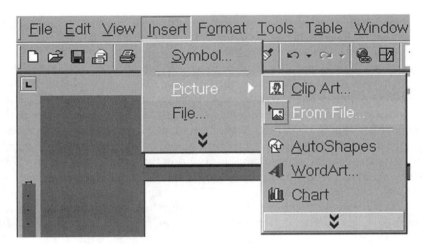

FIGURE C.7   Child menus spring from other menus to provide additional options.

chipping code   A pattern of several changes in the signal carrier to represent a single bit. These changes can be frequency, amplitude, or pulse-modulated. Chipping code is used in spread spectrum transmissions to provide a degree of redundancy to transmitted data. This provides a degree of protection against electrical interference to the signal.

chipset   A matched set of two (three, on some of the older systems) ICs that control critical system functions, including bus speeds, memory types, and capacity, and the type of hardware supported by a motherboard (Figure C.8). The chipset acts

FIGURE C.8   The chipset of a computer system is just as much the brains of the computer as is the CPU.

as an interface between the various hardware subsystems of the computer and the *central processing unit*. The early chipset model consisted of a *northbridge* and a *southbridge* chip. Occasionally, a manufacturer would include a third chip called an *Advanced I/O* chip. This is rarely seen today. The northbridge handled all high-speed functions, such as AGP video, the communications between the CPU and cache, and some functions of the PCI bus. The southbridge deals with data transfers involving lower bandwidth, such as serial and parallel communications, USB, and most expansion bus transfers. A more recent evolution of the chipset by Intel involves two chips as well. However, their functions are slightly reorganized. The memory controller hub handles memory and cache operations. The I/O controller hub handles the slower data transfers.

CHK file   A shortened term for a *CHecKdisk* file. The Windows utility called *Checkdisk* takes all the unlinked or orphaned files it finds and turns them into valid files that the file system can read. Since there is a very good chance that these files contain data that you really might need some day, rather than totally blow all those bytes of data into digital oblivion, they are saved as files with a .CHK extension. The idea is that if you discover a critical file has gone missing or is corrupted, you can examine all your CHK files to see if any of it is there. However, these files all get shoveled into the root directory, where you are always told you are not allowed to play, and since most people do not know they exist, CHK files generally go unnoticed.

chop   A 16-bit piece of data generated when music is sampled once during the digital recording procedure.

chroma   An abbreviation for *chrominance*.

chromatic aberration   A form of optical distortion caused when a lens does not focus all colors at the same point in space. Almost every lens exhibits chromatic aberration to some point because red light is very difficult to get to focus at the same point as the other colors. Blue and green light also focus to different points naturally, but not to the same extreme, and those two colors are easier to control. Most of the prominent lens manufacturers have lenses that focus all the colors at the same point. These lenses are called *apochromatic lenses*. Apochromatic lenses have a tendency to have relatively narrow angles of focus and can be a bit pricier than their counterparts, the *achromatic lens*, which lets the red waves focus where they want. Figure C.9 illustrates the concept of chromatic aberration.

chromatic dispersion   The tendency for a lens to disperse light of different colors at different angles. This is very similar to *chromatic aberration*, except it affects the way projection lenses transmit light rather than how imaging lenses focus light.

chrominance   This term refers to the collective attributes of a specific color. Chrominance takes into consideration *hue* (the relative color of light as determined by its actual frequency reflected from the surface of the subject), *saturation* (the relative richness of color, determined by the amount of black present), and *reflectance* (the ability of the object to bounce light off its surface).

CHS parameters   A description of a hard disk drive's geometrical layout. It defines the location and number of all cylinders, read/write heads, and how many sectors are contained in each track. CHS geometry was originally managed by a BIOS interrupt called Int13h. Int13h defined 1,024 cylinders, 256 R/W heads, and 63 sectors per track. Running the math out to its logical conclusion, you will see that this imposes

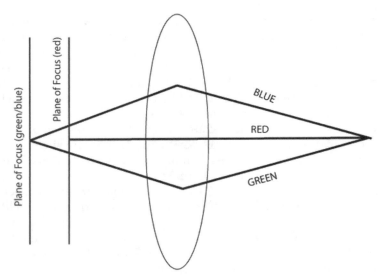

FIGURE C.9   Lenses that exhibit chromatic aberration do not focus all the colors of light at the same point.

a built-in limitation of slightly under 8 GB as the largest hard disk supported by Int13h. Subsequent *BIOS extensions* were developed that allow the larger hard disks in use today.

CIDR block   CIDR is an acronym for *C*lassless *I*nter*D*omain *R*outing. Another term for this is *supernetting*. CIDR allows a network administrator to take a series of smaller adjacent network addresses and merge them into a single larger address. It did this by creating a subnet mask that includes 1s in the network portion of the subnet mask. The resulting larger group of IP addresses created by this schema is the CIDR block.

cipher   The *algorithm* used to convert conventionally formatted data into a securely encoded format. The cipher determines the pattern of bit distribution, the use of public and/or private *keys* used to decode data. Without the possession of the appropriate key, another individual cannot break the code (in theory, anyway).

circuit   The overall collection of wires and components in an electrical device that perform a specific function. As the electrical current flows across the circuit, each device performs its magic until the signal that passes out of the circuit has been modified in the desired manner. Generally, an electronic device is a complex mechanism consisting of a large number of circuits.

circuit switching   A telecommunications technology that selects the best route for data to take, based on current network conditions, and then creates a virtual circuit over which all data from that session will flow. Since this is a temporary configuration, the next time those same two devices establish a connection the telecommunications provider will create a new virtual circuit for that session. The physical path of the new virtual circuit is unlikely to be the same as previous sessions. In other words, the devices switched circuits for the new session.

circular buffer   A dedicated area in memory, or in some cases a hardware *circuit* that holds incoming data for a device or program. It gets its name from the fact that data moves through the address or circuit as space frees up. Incoming data fills the space left by outgoing data. Circular buffers are commonly used in situations where the data is generated by one process or application, but is intended to be read by a different process or application. In order to assure that new data never overwrites unread data, the applications use separate read and write pointers.

circumflex   The "arrowhead" (^) on the keyboard, also called a *caret*. On most keyboards it is produced by pressing <Shift> + 6.

cladding   This is a plastic or glass lining that surrounds the core of a fiber optics cable. The inner surface of the cladding consists of a mirrored surface that reflects the beam of light back into the core. Some networking technologies take advantage of the reflective qualities of the cladding and encode different streams of data onto beams of varying wavelengths of light. The light or laser-emitting diodes in the transmitter shoot each channel over the optical fiber at a slightly different angle. On the receiving end these different light beams are translated back into digital form for use by that device or application. Figure C.10 shows a crude representation of this concept.

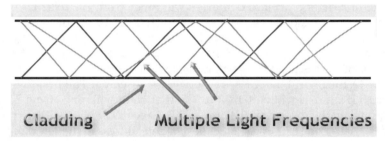

FIGURE C.10   The reflective nature of fiber optics cladding allows an angled beam to be bounced back into the core.

clamping voltage   The threshold voltage at which a surge suppressor kicks in and suppresses incoming current. Suppression can occur in a couple of different ways. It can absorb excess voltage through a device called a *metal oxide varistor* (MOV) and then drain the excess voltage through the ground wire, or it can simply divert the entire current to ground. Obviously, the latter method is not all that attractive to an electronic device, so most of the better ones take advantage of the MOV. Clamping voltages vary between brands of surge suppressor. On the average, they seem to clamp between 135 and 140 volts on a 115-V line. On a 5-V DC circuit, it can range as high as 7 V.

class   A predefined data type that describes the attributes of a group of objects that share similar characteristics. In particular, class defines the attributes that define an object's position in the hierarchy of the defined group. Networking devices examine a packet header to determine the class of data the packet contains. They will also examine the IP address to determine its type. IP addresses are configured according to their address class.

Class A An IP address class in which the first *octet* of the address defines the network portion of the address. The remaining three octets define the host portion of the address. The first bit of a class A address must always be 0. This limits the total number of theoretical class A network addresses to 126 ($2^7 - 2$, in that an address cannot contain all 0s or all 1s). These addresses will be numbered 0 through 127. A class A address that uses a standard subnet can support up to 16, 777,214 hosts. The first octet of a class A address will range from 001 to 127.

Class B An IP address class in which the first two *octets* of the address define the network portion of the address. The remaining two octets define the host portion of the address. The first two bits of a class B address must always be 1 0. A class B network using a standard subnet can host up to 16,384 networks, each of which can contain 65,534 hosts. The first octet of a class B address will range from 128 to 191.

Class C An IP address class in which the first three *octets* of the address define the network portion of the address. The remaining octet defines the host portion of the address. The first three bits of a class C address must always be 1 1 0. There can be up to 2,097,152 class C networks, each with 255 hosts. The first octet of a class C address will range from 192 to 223.

Class D Class D addresses are reserved by TCP/IP for the purpose of generating *multicasts*. They cannot be configured or used independently by an administrator. The first four bits of a class D address will be 1 1 1 0. The first octet of a class D address will range from 224 to 239.

Class E A range of IP addresses reserved for research. The first five bits of a class E address will be 1 1 1 1 0. The first octet will range from 240 to 254.

class code Information programmed onto a PCI device that tells the BIOS precisely what it is. Class code is recorded in a designated address in the device's *firmware*. During *POST* the BIOS interrogates the firmware to determine what kind of a device it is talking to. Class codes are not optional parameters for PCI designers. They are a required register in the device's configuration parameters. PCI specifications call for their presence on every PCI device. Each individual class of device is broken down into subclasses of device. Table C.2 lists the general class codes.

clean boot A method of booting an operating system with only the bare minimum set of drivers needed to run the OS. This allows you to attempt to figure out what device or devices might be causing the system to refuse to boot. In the days of MS-DOS, you could execute a clean boot by pressing F5. This bypassed the AUTOEXEC.BAT and CONFIG.SYS files, thereby not loading any of the drivers and programs listed. In Windows, F5 will boot to *Safe Mode*, which is the Windows equivalent of a clean boot. However, Windows offers several other options as well. Pressing F8 during the Windows boot process will bring up a boot menu that displays those options.

clean install The fresh installation of an OS over a newly partitioned and formatted hard disk. When reinstalling an operating system onto a computer or when installing a newer version, you may have the option of doing an *upgrade*, performing a *repair installation*, or doing a clean install. Both an upgrade and a repair installation will attempt to retain all user settings and saved files. The clean

TABLE C.2
Listing of PCI class codes

CLASS	CLASS VALUE	DESCRIPTION
0x00	BASE_BC	Devices built prior to class requirements (before PCI 2.0)
0x01	BASE_MASS	Mass storage controller
0x02	BASE_NETWORK	Network interface controller
0x03	BASE_DISPLAY	Display controller
0x04	BASE_MULTMEDIA	Multimedia device
0x05	BASE_MEM	Memory controller
0x06	BASE_BRIDGE	Bridge device
0x07	BASE_COMM	Simple communications controllers
0x08	BASE_SYS_PERIPH	Base system peripherals
0x09	BASE_INPUT	Input devices
0x0A	BASE_DOCK	Docking stations
0x0B	BASE_PROCESSOR	Processors
0x0C	BASE_SERIAL_BUS	Serial bus controllers
0x0D–0xFE	N/A	Reserved
0xFF	BASE_UNKNOWN	Misc

install blows everything away, forcing the user to start from scratch. The downside to the clean install is that the user has to start from scratch. If their files are not backed up, then the data is forever lost. The downside to the upgrade or repair is that all problems that result from incorrect user settings or an incorrect device driver move over into the new installation. In order to repair a corrupted OS, the only real solution is a clean install.

clean room Many server installations and manufacturing facilities require that the air be meticulously filtered to keep out even the smallest of particles. A room in which the air is filtered at all points, including the entrance and exit doorways, is an example of a clean room. Workers in a clean room are generally required to wear freshly sanitized uniforms from which all particles of dust and cloth fiber have been removed. Because of their amusing appearance, these uniforms earned the nickname *bunny suit*. In addition to the air filtration and special uniforms, special mats with a slightly adhesive surface adorn the floor at all entrances. Anyone entering the room must walk over this mat, removing loose particles from the bottoms of the bunny feet they are wearing with the bunny suit.

clear memory A verb. This term refers to the process of resetting all memory and hardware registers to null values. Generally, for this process to be totally successful, a simple device reset will not work. A *cold boot* that involves turning the device completely off and then back off again is required to completely clear memory.

clear text   Unencrypted text. Clear text sent over a data transmission is easily read by anyone who is able to intercept the transmission. Some of the older *dialup networking* protocols transmitted all data in clear text, including logon authentication credentials.

ClearType   In Windows XP and later, Microsoft incorporated a screen display technology that doubles the horizontal resolution of the graphics. The idea is that diagonal lines and text will be displayed more clearly. Since not all displays respond well to different horizontal and vertical resolutions, Microsoft does not enable this setting by default. If you want to experiment with ClearType, right-click on the desktop, select Properties, and in the window that pops up, click on the Appearance tab. Select Effects. One of the options will be to use either Standard view or ClearType.

click   (1) To press down once on the left button of a mouse or trackball. In most operating systems, some functions are activated with a single click, while others require to clicks in rapid succession (the double-click). Pressing down on the right mouse button is not surprisingly referred to as a right-click. With Windows and OS X, a right-click brings up a menu of options related to the object on which you right-clicked. (2) When analyzing Web page statistics, a click refers to each attempt to access a hyperlink. Monitoring what links get the most clicks is an indicator of what Web site features are attracting the most visitors.

click and drag   An operating system feature that allows a user to relocate an object by clicking on the *icon* representing the object, holding down with the mouse button, and dragging the icon across the screen. Click and drag can be used for different functions. If you click on a document icon and drag it over the printer icon, the word processing program that created the document will open and subsequently print that document on the selected printer. You can also click and drag a file from one folder to another.

click fraud   In the Internet advertising industry, a common practice is to pay the owners of popular Web site for hosting a banner on their site advertising your product. One method of calculating how much the owner is paid is per-click. Every time a user clicks on that banner, the Web site owner gets a few cents. Click fraud occurs when a dishonest or unethical practice is used to inflate the number of clicks. By having a thousand monkeys clicking on the banner a thousand times a day with a thousand different computers, a dishonest webmaster can make a lot of cash for a few bananas. Some *fraudmeisters* simply outsource the fake clicks to the Middle East where the labor is even cheaper.

click of death   Some of the earlier models of Iomega Zip drives had a problem in which the drive would suddenly start making a rapid clicking noise when a disk was inserted. Once that noise was heard, the disk involved was dead. It could never be used again. The drive itself either died immediately, or within a few disk reads. And in fact, if you attempt to use that disk in another drive, it will damage the second drive as well.

click speed   A term that describes just how quickly you must press down on the left mouse button before the system will recognize it as a *double-click*. Operating systems such as Windows and OS X have utilities that allow the user to adjust click speed to their own abilities. This is why someone who is accustomed to a slower click speed has trouble if another computer is set too fast. Want to have some fun? Set the speed to its absolute fastest and watch the average user try to figure why nothing opens when they double-click on it.

clickstream   The path of mouse clicks that a user makes to get from one point to another in a program or on a Web site. When analyzing a program or Web page for efficiency, designers look at the clickstream very carefully and study the program to see if there are features that should be moved higher up in the hierarchy in order to reduce the number of clicks required to get from beginning to end. Most Web-analyzing software is able to generate a clickstream analysis.

click-through   On a Web page, the process of clicking on a hyperlink to get to a secondary site is a click-through. Web sites that draw their income from generating traffic for other Web sites count on an accurate measurement of click-through rate. A single person clicking on a link is counted as a single click-through. If that same person clicks on the same link a second time within a certain predesignated period of time, additional clicks will not be recorded.

clickwrap   A software licensing technique that requires a user to click on a button signifying that he agrees to the terms of use defined in the end user license agreement. Some software manufacturers require that the user at least scroll down through the agreement before clicking on the "I Agree" button. There is some debate over the legality of an agreement that does not require the user to read what he is agreeing to. The term was derived from the old-fashioned licensing agreement on shrink-wrapped packages that stated acceptance of the licensing agreement was inferred by breaking the seal of the package.

client   (1) Any device or software that requires the services of another device or piece of software in order to perform its function. In a networked environment, any user's computer hooked up to the network is usually considered a client. (2) Software running from within an OS that allows the device to connect to a network. The client runs another specialized piece of software called the *redirector*, which determines if a request can be resolved on the local machine or if it must be forwarded to a remote device on the network for resolution.

client-based   A software model that splits responsibilities between host machines running on the network and one or more servers. The application runs on the host machine, making that machine the client. Data is stored on a centralized server and doled out to those with appropriate access. *See also* **client/server**.

client/server   A network in which one or more master computers keeps a database of users and/or dole out files on an as-needed basis. In the classic instance of client/server architecture, the server(s) perform one or both of two roles. In the first role, it authenticates each user or host that attempts to connect to it. The most common form of authentication is the *challenge/response* approach of asking the user for a password and then granting or denying access, based on whether or not the user can type. The second role of the server is to provide *services*. Services include providing access to files, to other devices on the network, or to other networks or the Internet. The list of services a server can provide is long enough to be the subject of a book in itself. The client (also called a *host* or *node*) is any device that hooks up to a network and draws its services from a server. The client is *not* the end user. In a client/server setup, security is much tighter because the logon authentication provided by the server dictates what users have what rights to which resources.

cliff effect   The tendency for a digital signal to be all or none. Digital information is readable all the way down to a certain threshold. After that it is totally unreadable. There is no gradual degradation of quality as the signal weakens. As a result there is an illusion of the signal going as far as it possibly can and then dropping off the edge of a cliff. You see this phenomenon illustrated with cell phones. The voice does not fade away gradually: it is either there or it is not. In borderline situations the call seems crackly because it is in and out constantly.

clipart   Images that are supplied with an application for use in documents created by that application. Generally, clipart consists of relatively crude line drawings with 256 or fewer colors. Thousands of Internet sites have sprung up offering millions of clipart images at prices ranging from totally free (and usually worth every penny) to relatively high. A precaution that should be taken with commercial clipart is to double-check the licensing agreement. There are some companies that charge one-time use rates for their artwork, while others charge royalties. With a royalty, you must pay the provider of the artwork for every copy of the piece you distribute.

clipboard   A piece of memory reserved by the operating system for holding data that was copied from one document until it can be placed into another document. The process of *cut and paste* requires the services of the clipboard. Early versions of Microsoft's clipboard were very limited in usage. Every time the users copied anything at all to the clipboard, no matter how small, the entire contents of the existing clipboard, no matter how large, were overwritten. Subsequent versions have gotten a bit more flexible and now it is possible to hold up to twelve different iterations of the clipboard in memory. This, of course, depends of the relative size of each piece being held. The clipboard is of finite size. If one piece of data is large enough to occupy the entire clipboard, then do not count on adding eleven more items.

clipping   (1) On a document, clipping occurs when the image bleeds over into the area of the paper that is beyond the printer's ability to cover. Some clipping also occurs on a display when the image extends beyond the screen's size. (2) An electronic waveform that is cut off unnaturally when amplitude is greater than the circuit can handle. For example, if an audio signal is driven harder than the amplifier's power, the waveform will hit the peak of amplification power. Any audio content that should exist above that point is abruptly cut off, resulting in a squared-off waveform. Mild clipping of an audio signal is usually acceptable in that only extremely loud signals are affected. Excessive clipping, on the other hand, can result in unpleasant distortion.

clobbering   A slang term for overwriting the contents of a buffer that is still in use. When an application stores data or instructions to memory, it does so expecting to find that information when it needs it. If the memory manager of the application erroneously allows different data to overwrite the existing data before it is used, this *clobbering* can result in corrupted data or even a system crash.

clock   (1) An internal circuit on a device that controls the timing of signals transmitted or received. Most modern clocking circuits are able to work with *multipliers*. This allows the circuit or device to maintain two separate speeds. An example of this is the *central processing unit*, which runs at a much faster speed internally than it does externally. (2) A circuit or device that keeps track of the actual time of day. The *real-time clock* (RTC) chip on a motherboard is usually a separate chip that gets backup power from a battery installed on the motherboard when power is shut off from the system.

clock cycle   A timing signal generated by exciting a crystal with an electrical current that synchronizes data movement throughout the system. When the crystal is excited it vibrates at a particular frequency. The vibration is called *oscillation*. The frequency of oscillation depends on the molecular structure of the crystal and its relative thickness. Since it is nothing more than an electrical current, a clock cycle resembles a sine wave with a rising half of the signal and a falling half. A full clock cycle is the amount of time that elapses between pulses of the oscillating signal. All data transfers occur between pulses. Data transfer typically occurs on the rising half of the signal, although some newer data transfer techniques, such as the one used for AGP video signals and DDR memory, moves data on both halves of the cycle.

clock doubling   A technique Intel used on some models of their 80486 microprocessor that allowed the internal processing speed of the chip to be double that of its *external data bus*. While this was groundbreaking technology in its day, today's processors operate at internal speeds many times faster than the external bus speed.

clock pulse   When an electrical current excites a clock crystal, it causes the crystal to vibrate at a specific frequency. The vibration is caused by energy fluxes that occur in the molecular structure of the crystal. A clock pulse is a single energy flux taken out of the stream of vibration.

clock speed   The number of times per second that the timing mechanism on a given device initiates a *cycle*. Microprocessors are frequently measured by their clock speed. With modern chips, clock speeds are measured in *megahertz* or *gigahertz*. Measuring overall performance based simply on clock speed can be a mistake in one respect because different processors can do more work in a single clock cycle than others. If one processor runs at 2 GHz and requires five clock cycles to process a command, and another one runs at 1.5 GHz but only requires three clock cycles, the "slower" chip is actually working faster. The 2-GHz chip is executing 400,000,000 commands per second, whereas the 1.5-GHz chip is pushing out 500,000,000 per second. This is a simplified example because different commands can vary greatly in the number of clock cycles they take to execute on a given chip.

clone   (1) Something that looks, feels, smells, and tastes like the real thing but it is not. The term became popular in relation to computers when dozens of companies tried to emulate the IBM PC and the marketing success that came with it. Since so much of the device was based on open standards, it was relatively easy for a company to purchase the parts it needed from wholesalers and assemble a PC-compatible computer that operated very much like the original IBM product. The key term to consider when deciding if a product is a true clone is the part about being *compatible*. Some companies in the 1980s, such as Tandy Corporation, put out personal computers that were "sort of" compatible. (2) To duplicate precisely. This involves more than simply copying all the files from one disk to another. Hidden information, such as file allocation tables and master boot records, must also be duplicated. Cloning software and hardware make it possible to create a number of identical duplicates of CDs, floppy disks, or hard disks by creating an image of the disk and then performing a bit-by-bit copy to the target disks.

closed-ended question   A question that leads to an answer that provides no further insight or leads to an abrupt dead end to the discussion. Most questions that lead to a simple yes/no response can be considered closed-ended because to continue the discussion an entirely new question must be asked.

closed port   (1) Any *TCP/IP port* that has been shut down and prohibited from accepting and/or transmitting packets over an interface on a device such as a firewall or a router with a configured access control list. By default most of the ports used by the operating system are configured to allow packets to pass even if there is no application running on the system that would make use of the port. This is the equivalent of an open door with a welcome sign to even a mediocre hacker. Firewall software will scan your system and tell you what ports are open but unused, and provide you with the ability to shut them down. (2) Any interface on a *layer 3* (or intelligent) switch or router that has been shut down to traffic. These types of devices can be configured with a form of security called *port security*. When port security is enabled, the port will only accept or transmit packets to an interface with a specific *MAC address*. If the accepted device is taken off the system and a new device is installed, the MAC address will be different and the port will automatically shut down, denying network access to the new device.

cloud   In the world of networking, the cloud refers to "out there." When passing information over the Internet, the cloud would be the unpredictable mass of devices and media over which data must pass to get from point A to point B. In some contexts, the cloud consists of all networks that are part of the Internet. On a local area network, it is the infrastructure that exists between any two points. Many times, you will see the *telecom*'s infrastructure referred to as the cloud.

cluster   (1) Combining multiple individual units or devices to work together as a single unit. A server cluster consists of two or more servers that appear on the network as a single device. Clusters can be configured in one of several ways. A high-availability cluster is a redundant system in which the backup server instantly takes over in the event the primary server fails. A load-balancing cluster consists of two or more servers that are on line together and share the workload of incoming requests. There is no fault tolerance in a load-balanced cluster, but network performance is greatly improved. A high-performance computing (HPC) cluster is an array of several servers that work together to form a single supercomputer. Tasks are processed across multiple nodes of the array, speeding up the completion of extremely complex processes. (2) Another term for *file allocation unit*.

cluster addressing   (1) A mapping method that a different version of file allocation table (FAT) uses to locate the individual file allocations units that make up an individual file. Each version of FAT uses a different form of cluster addressing. FAT12 uses a 12-bit cluster address, FAT16 uses a 16-bit cluster address, and surprisingly enough, FAT32 uses a 32-bit cluster address. (2) The ability to identify the topological location of a host by its IP address. This is one of the features of the newer IPv6. Cluster addressing is a feature that allows far more efficient use of routing tables by directing a packet to the appropriate topological domain before handing off to the local server.

CMOS setup   One of the programs loaded on the BIOS chip. This particular program allows user-defined parameters relating to BIOS settings to be configured. Keep in mind that when you make adjustments in the BIOS setup, you are not modifying the BIOS code in any way, you are merely providing certain parameters that BIOS calls will use. In the event that you make changes to the CMOS setup that prevent your system from booting properly, do not panic. On most systems, if you remove the battery from the motherboard and count to thirty—very slowly—and then replace the battery, you will force the CMOS configurations to return to their original factory defaults. This includes CMOS-configured passwords that an irate employee put on a company machine before leaving in a huff.

coaxial   A conductor that has both the signal conductor and the ground running along the same axis. Coaxial cable starts with a solid (and relatively thick) strand of copper wire called the *core*. A thin layer of insulation surrounds the core. Around the core is a layer of copper mesh that performs double-duty as both a grounding conductor and as a shield against electromagnetic radiation for the copper core. All of this is insulated in a tough outer shell of PVC (polyvinyl chloride) or rubber. Figure C.11 is a diagram of a piece of coaxial cable.

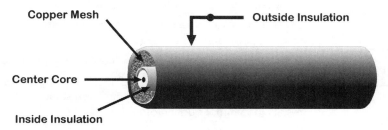

FIGURE C.11   A cross-section of coaxial cable.

code   The complete set of instructions that make up a program or data file. Program code is very much like a complex book. Each line of code represents a specific instruction. An interesting side note is that in the old days of computing, programmers were often paid not by the hour but for each line of code that they wrote. As you might imagine, this practice led to programs with a lot of unnecessary heft. Needless to say, programmers are not paid this way any more.

code density   The amount of memory space that a program requires to run. Overall code density dictates the minimum amount of RAM a device needs to support a particular application. Code density really comes into play when considering applications for very small devices such as personal data assistants or pocket PCs. Factors that have an impact on code density include the programming language used to write the code, the compiler used to render the code into executable form, and the efficiency of the programmer who wrote the code.

codec   (1) A coined term derived from two other terms, *coder* and *decoder*. A codec is an IC that has been programmed to convert data from one form to another. An example of this would be a chip that takes analog signals and converts them to digital, and vice versa. (2) Compressor/decompressor. This is a piece of software that takes data and compresses it on the fly for transmission over the medium or for storage. On the receiving end or when the data needs to be extracted, the codec performs the reverse function. All codecs, whether of the first or the second variety, can be identified by a designation. There are speech codecs, audio codecs, and video codecs. Table C.3 lists some of the more common types of codecs.

TABLE C.3
A listing of commonly used codecs

NAME	PURPOSE
AUDIO CODECS	
AAC	Advanced Audio Coding. Originally part of Apple Quick-Time, it is now the core codec for MPEG 4 audio streams.
AIFF	Audio Information File Format. The audio code used by Macintosh computers.
AU	The audio codec used by Sun and NeXT systems.
CDDA	CD Digital Audio. The standard audio file format used by commercially pressed compact disks.
DRM	Music with digital rights. Embeds copyright information into the file.
MP3	MPEG layer 3 audio. A highly compressed music format that results in minimal quality loss.
Ogg Vorbis Music	Open source standard.
RA, RAM	Real Networks streaming audio files.
WMA	Windows Media Audio. A Microsoft audio codec.
TELECOMMUNICATIONS CODECS	
A-Law	A European telephone codec that supports multifunction circuits.
μ-Law	A U.S. telephone codec that supports multifunction circuits.
GSM 6.10	Global Systems Mobile. A speech compression algorithm for cell phones.
G.711	Audio/videoconferencing standard from the International Telecommunications Union.
G.722	Audio/videoconferencing standard from the International Telecommunications Union.
G.723.1	Voice over IP standards from the International Telecommunications Union.

TABLE C.3
(Continued)

G.728	Audio/videoconferencing standard from the International Telecommunications Union.
G.729	Audio/videoconferencing standard from the International Telecommunications Union.
AMR-NB	Adaptive Multi Rate Narrow Band codec from Global Systems Mobile.
AMR-WB	Adaptive Multi Rate Wide Band codec from Global Systems Mobile.
MOTION PICTURE CODECS	
MPEG-1	Motion Picture Experts Group, Layer One Video Compression.
MPEG-2	Motion Picture Experts Group, Layer Two Video Compression.
MPEG-4	Motion Picture Experts Group, Layer Four Video Compression.
AVI	Audio Video Interleave. A Windows movie compression file format.
WMV	Windows Media Video. A Windows movie compression file format.
RM, RV	Real Networks Movie and Real Networks Video.
Indeo	An older movie codec developed by Intel and Microsoft.
H.261	Video conferencing standards from the International Telecommunications Union.
H.263	Video conferencing standards from the International Telecommunications Union.
H.264	Video conferencing standards from the International Telecommunications Union.
DivX	A file compression algorithm that can compress the audio and video content of a video to 10 percent of its original size.

coercivity   A measurement of the amount of energy it takes to reverse the polarization of a bit of data stored on magnetic media. Coercivity is measured in an oddly named rating called *oersted*. The higher the oersted rating, the more electrical current it takes to reverse the polarity. If you reverse the polarity of the bit, you change its value from 0 to 1 or from 1 to 0.

coil   An electrical component consisting of wire tightly wound around a core. Coils are used for a variety of purposes. One of these is to filter out AC current and low-frequency signals. Coils are used to stabilize a DC current that has been converted over from an AC source or to filter out rumble from an audio signal.

FIGURE C.12   A coil in a computer power supply.

A coil with a constant supply of electricity can be used as an electromagnet. Figure C.12 shows an example of a coil in a computer power supply.

colocation   This term defines a procedure in which a customer's equipment will be located on a service provider's site, or vice versa, in order to provide the best possible service. Colocation is often arranged when connection through a remote connection would degrade connection speeds too greatly, or when a large amount of administration work will be performed at the colocated device. Telecommunications providers often colocate connection equipment on the customer's site in order to provide the connection between the customer's network and the telecom. Also, it is not uncommon for the host of a very large Web site to allow the organization that owns the site to colocate their own server at the hosting company's facility. Naturally, there is a service charge that goes along with colocation.

cold boot   To turn a machine completely off, wait a few seconds for capacitors to discharge, and then turn the machine back on again. The purpose of this is to reset all device configurations as well as restart the operating system. This is opposed to a *warm boot* in which the user simply restarts the operating system without shutting the computer down. Also known as a *cold start*.

cold fusing   A process used by some phase-change printers that uses pressure rollers to press the ink into the paper. Printers that use this method generate images in which the color dots created by the printing process are flattened and blended in the image. The dyes used to create the image are embedded in the medium and are less likely to flake off than images created by laser methods. This is different from conventional laser printers that raise the temperature to nearly the incineration point of paper in order to melt the toner. Some printers offer the option of using either cold fusing or hot fusing by making the appropriate choice in the print options.

cold site   A facility remote to the network that contains all of the hardware necessary to install new network servers but does not have the actual servers, nor does it maintain copies of the operating systems, software, or data required. When an organization maintains a cold site, it basically keeps spare equipment around that will facilitate moving new servers in without the delay of preparing the infrastructure. In the event of a total disaster in which all network servers are lost, new servers are delivered and installed into the racks. Copies of operating systems, applications, and data backups must be shipped to the cold site. There can be a lengthy delay while the systems are brought up to speed and the data restored to the new systems. This contrasts to *warm sites* and *hot sites*.

cold start   *See* **cold boot**.

collaborate   To work together on a single project.

collaborative software   Any application that allows two or more people to work on the same project at the same time, each person working from a separate networked computer. In today's business environment, collaborative software has become an essential ingredient to success. Programs running on your computer allow you to set up virtual meetings without anyone ever leaving their desks. Documents can be prepared, critiqued, revised, and rewritten by groups of people, while leaving the original document intact in the event that someone decides to revert to the original. Shared calendars allow users to check on a coworker's availability at any given time without the need of interrupting anyone.

collator   A software program that takes multiple files and merges them into a single cohesive file. This is not quite the same as *appending* a file, in that the new data is not simply tacked on at the end. If the collator is merging two database files, the records of each data set are inserted and sorted as required. Collators do not necessarily have to work with entire files. They can act as "data miners" that look for specific records or types of records stored in multiple databases and merge them into a single target database.

collector   One of the terminals on a bipolar transistor. This is the electrode that gathers together and dissipates the electrons that created the current it "collected." Whether current flows or not depends on whether the current on the circuit reaches the *threshold voltage* required to open the switch.

collimate   To merge two linear paths into a straight and parallel line. This term is frequently used in relation to light. Optical instruments frequently need multiple beams of light to run parallel. The process of calibrating that device would be known as *collimation*. Collimated light results when lenses are used to refract all the colors light into parallel paths. A laser is a highly collimated beam of light, even though it appears as a single beam. The streams of photons are extremely parallel.

collision   On a *CSMA/CD*-based network, a collision occurs when two different devices attempt to transmit data onto the wire at the same time. When a collision occurs, each device broadcasts a *backoff algorithm*, instructing all devices to withhold transmissions for a predefined number of clock cycles. Collisions cause a delay in transmitting data. Network *congestion* occurs when too many users are on the network at the same time, which results in a significant increase in the number of collisions that occur.

collision domain   All of the devices on a network that must compete with each other for their turn to use the cable. Two devices that try to use the network cable at the same time are said to experience a collision, which causes the information to be dropped and each device must send its information once again. Collision domains can be limited by using a device that filters packets based on IP address or MAC address. When a *switch* is used on a network instead of a *hub*, each port on the switch is a separate collision domain. If you attach a hub to that port, then all the devices that connect to the hub share the same collision domain but devices on other ports of the switch do not. If only one device is connected per port on the switch, then each device is on its own collision domain.

colon   A punctuation mark that looks like a pair of stacked dots. The colon is used to separate groups of characters in a hexadecimal address or in an IPv6 address.

color depth   The number of individual hues that can be generated by a given display setting. This is directly related to the number of bits that are used by the display driver to create images. Table C.4 lists some common color depth settings used by Windows systems.

TABLE C.4
The color settings of Windows

COLOR DEPTH	NO. OF COLORS	DESCRIPTION
6-bit	16	Standard VGA, 16 colors selected from a larger palette
8-bit	256	Super VGA, indexed color
15-bit	32, 768	High Color with 5 bits for each color
16-bit	65, 536	High Color with 5 bits for red and blue and 6 bits for green
24-bit	16, 777, 216	True Color
32-bit	16, 777, 216	True Color + alpha channel

color gamut   The total range of colors that can be either created or displayed by a particular device. Even though the *bit depth* might suggest some ridiculously high number like 16,777,216 colors, the reality of the situation is that most devices cannot make such fine distinctions. For example, the pearl divers of Japan are considered to have the finest color vision of all humans, and they can distinguish between about 16,000 separate hues. That is their gamut. The ability of a device to distinguish between two subtly different shades of a similar color defines that device's gamut.

color laser   A form of laser printer that incorporates four separate toner cartridges in order to reproduce a wide *color gamut*. The colors used by laser printers are

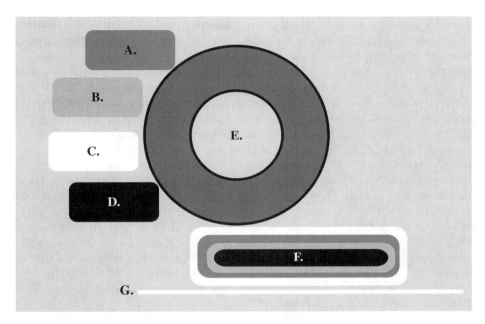

A. Magenta Toner   E. Imaging Drum
B. Cyan Toner   F. Intermediate Transfer Surface
C. Yellow Toner   G. Paper
D. Black Toner

FIGURE C.13   A color laser incorporates four toner cartridges containing the subtractive colors. An intermediate transfer belt or roller then moves the combined image onto the paper.

the *subtractive colors* of cyan, magenta, yellow, and black. In order to create the color image, separate prints are made from each of the four subtractive colors. Until the printer is ready to transfer these images to paper, they are stored on an *intermediate transfer belt*. Once all four images are on the belt, they get transferred to the paper and then the paper runs through a *fusing assembly* where heat and pressure bond the toner to the paper. Figure C.13 is a conceptual diagram of how a color laser creates an image.

color temperature   A measurement of light frequencies in degrees Kelvin. Since it probably comes to mind to question how something that you cannot feel at all, such as light waves, can possibly have a temperature, I thought it best to explain that as well. When scientists first noticed that the frequency of light waves affected our perception of color, their first studies involved how objects changed in color as they heated up. A black iron radiator was used in the experiments. As the temperature of the iron went from cold to hot, it transformed from black to red, then from red to yellow, then to white and finally to blue. So naturally, our concept of color temperature is that blue, which is created from the highest possible temperatures is a "cool" color, while yellows and reds, which result from much lower temperatures, are referred to as the warm colors. I suppose you are wondering how that came to be as well. So am I.

colorimeter   A light-sensitive device that is capable of measuring the relative values of the *additive colors* of red, green, and blue. A colorimeter is used for calibrating different devices to treat different hues in exactly the same manner. Without accurate calibration, the blue you see on a monitor does not print out on your color printer with the same hue. With proper calibration, you can adjust your monitor to match the output of your printer.

column   A vertical subset from a two-dimensional array of data. Spreadsheets lay data out in *rows* and columns. The column is the set of data that moves up and down on the page or screen. The row moves from right to left. Where a row and column converge is called a *cell*.

COM file   A executable file with the extension of .COM. COM files go back to the days of MS-DOS. For a COM file to work in DOS, it had to be under 64 K in size so it could fit into a single memory *segment*. As we all moved into the world of Windows, COM files become obsolete and we started to use .EXE files for primary executables. However, in order to remain backwardly compatible with DOS, a COM file exists that can call the EXE file.

COM port   A predefined combination of an IRQ and an I/O address configured for communications devices. COM ports 1 and 3 and ports 2 and 4 each share IRQs with one another, but make use of unique I/O addresses. The idea is that two communications devices would not be active at the same time. However, should both devices become active simultaneously, the system would experience a *nonmaskable interrupt* and the system would lock up like a tomb. COM ports are generally assigned to serial ports. A common error made by a large number of manufacturers is to label the serial ports on the back of a PC as COM port 1 and COM port 2. Insomuch as either of the serial ports can be assigned to any COM port, this is an error. Table C.5 lists the COM ports along with their assigned IRQ and I/O addresses.

TABLE C.5
COM port settings

COM PORT	IRQ	I/O ADDRESS
1	IRQ4	03F8
2	IRQ3	02F8
3	IRQ4	03E8
4	IRQ3	02E8

combo box   On a Web page or in an application, a combo box is a field that appears to be a simple text box. However, by holding the mouse cursor over the box or by clicking on an arrow, a list of options appears. When the user selects an option, that value fills the field.

combo card   An expansion card that performs two or more functions. A common example is a network interface card combined with a SCSI adapter or a fax/modem. Also, network interface cards with two different types of interface, such as an *AUI* and an *RJ-45* port or an RJ-45 and a *BNC* port, are called combo cards.

comma delimited   An export file of a set of database records that separates each field with a comma. Typically, the actual data is also enclosed in quotation marks. *"Night River Tales," "Short Story Collection,"* and *"2004." "2004"* is an example from a FileMaker Pro database. Most spreadsheets and databases are capable of importing and exporting comma delimited text files. These files may end in a .TXT extension, but more typically they have a .CSV extension.

command   A string of code that initiates a specific action that a program or device is asked to execute. Many commands allow a programmer to incorporate an *argument,* which is a value attached to the command that modifies or more strictly defines the action performed by the command. For example, *log* could be a command to calculate a logarithm. Log (x) adds the argument X, which can be a numerical value inputted by the customer or provided by an application. Most commands are issued by an application or program, which consists of a very long series of commands that the processor must execute in a specific order. Commands can be generated and issued by device controllers as well.

command interpreter   A program running as part of an operating system that takes user commands or programming level commands from the applications and translates them into machine-level instructions that the hardware can understand. It is possible for commands to be executed from within the interpreter or for the interpreter to call on and execute external commands. A command executed from within the interpreter is an *internal command.* For example, the old MS-DOS command interpreter is COMMAND.COM. By typing DIR at the command prompt, a user got a listing of all the files resident in the directory open by the system. This was an internal command. There was no DIR.EXE or DIR.COM file called by COMMAND.COM. On the other hand, when a user typed in the FORMAT C:\ command, COMMAND.COM called and executed FORMAT.EXE. This is an example of an *external command.* In the Windows environment, CMD.EXE replaces COMMAND.COM.

command key   On an Apple keyboard, the key that is used to modify other keys on the keyboard in order to launch commands from keyboard shortcuts. It is the OS X equivalent of the <Ctrl> key in Windows. You can recognize the command key by the special little diagram of an apple on the keycap (see Figure C.14).

command line   Any field in an application or operating system that allows the user to input commands. In Windows, if you click Start>Run, a field appears that allows you to type in textual commands. For many functions, many programmers or administrators prefer the command line. It offers direct access to the operating system and, through the use of *switches,* allows the user somewhat greater flexibility. The general user prefers to work from a graphical interface. It is not unusual to have a large number of operating system functions that run only from the command line. This prevents curious users from double-clicking on the icon to see what the command "FORMAT C:\" does.

command overhead   The number of instructions that must be executed in order to carry out a specific request, combined with the speed at which the device can carry out those instructions. Essentially this is the equivalent of a device's knee-jerk reflex. Command overhead directly impacts on how many clock cycles will

FIGURE C.14   *The Apple Command key is right next to the Option key on the Apple keyboard.*

elapse from the instant the CPU makes a request to the satisfaction of that request. While all devices are at the mercy of command overhead, you most frequently see the reference applied to disk drives.

command overlapping   The ability of a device to start processing a command even before the command issued prior to it has completed its cycle. The term is generally seen in connection with storage devices. It emerged as a technique used in later generations of IDE devices and became a standard feature of SCSI. However, similar techniques are used by a variety of devices. When a CPU does it, it is called *instruction pipelining*.

command prompt   In Windows, this is a screen that mimics the old MS-DOS screen where users can work with a command line interface without the limitations of the graphical command line. Many system management utilities are designed to run from the command prompt. IPCONFIG is a TCP/IP utility (Figure C.15) that works from the command prompt.

command queuing   Allows a device to store a series of commands in a buffer area, assuring that as one command is completed another one is rolled up to the gate and ready to go. Most devices benefit from command queuing. It originated in SCSI-II and was quickly introduced into parallel ATA devices. SCSI-III calls for all devices to support the feature and it is a native function of Serial ATA. PATA did not really gain much from the feature because of other technical restraints. A variation on the theme is *tagged command queuing* in which the commands are redistributed in the queue so that they are executed in the most efficient order. All queued operations related to data located on one region of the disk platter are completed before the *actuator arm* moves the heads to a new location on the disk. By arranging I/O operations related to specific geographic areas on the drive, both performance and drive longevity are enhanced.

comment   A nonexecutable line in a program or batch file that is only present to act as an explanation. In order to prevent a comment from being misinterpreted by the *command interpreter* as being an unknown or invalid command, comments are usually preceded by an asterisk or the abbreviation REM (for remark).

FIGURE C.15   The Windows command prompt.

commit   (1) To reserve for use by a specific program or thread. When an application is launched, the operating system must commit a certain amount of memory for use by that application. The OS will also commit a percentage of CPU time for the newly launched application as well. (2) To save the results of updating a record, making the new information permanent.

common carrier   A telecommunications service provider that is under the watchful eye of several government regulatory agencies. These organizations provide the basic services we all count on for telephone and Internet services. The primary common carriers are AT&T, MCI, Verizon, and others like them.

Common Desktop Environment   An applications programming interface that defines an operating environment that all applications running under the operating system will share. This assures that as users move from one application to another, they do not have to relearn menus, keystrokes, and basic commands.

compact disk (CD)   What started out to be a medium for digital music was quickly adopted for storage of larger collections of binary data as well. It was not long before the compact disk went from being a luxury to be a standard component on all desktop computers and virtually all laptops. A compact disk consists of a 4.5" plastic disk with a very thin layer of medium. The original CD used aluminum with holes punched into the surface to absorb the laser beam that read the data. Recordable disks use cyanine dye and rewritable disks use a complex metallic alloy. In order to encode data onto the reflective surface (called *land*), a series of holes (called *pits*) is embedded. A laser beam shines down on the disk spinning beneath. As the pits fly by underneath the beam, the light is absorbed, whereas it is reflected from the land. This alternating series of reflection/nonreflection is picked

FIGURE C.16   *While this CompactFlash card stores only 512 MB of data, they are available in much larger sizes.*

up by a photosensor, which converts the flickering beam into a pulsating electrical current. A *digital analog converter* turns the current into a stream of 1s and 0s.

CompactFlash   A very small card (Figure C.16) containing *flash memory* originally developed by SanDisk corporation. The CompactFlash card is a small rectangular card 36.4 mm × 42.8 mm × 3.3 mm in size. A 50-pin PC/ATA interface connects it to the devices that use it. When they originally came out, they were a huge hit because a CompactFlash card, as small as it was, could store an immense 4 MB of data. Now it is hard to find one smaller than 256 MB and they come in sizes up to 12 GB. CompactFlash is a very popular memory medium for digital cameras.

compand   (1) A combination of compressing and expanding. In analog musical recording, the process of companding is used to modify the reproduction of audio signals by compressing the *dynamic range* of passages that are too wide for the medium to record, and expanding the dynamic range of very low-level passages. This allows the storage medium to record the entire range of the musical experience onto a limited medium. On playback, the same circuit reverses the procedure so that those listening hear the music more naturally. (2) A technique used in digital transmission of audio signals that reduces the number of bits that are used in sampling the loudest passages of the audio signal.

comparator   Any device or software program that examines two or more objects and measures the factors that make them equal and those that make them different. A comparator might be used to determine if two files that have the same name actually contain the same data. In forensics, a comparator can be used to analyze facial features to decide if the features in a semilegible photograph are similar enough to a clear photo to provide positive identification.

compatibility   The ability of two components to work together or for a piece of software to work in harmony with a piece of hardware. In the early days of computing, different brands of computers had so many differences that any semblance of compatibility was something a computer engineer could only dream about. As systems evolved, compatibility became a major issue and different organizations evolved to oversee the development of standards that would assure compatibility. Even in this modern age, compatibility issues are always rearing up to bite us in the back of the neck.

compatibility mode   (1) A unidirectional signal that is used to send data to the printer. This is also known as *Centronics mode*. Signals that run in compatibility mode are very slow, running at approximately 150 KB/s. (2) A feature built into some operating systems that allows them to run programs written for a different OS or to read data that was compiled on a different system. Generally, running in compatibility mode results in a major performance hit.

compile   The process of taking the code from an application that was written in a high-level programming language and translating it into a series of machine-level commands that the computer can recognize. Generally, compiling a program requires the services of a secondary application, oddly enough known as a *compiler*. Some database applications such as FileMaker Pro Developer include a compiler that allows databases to be converted into stand-alone *runtime* applications. Some operating systems must be recompiled any time a significant chance is made.

compiler   The application used to *compile* high-level programming language into machine language.

component   Just one of the many objects that make up a larger, more complex object. An automobile looks like a very large object parked on the side of the road. But on closer inspection, you can easily see that thousands of smaller objects, or components, were assembled to create the automobile. Computers are an assembly of components. Certain components are so fundamental to the construction of a computer that entire industries are built around them. Intel started out as a chip manufacturer.

component video   A method of transmitting a video image in which each of the primary colors travels over a separate channel. VGA graphics is a form of component video in that the red, green, and blue signals each travel over a separate wire. RGB and S-Video are examples of component video.

composite video   A method of transmitting a video signal in which all aspects of the video signal follow a single channel. Cable television and broadcast television are examples of composite video. NTSC and PAL are examples of composite video standards.

compound document   A single file that can be opened in an application that contains a variety of different forms of data. For example, a multimedia file with text and a video clip with audio accompaniment is a compound document. Compound documents do not have to be multimedia to qualify. A text document with an embedded photograph or a spreadsheet with an embedded text file both would be considered compound documents.

compress   To make a digital file require fewer bits to hold the same information. Data compression can occur in a number of different ways, but all involve taking a long series of data that is either all the same digit (0 or 1) or close enough to being all the same that the rare exception is ignored. Data compression can either be performed as *lossless* compression or *lossy* compression. With lossless compression, when the data is extracted it is returned to its original form exactly, with no bits altered at all. With lossy compression, it is assumed that a few altered bits here and there are acceptable. Some forms of data cannot be altered in any way. An executable file is an example of this. Only lossless compression can be used. A graphics file, on the other hand, can stand to lose a few bits here and there. Who is really going to notice if one pixel in the blue sky is a different shade of blue? That is why a lossy compression algorithm such as *JPEG* works fine with graphics.

compression ratio   The degree to which a file can be compressed. Compression ratios are iterated as a reverse denominator. A compression ratio of 2:1 means that the compressed file is exactly half the size of the original.

computer   Any device that can accept the input of user data, process that data according to a specific set of instructions, and then provide the results of that processing in the form of output to the end user. To qualify as a computer, a device will follow the general computer model. Functionally, it must be able to perform the basic operations called the *Three C's of Computing*. A computer must be able to Calculate, Copy, and Compare data. In order to perform these functions, it needs as a minimum a *central processing unit*, *random access memory*, *storage*, and a controlled *input/output* stage. Figure C.17 shows a conceptual diagram of the basic computer model.

computer book   The one thing that you DO NOT want to get involved in writing when you grow up if you have any illusions at all of making a decent living.

computer forensics   A careful study of a computer system that is suspected to have been used in a crime or for other illicit purposes. Investigators use a collection of specialized techniques and procedures to extract, preserve, and analyze digital information so that it may be presented as evidence in civil or criminal proceedings. For the evidence collected by a computer forensics specialist to be accepted in a court of law, that person must have followed strict guidelines as prescribed by law and documented every step used to obtain the evidence presented. This prevents a crafty defense team from insisting that the evidence collected either is not valid or that it did not come from the source claimed. Specialized software allows an investigator to perform some pretty nifty tricks on computers. Some utilities can compare the contents of a file to its extension to see if attempts are being made to camouflage the file contents. For example, pornographic images might be renamed with a .DOC extension. For an individual to examine every file on a computer to verify its contents would take weeks, or even months. A computer can do it in a couple of hours. Other utilities can extract deleted files that were removed from the recycle bin, and still others can extract the contents of a drive that has been wiped.

computer literacy   A person's relative competence with computers in general. This is somewhat of a generic term in that in the office environment, computer literacy might be defined by how intimately a person knows the ins and outs of the office productivity suite used by the organization. Yet to a technical shop, people might be more interested in your ability to navigate operating systems. Overall, computer

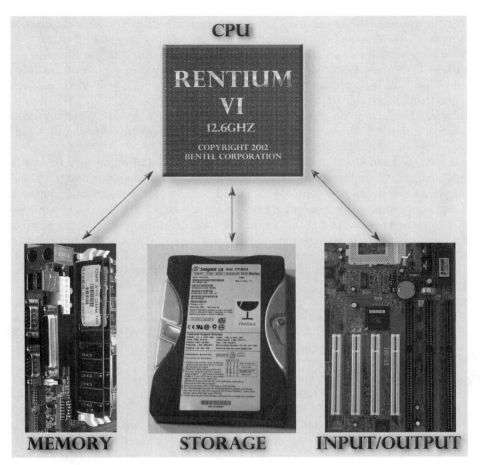

FIGURE C.17   The basic computer model.

literacy is best described as having more than the minimum level of knowledge and ability to do the required job at hand.

computer on a chip   This is a slang term for a single integrated circuit that contains a microprocessor, RAM, ROM with a basic OS built in, an I/O circuit, and some form of clock circuitry to synchronize it all. These chips are commonly used on computerized objects ranging from toys to the computer that controls the automobile you drive.

concatenate   To link two disparate structures together to form a single unit. When data is *appended* to an existing file, you are concatenating the files. As far as I know, there is no law against concatenating in public, as long as it is with computer files.

concentrator   A device that takes multiple incoming signals from different channels and combines them all into a single stream. Many network devices act as concentrators. Ethernet switches and hubs can be considered as such. Internet service providers use high-speed concentrators to conglomerate all of the incoming signals from all their users and dump them onto the backbone.

concentric   A series of circular tracks that gets larger from the center of the disk to the edge. This is as opposed to a spiral track that is actually a single track that coils from the center to the edge.

concurrent   Occurring at the same time. When you have Microsoft Word running on your computer at the same time as Netscape Navigator, the two programs are running concurrently.

concurrent use licensing   A licensing policy that, instead of requiring a license for each user, dictates how many different users can use the software at one time. An organization that has 300 employees but runs them on three shifts of 100 per shift would only require 100 concurrent licenses instead of 300 individual user licenses. Concurrency is managed at the server level. In the aforementioned situation, if someone chose to work overtime and did not log off, then one person on the next shift would be refused access. But as soon as the one working logged off, that license becomes available and the other person can start working and the two of them can stop fighting.

conductor   Any substance that encourages the flow of electricity. The term also describes the man or woman standing at the podium waving a white stick in front of the musicians. The better conductors can actually wave their stick at exactly the same rhythm at which the musicians are playing their music. Railroad conductors encourage the flow of train cars along a track.

conferencing   The ability to bring multiple users into a single communications or computing session. While teleconferencing has been with us for a while, computer conferencing is now taking a firm hold. Teleconferencing allows several people to participate in the same telephone conversation at the same time. Computer conferencing does basically the same thing, but adds a number of additional benefits. All the people involved in the conference can have the same application open with the same data file displayed. Digital video streams allow the users to see one another and they converse among one another using *voice over IP* (VoIP) technology. Do not try this stunt with an old 486 computer running Windows 3.11 for Workgroups.

configure   A process of choice. To configure something is to decide from a variety of different options which specific options to use when building a system or when setting up the operating system and applications to run on a system. A computer goes through a number of configuration processes. First, the designer decides what parts to use when building the system. Once the system is fully built, certain settings in the *CMOS setup* might need a little tweaking here and there. This is the hardware configuration. Then when the operating system is installed, a number of different decisions must be made in terms of how that part of the system will be configured. Options such as networking, display configuration, printers, and desktop colors must all be selected and configured. Finally, the applications are selected and installed. That is the part that never ends.

congestion   A situation that occurs when there is more traffic than the medium can support. We have all encountered congestion in downtown traffic at rush hour. Networks experience the same thing when 5,000 users all try to log in at once at 8:00 in the morning. Just as traffic congestion slows you and your car down, so goes the network. Logons can take forever, and if you need to download a large file during the logon rush, it might be a good time to go get coffee and donuts.

connection ID A randomly generated number that the server application assigns to each session to assure that data is kept together and in sequence.

connectionless A networking service that establishes no virtual link between transmitting devices and makes use of no error control. With a connectionless service, a computer throws data out onto the network and just assumes it will get where it is going. If not, oh well. When you browse the Internet, you use a connectionless service.

connection-oriented A networking service that does establish a virtual link between transmitting devices and incorporates end-to-end error control. With a connection-oriented service, for each packet of data transmitted, the computer on the receiving end is expected to send an *acknowledgement packet* (ACK). If the transmitting computer has not received an ACK after a certain period of time has elapsed, it will retransmit the packet. This process assures that the data arrives intact at the intended destination. When you download a large file over the Internet, you are using connection-oriented services.

connectivity The existence of a successful data or electrical link between two points. Connectivity is not dependent on whether or not the two points can communicate. For example two computers on which the networking configuration is wrong may not be able to communicate, but a cable tester proves that current can flow successfully from one device to the other. This shows that there is connectivity between the two devices.

connector Either the terminal at the end of a cable or the socket on a device where the cable connects that allows the cable to hook up to the device. Unless a cable is *hardwired* it will have a connector. Most connectors used in the computer industry are under the control of one of the many organizations that oversee standardized specifications. This assures the greatest degree of *compatibility* that is possible. The RJ-45 terminal shown in Figure C.18 is just one of hundreds of different connectors used in the computer industry.

coresident Any two (or more) programs or data files that share a particular block of memory. No two pieces of data may occupy the same exact address.

console The control panel of any device. In the old days of computing, when the actual computer was an enormous mainframe devices humming away in a climate-controlled room, the user's terminal was called the *console*. In a *thin client* network, this terminology is still used. However, the control panels on a printer or on a power plant are also examples of consoles.

constant A fixed value in a program or database that never changes, no matter what might happen to the other data around it. Constants can be used in a wide variety of ways. If you have a value that must fall between 1 and 10, then 1 and 10 are your constants. The values that fall between are *variables*. In a price list where there is no discount structure allowed, then you might program the price of an object as a constant, with the invoice total being a variable based on the constant multiplied by a factor that the user inserts as quantity. If you charge sales tax, then the percentage charged by your state and locale would be entered as a constant.

Constant Bit Rate Any form of data transmission that requires that the speed of bit transmission not vary. An example of this would be the data read from an audio

FIGURE C.18 The P4 connector shown here hooks up a secondary power source to Pentium 4 CPUs.

CD. The music is sampled at a rate of 41,100 times per second and each sample is 16 bits. For the music to sound right, it must be played back at this same speed. (This example does not take into consideration the technique of *oversampling* used by engineers to eliminate noise from the recording.)

consumable   Supplies that are constantly used and must be replenished. Ink, toner, and paper are consumables. Consumables are not covered under most warranty agreements. They are also a primary source of profit for many manufacturers. You didn't really think they make a lot of money on a $79.00 printer, did you? But have you ever asked yourself why the printer, complete with ink cartridges, cost $79.00 when the replacement ink cost $59.00? Give away the razor and then charge for the blades.

contact   The point where a wire comes in contact with the socket or switch. This is the point where the current passed from one *conductor* to another. Since the contact is frequently a point of data loss or distortion, it is critical that where the two metals touch that corrosion be avoided. As a result, it is not uncommon for a *noble element* such as gold to be used on contacts because noble elements do not corrode.

container   (1) A collection of objects on the system or network that has been gathered together into a single administrative unit. In a system such as Active Directory or Directory Services, any container object is an object that can hold other objects. A folder on a hard disk or a user group would both be considered containers. (2) Within a database, a container is any field or table that can hold a data file. For example, in FileMaker Pro, it is possible to create a field that holds documents from a word processor in their entirety or graphics files in any format. It is even possible to store a musical score. When this file is needed, it can be extracted from the database without going to a different directory or computer.

contention   A conflict that occurs any time two or more objects attempt to access the same resource at the same time. In a networking environment, contention might result in a *collision*. Generally, if the resource is a physical resource, such a file on the server, the second and subsequent attempts to get in will simply be blocked.

contention window   The number of time slots a device will wait after a *collision* occurs on a *CSMA/CD* network. This is the value used to set the *backoff timer*. The contention window starts small, gradually increasing in size until the two objects competing for bandwidth finally gain access to the network.

context   (1) Any text or data presented around or alongside a statement or instruction that might have an impact on how the data will be interpreted. If a politician says, "There is no remote possibility that I cheated on my taxes" and the news quotes him as saying "…I cheated on my taxes," the newspaper is quoting the man out of context. (2) In terms of a computer system or network, the context refers to the current status or mode in which the system is running.

context sensitive   Relevant to what a user is doing at the moment. Many applications or operating systems have a help system that is able to take a snapshot of the system and calculate what a user is doing at the time he presses a hot key to bring up the help program. By providing information relative to what the user is doing, the application is providing context-sensitive help.

contiguous   Any two objects or pieces of data that are side by side and/or touching. When referring to files on a hard disk, contiguous files are those that are all together in adjacent *clusters* on the disk platter. When files are not contiguous, they are considered to be fragmented. This means that part of the file is located in one place on the drive, part of it is over there, and other parts are there, there, there, and there. A utility such as Microsoft's Defrag takes fragmented files and makes them concentric.

contingency   A plan of action that you can fall back on in the event that your usual method cannot be used. Businesses that completely rely on computers to produce invoices need to have a method of manually creating invoices in the event that the systems are down for any length of time. This is their contingency plan. Having another ride to work in case your car breaks down is a contingency plan. Any organization with significant amounts of data stored in digital form needs to have a contingency plan for retrieving that data in more conventional means should the computers become unavailable.

continuity   The ability of a signal to travel from the beginning to the end of a circuit. Any time a computer loses the network, the first thing a technician should check is continuity. Was the network cable dislodged from the network card? If so, continuity is lost. Continuity includes all cables and devices that exist between two hosts on a network. If a router or a hub goes down, continuity will be lost. Status lights on interfaces are a good indication of electrical continuity. Also a utility such as *PING* can let you know if continuity exists.

continuity module   A null memory module that fills the empty banks on a system using Rambus memory. Unlike other types of memory, Rambus does not tolerate an empty slot on the system. This is similar to an unterminated SCSI chain in that an empty slot results in none of the memory being recognized. Adding continuity modules to all slots not occupied by memory provides the termination required.

continuous form   Preprinted forms that are printed on long rolls of paper. Continuous forms are frequently created and/or filled out on printers such as *dot matrix* or *line printers*. Each individual form on the roll can be separated from the roll because of perforations. In order to run the paper through the *tractor feed* transport mechanisms of these kinds of printers, continuous forms generally have holes punched along each side of the page. Gears in the printer mesh with the holes and pull the paper through the printer.

continuous loop   A set of code that sends the processor back to its beginning over and over again. Continuous loops that offer no user feedback can make the system appear to be locked up, when indeed it is doing precisely what it was asked to do. *See also* **endless loop** *and* **infinite loop**.

contrast   The relative difference between bright objects and dark objects in an image. On a computer monitor, contrast is a user-adjustable setting. Typically, there will be a button or dial with a diagram similar to that shown in Figure C.19. Most photo editing programs also provide methods of altering image contrast in photos or other graphics. Images with excessive contrast have bright areas that are washed out and dark areas that are practically black. If there is too little contrast there will be little in the way of highlights and shadows, and the image will look flat and murky.

control   A subroutine within a program that proves a specialized function. An example of a control in a database application would be a button that launches a query. Controls can be quite small, or they can be very complex applets that run within applications. A script that performs a series of complex mathematical calculations on a user-inputted number and then returns the value to a predefined field in the program is a more complex control.

FIGURE C.19   *The contrast control for most monitors carries a label similar to this.*

control character   In the original version of *ASCII*, certain characters were embedded in the set that were not considered printable characters. Instead they communicated certain functions to the printer, such as a line feed or a page break. These characters were also known as *control code*.

control code   *See* **control character**.

Control key   Two keys on an IBM-compatible keyboard that alter the behavior of all other keys on the keyboard. It is pressed at the same time as another key in order to launch a command or *macro* instead of simply typing the companion character. Three ways you will see this key abbreviated in literature are <Ctrl>, Ctl, and with a carat. Examples are <Ctrl> S to indicate that the control key is being used in conjunction with the S key. It might also be shown as Ctl-S or ^S.

Control Panel   A Windows utility that allows the user to change the configuration on practically every aspect of his computer system. Control Panel is divided up into a number of *applets* that manage specific functions. For example, the Network Applet is where the user goes to change configuration settings for different networking *protocols* such as TCP/IP or IPX/SPX. Control Panel can be accessed by clicking on Start>Settings>Control Panel, or by double-clicking on My Computer and then double-clicking on Control Panel.

control set   A collection of registry settings that defines the system configuration for Windows during the boot process. There are a minimum of two control sets stored in the registry, and there may be three or four. The current control set contains configuration data that is used to start the operating system and to initialize devices based on the user's current preferences. A second control set called *last known good* contains configuration data that was accurate the last time the system booted successfully. Last known good is rewritten on every successful boot. A successful boot is defined as the ability of the OS to boot as far as the logon screen. If it crashes and burns after that, you will have a perfectly useless last known good that crashes and burns after the user logs on. Windows users are accustomed this sort of behavior.

control signal   Data that travels across a network or between devices on a system cannot just be sent, hoping that the information will arrive. Two different devices might operate at different speeds. Some devices, such as modems, operate at different speeds at different times, depending on conditions. Additional signals for *timing, synchronization,* and other functions are added to the data to keep different devices talking to one another. These are the various control signals. The data itself, oddly enough, travels along the *data signal.*

control unit   On a *central processing unit*, this is a subcomponent that acts as the "commander in chief," if you will. This component is in charge of keeping track of the task at hand, determining what needs to be done next, and which of the other subcomponents needs to do it.

controller   A circuit that is either installed on a device, or in addition to a device that processes commands for that device. The controller will generally have a chip that holds the *firmware.* The firmware contains all the commands that the device understands and requires in order to function. In addition, most controllers contain *buffer* memory to hold data or commands that are on the way into or out of the device. Some devices, such as *IDE* drives, have the controller circuitry built right onto the device. Others, such as a *SCSI* device, will either have the circuitry installed as an add-on *expansion card* or it might be built into the motherboard.

conventional memory   The first megabyte of RAM, divided into 640 K for running programs and 384 K reserved for system use. This dates back to the days of MS-DOS when all systems had to run programs in the lower 640 K of memory. When the PC was first released, IBM decided that 1 MB of RAM was "all a computer user would ever need." The 640 K were assigned for running programs and 384 K were devoted to system use for things like device drivers and *shadowing* the system BIOS. This 384 K was called *upper memory* or *high memory.* Anything beyond 1 MB is classified as either *extended memory* or *expanded memory.*

convergence   The accuracy with which multiple beams of electrons or light can focus on the same point. *CRT* monitors rely on accurate convergence to deliver a sharp image without distortion. If convergence is off by the slightest amount, resolution suffers and colors are not reproduced accurately.

converter   Any device or circuit that takes a signal, a medium type, a form of computer code, or a set of frequencies and changes it to a different format. A digital/analog converter takes binary data coming from a computer or digital device and turns it into an electrical waveform. The analog/digital converter performs the opposite magic. An AC converter takes household current from the wall and turns it into DC current that a device requires in order to operate.

cooked   Data that has been manipulated in some way to alter output results. If an algorithm is used to perform a specific calculation on data when it is processed, that data is cooked. If an accountant is "tweaking" the books to hide discrepancies or to make the stockholders think they actually own something of value, the books are being cooked.

cookie   A small file that a Web site stores on your computer. Cookies might be *transient* or permanent. A transient cookie only stays on your computer as long as you are connected to the site. A permanent cookie stays even after you leave. The cookie contains data specific to you and/or your system. By storing this information, the next time it is needed you do not have to provide it again. Cookies are why you can come back to a Web site several days after your first visit and a message flashes on the screen, welcoming you back by name.

cool   A shift in the color of an image toward the blue side. For a more detailed explanation *see* **color temperature**.

cooperative multitasking   The ability of an OS to simultaneously run more than one program, placing responsibility on the application for relinquishing control of the system. With cooperative multitasking, an application that has control of the system virtually owns all system resources. It may be able to relinquish control of the system only under certain circumstances, such as when waiting for user input or after a thread of code has run through the processor. Processes running in the background will not have access to CPU or memory resources until the running process is completed. With cooperative multitasking, if the system that controls the system crashes, it can bring down the entire computer. All versions of Windows 3.xx made use of cooperative multitasking. All modern operating systems employ *pre-emptive multitasking*.

coprocessed   Any adapter or device that is equipped with a microprocessor that offloads some of the work of the PC's CPU. Most expansion cards today employ some form of coprocessing. Modern video cards have extremely fast processors in order to keep up with the demands of new video games. Virtually all SCSI controllers have coprocessing capability.

Copyleft   A coined term that describes the lack of a copyright applied to open-source software. Specifically the term arose from the ranks of Linux aficionados who derided the stringent licensing agreements one had to accept in order to install software.

core router   (1) A router that exists within the confines of a specific network. Core routers do not forward packets to any destination outside the assigned network. They are used to subnet a larger network into smaller segments in order to make more efficient use of bandwidth or to tighten security within the network. (2) A high-speed router that operates within the backbone of the Internet. In order to function as an Internet core router, the device must be able to communicate with all Internet protocols and to be able to operate at the maximum speed of all supported protocols. A typical core router operates at 10 GB/s throughput. Some links are even faster.

CPU *See* **central processing unit**. The primary chip that handles the majority of a computer's functions. It also directs the actions of other microprocessors in the system.

CPU bus This is the information path between the CPU and other primary controller chips in the system. By itself, the CPU cannot talk to the keyboard. It has no idea what the signals coming from that device mean. Located among the chips you see planted here and there along the surface of the motherboard is one that holds a program that does nothing but translate keyboard signals into pure binary code that the CPU can digest. All the chips that perform functions of this nature are located along the CPU bus. These are the devices that can communicate directly with the CPU, at the CPU's speed.

crash dump A direct copy of the entire contents of system RAM copied to a file on the hard disk. The idea is that astute programmers can use this information to recreate what was going on with the system at the moment of the system crash. To the average user, the crash dump file is about as useful as an ejection seat in a helicopter. In reality it is of only limited use to the programmers. It can point someone in the right direction, but facts being what they are, the crash dump is data that was written to the hard drive by an operating system that has already failed.

credentials Information provided by the user, including but not restricted to the user ID and password, that grants that user access to a system or network. On a more secure network, user ID and password might be supplemented by *biometrics* or with a security card or token.

cross-linked file Data that originated in totally different files, but now thinks that it belongs together. This happens when the operating system writes data from two different files into the same FAU. In reality only a single file can occupy any given FAU. Even if the data occupying that FAU only takes up a fraction of the available space, as far as the file system is concerned, that cluster is full. In those instances where data from a second file is successfully copied into the FAU, the data from both files is now corrupted. Microsoft's ScanDisk utility "fixes" these clusters by taking all FAUs linked to the affected one and copying them all into a .CHK file. This is a file stored in the root directory of the system that carries a name consisting of FILEXXXX.CHK, where the Xs are replaced with a sequential series of numbers, starting with 0000. (Note: A CHK file might also contain a *lost cluster.*)

crossover cable A twisted pair cable that has the transmit and receive signals reversed from the conventional wiring standard. This allows two devices to talk directly to one another without the need for a hub or switch in the path. Crossover cables are a convenient tool for any network administrator. It allows a person to interconnect any two PCs or other devices with network interfaces without the need for intermediary hubs or switches. Some devices such as routers and switches allow you to directly link to the device through a crossover cable in order to configure the interfaces. Table C.6 shows the wiring diagram for a standard crossover cable.

crosstalk The tendency of an electrical current to "leak" from one conductor to another when they are run alongside one another. Crosstalk occurs any time

TABLE C.6
Wiring diagram for crossover cable

PIN NO. END 1	SIGNAL TX	569A	568B	PIN NO. END 2	SIGNAL RCV
1	Transmit (+)	White/Green	White/Orange	3	Receive (+)
2	Transmit (-)	Green	Orange	6	Receive (-)
3	Receive (+)	White/Orange	White/Green	1	Transmit (+)
4	Not Used	Blue	Blue	4	Not Used
5	Not Used	White/Blue	White/Blue	5	Not Used
6	Receive (-)	Orange	Green	2	Transmit (-)
7	Not Used	White/Brown	White/Brown	7	Not Used
8	Not Used	Brown	Brown	8	Not Used

two wires run parallel along the same axis. The effect can be greatly reduced by twisting the adjacent conductors instead of allowing them to run flat. The more times per linear inch the cable gets twisted, the more reduction that results.

current The electrons that flow across a conductor in a fixed amount of time. Electrical current is measured in *amperes*. Current does not necessarily need to have wires to flow. Lightning is an example of an electrical current that flows from the ground to the sky through the molecules of the air. Current can be manipulated in an electrical circuit by adding devices such as *resistors* or *capacitors*.

cursor (1) A graphical element used by an operating system or application to point to a position on the computer screen. The most common cursor these days is the arrow you move around the screen with a mouse. Operating systems such as Windows and Linux rely heavily on a *point and click* interface. The user positions the mouse cursor over an active object and clicks in order to perform some specific function. There is more than one kind of cursor, however. In addition to the mouse cursor, the vertical line that shows your relative position in a word processing document is also a form of cursor. In the old days of MS-DOS, a horizontal line on the screen showed your relative position. (2) Devices called *digitizing tablets* make use of a special device to replicate the movements of a pen over paper, allowing a user to draw freehand images. These devices are often called cursors as well.

cut and paste A process by which a user selects a block of data (usually using the mouse), copies that data to memory, and then subsequently copies it once again to another location in the same document or to a different document all together. Cut and paste is not simply copying data, however. The concept of "cutting" suggests that the data is deleted from the original location and moved to the second one. For cut and paste to work, a dedicated section of memory must be able to store the deleted information until such time as it is copied to the new location. This memory is often called the *clipboard.*

cyanine dye   A bluish-colored dye that was used in the recording layer of early generations of CD-R media. Cyanine dye has long been used in the photographic industry to sensitize photographic emulsions. Films that were sensitized with this substance were sensitive to a much wider range of wavelengths. When engineers were looking for a medium that could be used for recording digital data optically, they turned to the world of photography to see what they were doing. When zapped with a laser, the reflective nature of cyanine dye is drastically changed. By putting a layer of this dye over a highly reflective layer of some metallic substance, you had a substrate that worked for digital recording. Areas zapped by the laser do not reflect light back to the photosensor. The laser used to read back data "sees" through unburned areas to the reflective layer below. The biggest problem with cyanine dye was that it was perceived to have a substantially lower lifespan than some of the other competing media, such as *phthalocyanine dye.* You can tell if your CD-R is made with cyanine dye because it will have a distinct blue-green color to the data surface.

cybernetics   A study of how mechanical processes relate to human processes. The mathematician Norbert Weiner originally used the term to describe how computers could eventually mimic human thought processes and behavior. These days, a shortened abbreviation of the term, *cyber,* is tagged onto just about any word to give it computer-related connotations. Cybercrime can describe just about any crime that makes use of computer technology. A cybercop is an investigator who looks into high-tech crime. (It's also a really bad science fiction movie.)

cybrarian   A coined term to describe an information specialist who does most of his research on the Internet or using other online sources. It is an abbreviation for *cyberlibrarian,* which is also a coined term.

cycle   Any unique event that is continuously repeated. In electronics, the most common usage of the term is in relation to electronic waveforms. Signals such as the carrier wave used to transmit data show up on an oscilloscope as a *sine wave.* The wave has a crest, which is the rising half of the cycle, and a dip that represents the falling half of the cycle.

cycle rate   This is another term for *clock speed.* It represents the amount of time it takes for a continuously repeating event to complete one instance of that event. For example, a clock circuit keeps a PCI device synchronized. Each "tick" of this clock represents one clock cycle. The cycle rate is how many times per second.

cylinder   A virtual structure created by the tracks that line up vertically on the surface of each of the platters. Most hard disks have multiple platters and each platter has two surfaces. A *track* is a ring of adjacent *sectors* that form a circle. If you take all of the tracks that line up perfectly along all disk surfaces, these constitute a cylinder. Figure C.20 illustrates this concept.

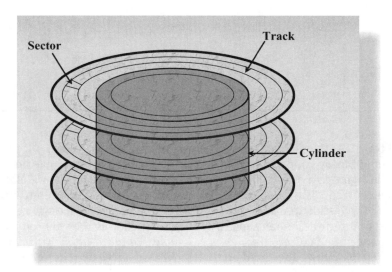

FIGURE C.20   *The cylinder is all of the tracks in a hard disk that line up.*

D

D/A converter (DAC)   Digital-to-analog converter. An integrated circuit that takes a stream of binary code and processes it in such a way as it outputs an analog electrical signal to a circuit. In most cases the analog signal is a modulated electrical current. The analog signal can then be sent over more conventional signals to its destination. D/A converters are used in any device where 0s and 1s are used to interpret human senses. Three specifications relevant to measuring the performance of a DAC are *frequency response*, *signal-to-noise ratio*, and *dynamic range*. Digital audio, video, and tactile feedback devices all require the services of a D/A converter.

daemon   A Unix program that is constantly running in the background, ready to respond whenever the OS or an application calls on its services. Most daemons are initialized when the OS mounts, but in some cases they can be called on to launch by a service or application. Examples of daemons are the Unix Printer Daemon that functions as a multiuser print spooler and the Unix Task Scheduler that manages CPU and memory access for multiple applications.

daisy chain   (n) A series of devices or circuits that are connected, one after another, in a continuous line. An example of a daisy chain is the SCSI chain. A single cable connects to the host adapter and each device hangs off of a separate controller on a single cable (Figure D.1) . The Universal Serial Bus (USB) and Firewire

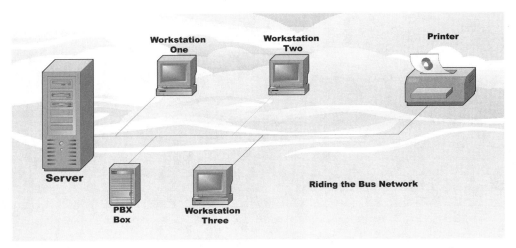

FIGURE D.1   *In a daisy chain such as in this illustration of a bus network, the signal passes through each and every device on its way to the end of the chain.*

FIGURE D.2   Daisy wheels got their name from the fact that the characters radiated from a center hub like the petals of a daisy radiate from the middle of the flower.

are also examples of daisy chains. In a daisy chain, any signal intended for the device on the end must pass through each and every device on its way to the final destination. (v) To connect multiple devices in a continuous chain.

daisy wheel   A printhead device such as the one in Figure D.2 used on early impact printers that contained a physical image of each character available in the character set. The individual characters reside on the end of a flexible rod. When the printer wants to imprint the character onto paper, it projects a small hammer head onto the base of the character, projecting it against an inked ribbon. Daisy wheel printers were popular for a short while because they provided print quality as good as that of a *typewriter*. Also, since the daisy wheels could be changed, different type faces were available to printers that featured them.

damping   A process by which undesirable vibration or noise is reduced or eliminated. Electrical circuits are dampened when unwanted electrical noise is filtered out. Damping is a form of physical resistance applied to the oscillation that generates the vibrations, or electrical resistance to reduce electrical noise. The term originates from the fact that moisture tends to make a substance less brittle and thereby less prone to make noise.

dangling reference   In programming or Web development, it is not uncommon for a link or pointer to point to a reference item that no longer or never did exist. In programming, a command might reference a data set that was removed or never created. A Web page can have links that point to nowhere. Dangling references are not limited to computers either. Even the written word is occasionally afflicted by this malady. For example....

dark fiber   (1) Fiber optic cabling that has been put into place but not yet connected to the network. The term came about in the mid-1990s of the twentieth century when vast amounts of fiber optic cabling was laid in anticipation of greatly increased demand for bandwidth. Early into the new millennium, large amounts of this cable had still never seen a single photon. The fiber optic cable that is used is conversely known as *lit fiber*. (2) In the communications industry, dark fiber is available fiber circuitry that is given to carriers with no carrier signal provided. It is up to the provider to supply their own signaling apparatus.

Darlington circuit   A circuit that amplifies a signal by passing it through two bipolar transistors paired together. As the current passes through the first transistor, it receives the first stage of amplification. The second transistor then amplifies the signal yet again. In most modern circuits, the transistors have effectively been integrated into a single *IC*. The circuit is named in honor of its inventor, Sidney Darlington of Bell Labs.

DAT file   A digital file that stores raw data. Generally, these files end with a .DAT *extension*, which, coincidentally, is why they are called DAT files.

data   (1) On a universal level, data is any information that is used in day-to-day affairs. Your PIN number, social security number, name and address, and all the other information that makes you unique is all data. A single piece of information is a *datum*. Data is the plural form of datum. (2) From a standpoint of computer processing, data is the information being processed by the computer. It is *not* the code used in running applications. Examples of data would include digital images, word processing documents, MIDI files, digital music, and so on. Application files, such as .EXE files, .DLL files, and such are considered *instructions*.

data bank   An electronic storage facility for all of the information used by an organization. This differs from a database in that the database consists of a large collection of related information and is accessible through a dedicated application. The data bank is very likely to encompass multiple databases and a variety of information from a number of different applications. The data bank will most likely house all of the individual files for the users on the network in separate directories.

data bits   (1) The number of bits required to represent a single character. In the old ASCII set, characters could be either 7-bit or 8-bit characters. With Unicode, each character is 16 bits wide. (2) The format that information takes at the physical layer in networking as it is transmitted over the network medium. In transit, each bit is considered a separate entity. However, on the transmitting and receiving ends, it is the data *packet* as a whole that must arrive intact.

data bus   The path that data takes between the source and destination devices. Many devices, including the CPU, incorporate a separate *internal data bus* (IDB) and *external data bus* (EDB). The IDB is the path that data follows as the device performs its particular magic on the data. The EDB represents the conduit for data to follow between one device and the next. A complex problem that computers face in every data transaction is that not all data busses are of the same speed or *bit width*. Therefore, circuits for buffering data and for synchronizing transmission speed are required in order to assure the integrity of the information transmitted.

data cache   A CPU maintains numerous sets of registers that hold data and instructions until the control unit is ready to put it to use. Once the prefetch has located and retrieved the data or instructions, it needs a place to store that information until the control unit is ready to send it down the processing pipeline. The CPU maintains two of these storage registers. The data cache is one and the *instruction cache* is the other.

data compression   This is a method by which the physical number of 0s and 1s required to encode a specific piece of information is noticeably reduced. The most common methods of data compression involve taking repeating bits or patterns of bits and replacing a long stretch of data with a mathematical expression that represents those bits. For example, in a digital image that contains a vast expanse of white, a long series of bytes that define white would look like a very long string of 0s. Instead of repeating the 0 bit 120,000 times, which I *won't* do on this page to show you, the algorithm would replace it with the mathematical expression of $120,000 \times 0$. Instead of 120 Kb, the string is now only a few bytes long. Data compression can be used prior to storing data or prior to transmission. Either way, in order to properly use the data after compression, the appropriate decompression algorithm must be available on the other end. The effect of compression and decompression of data varies with the algorithm used. *Lossy* compression techniques assume that if a few bits here and there get dropped, it's no big deal. This is useful for storing information such as music or graphics intended for display on a monitor. *Lossless* compression techniques take the approach that no lost bits are tolerable. Images intended for printed form and executable programs are best suited for lossless compression. Lossless compression cannot compact a file as small as a lossy protocol.

data conversion   Data is stored in files. Various types of data work best with specific file formats. Occasionally it is necessary to convert from one file format to another. This is the process of data conversion. Reasons for converting data are many. You might be moving information from one spreadsheet to another, or you might be trying to embed data from your spreadsheet into a word processing document. In either case, for you to be able to successfully use the material, the application that is attempting to process the data must be reading it properly. Word processing documents are stored in a different format than spreadsheet documents. You also might be moving data between platforms. A word processing document on a Macintosh computer will be in a different format than the same document created on a PC. However, in most cases, there are few problems associated with reading documents between platforms. Several factors that come into play when converting data format include (among many other things):

1. How is the document formatted?
2. What information is included in the data header?

3. What parts of the file are user data and what parts are control data used by the application?
4. Does the data travel over the wire from the most significant bit to the least significant bit, or vice versa?

data corruption   A situation that arises when the precise order of bits that comprise the data in a system cannot be read back or are not read back in precisely the correct order. Data corruption can occur during transmission and retrieval or it can occur during storage. It happens because of a number of reasons. On magnetically encoded media, it can be because the polarity of the medium where some bits are stored is either reversed or loses sufficient energy as to not be read back correctly. On optical media, it might occur because of physical damage. Error correction algorithms, such as *checksum* and *cyclical redundancy check*, were designed to combat corruption. Data corruption can also occur on a file system level. *Lost clusters* and *cross-linked files* are both examples of data corruption that can occur when an error is committed by the file system.

data encoding mechanism   The method used by a device to convert digital information into an electronic format recognizable by the target device. In general, digital information must be transmitted over the medium in an *analog* format. In order to read and write nondigital information as digital, some form of mutually acceptable code must be used between devices. Different encoding methods for electrical signals include *amplitude modulation* and *frequency modulation* as well as variations of the different themes. Optical carriers might use rhythmically encoded light pulses to encode data. Think smoke signals over electricity or laser and you'll have the idea.

Data Encryption Standard (DES)   A secure set of methods by which data can be confidently encoded on one side and decoded on the other.

data error   This is a situation that arises when data that is stored on a specific medium cannot be read back. Sometimes the error will read back as "I/O Data Error." Such *data corruption* occurs either because of physical damage or because magnetic media are either exposed to magnetic energy or other electrical interference. In many cases third-party data recovery utilities might be able to recover the information.

data format   The physical structure that data assumes when it is either stored as a file or when it is transmitted over the wire. When stored as a file, the data can be collected in one large contiguous pile. (Note, however, that the disk controller may or may not store it on a hard disk in a contiguous manner. *See* **fragmentation** for more information on that.) When stored on a disk, data assumes the *file format* required by the OS, in combination with the application that created the file. However, in order to transmit data over the network, it must be broken into smaller segments and each segment transmitted individually. As such, the data format changes rather dramatically. While the end users at either end of a transmission should never see any difference in the data, the format that the bits and bytes assume during storage and that which they assume during transmission are completely different.

data mirroring   The storage of identical sets of information on two different sets of media. Data mirroring differs from data replication in that mirroring is accomplished in real time. The data that is currently active are copied to both locations simultaneously. The most common form of mirroring is with a RAID 1 array. When a computer is configured with one of these arrays, data is automatically mirrored as they are created. On a higher level, server *clusters* mirror data for an entire network. Cloning software can be used to create a mirror of a drive onto drives that were not previously part of the data image. Figure D.3 illustrates the concept of mirroring in a RAID array.

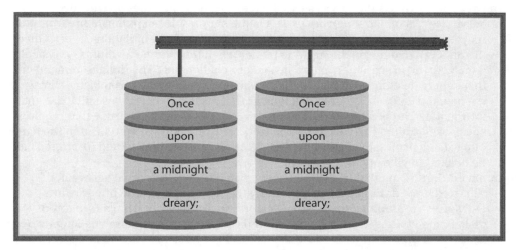

FIGURE D.3   Data mirroring is simply a process of writing data to two separate locations at once.

data phase   The portion of an I/O operation that performs the actual transfer of information from device to device. A typical I/O operation consists of several phases. The device requesting the data makes a request. The device hosting the data needs to process the request, locate the desired information, and move it to the bus. Because of this additional overhead, for many devices, the data phase eats up as little as half the total time required to perform a single operation. The remaining time is spent setting up the operation, finding and locking onto the data, and cleaning up the session when the I/O operation is complete.

data port   (1) On a computer system, a data port is any externally accessible I/O port. The serial, parallel, USB, and modem ports are common examples. You'll also frequently see the infrared sensors for wireless peripherals, such as a printer, called the *data port*. (2) Many hotels offer a local connection to the Internet as part of their service. In each room that offers this service, an *RJ-45* jack will be installed in the wall. The user plugs her computer into the data port and logs on using an ID and password provided by the establishment. For the traveling businessperson, the question asked before a reservation is confirmed is, "How fast is your data port?" rather than "Do your beds have Magic Fingers?"

data pump   Any circuit that generates the analog signal used to carry digital information. Different devices use different circuits. For example, the *universal asynchronous receiver/transmitter* (UART) is one of the chips in the data pump for a modem. Multiple processes go on in transmitting data over an analog path. First of all, the method of signal modulation is a function of the data pump. Electrical circuits might use *frequency modulation, amplitude modulation,* or a combination of the two to encode data. Optical signals will pump out the data using patterns of light pulses. Next, the device for generating the actual signal comes into play. An example of this would be the laser diode that generates the bursts of light that go out over a fiber connection.

data recovery   This is the process by which lost or damaged files are retrieved. Varying levels of data recovery exist. On the simplest level, pulling a file from the recycle bin of Windows, or the trash bin of OS X is a form of data recovery. Once the data is deleted from the recycle bin, or when the storage medium is physically damaged, the process becomes a little more challenging. The thing to remember is that simply deleting or erasing a file does not remove the electromagnetic image of the actual data from the drive. As long as the magnetized particles still exist, that information can be recovered. Data recovery is an area of expertise that requires specialized training as well as specialized hardware and software. But in the hands of a trained professional, even a hard disk that is repartitioned and formatted can be coaxed to give up its secrets.

data shredding   Data that has simply been erased from a disk drive isn't really removed. (*See* **data recovery**.) By using the right combination of hardware and software, a trained professional can retrieve data even from a formatted disk. Some utilities make the process of data recovery a bit more challenging by attempting to permanently erase the residual magnetic fluxes that encoded the original information on the drive. The most common method of shredding data is to write a series of 1s over the sectors that used to host the data and then erase them. Then the software writes a series of 0s across those same sectors and erases those. This process is repeated several times over. Data shredding makes it exceedingly difficult for even a highly trained data recovery expert to restore the original data. It does not, however, make it impossible.

data stream   (1) This is a colorful term for the flow of electrons or photons across the medium that carried the encoded information. When referencing the data stream, the information itself isn't the topic of discussion, but rather the movement of the data over the medium. When working with broadband technologies, such as DSL, the data stream contains the combined information sent by every user sharing the medium. (2) In telecommunications, the data stream is the collection of related data structures, including cells or packets, that constitute a single transmission.

datacom   Shortened term for *data communications*. It refers to any and all equipment, media, or software used for the transmission and reception of data. In many cases, data and analog voice signals travel over the same wires. Datacom equipment works specifically with digital information. Digital voice would fall under this category because it is transmitted in a binary bit stream.

datagram   (1) In reference to the *User Datagram Protocol* the datagram is a self-contained bundle of data that contains all the information it needs to travel from point A to point B. By definition, a datagram cannot rely on any previous exchanges of data between devices or expect the help of any of those to follow in order to make its trip. This is different from a *packet* in that a packet is likely to count on synchronization packets, acknowledgment packets, and other data forms to assure accurate delivery. AppleTalk uses the datagram in their *Datagram Delivery Protocol*. The protocol is useful for exchanging quick messages over a network connection, but provides very little error correction support.

Datagram Delivery Protocol (DDP)   DDP is a connectionless data transfer protocol in the AppleTalk suite that moves data in discrete packets over the network. There is no flow control and no error correction involved, so it is primarily used for short communications bursts and not for the transfer of files. It is frequently the protocol of choice for networked games. Since DDP packets are stand-alone entities, each packet must include all addressing information, including destination and source network and hardware addresses.

datum   A single piece of information. Collectively, more than one datum would be data, which is pretty much the only form of this word you'll ever see in the real world. Originally, the term was derived from the Latin word *dare*, meaning "to give." The scientific world used the term for centuries as a description of an individual piece of scientific information that supported a complex idea. The computer industry accepted the term as any piece of information (as opposed to a command or instruction).

D-channel   A shortened term for the delta channel. This is a 16-KB/s or 64-KB/s channel used by ISDN for control data, including synchronization, ACKs and NACKs, and other nonuser data. Two communicating devices will use this channel for exchanging control data, leaving the *bearer*, or B-channels, free for user data. The basic rate interface (BRI) service of ISDN provides a single 16-KB/s D channel, while the primary rate interface (PRI) provides a 64-K D-channel.

decibel   A measurement of the quantity of energy. While decibels might be used as a measurement of electronic signals or other forms of energy, it is most frequently seen as a measurement of sound volume levels. Technically, it is 1/10th of a bel, which is quantification of how much volume a particular sound loses when measured a mile away from the source. Decibels are a logarithmic value and are measured against a calibrated reference level.

decimal   Any one of the numbers used by the base10 counting system, consisting of ten characters, 0 through 9. It is also an alliteration of any negative power of 1. A negative power of 1 results in a fraction and is displayed as a period followed by numbers, such as .01. It is from the Latin *decimal*, which means "in tenths" or "tithe."

decode unit   One of the subcomponents of a CPU that translates machine code into simpler instructions. Most instructions that come into the CPU are far too complex for other microcomponents of the CPU to handle. The decode unit breaks these instructions down into the simple binary commands that the CPU understands.

dedicated application server   A single computer running on a network whose job it is to run a specific program for the users and process data from that program on their behalf. An example of a dedicated application server is the e-mail server. The traffic and processing power that is required to provide e-mail services to hundreds of users would greatly tax the resources of a single server that was also responsible for authentication or file services.

default gateway   The route through which all packets that contain addresses that the transmitting device cannot resolve will be sent. Generally, the default gateway is the port on a router that acts as the portal to either another network or to the Internet service provider, who acts as the gateway to the outside world. When a computer is configured with TCP/IP, a component of the address called a *subnet mask* defines which part of the address points to the network and which part points to the host address. If the destination address in a packet involves an external network, the packet will be forwarded to the IP address configured as the gateway. If no gateway is configured, that packet will be dropped.

defined context set   When data is sent over a network connection, the form will be modified in several ways. In addition to control data being merged with the user data in packets, the actual format of data is modified. The methods used to transmit data and the format data will assume during transfer is called it *presentation context*. During a lengthy session multiple data forms may need to be transferred; hence, the presentation context may change from time to time throughout the duration of the session. The collection of contexts agreed upon and used during a session is the defined context set.

deflection yoke   A circular array of powerful magnets that act to deflect a beam of electrons from its natural path. These are used in CRT monitors, televisions, and rear-projection TVs as part of the image-forming apparatus. The device consists of a large coil (or an array of coils) through which an electrical current is passed. The result is a relatively powerful electromagnetic field. When a beam of electrons is directed through the field, the electrons are deflected at an angle determined by the position of the source of magnetic energy at the instant of deflection.

Defrag   A utility specific to Microsoft operating systems that will take files that are scattered all over the disk and reassemble them into a contiguous order. Other operating systems have similar utilities with different names.

defragment   When files are opened, data added, and the closed repeatedly, those files end up stored on multiple disk sectors spread out across the hard disk. This fragmentation results in degraded performance. Several utilities have been written by various developers to bring files back together and relocate them in contiguous space. To defragment a file is to bring it back together in one piece.

demultiplexing   The separation and resequencing of multiple messages coming off a single communications link.

depth queuing   A mathematical algorithm that recalculates the hue and intensity of colors in respect to increasing distances.

deterministic   Any approach that is guaranteed to achieve the desired results.

device driver   A piece of software running on the system that provides the command set for a specific piece of hardware.

device ID   A unique number assigned to each device on a SCSI chain, including the host adapter, that identifies it to other devices on the chain.

DHCP lease   The amount of time a Dynamic Host Configuration Protocol (DHCP) client is allowed to hang onto a lease assigned by a DHCP server.

dialogue   The two-way transfer of data between devices, including control data used to maintain the session.

dictionary attack   An attempt by a hacker to break into a network by barraging the server with a database of user IDs and passwords.

dielectric layer   A transparent layer of material above and below the recording layer of a CD-RW that dissipates the heat built up in the CD during the recording process.

differential backup   A backup that copies all files added or changed since the last full backup. A differential backup does not clear the archive bit located in the file header.

differential signaling   A method by which a single data wire on a parallel cable is matched up by a wire carrying the inverse of the signal being carried by the data wire.

digital   Information that is created by encoding a series of 0s and 1s. All computers use digital information. These days virtually everything you see or hear from the media is digitally managed. Television, telephone, radio, and recorded music have all become an integral part of our digital world.

digital noise   Unwanted color artifacts introduced into a digitized image during capture and/or by imaging software during the capture or processing of that image. A digital image is nothing more than a mosaic of differently colored dots called *pixels*. A pixel is created when light strikes the image sensor and is converted into a digital pattern. For every hue and intensity level there is a unique string of bits to translate the analog information captured into the digital bit stream. Excessive or insufficient exposure to light can cause sensors to generate random bit strings, or to inaccurately represent the light form that is translating. Both of these situations are examples of noise. If the sensor gets too hot, it will generate random noise. Noise is most obvious in areas of uniform tone, such as a dark sky or a smooth gray wall.

digital signature   A small token of *binary* information that is attached to a transmission that verifies security. Digital signatures can assure you that the information you are receiving from a Web site is authentic and secure. You can use a digital signature to assure others that you are who you say you are. In order to maintain credibility, for a digital signature to be valid it must be issued by one of the recognized *certificate authorities*.

Digital Subscriber Line (DSL)   A form of broadband communications that is delivered over telephone lines, providing high-speed digital connections to the general public. DSL is available in a variety of forms, including:

- ADSL   Asymmetric DSL
- BDSL   Broadband DSL
- CDSL   Consumer DSL (Rockwell Corp.)
- FDSL   Fixed Directory Subscriber List
- HDSL   High-Bit-Rate DSL + High-Data-Rate DSL
- IDSL   Integrated Services Digital Network DSL
- RDSL   Rate-Adaptive DSL
- SDSL   Single-Line DSL + Symmetric DSL
- VDSL   Very-High-Bit-Rate DSL
- VADSL   Very-High-Rate Asymmetric DSL
- VDSL   Very-High-Data-Rate DSL

diode   An electrical component that freely permits the flow of electrons in one direction but resists electron flow in the opposite direction. A diode consists of two electrodes. One is called an *anode* and the other a *cathode*. A diode is similar to a transistor in that voltage must reach a certain threshold level before it will pass over the device. With a diode, this threshold value is called *forward breakover*. Because of the nature of the diode, it makes a good component in designing signal-limiting circuits and they make good switches for circuits that you want to turn on automatically when voltage is present on the wire. Some diodes are designed to emit light when current passes. These are the popular *light-emitting diodes* (LEDs) used on just about every electronic device known to man.

direct current (DC) An electrical current that exhibits a steady directional flow from a source of relative positive voltage to a target of relative negative voltage. Direct current circuits all possess a singular positive pole and associated negative pole. Current travels from positive to negative. Because of its unidirectional nature, the direction of DC never changes the way common household current (alternating current, or AC) does. The most common source of DC current is a storage battery or a photovoltaic cell. However, AC can be converted to DC through a voltage transformer. A circuit called a *rectifier* limits the movement of AC to one direction and a filter eliminates the pulses caused the direction changes inherent in AC. Most electronic equipment manufactured uses DC in at least some of its circuits. A computer cannot function without DC. The changes in current would be dumping the information from memory and the CPU 60 times a second.

directory A container node of a file system that can contain other directories or files. The file system on a computer is a hierarchical system that is broken down into multiple levels. The highest level is the *root directory*. This is the basic directory on a hard disk partition that hosts all other directories or subdirectories. The root is generally not given a specific name, but rather identified by a letter followed by a backslash (in Microsoft operating systems), with a forward slash or simply /root in some operating systems. Beneath the root are the named directories. For example, when you install Windows, it creates a directory called Windows. Other directories can also exist beneath the named directories. These are called *subdirectories* or *folders*. While these two terms are often used interchangeably, in general, the term folders is reserved as a term for repositories of user data or data saved and stored by applications. Subdirectories contained within subdirectories contained within directories are *nested directories*. In virtually all file systems there is a limit to the number of levels to which you can create nested directories. This is a limitation imposed by the length of directory path supported by the OS.

directory attribute A single bit that identifies an entry in the directory table as being a subdirectory rather than a file. In the *FAT* file systems, each file stored on the hard drive has an associated entry in the file allocation tables. The *attribute* byte defines the type of entry it is. An attribute value of 0001 0000 in the attribute byte indicates that the entry defined is a directory and not a file. As such, the defined entry is considered a *container object*. The NFTS file system also makes use of directory attributes. However, since NTFS doesn't make use of a file allocation table, attributes are defined somewhat differently. NTFS uses a *master file table* (MFT), which consists of a relational database stored on a hidden partition on the hard disk. The MFT contains a unique record for each file or directory on the hard disk. Since the attribute record in NFTS is larger than a single byte, more attributes are possible. The directory attribute is one of those stored in this record.

directory table (1) A database of all file names used by an application and the directories with which they are associated. Specifically, with Microsoft operating systems, the Windows Installer opens the directory table first and scans it in order to determine the directory structure required to properly install the product. The directory table directs the installer to the proper location to find the source file as well as the target location for the uncompressed copy of the source. Other information pertaining to file system security is also contained here. (2) In the FAT file system, the directory table is an encoded file that defines the contents of a specific directory. In FAT32, this table contains a 32-byte entry for every file or directory on the hard disk. Each of these entries contains the file name and extension, file *attributes*, the date and time that the file was created, and a pointer to the first cluster on the drive that holds data for that file.

disk duplexing   A form of fault-tolerant data protection provided by storing identical volumes of data on two separate physical disks. Two different approaches have evolved to the dual disk approach. One of these, *disk mirroring*, involves two independent disks attached to a single disk controller. Disk duplexing takes the next step in fault tolerance by hanging each disk off of a separate controller. This way, in the event of a controller failure the system isn't brought down. Any time you incorporate either of these forms of data protection, you will experience a slight hit in performance during the write phase of a hard disk I/O operation. However, this is negligible and easily offset by the data protection offered. Figure D.4 shows an artist's rendition of disk duplexing in operation.

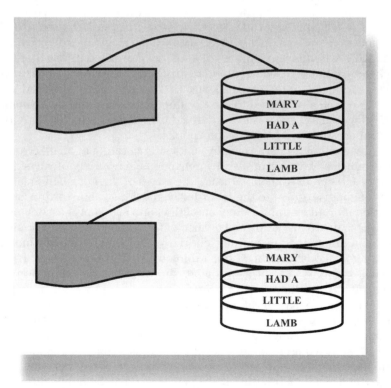

FIGURE D.4   *With disk duplexing, identical copies of data are copied to two separate drives, each one attached to a different disk controller.*

disk editor   A piece of specialized software that allows a user to examine and alter the contents of a disk drive bit by bit. Disk editors even allow access to parts of the drive not normally accessible by the user, such as FAT. Disk editors differ greatly from file editors or text editors in several ways. Disk editors bypass the file system of a computer and allow the user to examine and manipulate the contents of individual disk *sectors*. General user programs can only read data in *file allocation units*. Because of this, a disk editor allows someone to edit contents of the hard disk that are normally not seen by the user. This includes the *master boot record*, *volume boot records*, file headers, and directory tables. This is a good thing in that it is the only way a user can alter such contents. It is a bad thing in that there is no such thing as "undo." If you edit the wrong thing, there is the potential that you could render a system unusable.

disk mirroring   *See* **disk duplexing** or **data mirroring**. This is a process of exactly duplicating the data on a system on two different drives hanging off a single controller.

disk slack   Wasted disk space caused by inefficient storage of data by the file system. Information stored on a hard disk is a stream of 0s and 1s. An individual file consists of a block of binary code and can range anywhere for a few bytes to several gigabytes. Disks are broken down into sectors of 512 bytes, and these sectors join together to form *allocation units*. Depending on the file system in use, an allocation unit can be made up of anywhere from 1 to 64 sectors, or 512 bytes to 32 KB. A single allocation unit can only hold the data from a single file. If your file system is using 32-KB FAUs, and you store a 128-byte file, more than 99% of that FAU will be empty but it cannot be used to store data from any other file. It goes unused. Disk slack is the total amount of unused space tied up in partially filled FAUs.

diskette   A term typically applied to the 3.5" floppy disk in order to distinguish it from the 5.25" floppy disk. The term was derived from the fact that the 3.5" format was much smaller and could fit into a shirt pocket.

distortion   Any unintentional or (usually) undesired altering of an electronic signal, image, or musical waveform. Distortion happens in a variety of ways. In an image, it can appear as unnatural curvature at the edges of the image. In music, it can be additional noise added to the recorded signal. Musical distortion isn't always unintentional or undesirable. Many amplifiers and signal processors enjoy great success in the marketplace because of their ability to induce controlled distortion. A great example is Jimi Hendrix. Would Jimi have been Jimi playing a nylon-stringed acoustic guitar? I don't think so! Distortion of a signal in a computer system is less forgiving or pleasurable. It can result in data corruption or loss.

distributed application server   *Application servers* are powerful computers that are dedicated to the task of running a single application. An example of this is an e-mail server on a network. One computer could be used to bring in all of the e-mails for a large company and distribute them to tens of thousands of employees. It could … but it would result in tens of thousands of unhappy employees. Performance would be severely impacted by tryng to serve this many users with a single server. On a network this size, it is best to have the application running on several servers that share the workload. This makes more efficient use of network bandwidth and it allows all the servers to share the load. Figure D.5 illustrates the concept of a distributed application server.

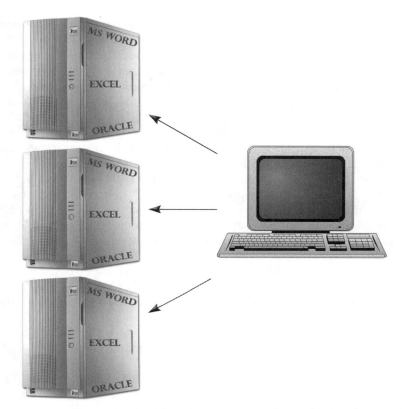

FIGURE D.5 *A distributed application server scheme divides the workload of a heavily used application across multiple computers.*

Distributed Queue, Dual Bus (DQDB) A networking standard that allows multiple-user access over two or more disparate connections. FDDI is a protocol that uses DQDB. It allows a 150 mb/s transfer rate over two separate fiber lines, with a separate queue assigned to each carrier.

distribution server Any server that collects content and dispenses it to multiple users across the network. A common form of distribution server is one that houses the installation files for applications needed by users. When a new application is needed, it can be installed from a network source instead of requiring the original CDs. Antipiracy is accomplished by maintaining license catalogs on the servers and tracking to whom, when, and how many times the application was installed. This process is not generally necessary if a *site license* has been purchased.

dithering A process of blending the colors of adjacent areas in an image to make the appearance more natural. Color and density values of adjacent *pixels* are measured and the values of all bordering pixels are averaged into the newly created one. Dithering comes into play most predominately in the following circumstances. When two colors come together in a sharp edge, but a sharp edge isn't a natural part of the image, the transition between the two colors is softened through dithering. Secondly, when a scanner is configured to capture an image using *interpolated resolution*, it has to "make up dots" on the fly. The values of those dots must be approximated because they weren't created optically. A form of dithering is used to generate these new pixels. Finally, when an imaging software package resizes an image to a higher resolution or to a larger size with the same resolution, new pixels must be created. Dithering is one of several methods used to create realistic values for the new dots.

DNS   Domain Name System. A TCP-IP protocol that translates user-friendly names of websites or devices into the IP address needed to find the host.

docking station   A device to which a laptop computer can be attached that provides additional hardware support, including I/O ports, PCI slots, and drive bays. Docking stations provide all the standard I/O connectors of a desktop computer and also allow additional drives and/or PCI cards to be installed that are not part of the original laptop's configuration. A typical docking station offers the following:

- Standard I/O ports installed include serial, parallel, video, two PS/2, four USB, VGA, DVI, S-Video, and audio ports
- One half-height standard PCI slot and one internal media bay with battery charging support
- RJ-45 and RJ-11 jacks for network and modem hookups
- Cable lock security with latch

domain   (1) A collection of all resources and users that fall under the control of a single administrative unit. In the case of a Windows network, the administrative unit would be *domain controller*. A centralized database maintains the security records for all objects and resources on the network, including end users (considered an object). Each of these entities has its own entry in this database, which identifies all permissions and privileges. When the user logs on to the network, she provides a user ID and password, which is compared to the database. If the credentials match, the user is allowed access to any resource for which she has been assigned *permissions*. Because of this, the domain model is considered a relatively secure network. In addition, domains can be joined through a collection of *trusts*, allowing for networks that are essentially unlimited in size. (2) A virtual host on the Internet that is assigned a unique *fully qualified domain name* (FQDN). To the end user, www.mwgraves.com appears to be a unique entity on the Internet, while in reality it is one of many Web sites hosted on a single server at a large Internet service provider.

domain divider switch   A device that allows external SCSI devices to be shared by multiple host computers (Figure D.6). SCSI resources are on separate busses, divided into groups called *domains*. Each domain resides on one side of the switch or the other. When the switch is thrown open, each domain is accessible only to hosts that access that specific bus. Hosts enjoy the full bandwidth but do not have access to resources on the other domain. By closing the switch, both domains are open to both busses. Bandwidth is compromised, but access is improved. Domain divider switches can be used for multiple purposes. In addition to simple device sharing, they can be used as *load balancing* devices or as fault-tolerant switches providing automatic rollover to one device when the other fails.

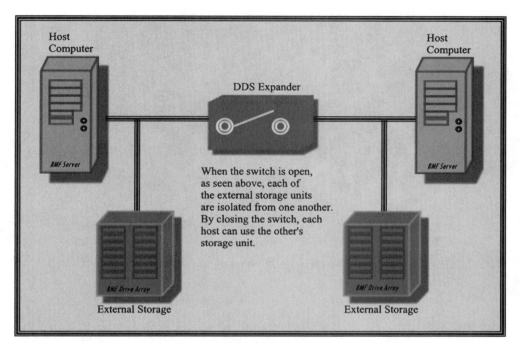

FIGURE D.6 A domain divider greatly increases the versatility of an SCSI implementation.

domain validation   A process by which an SCSI host adapter sends out a series of commands to each device on the chain and calculates each device's maximum data transfer rate. The response of each device indicates the best methods to use in transferring data between devices. A *synchronous data transfer request* determines the maximum speed that can be used. A *wide data transfer request* determines the bit width that is mutually compatible between the two devices. A *parallel protocol request* assumes parallel speeds in excess of SCSI-II standards and is used to negotiate speeds up to and including the ultra-640 standards. In addition to setting these three modes, other parameters, including clocking and the size of data units, are negotiated.

dot pitch (dp)   Dot pitch is the industry standard measurement for resolution on a computer monitor. Unfortunately, not all monitor manufacturers follow the same industry standards in defining what it is. A single pixel consists of three dots of glowing *phosphors* that, when their hues are mixed, create the colors you see. Each phosphor glows in one of the primary colors. By definition, dot pitch measures the distance between two adjacent *like-colored* phosphors. However, some manufacturers, in order to inflate their specification, measure the distance between adjacent pixels, regardless of color. As you can see in Figure D.7, there is a distinct difference between these two figures. One company's .22dp monitor might be the equivalent of another company's .26dp monitor, if not measured identically.

dot server   This is a slang expression for any one of the name servers distributed around the world that host the *Domain Name System* (DNS) resource records.

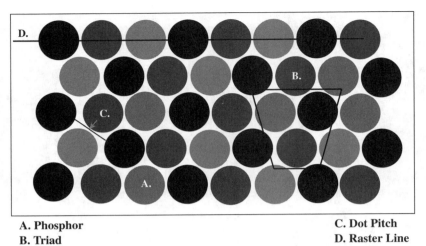

A. Phosphor
B. Triad
C. Dot Pitch
D. Raster Line

FIGURE D.7   Dot pitch is the distance between two adjacent like-colored dots.

In order to distribute the load of the entire population of the Internet asking the same server to look up a DNS name every time it can't find a host, domain names are divided up into a number of different zones. Each of these zones manages the database of URLs and IP addresses for Web sites with a particular suffix (for example, .com or .gov). There are two types of name server. An authoritative name server maintains a primary database and is never overwritten. For the authoritative name server there is nowhere "upstairs" to go if it can't resolve a domain name. If the authoritative name server can't resolve the name, the name doesn't exist. In order to shield the authoritative name server from a barrage of unnecessary queries, *caching servers* maintain databases of frequently accessed host names. Because of the heavy workload imposed on a dot server, it shouldn't come as much of a surprise to learn that it isn't just a single server that fulfills the role, but rather large clusters of load-balanced and fault-tolerant servers. The individual servers are generally high-end mainframe computers capable of several trillion operations per second.

double-buffering   This is a technique used by a number of different devices in order to speed up I/O operations. The use of two separate memory buffers allows the results of one operation to be stored, ready for transmission to the receiving device, while the next operation is being queued to the buffer. Video cards commonly use double-buffering so that as a frame is displayed on the monitor, another frame is in the queue, ready for display, while yet a third is being assembled by the graphics adapter. The buffers swap roles as needed. While one is writing to the target address, the other is collecting new data. When the first one finishes its chore it starts collecting data while the second writes its data.

double-transition clocking   The movement of two transfers of data on a single clock cycle. Data is transferred using an electrical current that has the characteristics of a sine wave. There is a rising end and a falling end to the wave.

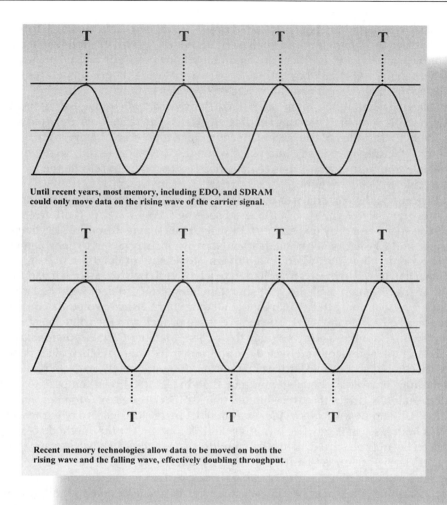

FIGURE D.8   Double-transition clocking allows data to move across the bus on both the rising and falling ends of the signal.

In the dinosaur days of computing, data could only be transferred on the rising end. Double-transition clocking allows data to move on both ends of the clock cycle, as illustrated in Figure D.8. Devices that incorporate this technology include AGP and DDR memory.

drive bay   A metal frame within a computer enclosure (which may or may not be removable) that supports disk drives. Typically, drive bays come in two different sizes and they may be internal or external. Internal drive bays house devices that do not need to be accessed directly by the user, such as a hard disk drive. External bays are used for removable media or for devices that allow the user to interconnect external devices. Drive bays are typically either 3.5" or 5.25" frames. A 5.25" bay is typically 1.75" high and is frequently called a *half-height bay*. This nomenclature is a throwback to the computer era's equivalent of the Ice Age when a full-height bay was 3.5" by 5.25". Even today there are a number of devices, such as tape backup units, that require full-height bays. The 3.5" bays are 4" wide (hence the reference to a 3.5" bay) by 1" high. *Drive rails* allow the 3.5" devices to fit in the 4" bay.

drive rails   Devices that attach to the side of a disk drive that allow the user to install or subsequently remove it without needing any tools. The drive rails are attached with screws to the sides of the device. Receptacles mounted in the *drive bay* assure that the rails snap firmly into place when the drive is inserted. To remove the device in the future, all one has to do is depress two tabs to release the lock and the drive will slide right out.

drive translation   In the early days of computers, all hard disks were read through a BIOS interrupt called *INT13h*. INT13h was based on *CHS geometry*. It offered a 24-bit address space and provided support for disk drives that featured 1,024 cylinders, 256 heads, and 63 sectors per track. Mathematically, this works out to approximately 8 GB. In order to allow the system to address systems larger than 8 GB, one of two things had to happen. We either had to teach INT13h new tricks or we had to scrap it all together and come up with something new. The problem with the latter approach was that doing this would render all older hard disks obsolete (as if that wasn't going to happen anyway). The new tricks approach was the route design engineers chose to take. They were able to do this by adding *BIOS extensions* to the mix. The INT13h extensions increased the address space from 24 bits to 64 bits. In theory, this would give us hard drives up to around 18 million terabytes. In reality, the limitations have so far been greater than that. In fact, the first attempt to expand INT13h resulted in drives that were limited to 528 MB. Subsequent attempts, such as extended IDE and *Logical Block Addressing*, did a better job. Instead of expressing hard disk addresses in geometric terms, as did INT13h, the various methods of drive translation lay out the hard disk in a linear addressing method. They translate those addresses into terms that INT13h can understand.

drop   This is a term for a singular run of cable that links a networked device to a central location, such as a server closet. In a typical business, computers, printers, and other devices are scattered across the facility and installed wherever it's convenient. Technicians then string a cable from that location to the server room. Since it was a common practice to run cabling in the ceiling, it generally looped down through a conduit in the ceiling of the server room. Each cable then connects to a patch panel. In order to make life easier on the technicians who will service the site in the future, it is a good practice to clearly label the jack at each location with a unique letter/number combination and then label the other end of that cable with the same number. This becomes the drop number.

D-sub   D subminiature. Also called *DB connectors* or *D-shell connectors*, they are so named because of the D-shape of the plug. Technically speaking, most of these plugs are not really DB connectors. In every case but one, international DIN designations use letters A through E in conjunction with the D. For example, what we commonly call DB-15 is really DE-15 under DIN specifications. Table D.1 defines the common D-sub connectors.

dual core processing   When Intel released their Pentium 4 Extreme Edition, they gave us our first dual-processor CPU on a single chip. Well, sort of, anyway. This new

TABLE D.1
A listing of DB connectors and their usage

DB NO.	DIN NO.	DESCRIPTION
DB-9	DE-9	A male 9-pin connector commonly used on serial connectors
DB-15	DA-15	A two-row 15-pin connector commonly used on AU connectors and on MIDI ports
DB-15	DE-15	A 15-pin connector with three rows of pins used on VGA cables and cards
DB-19	N/A	A connector used with NeXT and early Macintosh computers
DB-25	DB-25	The 25-pin connector used on the computer end of parallel printer cables and on 25-pin RS-232 serial cables or connectors
DB-37	DC-37	A 37-pin connector used on RS-423 cables and connectors
DB-50	DD-50	The 50-pin connector used by SCSI devices
DB-68	MD-69	A 68-pin connector used by SCSI devices

chip offered two completed dedicated processing cores and a set of instructions called *Hyperthreading Technology* (HT). Each processing core gets its own dedicated L1 and L2 cache, and by providing a high-speed frontside bus, the CPU is fed with data much faster. Dual core processors literally perform (within a few tenths of a percentage point) as well as dual processor systems in most situations without the additional overhead required by multi-CPU systems.

dump-charge   This is a process of cycling a rechargeable battery by draining it completely of any charge and then giving it a full charge. Repeating this cycle a couple of times will extend the life of certain types of rechargeable battery. Batteries such as nickel cadmium (Ni-Cad) exhibit a phenomenon called *memory*. This occurs when a battery is never discharged completely. Over time, the abbreviated charges that the battery receives gradually metamorphose into becoming the total charge that the battery can hold. As a result, the usable time for the battery gets reduced slightly on every subsequent charge, greatly reducing the overall life of the battery. Dump-charging the battery reduces this phenomenon and increases the life of the battery.

duplex   A communications method by which a device can be transmitting and receiving at the same time. Duplex communications occurs in one of two fashions. Half-duplex describes a situation in which each party can send and each party can receive, but they can't do both at the same time. Full duplex communications assumes that each device can both transmit and receive at the same time. Ethernet networks are an example of full duplex. There are four pairs of wires. Two of these pairs are dedicated to data transmission and the other two handle incoming data.

dynamic   Any process that works interactively with another process. Any dynamic process is one that is constantly subject to change, able to perform an operation or execute a change on the fly. For example, tables that automatically update themselves when data is changed in an external source are dynamic tables. Routing tables that provide address resolution in routers are frequently dynamic tables. Dynamic buffers are areas of memory that are present when needed and closed down when not. Some operating systems perform dynamic file compression. Files are compressed as they are written to disk and decompressed when opened. The user doesn't have to take any action to make this happen; it occurs dynamically.

dynamic disk   For many years, hard disks have been defined by a specific set of features. There were primary partitions, extended partitions, and logical disks. With the release of NTFS, Microsoft introduced the concept of dynamic disks. Dynamic disks make use of a single partition across the entire disk, divided into volumes. There can be multiple volumes on a single disk or a single volume can span multiple disks. Instead of partition tables, a dynamic disk is mapped out within a string of data known as *metadata*, which is stored in a nonpartitioned section of the disk. In operating systems that support dynamic disks, a basic disk can be converted to a dynamic disk. Reverse conversion is generally not possible. With Windows 2000 and later operating systems, in order to use advanced disk configurations such as RAID the disks must be converted to dynamic disks.

Dynamic Host Control Protocol (DHCP)   One of the biggest problems facing network administrators is keeping track of all those IP addresses and who has what. The Dynamic Host Configuration Protocol was designed to alleviate most, if not all of those problems. DHCP is an extension of BootP and allows for dynamic configuration of network clients.

DHCP works in a similar manner to BootP, with a few enhancements and one notable limitation. The enhancements are that DHCP allows the administrator to put all the available IP addresses into a pool and dole them out for a limited time. This time is known as the DHCP lease. Leases can be for as long or as short as the administrator wishes them to be. By assigning a very short lease, such as one hour, to an IP address, that address essentially becomes available once that person logs off of their machine. It can then be handed out to the next person who wishes to log on. This is useful when there are a limited number of addresses available and you don't want them tied up for any extended period. ISPs frequently use this technique. Longer leases are useful when there are plenty of addresses to go around.

Once that lease has been configured, the client machine can keep the IP address for that amount of time. When the lease reaches 50% of its maturity, the client will begin sending messages to the DHCP server that issued the address to renew the lease or reassign a new address. At approximately 75% of maturity, the client begins broadcasting to all hosts, looking for any DHCP server that will give it a new IP address.

Other advantages of DHCP are the number of options that can be configured by an administrator. Nearly every parameter of a client TCP/IP configuration can be handed out by DHCP. In the event that something changes, such as the static address of a DNS server or a router interface, those changes can be placed into the DHCP options and then everybody's lease set to 1 minute. The next time a person restarts their machine the new configuration will automatically take effect. If you have a network of 2500 users, which do you think might be easier; the DHCP method, or trotting around to 2500 different machines manually changing their configuration?

The limitation, if you want to consider it that, is that DHCP does not allow for the distribution of a boot file. Machines configured for DHCP can obtain configuration information remotely, but to boot remotely, they will still need a BootP server. Both DHCP and BootP use ports 67 and 68 for their operation.

dynamic range The difference between the largest and the smallest values within a variable that can be measured in a progression of values. For example, the human ear can hear sounds from approximately 20 Hz to 20,000 Hz when a person is young and has good hearing. This range gradually drops as that person ages. In addition to frequency, there is a range of sound volume that the human ear can detect. A single frequency at a single intensity would result in a single sound. If you mix a variety of sounds, such as you have with a symphony orchestra, you will have a wide variety of frequencies from the bass drum to the highest notes of the piccolo. Some of these instruments play louder than others. Most musicians and recording engineers take only volume into consideration when measuring dynamic range. Dynamic range of sound is measured in *decibels* (dB). A higher number means a greater range between the softest and loudest passages. Generally, dynamic range is reduced when a recording is made of a natural phenomenon. The recording of Beethoven's Symphony No. 5 will not possess the full dynamic range of the original performance. Dynamic range of an image is measured in *gamma* and is a measurement of the difference between the brightest and the darkest tones on the image.

dynamic routing *Routers* perform their task of sending data to the correct location by knowing which wire is the correct "highway" for that data to take in order to get to its destination. In order to do this, they rely on *routing tables*, which tell the router which port to use to send data to a specific network address. In the early days of routers and internetworking, routing tables were statically configured, meaning somebody had to write them up in a text editor and then export them into the router's memory. More recent routing protocols ask neighboring routers if they can borrow their routing tables and then use the neighbor's tables to update their own. When a new router configured to use dynamic routing comes online, the first thing it does is send out a broadcast message from all ports asking for an update of routing tables. Every router that receives this broadcast will respond by transmitting the requested tables (unless configured *not* to respond to these requests). The new router builds its tables accordingly.

E

e-cash A method of making payments over a computer connection using a software-based transaction system. A financial institution such as a bank must be involved in order to back up the electronic transfer of funds with real money. The financial institution issues a user a certain amount of money, which is physically stored on the user's computer in a binary file. To secure the funds, another institution is used as a digital signer. The digital signature verifies that the funds being used are valid. Using e-cash, a person can shop online and make payments without exposing critical information, such as his credit card numbers, over an Internet connection. Most banks offer some form of online banking, but this is not considered e-cash because the payments are made out of existing cash deposits. Several major players in the e-cash market include Digicash and Ecash, Inc.

E-carrier A fiber optics digital transmission line capable of moving data at high rates of speed. E-lines, as they're called, are defined by the International Telecommunications Union (ITU) and are used in most countries except the United States and Japan. Similar to the *T-carriers* used in the United States, E-carriers are composed of several 64-Kb/s lines (called DSO channels) that are multiplexed for form a single high-speed carrier. Table E.1 lists the commonly used E-carriers.

TABLE E.1
The E-carriers of Europe

CARRIER	DESCRIPTION	BANDWIDTH (M/b/s)
E1	32 DSO channels	2,048
E2	4 E1 lines multiplexed	8,448
E3	16 E1 lines multiplexed	34,368
E4	64 E1 lines multiplexed	139,264
E4	256 E1 lines multiplexed	565,148

e-commerce Electronic commerce. This is a term that defines any business transaction that occurs over the Internet or through other electronic means. Typically, for e-commerce to be safe and secure, transactions need to be performed over a secured connection. To be sure that your connection is secured when performing a transaction with a Web-based entity, make sure that the URL of the Web page begins with https:// rather than http://. The *s* indicates that it is a secured Web site. Data moving back and forth between your computer and the server will be encrypted. Sensitive information such as account numbers, passwords, and social security numbers will not be displayed on the screen. If a screen expires, it cannot be automatically refreshed. Any forms of online banking, online shopping, or online auctions are obviously forms of e-commerce. Less obvious examples include real estate agencies with passive listings, Web sites that offer unbiased reviews of products, and Web pages that act only as a listing of links to other e-commerce sites.

Easter egg　This is a term for hidden (rarely malicious) code that is buried inside an application. The code will be launched only if a specific trigger event occurs. The trigger event might be a specific key sequence or it could be set off by a specific date and time. Programmers plant most Easter eggs as their little hidden joke. For example, in one popular game, typing in a secret code during one level caused the heroine to suddenly lose her clothing.

echo　An automated response from a device or application. The idea of the response is so that the user can verify that his request was correctly received and interpreted. The echo response is invariably a direct replication of the data sent by the user, which is how the term got its colorful name.

edge connector　On expansion devices or other components' construction on circuit boards, wiring terminals are generally metal-plated tabs along one edge of the board that attach to the traces in the board. These terminals make up the edge connector, which mates to the receiving device in a slot. The PCI card in Figure E.1 is an example of an edge connector.

FIGURE E.1　Most expansion cards, including this PCI device, use edge connectors to interface with the motherboard.

edge router　*See* **border router**.

edge-triggered　Any response that elicited and/or was controlled by a direct change in the electrical signal coming from a pin or wire on a device. The voltage is applied and the device depends on the interrupt controller to "remember" that it sent the signal. Because edge-triggered circuits depend on a physical signal and not a logical event, in order for two edge-triggered devices to share the same interrupt line, they must be designed to do so. When not signaling for an interrupt, the device must release the line so that other devices can use it. This can be accomplished by adding resistors to the circuit. If an edge-triggered device is not configured to share interrupts, then any other device on the system that shares the interrupt will cause a system lockup if both are active on the circuit at once. Older *ISA* devices are examples of edge-triggered devices that were not designed by default to share interrupts.

Edlin   This is a now-obsolete text editor that shipped with various versions of MS-DOS. Edlin was crude and archaic. Besides being difficult to use and virtually impossible to edit once a line was copied to memory, it was still an unpopular tool among computer professionals in its day.

effective computable   Any function or equation for which a routine can be written to solve. Any mathematical equation such as 2+2 would be an effective computable. However, things that might not immediately come to mind also fit the definition. A graphic displayed on a screen is the result of several complex mathematical equations. Therefore, that image is an effective computable. Generally, the term is used by programmers to describe specific functions.

eight-bit clean   Some early character sets, such as ASCII, included characters that made use of only 7 bits in a byte. The eighth bit could be used as a flag in programming functions or as a parity bit, if so desired. For many years, all character sets have used all eight bits of every bite. *Eight-bit clean* is a term for any coding mechanism that uses eight of eight.

eject   The process of removing a disk from an external drive bay.

electroluminescent display   A form of thin-panel display that consists of a layer of phosphorescent material sandwiched between two wire grids. Each of the grids is wired perpendicular to the other. Where they intersect, a pixel is formed. Varying levels of signal are applied to the wires of each grid, and the composite value of the two wires determines how brightly the pixel will glow. Electroluminescent displays have become obsolete as varying forms of LCD or plasma display have taken their place.

electromagnet   A device consisting of a conducting core (usually iron) wrapped with one or more coils of wire. The two ends of the metal rod protrude from the coil. When electricity is applied to the wire, the core develops a magnetic charge. The strength of magnetism is a function of the number of coils and the amount of current applied to the wire. When no current is applied, there is no magnetic charge. One implementation of an electromagnet in the computer system is the read/write heads in a disk drive.

electromagnetic interference (EMI)   Any spurious noise introduced into an electrical signal as a result of any form of energy that is part of the electromagnetic spectrum. This would include radio waves, cosmic radiation, and any form of visible light wave (although if light is visible, it is usually of no concern to an electronic signal). There are various sources of EMI. Unshielded electronic devices, such as a space heater, can emit large quantities. If you live in close proximity to a power station you are most likely bombarded with this energy. EMI can be countered by using metal foil to shield the medium carrying the signal.

electron   One of the subatomic particles that make up an atom. The electron is a negatively charged particle that circles around the core of the atom (called the *neutron*). Electrons circle the neutron in one or more orbital shells. With many elements, the outer shell of electrons may be susceptible to migration. This occurs when the pull of another atom is strong enough to attract the electron over to that atom. Electronic signals depend on this behavior. The more easily an element gives up the electrons in its outer shell, the more *conductive* it is. Conductors carry an electrical signal very well for this reason.

electron gun   A cathode that, when heated, emits a stream of electrons from the positive pole. Electron guns consist of several key components. One of these is a cathode, which emits a burst of electrons when energized. A series of electrodes focus those electrons into a beam. This beam passes one or more *anodes* that bring the beam down to pinpoint focus and send it off in a targeted direction. Electron guns are a key component on *cathode ray tube* monitors.

electron tube   This is another name for a *vacuum tube*. A glass tube from which all atmospheric gasses have been evacuated will allow electrons to move about more freely. An electron tube consists of two or more *electrodes* within the vacuum. One of the electrodes is called a *cathode*. When heated, the cathode emits a burst of electrons. Another electrode, called an *anode*, attracts these stray electrons. Electron tubes perform a variety of functions. They can act as switches that activate when the voltage is high enough to heat the cathode sufficiently to emit the electrons. They can be used to amplify signals or they can be used to create a focused beam of light. These are only a few of the many uses for electron tubes.

electrostatic field   In nature, all objects possess some sort of electrical charge. It is the nature of being constructed from molecules with differing numbers of electrons in the outer shell. Any time two objects with different charges exist in close proximity to one another, an energized "wall" develops between them. A difference in charge occurs any time there are more free electrons on one side of the field than on the other. The side with the most electrons will carry a negative charge, and the opposite side will carry a positive charge. It is a static charge because the electrons that make up the charge are not moving along any conductors, but are a part of the molecular matrix that exists between the two objects. Electrostatic fields can play havoc with data transmissions because the electrical activity can alter the signal traveling along the media, resulting in data corruption. Since metallic objects tend to deflect electrostatic charges, shielding the media with metal foil can greatly reduce the impact.

element   (1) One of the basic substances of nature that make up matter. Elements consist of only one type of atom, each of which contains the same number of *protons* in the nucleus of the atom. An element cannot be broken down to any simpler form using natural means. Multiple elements can combine to form compounds. There are 118 elements listed on the *periodic table*, which is the listing of all the elements. (2) In an array of data, an element is a single data entity that is part of that array. For example, a spreadsheet consists of many columns of data combined with many rows. Where a column and a cell intersect, a single cell is defined that contains a data element.

ellipsis   A punctuation mark consisting of three dots in a row. The typical use of an ellipsis is to indicate that there are words or portions of words omitted from the text. If I were to … you might consider that a place to use an ellipsis. Another place where it is commonly used is between numbers to show a range. In the example 1…45, you can interpret the entire range of numbers between 1 and 45 and not simply those two numbers.

else   A programming or scripting statement that points to an alternative action in the event that a previously stated condition (such as an IF statement) is not met. In the statement "IF X=7, Y=SUM(E1:E24)" it is clear what should happen if the expected value of 7 is recognized. By following with the statement "ELSE (Y=SUM(F1:F24)" there is a clear indication of what to do if the expected value is NOT recognized.

em   A specification for a typeface that is derived by measuring the total height of a capital M within the range of characters for the typeface. *Em space* measures with the width of that character. Another place where you will see the term used is in respect to the *em square*, which refers to an imaginary square that you could potentially draw between two single-spaced lines of type using the same size of typeface.

e-mail   Electronic mail. A message sent from one user to another across a computer network or the Internet. While primarily a text message, e-mails can also contain graphics, embedded music, and other forms of medium. In addition to the basic message, an e-mail can also contain attachments, which can be any type of file. For an e-mail system to work, there must be a protocol in place to process incoming messages and another to process outgoing messages. The two most commonly used protocols for incoming messages are the *Post Office Protocol* (POP) and the *Internet Message Access Protocol* (IMAP). The most commonly used protocol for incoming messages is the *Simple Mail Transfer Protocol* (SMTP). E-mail messages are directed to the recipient by way of the *e-mail address*. The e-mail address consists of a unique user ID along with the name of the domain for which that user is a member, separated by an ampersand (@). An example would be noah@ark.com.

embedded   Contained within another object. An embedded file is a complete autonomous file that has been made a part of a larger file. For example, a graphics file that is inserted into a word processing file in order to illustrate the document is an embedded file. Sometimes, in order to keep file size down, a program will use embedded links to a file rather than the entire file. That works as long as both files are concurrently present on the computer that is displaying the document.

embedded command   In many applications, such as a word processor, there are number strings of code contained in the document along with the user's text that indicate things such as formatting, line feed, and other elements of document structure. These invisible strings of code are the embedded commands. Many applications allow the user to view place marks for these commands, even if he can't see the actual code. Figure E.2 is the beginning of this chapter with the option to view codes enabled. In this illustration, you can see the paragraph marks, character spaces, and tab marks. The brackets around the E indicate that the letter has been bookmarked.

emoticon   A term coined to describe various combinations of letters, numbers, and punctuation marks that people use in electronic communications (such as e-mail

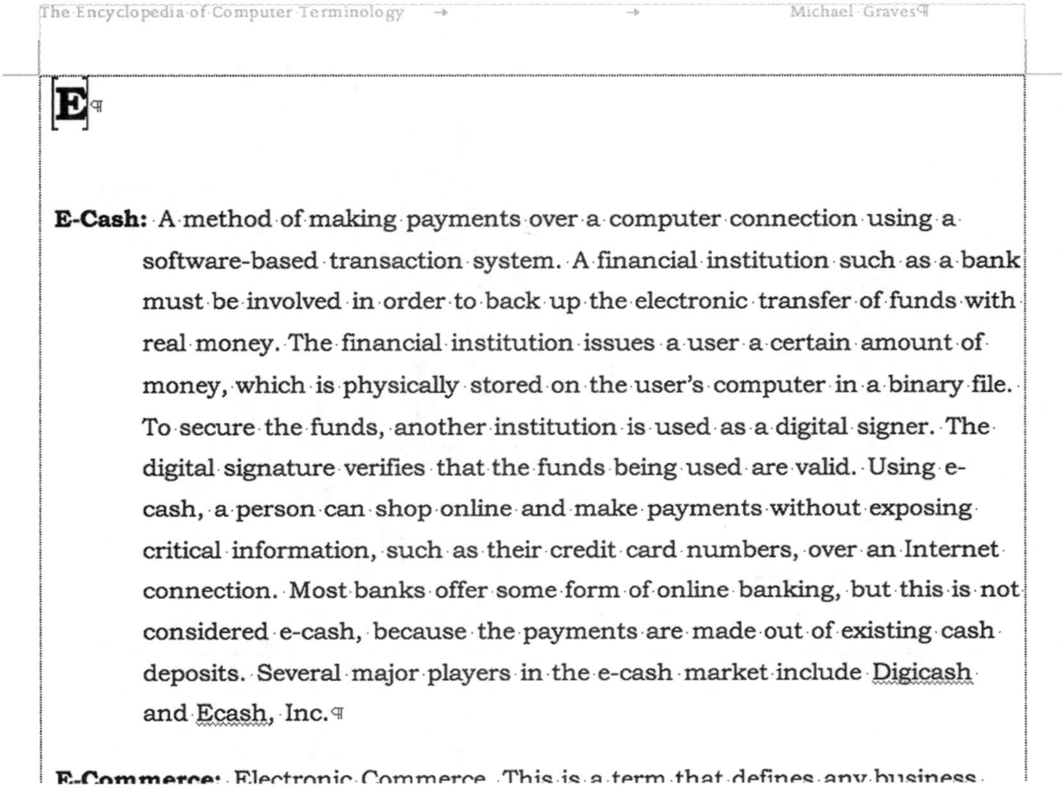
The Encyclopedia of Computer Terminology → → Michael Graves¶

E¶

E-Cash: A method of making payments over a computer connection using a software-based transaction system. A financial institution such as a bank must be involved in order to back up the electronic transfer of funds with real money. The financial institution issues a user a certain amount of money, which is physically stored on the user's computer in a binary file. To secure the funds, another institution is used as a digital signer. The digital signature verifies that the funds being used are valid. Using e-cash, a person can shop online and make payments without exposing critical information, such as their credit card numbers, over an Internet connection. Most banks offer some form of online banking, but this is not considered e-cash, because the payments are made out of existing cash deposits. Several major players in the e-cash market include Digicash and Ecash, Inc.¶

E-Commerce: Electronic Commerce. This is a term that defines any business

FIGURE E.2 Embedded commands, such as paragraph marks, are shown. The brackets around the E indicate the letter has been bookmarked.

and chat rooms) to convey an emotion. Table E.2 lists some commonly used emoticons, although it barely scratches the surface of all the ones used. The fact that somebody might actually know them all is somewhat frightening.

emulator Any device or piece of software designed in such a way that it assumes the features and attributes of a completely different device or software. For example, a DOS emulator is a piece of software that allows a user to run programs originally written for MS-DOS on a Windows platform. In addition there are emulators available that allow programs to run on completely different platforms. It is possible to get emulators to run Nintendo, Amiga, or Atari games on a PC, to run PC games on a Macintosh computer, and so forth. One should take care in using this type of software. Many companies prohibit the use of their products over emulators and it is a violation of copyright.

enable To activate or make operational. Once a piece of hardware is installed on a system, it might be necessary to take some additional step in order to make the system recognize the new hardware. Conversely, one might want to disable the hardware if it is not being used and resources need to be freed up for another

TABLE E.2
A brief listing of commonly used emoticons

KEYSTROKES	INTENDED EMOTION
%-)	Baffled
</3	Broken Heart
H-)	Confused
>:)	Devilish
:#)	Drunken smile
>:->	Evil grin
>=)	Evil intentions
:-P	Sticking tongue out
:P~	Sticking tongue out
:P	Sticking tongue out
<:-L	Feeling stupid
:-!	Foot in mouth
X:-)	Goofy grin
:-*	Kiss
XD	Laughing smile
<3	Love
:-C	Real unhappy smile
:-(	Sad
:(	Sad
:`(	Sad smile
:->	Sarcastic
:-(*)	Sick
:-X	Sloppy wet kiss
:)	Smile
:-)	Smile
=-)	Smile
(:	Smile
=)	Smile
:>	Smile
:-o	Surprised
:-&	Tongue-tied
8)	Wide-eyed smile
8-)	Wide-eyed smile (Goggle-eyed)
;)	Wink
;-)	Wink

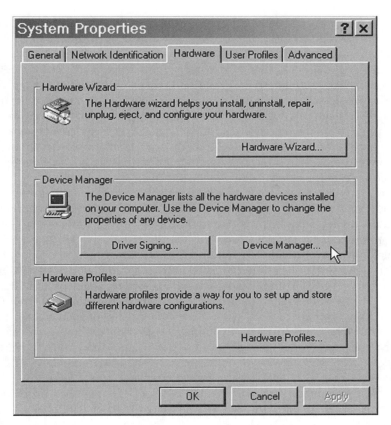

FIGURE E.3   Hardware devices can be enabled and disabled in Hardware Profiles in the Windows Device Manager.

device. Operating systems typically have some method of enabling and disabling hardware. In Windows, one goes into Device Manager, selects the device, and opens the device properties. There is a pull-down menu, as shown in Figure E.3, that allows the user to do this.

encapsulation   This is a process by which information that is to be transmitted over a network connection is broken down into sections small enough to fit into a packet and then the required control information is added to each segment. When data is prepared for transmission, it undergoes several steps along the way. The data to be transmitted is segmented into pieces small enough to transmit. Then the segment passes through several routines, each of which adds certain information. The *MAC address* of the transmitting and receiving devices is added, as is a logical *network address*. In addition, any time there are multiple packets to be transmitted, a unique packet number, along with sequencing information, is added as well. Some form of error correction is needed so that data will be added. The overall process of segmenting the data and tucking it into all of this control information is the process of encapsulation.

encode   (1) The process of taking any analog source material and turning it into digital information is a form of *encoding*. The letters of the alphabet, numbers and punctuation, and so forth all need to be converted into a series of 0s and 1s before the computer can process them. Likewise, a file such as a scanned photograph must be converted into binary information before the computer can make use of it. (2) The process of turning digital information into an electronic or optical signal that can be transmitted over a medium or stored on a medium and subsequently restored to a digital format. For data to be transmitted over the network, an electrical signal or light wave must be modulated in a controlled fashion so that the receiving device can interpret the modulations correctly and regenerate the digital code from the electrical or optical signals.

encrypt   To scramble a message or data in a controlled fashion so that only those who know how to decipher the message can read the information. For encryption to work, a digital key must be provided to the intended recipients that allow them to restore the data to its original format. This key basically identifies how the message or data was scrambled and provides the direction for putting it back together. Common forms of encryption techniques include *block cipher* and *substitution cipher*. Over the years, several encryption security standards have evolved. The two most common are the Data Encryption Standard (DES) and the Advanced Encryption Standard (AES). The first version of DES emerged in 1976 as a federal standard for data encryption. Several versions have come and gone in the intervening years. AES was adopted as the official standard for government encryption in 2001. It uses block cipher with 128-bit blocks and keys of 128, 192, and 256 bits.

end of life   This is a phrase that indicates the official retirement of a product. When a piece of hardware or software goes end of life (or EOL, as is often seen), it means that the manufacturer will no longer support the product. Most manufacturers distinguish between end of production and end of life by providing support after production has ceased, whereas for some, EOL means end of production and of support.

end tag   In HTML, the end tag (/p) identifies the end of the page.

end user   The person actually working (or playing) on a computer. Various terms tend to confuse novitiates in the business by appearing to mean the same thing. Client and host are occasionally confused with the end user, but in the world of computing, neither term is used in reference to a human.

ending delimiter   One or more bits at the end of a stream of data that acts as the boundary marking the end of that data stream. Devices that use *asynchronous communication* rely on starting and ending delimiters to identify the portion of the signal that is user data.

endless loop   Occasionally, an error in programming can result in the same string of code being executed over and over again, with the end of the string calling the beginning back again. This is the endless loop, or *infinite loop* as it is also called. A program that enters this state will appear to have locked, even though it is constantly engaging the CPU and (possibly) memory. The problem with the endless loop is that while the application has stopped responding to the user, as far as the system is concerned it is still alive and well. Endless loops aren't always errors. They might be intentionally programmed into specialized applications that are designed to perform the same task over and again until stopped. The difference between the intentional loop and the bug is that there will be a programmed break sequence in the intentional version that allows the user to stop processing at any time.

engine In the world of hardware, an engine is any collection of components that work together to perform a singular function. An engine differs from a device in that the device is a stand-alone unit, whereas an engine is only a functioning part of another unit. For example, the print engine in a laser printer is the group of parts that transfer the image to paper. It cannot do its job without the support of other components that generate the image and still others that move the paper along its path through the printer.

enhanced I/O controller hub The IC in the newer Intel chipsets that manages all function other than memory and AGP. This chip assumes the functions that the *southbridge* chip took on in other chipsets, including serial and parallel ports, USB, IDE, floppy disks, and so forth that require limited I/O bandwidth.

enhanced mode Early versions of Microsoft operating systems had to overcome a limitation imposed by the first microprocessors called *real mode*. Real mode assumed 1 MB of RAM and a maximum of a 16-bit data path. When Windows rolled out, its big claim to fame was 32-bit architecture and the ability to take advantage of *protected mode*. Processors recognize two modes. These are real mode and protected mode. The 80286 microprocessor had a minor issue in that while it could jump from real mode to protected mode without issue, it couldn't go back to real mode again without resetting the CPU. Resetting the CPU essentially reset the computer, which had a negative impact on the emotional well-being of the user who saw sixteen pages of unsaved text reboot before his very eyes. Enhanced mode was an operational mode specific to Windows that forced the OS to run in protected mode all the time. In order to do this, it took advantage of several features specific to the 80386 microprocessor, including the ability to use *virtual memory* and to function in *virtual real mode*. Therefore, while an old computer running Win3x on an Intel 80286 could play some of the games offered by the OS, in order to play the whole deck, one needed a 386. This is an historical artifact that we can thankfully put behind us.

enterprise Technically speaking, an enterprise is any business entity. However, in the world of networking, it is a term reserved for very large installations, typically consisting of multiple networks or subnets. In an enterprise-level network, there are three key assumptions that must be made. The first is that there will be many users and resources, and the second is that the users must never lose access to the resources. The last assumption is that every user thinks he is performing the most important work and therefore needs the network available at all times. Therefore, a network targeted toward an enterprise will incorporate a high degree of *fault tolerance* and *load balancing*. Typically, clusters of servers will perform functions that a single server would typically handle on a smaller network.

entity name (1) In the name binding protocol the entity name is a user-friendly host name used for identifying hosts on the network. The entity name is associated with a name string that can be up to 32 characters in length. The name string identifies specific characteristics of the entity. (2) An HTML code that lets you insert special characters into your Web pages (such as ©, ®, and Æ). Entity names are easier to use than character references, but are not supported by all browsers. Entity names in HTML code are case-sensitive.

environment   When an application runs on a computer, it needs to be able to call on any of the resources it needs to perform its functions. When the application first launches, the operating system will provide the basic needs such as an available memory space, allotments for CPU space, and access to system resources (such as IRQ channels, I/O, storage, and cache). All the variables specific to the application make up its environment.

ephemeral port   TCP/IP uses numbered *ports* to identify the application or process that is generating code, or which is the target process to receive incoming code. There are a total of 65,535 ports available. Ports 1 through 999 are known as the *well-known ports* and were assigned by IANA to specific common protocols. An ephemeral port is a port created by a client application that identifies the place where all incoming data intended for that application will go. It is dynamically assigned by the application when it is needed and broken down when the transfer of data is complete. Unlike well-known ports, an ephemeral port is assigned from a range of ports up to 4,000 ports wide. Once one port has been used by an application and the session is closed, a new port number from that range will be assigned the next time that application needs a port number. This process will be repeated for each connection until the application runs out of port numbers in that range. Then it will start at the beginning and run another lap.

ergonomics   This is a relatively new area of study combining anatomy with engineering. Ergonomics looks at how the human body interacts with physical objects and looks at ways to improve the design (of the object, not the body) so that it can be used more comfortably and efficiently. An ergonomically designed product will place less stress on the parts of the body that interact with it. The idea is that if the body encounters less resistance, maladies such as *repetitive stress syndrome* will have less effect.

error   Any condition that arises when the expected results of an action or calculation do not match the actual results. Errors are the result of faulty design, faulty programming, or faulty operation. For example, if you press on the "Y" key of your keyboard and a "W" appears on the screen, you would interpret that as an error. Computers can ignore or easily recover from most errors. However, some errors can result in a computer locking up. These are generally called *fatal errors*. Fatal errors can be the result of asking the computer to perform an impossible task, such as dividing by 0.

Error Correction Code (ECC)   ECC is a form of detecting and correcting errors that occur when copying data to memory or storing it to a drive. With ECC, data is divided into blocks. A mathematical function is performed on that block of data and stored in a separate address. When that data is retrieved, the same algorithm is applied and the result compared to the value stored. If the two results match, then the data is considered viable and will be passed along. This is the error detection phase. The correction part comes into play whenever the results do not match. In this case, the device will be asked to retransmit that block of data and the process will be performed once again.

escape   To break off or abort. Once a process is begun on a computer, the general idea is that it will be performed to its conclusion. In the event that the user changes his mind and decides not to do something, programmers provide a method of breaking out of the process. Generally, this is accomplished by way of the <Esc> key, a convenient abbreviation for the word. There is a code specifically for the escape function built into the ASCII character set (and all subsequent character sets based on ASCII) that induces this function. It is ASCII character 27. Devices that use ASCII control characters, such as a printer, will abort a print job when the escape command is received.

Ethernet   Ethernet is a networking standard that makes use of a technology known as *Carrier Sense, Multiple Access/Collision Detection* (CSMA/CS) to provide access to network media. This term is derived from the idea that, in order to gain access to the wire, an Ethernet device will constantly monitor the carrier signal and wait for it to be idle before transmitting data. As soon as the device detects an idle carrier, it will send out its packet. An event caused by two devices transmitting at the same time is called a *collision*. When a collision is detected, both devices will issue a packet through a process called the *backoff algorithm*. Each device will calculate a random interval to wait and then transmit again. With each subsequent collision by these same transmissions, the interval will increase in time. Under Ethernet, in order to transmit data over the network, the information is first broken down into chunks of information small enough to send in short bursts. This prevents a single large file transfer from occupying the entire network until the transfer is complete. Each chunk of data is *encapsulated* by the networking protocols to be accompanied by a source MAC address and network address, a destination MAC and network address, and a variety of other pieces of control information used by the protocols so that the entire file arrives intact at the correct destination. The original Ethernet standards were based on specifications developed in a cooperative effort between Digital Equipment Corporation, Intel, and Xerox. In deference to the companies that developed the standards, these were known as the *DIX standards*. These standards described a 10-Mb/s signal that moved over coaxial cable. Eventually, Ethernet would evolve to include speed up to a gigabit per second and move over a variety of media.

event   Any action or reaction of the part of the operating system, application, or device driver that elicits a response from the system. If that system is unable to respond correctly, it triggers an action by the OS to make a record of the activity (or inactivity). This response is an event. In some operating systems, such as Windows NT and later, an application called *Event Viewer* archives these events in a searchable database and an administrator can use them for analysis or troubleshooting.

Event Viewer   One of the better troubleshooting tools provided by most Windows operating systems is one called *Event Viewer*. Event Viewer collects information on different activities that are generated by either hardware or software action. These events range from benign to critical, and Event Viewer frequently can provide information that helps the administrator diagnose what led up to the event.

Event Viewer reports three degrees of severity in its logs, as illustrated in Table E.3.

TABLE E.3
Severity classifications for Event Viewer, one of NT's more powerful tools

SYMBOL	SEVERITY	DESCRIPTION
	Information	Describes the successful operation of an application, driver, or service.
	Error	A significant problem, such as loss of data or loss of functionality.
	Warning	An event that is not necessarily significant, but may indicate a possible future problem.

There are three ways to get to Event Viewer. The first is to click Start⇒ Programs⇒Administrative Tools⇒Event Viewer, and another is to click Start⇒ Run and type "eventvwr" into the command line. The third way is to type that same command at the command prompt. How ever you get there, the result will be similar to the screen shown in Figure E.4.

The NT Event Viewer maintains three separate event logs. These are the application log, the system log, and the security log. I've already mentioned that the application log is where Dr. Watson stores the event notifications that it generates when an application error occurs. The security log is used only if the system administrator has enabled a function called *auditing*. Auditing is a method by which a user's activities on the system can be tracked. A large number of events, including logon attempts, attempts to access system resources, and literally hundreds of others can be tracked in NT. It is the security log that hosts the event notifications that are generated by auditing.

The log that is used most frequently is the system log. Here is where situations relating to system and network performance can be analyzed. When an error is generated, an event message will be generated. There is frequently good information within this message relating to what caused the error.

executable   Any string of binary code that contains the machine language necessary to perform a function or run an application. If the microprocessor interprets the code as being a program, it is an executable. Most executable code can be identified by the extension used on a file name. For example, the extensions .COM, .EXE, and

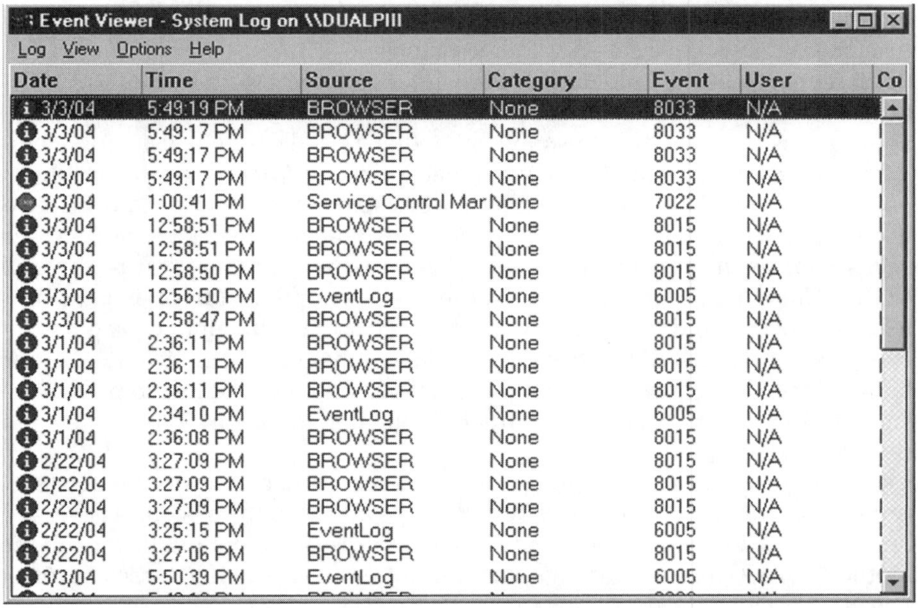

FIGURE E.4   The Windows Event Viewer.

.BIN all point to executable files; .APP points to an executable file on a Macintosh computer. However, the extension is not what makes it executable. Renaming NOVEL.DOC to NOVEL.COM will not make the document file an executable program. Likewise, not all executable programs contain exclusively a listing of commands. Comments and remarks can be added to the binary file to provide debugging or housekeeping functionality to the file.

executable marker   A 2-byte pointer in the MBR that directs the boot sequence to the first line of code for the primary kernel file of the OS installed. The executable marker is simply a sector address for the hard disk and does not contain executable code. A common attack for some early forms of virus was to erase or alter the executable marker so that the system could no longer launch the OS.

executive services   (also known as *native services*) A subset of operating system functions that form the application programming interface. Among these functions are:

- Device I/O
- Virtual memory management
- Multitasking
- Multiprocessing
- Process communication
- Security

User applications call on these services as required. As such, the applications can be said to run on the executive level. However, the applications don't directly interface with the executive services. They send their requests to an API, which in turn calls on executive services for assistance.

expanded memory   In the old days of MS-DOS, computers were limited to 1 MB of memory. The lower 640 K, known as *conventional memory*, was where applications ran. Anything the application didn't need could be used for user data. The 384-K space above conventional, known as *high memory*, was the place for system data. Early computers were able to add memory above 1 MB by using expanded memory. Address spaces above the first megabyte of RAM were accessed through a technique described in the *expanded memory specification* (EMS). Under early versions of EMS, there was a limit of 8 MB of expanded memory and it could be used only for storing data. It could not be used for executing programs. EMS 4.0 and later allowed the running of executables and bumped the limit up to 32 MB. While operating systems continue to provide support for expanded memory, virtually all memory above 1 MB is now accessed through *extended memory*.

expansion bus   A collection of circuits on a motherboard, along with associated protocols, that allows accessory devices to be added to the system. These devices come in the form of printed circuit boards that mount into slots on the motherboard. Over the years, a number of different expansion busses have come and gone. Among these are:

- Industry Standard Architecture (ISA)
- VESA Local Bus (VLB)
- Peripheral Components Interconnect (PCI)
- PCI-X
- PCI Express
- Accelerated Graphics Port (AGP)

The expansion bus straddles several of the primary system busses, including the *address bus*, the *power bus*, and the CPU bus. Figure E.5 shows a typical expansion bus on a motherboard. Technically speaking, the expansion bus isn't limited to just the cards that you can install. USB and Firewire devices also fall under the definition of expansion ports.

Explicitly Parallel Instruction Computing (EPIC)   A processor architecture that allows multiple CPUs to execute code and instructions in parallel, without the need for complex on-die circuitry. In order for a computer to take full advantage of the technology, the applications must be written with EPIC in mind. Instructions are coded for execution in multiple operations wherever possible. This allows a single instruction to be handled by multiple execution units, such as exist in the multiprocessing environment. These execution units are managed by the compiler and not by the processor's control unit. Multiple instructions are grouped together in a bundle. Along with the instructions, the bundle also includes information that shows dependency factors along with pointers to show what instructions are linked with what. This, coupled with multibranch prediction, allows for two or more processors to work on the same set of instructions at the same time.

Extended Capability ID   Information programmed onto a PCI device that defines any enhanced features beyond the basic features of its device class that it may support. This information resides in a header stored in the firmware of the device.

FIGURE E.5   *The expansion bus consists of all those slots you see on the motherboard, as well as additional ports such as your USB and Firewire sockets.*

extended memory   *See* **expanded memory**.

extended partition   Disk drives may be divided into partitions the way a house is divided into rooms. In a *basic disk* there can be four primary partitions and one extended partition. The extended partition is a secondary partition defined in the partitions tables, which can be subsequently divided into logical drives. Although there can only be one extended partition, there can be numerous logical drives. In Microsoft operating systems prior to Windows 2000, the number of logical drives was limited to the number of letters in the alphabet. However, more recent versions allow *volume mount points* to identify a logical drive. The mount point can be given any name that the file system in use deems legal, and can point to a place on the same physical drive or to a different drive altogether.

Extensible Firmware Interface (EFI)   Software that acts as an interpreter between the firmware installed on a piece of hardware and a computer's operating system. EFI started out as a brainchild of Intel as a method of limiting the negative impact that the system's reliance on BIOS had in an era where technological advances were happening much faster than BIOS manufacturers could keep up. The EFI interface defines the boot services of the system, including information regarding various bootable devices, system busses, and file systems. In addition, basic device drivers for nonspecific hardware common to most PCs are included. The driver interface is designed to be processor-independent so that the same interface can be used on different platforms. Because of this, many devices, including graphics and network, enjoy rudimentary support until the advanced drivers specific to the OS are loaded after the boot process is complete.

external data bus (EDB)   (1) The wires that move data from outside the CPU to the internal registers of the CPU. The external data bus is generally seen as divided between the *frontside bus* and the *backside bus*. The frontside bus interfaces with the chipset and system RAM, whereas the backside bus links up to L1 and onboard L2 cache. (2) The busses that exist between a computer and its peripherals. These would include Firewire and USB devices along with serial and parallel ports.

external host rate   Also known as the *external data transfer rate*. This a specification that measures how fast data moves from a drive's controller to RAM. Generally, the host rate can be measured in two ways. Burst rate is a measurement of how fast very small streams of data can move across the bus in an ideal world, with the transfer being the only process active on the system and the data is going downhill with a tailwind. A more accurate measurement of the external host rate is the device's sustained host rate. This is a measurement of the speed of data transfer when a large file is being moved and has to compete with other processes on the system for resources. As you might imagine, there is frequently a vast difference between burst and sustained rates.

F

failover   Clustered servers are frequently used as fault tolerant resources. The idea is that two servers each hold identical data and provide identical services. One server acts as the primary server, and the other runs passively on the side, ready to kick in if the primary server fails. The process by which the backup server automatically kicks in after a primary server failure is called failover. One server fails, the other moves over. Failover should be periodically tested during off hours to make sure that the process will be successful in the event of an actual failure.

farad   The major measurement of a capacitor's ability to store energy. A farad is one *coulomb* (6.24×10^{18} electrons per second) of charge between the plates in a capacitor with a difference potential of 1 V. What this means is that, on a capacitor with a value of 1 farad, a voltage change of 1 V per second will result in a 1A current. In most DC circuits this is a tremendously large potential and only a few devices use capacitors that even approach this value. Most capacitors are measured in microfarads (1/1,000,000 of a farad). Some audio amplifiers use very large capacitors in their power supplies. Larger capacitors allow for cleaner amplification at very high output.

Fast SCSI   *See* **Small Computer Systems Interface**.

fatal exception   Any event that requires that the application generating the event be closed down. By definition, an exception is any unexpected value or response to a command or calculation. Most programs are fully capable of recovering from most exceptions they encounter. If the application can't recover from the error, it will pass it on to the operating system and ask it to resolve the problem. The OS has several different layers through which the exception can pass in an effort to resolve the issue. The fatal exception is the one that can't be recovered. These can include programming errors, such as a request to divide any number by zero, or a hardware event that returns a nonmaskable interrupt. Frequently, a fatal exception generated by the OS will result in a system lockup, requiring a restart.

fault tolerance   Computer systems and networks are very complex assemblies of a vast array of components. In a system or network in which any down time is unacceptable, it is necessary to find ways to prevent the failure of a single component to cause system failure. With a fault-tolerant system, you will never have any single point of failure. In the event that a component does fail, you should be able to isolate that part from the rest of the system and repair it without incurring down time. Equally important is the fact that the failure of one component doesn't result in the failure of other components in the chain. Fault tolerance can occur on a software level and on a hardware level. Software fault tolerance keeps the data from going away in the event of failure. Methods of software fault tolerance include RAID arrays, backup/recovery schema, and file recovery methods. Hardware fault tolerance requires that components that fail had a failover partner and that the failed component can be replaced on the fly. Devices that can be replaced in this fashion are said to be *hot swappable*. Hot swappable devices include power supplies, PCI components, memory, and hard disks. All Firewire and USB devices are considered to be hot swappable.

faux parity   In the old days of memory manufacture, a form of error detection commonly used was parity. With parity memory, there were 9 bits for each byte of data. The number of 1s in a byte of data was counted. If an even number of 1s was detected, the 9th bit was set to 1. If an odd number was detected, the bit was set to 0. Faux parity was a memory package that contained a null chip that fooled a system into thinking parity memory was installed, when in fact it was not. Faux parity offered nothing in terms of error detection.

fax board   An expansion device that can convert documents on a computer into a Group 3 fax document and then transmit it over a telephone line. A typical fax/modem is the most commonly seen implementation of this device and still sees a lot of use in areas of the country where high-speed Internet service is not available. A less common version of the fax board is a specialized multiline device installed in dedicated *fax servers*. These devices offer anywhere to two to twenty-four ports (for the price of a new midsized card).

fax server   This is a dedicated server or server application that transmits documents for a number of network users over a telephone wire or Internet service to another user's fax machine or fax application. Because of the processing load and bandwidth demands of a fax server, it is most common to see a dedicated server assigned to faxing functions on a network. Fax servers can work over conventional analog telephone lines or can connect to a digital connection, such as a T1 line. While it is possible to construct a fax server that accesses only a single telephone line, that sort of defeats the purpose. Most fax servers incorporate a fax board that features two or more separate connections for telephone lines. With only a single port installed, if any fax is in progress (either incoming or outgoing), incoming faxes will be blocked and the device trying to connect will receive a busy signal. Outgoing faxes will simply be queued and sent out when the port is no longer busy. With a multiport board, when either an incoming or an outgoing signal is detected, the fax board will automatically roll over to the next available port. Another advantage is that a fax server can queue outgoing faxes and send them out at a particular time. This allows the faxes to be transmitted at a time when rates are lower.

file   A collection of data that is intended to stay together and, if separated, renders the whole collection useless. Typically, to qualify as a file, a string of data needs to fulfill several criteria.

- It is a single sequence of 0s and 1s with a finite length.
- The data is permanently stored onto some form of nonvolatile storage medium.
- It can be located by way of a directory path, which identifies the primary directory and all subdirectories that lead to the file.
- A conventional file system, such as FAT32 or NTFS, can locate the data through its conventional means.

Typically, files are assigned attributes, which define certain characteristics or behavioral patterns of the data. Standard attributes include *hidden, read only*, *system*, and *archived*. Most file systems also allow the file to be assigned permissions that determine what users are able to do with the file.

File Allocation Unit   This is the number of hard disk sectors that are required for the smallest unit of data that a specific disk can store. This number is codependent on the file system used and the size of the partition that holds the cluster. Only data from a single file can occupy a cluster. Even if a cluster is 16 K in size and the file it holds is only 1 K, no other file can make use of the wasted 15 K. (*See* **disk slack**.) Tables F.1 through F.3 list some common file systems and their cluster sizes.

TABLE F.1
FAT16 specifications: file allocation unit size by partition size

PARTITION SIZE	FAT TYPE	CLUSTER SIZE
16 to 128 MB	12-bit	4 Sectors (Approximately 2 K)
128 to 256 MB	16-bit	8 Sectors (Approximately 4 K)
256 to 512 K	16-bit	16 Sectors (Approximately 8 K)
512 K to 1 GB	16-bit	32 Sectors (Approximately 16 K)
1 to 2 GB	16-bit	64 Sectors (Approximately 32 K)

TABLE F.2
FAT32 specifications: file allocation unit size by partition size

PARTITION SIZE	FAT TYPE	CLUSTER SIZE
<512 MB to 8 GB	32-bit	8 Sectors (Approximately 4 K)
8 to 16 GB	32-bit	16 Sectors (Approximately 8 K)
16 to 32 GB	32-bit	32 Sectors (Approximately 16 K)
32 to 2,048 GB	32-bit	64 Sectors (Approximately 32 K)

TABLE F.3
NTFS specifications: file allocation unit size by partition size

PARTITION SIZE	FAT TYPE	CLUSTER SIZE
0 to 260 MB	Metafile	1 Sector (512 bytes)
261 to 8 GB	Metafile	8 Sectors (Approximately 4 K)
8 to 16 GB	Metafile	16 Sectors (Approximately 8 K)
16 to 32 GB	Metafile	32 Sectors (Approximately 16 K)
32 to 2,048 GB	Metafile	64 Sectors (Approximately 32 K)

file control block (FCB)   A component of an operating system that stored specific information about each file that was opened by the system. This information included such items as creation and access dates, permissions, pointers to sector locations, and ownership information. In the old days of MS-DOS, under the OS default, the user could open only four files at any given time. By adding a line to the *CONFIG.SYS* file such as FCBS=16,0 this number could be increased (to 16 in this example) up to 255 open files. While increasing this number allowed more files to be opened at once, it also decreased the amount of memory that remained available for programs once the OS loaded. Today's operating systems continue to use FCBs to represent files, but aren't under such restrictive limitations.

file filter   An application that converts a file from one format to another. Documents created by one application might not be in the same format read by another application. For example, while Microsoft Word and WordPerfect are both very good word processors, they both use unique and different file formats. Fortunately, both include a file filter that allows a document from one to be used in the other.

file format   The structure your data assumes while stored on the system. Technically speaking, all data on a system is nothing more than a string of 0s and 1s. The computer needs to know where one file ends and the next one begins. In addition to this very simplified information, it also needs to know what kind of file it is. Word processing documents contain a completely different type of information than a graphics or music file. An executable file is almost exclusively binary data and includes no text. A pure ASCII text file is the opposite. It contains nearly all text with virtually no control data. As such, nearly every file format is represented by one or more *extensions* specific to the format. Most people familiar with computers already recognize .JPG as being a graphic file and .MP3 as being a music file. Renaming a text file with an MP3 extension won't change the type of file it is so the music player can read you to sleep with the story you just wrote. The file format is completely different. Each file format is defined by a set of specifications that dictate how data is encoded and how file data is integrated from control data. Because a file is really nothing more than a container for data, the structure of the container dictates how the data is used by an application. This is why a word processing document by one brand of word processor might be unreadable to another word processor. *File filters* are frequently available to convert files from one format to another.

file striping   *See* **bit striping**.

file system   The mechanism used by a computer system to map the specific locations of information stored in nonvolatile storage. On the most basic level, the file system keeps track of the names of each and every file stored on the system. As such, the length and structure of a file name is under direct control of the file system. It is also directly responsible for keeping track of where all the data is stored. File systems keep track of physical locations as well as logical locations. A physical location would be the specific head, track, and sector where the first bit of data for a file resides. A logical location might be a pointer to a location. For example, file systems can locate files stored on a network server, but they can't store the information about that file in local file tables. All media require the support of a file system. However, the file system used by a CD-ROM is different than that of a hard disk drive.

A typical file system is hierarchical, meaning it defines the location of data in layers. In a hierarchical system, a hard disk can be divided into partitions, which subsequently can be broken up into directories. Multiple subdirectories reside beneath the primary directories and files can reside beneath any directory or subdirectory. The file system keeps entries for every piece of data stored on the system that includes a lot of information about each file. Such information includes the location of data as described, but it also can include information such as file attributes and permissions. Some file systems allow data to be compressed and decompressed on the fly and some allow data to be encrypted and decrypted on the fly.

File systems can be *journaling* or *versioning* in nature. A journaling file system gets its name because it keeps a journal of all files. Before a change to any given file is written to the system, the journal entry for that file is updated with critical changes, such as file size, sector locations, and so forth. A versioning file system allows a file to exist in multiple incarnations. When changes are made to the file and then saved, the original file is renamed and stored intact. This way if the user decides that the changes weren't for the better, she can go back to an earlier version. Most versioning file systems allow the user to configure how many versions to keep before overwriting the oldest version. Table F.4 lists a number of commonly seen file systems with a brief description of each.

TABLE F.4
File naming convention specifications

FILE SYSTEM	OS	FILE NAME LENGTH	DATABASE
FAT12	Microsoft	8.3*	File allocation tables
FAT16	Microsoft	8.3	File allocation tables
FAT32	Microsoft	255†	File allocation tables
NTFS	Microsoft	255	Master file table
HPFS	IBM‡	256	Metafile database
HFS	Apple	255	Unicode database
ISO 9660	Multi	Varies§	Descriptor database
UDF Plain	Universal	255	Block mapping
UDF VAT	Universal	255	Block mapping
UDF Spared	Universal	255	Block mapping with sparing table

* File name was limited to eleven characters, but a maximum of eight could be used for the file name, with three characters reserved for the extension.

† There were 255 characters included the file extension, which can be any length.

‡ Jointly developed between Microsoft and IBM, but IBM retained ownership after the partnership was dissolved. Early Microsoft products included some support for HTFS.

§ ISO 9660 defines three levels of file name. A Level 1 file name emulates the MS-DOS 8.3 file name. A Level 2 file name loosely emulates the long file names supported by FAT32 and NTFS, but must include a 1-byte counter along with file name byte counter. This typically limits ISO 9660 files to 155 to 160 characters.

File Transfer Protocol   More commonly known as FTP, this is one of the many protocols of the TCP/IP suite. FTP is used for exchanging larger files between devices on a network or the Internet. FTP is a connection-based protocol in that each system will negotiate with one another to arrive at a connection speed and protocol suite. FTP makes use of one of several error correction algorithms to assure error-free transmission of data. FTP operates over port 21 to accept incoming connections and port 20 for outgoing. A client will open a random port above port 1023 for the actual transmission of data, and this random port will be bound to port 20 for the duration of that session. On a future session a different port above 1023 is likely to be chosen.

For FTP to work, one device acts as a client and the other as a server. An FTP client opens a session in order to store or retrieve data on an FTP server. All modern network operating systems provide options for configuring a server as an FTP server. FTP client software can provide some very effective browsing functions once the connection has been made. However, FTP can also be run from a command prompt.

Users access the FTP servers in one of two ways. Anonymous login allows any user to attach to the FTP server. Secure login requires that the user provide a user name and password. Once a session has been initiated, a user can manipulate files on the server remotely using a variety of commands. This includes copying and deleting files, editing and renaming files, and so forth. In order to prevent unauthorized access to files, the server administrator may prevent anonymous logins or may limit anonymous logins to specific directories on the server. Various authorization levels can be configured to limit access to other directories.

firewall   A device or piece of software that examines all traffic going in or out of a network and uses a preconfigured set of rules to determine whether or not that data is allowed to pass. Firewalls can either be a dedicated piece of hardware or simply software running on a system. The name is derived from a fire-fighting term in which an impenetrable and inflammable barrier is placed between an uncontrolled fire and the undamaged area. The idea was that the barrier will stop the uncontrolled fire in its tracks. Sometimes it even works.

Configuration of a firewall is based on the assumption that packets entering a network can either be trusted or they can't. Trust level is determined by examining each packet as it passes through the firewall and looking for specific information. First-generation firewalls use simple packet filtering. Packets could be filtered by protocol, IP address, or MAC address. Packets must conform to a set of rules in order to pass. Either a preconfigured set of default rules can be used or an administrator can set a specific group of rules. Any packet that doesn't follow all the rules gets blocked. Blocking a protocol is as simple as blocking the *TCP/IP port* assigned to the protocol.

The weak point in the process was that once a connection was enabled, it could be hijacked and taken over by an intruder. The next generation of firewalls incorporated stateful packet filtering. This technology incorporates the same levels of packet filtering but also examines the status of the connection. This allows the firewall device to determine if a particular connection is identical to the one it allowed to originate. Application layer firewalls take this to the next step. They can examine the packets for the protocol used to generate the packet and then determine if the correct port is being used for the transmission. This allows the device to detect when a protocol is being used to redirect data through a nonstandard port that was inadvertently left open.

Most modern operating systems incorporate some form of software-level firewall in their design. Most of these offer multiple options for the default rules. A high security implementation will block just about any traffic from outside the network. Medium lets most traffic through as long as it is on the conventional port for the defined protocol. Low security lets just about anything through. However, the user will be prompted for each new connection and asked whether to allow or deny the traffic. Along with the request for permission will be some variation of the question, "Do you want to apply this rule to all traffic of this nature?" If you answer "Yes," you are effectively setting a custom rule. A newly installed firewall can drive you batty with the constant barrage of "Allow/deny" requests.

Firewire   The term is a registered trademark for Apple Computer Corporation's implementation of IEEE 1394. This is a high-speed serial SCSI connection used to connect external devices. (There is a set of specifications for IEEE 1394 backplanes defined, but you rarely see them installed on a system.) The original Firewire specifications called for a 400 Mb/s, whereas recent implementations of the bus extend that speed to 800 Mb/s. Firewire is fully Plug and Play-compliant and is hot swappable by design. Up to 63 devices can be hooked up to a single chain.

The Firewire cable is a six-conductor cable (Figure F.1). Four of the conductors carry signal and the other two are power connectors that can supply up to 45 W of power. Each device that is added will automatically configure itself and all devices will share a single set of resources (as well as the total bandwidth

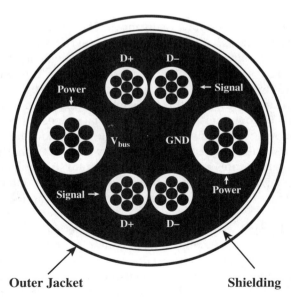

FIGURE F.1   This cross-section of a Firewire cable shows the function of each of the six conductors. In-diagram abbreviations are as follows: D+ Data signal, positive; D– Data signal, negative; GND Ground; V_{bus} Virtual bus.

available.) To facilitate configuration, every Firewire device manufactured carries a unique 64-bit device identifier assigned by IEEE. A ROM chip on the device identifies any protocols the device supports, along with any unique capabilities. The maximum cable length for a single Firewire segment is 4.5 meters. Up to sixteen segments can be daisy-chained using external repeaters or active Firewire hubs.

firmware   Any software that is embedded onto a piece of hardware. Most devices attached to computers make use of some sort of firmware. The computer itself depends on the *BIOS chip*, which is a form of firmware. In earlier years, firmware resided on *read only memory* (ROM) chips and provided machine language instructions that told the computer how to communicate with the device. Faster computers required faster source material, and modern firmware resides on a form of *flash memory*. Not only is this medium faster, but it also allows the firmware to be updated as needed. It isn't uncommon for the firmware on a device to automatically update every time the device driver loads. This way updates are added regularly.

flat addressing model   A method of addressing in which there is only one level of address for every node on a network or on a storage device. All addresses are thrown into the same pool and a device has to dive in to find a specific address. Flat addressing has been used on a limited number of file systems, including an earlier version of the Apple OS. In a flat memory addressing model, there is no distinction between the addresses used for code or those used for user data or virtual memory. It's all one great big pile, and to find data, an application or device depends on the services of a controller chip to map the addresses.

flicker fusion   Motion pictures don't really move. They consist of a long sequence of individual still images that are displayed several times per second. If the rate is fast enough, the brain will cease to register the individual images and interpret the stream of images as a single flowing motion picture. The rate where individual frames cease to register is the *flicker fusion threshold*. If the motion picture is displayed at a frame rate below this threshold, it will appear jittery and ragged. This is the effect of the brain registering the individual frames. Once threshold has been reached, the moving image smooths out. Frame rates much beyond threshold do little to improve quality but can impose a heavy load on the hardware generating the images. Common rates are 15 frames per second (fps; considered slightly below flicker fusion, but acceptable for webcast motion picture content), 24 fps (the most common rate for computer images), and 30 fps (a motion picture industry standard).

floating height   The read/write (R/W) heads for magnetic drives, such as hard disks and floppy disks, do not actually come in contact with the platter. In fact, at the speed with which the disks rotate, to do so would cause permanent damage to the drive. The heads actually float on a cushion of air a few nanometers above the surface of the platter. The actual distance between the heads and the platter is the floating height. Another term for this specification is *head gap*. Since any contact between the head and the platter while the disk is spinning will result in a head crash, floating height is carefully monitored by most drives. If it drops below a certain point, the drive's controller will issue a warning. Figure F.2 illustrates the concept of floating height.

floating point unit (FPU)   Mathematical calculations can be classified into two types. An *integer operation* is a calculation involving whole numbers with no fractions or decimals. Once fractional numbers come into play, the system must

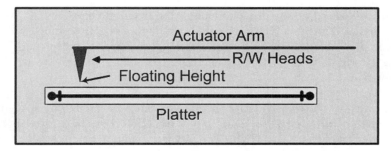

FIGURE F.2   *Floating height is the distance between the R/W heads on a drive and the platter while the drive is spinning.*

deal with a decimal point that can appear anywhere in the number. Fractions won't always be a convenient two places to the right of the decimal point. The FPU is a subcomponent of a microprocessor that is responsible for these more complex mathematical calculations. The FPU acts as the "scientific" calculator of the CPU. It does the more advanced math functions. In the early days of computing, the FPU was a separate processor called the *math coprocessor*. Starting with Intel's 80486 microprocessor, this chip was integrated onto the central die of the CPU. All CPUs feature at least one FPU, and the majority of processors manufactured today possess multiple FPUs. For example, the dual-core processors used on Macintosh computers feature 4 FPUs per processor. Other CPUs offer even more.

flow control   In an ideal world, when two devices need to communicate over the network, both devices would speak the same language and speak at the same speed. The reality of the situation is that different devices are capable of processing data at different rates. *Flow control* is a general term that refers to a variety of processes by which data is transferred between devices at a speed that is mutually acceptable and does not result in data loss. Flow control can be as simple as XON/XOFF, which is a method used in serial communication. One wire carries a signal that indicates that it is requesting permission to send data. When the other device is ready, it issues a clear to send (CTS) signal over a different wire. Data moves from one device to the other until the other device has as much data as it can handle. Then the receiving device drops the signal on the CTS wire. Transmission stops until the signal is restored.

A more complicated scheme is *sliding window*. With sliding window flow control, a certain number of packets are sent out and then the transmitting station sits back and waits for acknowledgment (ACK) packets to return for each packet it transmitted. If ACKs arrive for all transmitted packets, then the same number of packets is sent on the next transmission. If not, then the window is adjusted to the number of packets successfully transmitted on the previous transmission. The process continues.

flux reversal   Data is recorded onto magnetic media by applying a magnetic charge to the particles in the medium's coating. A recording head applies a small electrical current to a *bit cell* on the drive and aligns the magnetic particles. A flux reversal is a transition of magnet charge from a positive to a negative state, or vice versa. For example, the particles on the bit cell might be aligned to represent a 0. In copying new data to that bit cell, the charge is reversed to indicate a 1. This is a flux reversal.

fogging   A technique of implying distance in an image by making objects that are farther away less distinct. A graphics adapter can generate fog by applying changes to the *alpha channel* in 32-bit color. In nature, this occurs because particles in the atmosphere tend to disperse light. The farther you are from an object, the more dispersion there is. Software developers emulate this effect by using a fog gradient. As perceived distance increases, so does the intensity of the fogging effect.

font   Specifically, a font is a set of symbols that represents a specific character set for a specific typeface. Whereas a typeface is any collection of alphanumeric symbols that share a particular style, a single typeface can consist of multiple fonts. Each stylistic variation, such as **bold** or *italic*, represents a separate font within a typeface. Size is another stylistic variation that separates fonts. A 10-point Times New Roman font is different from a 12-point Times New Roman font, even though both character sets represent the same typeface. As you might imagine, a single typeface can be represented by hundreds of fonts.

form factor   This term is used in different ways between different industries. In engineering and design it refers to a preconfigured size, orientation, and design layout for a particular component used in order to assure compatibility among manufacturers. It basically defines that packaging of a specific component. A computer enclosure may be a desktop, a tower, a rack-mounted system, or a blade. This is one factor that defines the enclosure's form factor. On a motherboard, orientation of expansion slots in relation to memory slots and CPU sockets can define form factor, as well as other physical characteristics such as size and location of connectors. In order for two devices to coexist, both of them must feature mutually compatible form factors. In short, you don't shove a round plug into a square receptacle.

fractional T1   If you refer to the entry on T lines, you will see that a T1 line consists of twenty-four 64-Kb/s data transmission channels, yielding 1.544 Mb/s total throughput. T1 lines are also dedicated lines that are available full time to the leaser. For an organization or individual that needs a dedicated telecommunications link but doesn't need that much bandwidth, many telecoms offer the 64-Kb channels in groups. The most commonly offered options are four channels (totaling 256 Kb/s bandwidth) and six channels (offering 384 Kb/s). T1 lines can carry voice or data, or the channels can be isolated to carry both voice and data. While fractional T1 is still an available option, services such as DSL are rapidly moving in on its territory.

fragmentation   When files are repeatedly opened, modified, and then closed, it is not uncommon for a single file to be stored in multiple hard disk sectors spread apart on the hard disk. This is fragmentation. Fragmentation can lead to degraded performance and should be corrected. Defragmentation utilities, such as Microsoft's Defrag, will restore files to contiguous sectors on the drive.

frame   (1) Motion pictures are nothing more than an extended series of still photographs representing a fraction of a second in time for the subject being filmed. Each individual image is a frame. When played back, the sequence of still images is displayed in a rhythmic fashion, with several different images showing in a second. The number of images displayed in a second comprise the *frame rate*. Video cards in a computer have to be able to process these frames in a timely manner and display them smoothly and seamlessly or the motion picture will jitter.

(2) In data transmission, large blocks of data are broken down into smaller pieces before they are sent over the wire. Each chunk of data is bundled in a process called *encapsulation* with control information that provides addressing, flow control, and other protocol-specific information. Each parcel of data, along with its control information, makes up a single frame.

(3) In a computer enclosure, the frame consists of the primary support members that maintain the shape of the enclosure. The frame is encased in a skin of metal or plastic panels that makes the enclosure more attractive.

frame buffer   This is dedicated memory installed on a graphics adapter that holds the next fully bit-mapped image that will be displayed in the time that the current image frame is on the screen. Most video cards currently manufactured have a frame buffer for one completed screen and another that the card will use to assemble the next screen. For even faster video throughput, it is possible to buy dedicated frame buffers. These are hardware devices installed alongside a video card that accepts an offloaded frame from the card and holds it in memory until it is time to feed it to the monitor. Since this allows faster image processing, higher frame rates are possible, leading to smoother animation.

frame rate   The number of times per second that an imaging device, such as a video card, can process and display individual frames of a motion picture. Frame rate must be selected judiciously. If it is too slow, the motion picture will drop below the *flicker fusion threshold* and will appear rough and jittery. A very fast frame rate leads to smooth animation, but if it is too fast, it can impose a heavy load on the hardware generating the frames. The motion picture industry films at either 30 or 60 frames per second (fps). However, broadcasting or recording at the maximum rate can make it difficult to transfer the images to the screen fast enough. A process called *interlacing* cheats the speed by displaying every other line on the screen during one frame, and the alternating lines on the next screen. Although this maintains speed while reducing overhead, it has a negative impact on quality. *Progressive* scanning displays every line of every frame.

frame relay   A packet-switching WAN protocol that makes use of layer 2 networking services. With frame relay, data is sent out in variable-sized data blocks called *frames* (thus the name). The data frames offer no data correction services. However, a frame check sequence is added to each frame to allow the detection of errors. This sequence is a variation of *CRC*. If errors are found, the offending frame is simply dropped. It is the responsibility of the end points to manage errors. The fact that a frame was dropped gets communicated to the transmitting device and the frame gets retransmitted.

Service providers can make use of a variety of media to carry frame relay; however, the most commonly used are T1 and fractional T1. This allows for transmission speed of up to 1.44 Mb/s. Regardless of the medium used, the service provider will set up a *virtual circuit* for each communications session. For any given session, a route is determined through the fastest available circuits between communicating stations. Once the session is over, the circuit is broken down. The next communications session between those same two hosts will most likely involve a completely different route, depending on circuit conditions that exist at the time.

fraudmeisters   A slang term for anyone who actively commits illegal acts, either for fun or profit. There is a certain *class* of person for whom an honest dollar just isn't appealing. If there isn't a dirty way to earn a buck, then that buck just isn't worth earning.

frequency   The number of times in a specifically defined timer interval an event occurs. The usual measurement is in hertz (Hz): 100 Hz is 100 times per second, 1,000 Hz is 1,000 times per second. Other measurements frequently seen are frames per second (fps), revolutions per minute (rpm), and beats per minute (bpm). In a computer, frequency measurements are greatly impacted by the accuracy of the clock crystals used by the system.

frequency response   A measurement of a device's ability to accurately record or play back sound over a wide frequency range. It is measured in hertz (Hz) and will be offered in a range from the lowest to the highest frequency reproducible. For example, a speaker might be advertised as having a frequency response of 20 to 20,000 Hz. The usefulness of this measurement is entirely dependent on the range of acceptable output (in decibels or dB) of the signal at the measured ranges. For example, two speakers might be advertised as having 20–20KHz frequency responses. However, one of them specifies that the measurements were taken within an acceptable range of plus or minus (±) 3 dB. The other is measured at ±20 dB. A 20-dB drop in amplitude will render the signal much more quietly than a 3-dB drop. Therefore, a usable frequency response measurement will include the decibel range. To put this in perspective, a young person still in her teens might be able to sense a 20–20KHz range. However, sound sensitivity drops greatly as a person ages. If you measure that same person 40 years later, she'll be lucky to have a 40–14 KHz range in her hearing.

frontside bus (FSB)   This is a bidirectional data port on a CPU that moves data between the computer's chipset and the processor. On a computer that has external L1 cache, the cache will also be connected through the FSB. The FSB is measured in both bit width and clock speed in order to calculate overall bandwidth. A typical Pentium-class CPU has a 64-bit FSB. Its clock speed will be measured from 100 MHz to as much as 1,333 Mhz. Some caution must be taken in the actual value of some higher clock speeds. Most modern CPUs now use *quad-pumped* data busses. This means that the CPU has actually been endowed with four separate FSBs. On the aforementioned 1,333-Mhz FSB, it is actually

4×333 Mhz. As long as the operating system and all of the applications running on the OS have been written to take advantage of a quad-pumped FSB, the user will enjoy the maximum bandwidth. Some older applications may not be able to take advantage of the technology; however, the system will still benefit by allowing other applications to make use of the available pipelines.

FTP server   A server or server application that stores large files and makes them available for distribution over the network or Internet by way of the *file transfer protocol*. *See* **FTP**.

full backup   This term would appear to reference a complete and total backup of all data on a hard disk. In reality, a full backup does *not* copy all files on the hard disk. Certain system files, including the registry, are not copied, and a full backup will not include the MBR or FAT. Also, any files that are opened by a user won't be backed up. Files copied during a full backup will have the archive bit in the file header reset to zero.

full duplex   The ability to send and receive data in either direction, moving both directions at the same time. Your cell phone is a device that makes use of full-duplex operation. Full duplex can be engineered into a device in two ways. One method used by Ethernet networks uses a separate set of conductors for each direction of communication. Wireless communication techniques more commonly use frequency-division duplexing. This places each direction of a separate channel to prevent overlap.

full height   A term that describes an external drive bay that is 3.5" from top to bottom and 5.75" wide. The majority of external drive bays on computers manufactured today are either half-height (1.75" × 5.75") or one inch (1" × 4"). However, some devices still manufactured, including many tape drives, are full-height devices. A full-height bay can usually be made from two adjacent half-height bays by removing a small divider on either side of the enclosure.

Fully Qualified Domain Name   FQDN for short; this is an identification of an Internet location that completely describes the path to that location, including the root domain, the top-level domain, and all subdomains. Included in the path will be the name of the host. An FQDN can be distinguished from a generic domain name by the fact it will be concluded with a period at the end. For example, http://www.mwgraves.com is an example of a valid domain name. The URL http://photographs.mwgraves.com. represents the FQDN for the photographs node in that domain.

fuse   An electrical component that consists of a filament that vaporizes when more than a certain amount of current tries to pass. Fuses come in three basic forms. A cartridge fuse is a glass or ceramic tube encasing the filament in a vacuum. Plug fuses either screw into a socket or plug into terminal. The idea is that if current reaches a critical point, a device is protected by removing the source of the potential damage (i.e., the electricity itself). The common sentiment among many electricians and engineers is that all too often a fuse will protect itself by blowing the circuit first.

G

gamma A term referring to the relative brightness of an image. When displaying an image on a monitor, the relative intensity of any value should be directly dependent on the input voltage. If we were living in the perfect world, all devices would have a gamma of 1. This would suggest a totally linear relationship between input voltage and brightness. In reality, brightness values exhibit a curve with a distinct *toe* and *shoulder*. The toe represents darker values that flatten out with lower voltages because the monitor is not sufficiently sensitive to separate the darker values generated by close values. The shoulder represents the brighter values that can't be separated.

gamut The total range of color hues an imaging device can either display or print. All devices derive their hues by mixing either the *primary colors* (red, green, and blue) or the *subtractive colors* (cyan, magenta, and yellow). In the real world, there is no limit to the theoretical number of colors that can be generated by mixing these colors. People and devices are much more limited in scope than nature. The average human being with good eyesight can discern approximately 10,000 different hues. A graphics adapter using 24-bit color can render over 16 million colors. A computer monitor, however, might be able to render 50,000 to 60,000 different colors (as measured by electronic sensors) while a printer is liable to be more limited in gamut than the human eye.

gate A low-level bit of logic used by microprocessors to crunch data. Programmers make use of the logic gates that I discussed earlier to filter electrons through a circuit in such a way that they cause the final switches to fall into a position that will be interpreted as the answer we're looking for. More simply put, the results of turning on or off one set of switches can be made to affect how another set of switches gets positioned. The simple logic gates are described here.

The NOT gate This is, by far, the simplest of gates. A NOT gate looks at the position of a single switch and outputs the exact opposite value to the target switch. Therefore, as you can see in Table G.1, a bit set at zero that moves through a NOT gate will be outputted as a 1. Conversely, a 1 will emerge as a zero.

TABLE G.1
The NOT gate

SWITCH NO. 1	TARGET SWITCH
0	1
1	0

The AND gate   This gate takes the positions of two different switches and compares them. Then, depending on whether or not there is a match, either a zero or a 1 gets sent to the next level. Take a look at Table G.2. If switch no. 1 and switch no. 2 are both 1, then the value 1 will be sent to the target switch. Any other combination will set the target switch to zero.

TABLE G.2
The AND gate

SWITCH NO. 1	SWITCH NO. 2	TARGET SWITCH
0	0	0
0	1	0
1	0	0
1	1	1

The OR gate   The OR gate looks at the values in switches no. 1 and no. 2 and if either switch, or if both switches, are set to 1, the value of 1 will be directed to the target switch. Table G.3 illustrates the possible combinations.

TABLE G.3
The OR gate

SWITCH NO. 1	SWITCH NO. 2	TARGET SWITCH
0	0	0
0	1	1
1	0	1
1	1	1

These are the basic three logic gates. Other logic gates that are occasionally described include the NAND gate and the NOR gate. These are achieved simply by combining either an AND gate with a NOT gate or an OR gate with a NOT gate. Therefore, in reality, they are actually two separate gates being used simultaneously. Logic gates may seem complicated at first, but the way they work is actually elegantly simple. The position of two (or more) switches has the effect of determining the position of other switches, generating a new bit of information.

gateway   (1) Any device or interface on a computer network that interfaces with another network. By default, hosts on a network can only communicate with other hosts on the same network. Therefore, in order to send and receive messages from beyond, there has to be a portal. Various devices that can act as gateways include secondary network interface cards installed in a computer, routers, layer 3 switches, and bridges. (2) An IP address in the TCP/IP configuration of a computer that points to the device on the network that acts as a portal to the outside world. This is sometimes called the *default gateway*. (3) When capitalized, a service running on Microsoft operating systems that interfaces with a Novell NetWare network. The Gateway Services protocol runs on a Windows 2000 (or later) computer and provides cross-platform support.

gauge   (1) An instrument of measurement. Gauges are used to measure air or hydraulic pressure, temperature, and a myriad of other things. (2) A measurement of the thickness or diameter of a substance such as sheet metal or wire. Larger numbers indicate smaller sizes.

geek   An individual whose life revolves around technical toys and trickery. A typical geek can tell you every single detail about his computer, but has no idea how to fix an omelet. Geeks can be subdivided into hardware geeks and software geeks (more commonly known as *hackers*). The hardware geek will tell you about every single video card on the market with a Amazatronics chipset and Draconics memory, while the software geek will bore you with every detail of the APIs each card supports. The archetypical geek is unattractive, has bad manners, and no social life. His last date was to take himself to dinner and make sure his other half had a good time. His after-dinner chitchat centers on how many transistors the next Intel CPU is reputed to have. Don't ask a geek to update you on baseball scores. He has no idea what baseball is. A geek's idea of a good time is sitting in an easy chair writing computer encyclopedias (Figure G.1).

FIGURE G.1   A typical geek at work on an encyclopedia of computer terminology. (Photo by Christopher Graves).

general protection fault (GFP)   Intel processors are designed with a number of features that prevent them from doing unwanted things, such as actually provide an answer when you ask it to divide by zero. These protection mechanisms include such things as memory address protection, IRQ monitoring, maskable and nonmaskable interrupts, and a number of other things. Most protection mechanisms amount to a firmly enforced set of rules that applications and data must adhere to. When one of these rules is broken, the CPU will stop executing that thread and generate a protection fault. Most GPFs result in the offending application shutting down, while the system and other applications remain unaffected. Unfortunately, even with today's modern CPUs, only one GPF can be managed at a time. If a second fault occurs before the processor recovers from the first, then a double fault will result and the processor will shut down.

If you are running a Microsoft OS, you may have no way of knowing that your problem is the result of a GPF. Depending on the version of OS you happen to be running, you might be informed of an "Unrecoverable Application Error," an "Illegal Operation," or actually be told that you've experienced a "General Protection Fault." Likewise, you may learn that the program you're running "Has Encountered a Problem and Needs to Close," that your program "Will Now Close," or that your program "Has Stopped Responding." Unix and Linux are a little more intelligent in their error-reporting methods and will actually tell you if your problem is memory- or CPU-related.

General Public License (GPL) Most software distributed in the world is of a commercial nature. You do not own the code or the software, but rather the right to run the software on your computer. The right to run an application is your *license.* Every product ships with some form of license, specifically spelling out your rights under the agreement and what you may not do with the software. Among the restrictions you are likely to encounter are the number of computers onto which you may install the software, what (if any) changes you can make, and what rights (if any) you have to redistribute the software. There is rather vociferous support for developers to make software available on the market for no charge. However, even free software comes with restrictions. The General Public License restricts a developer from adding restrictions to software. GPL assures that software released under its protection may be freely distributed and modified, or that slices of code from a GPL-licensed program may be used within other programs to add features or interactive support. No product that is protected under a GPL may be subsequently recompiled and released as a commercial product. The source code for all GPL-licensed software must be freely available to the public; in most cases, it defines limitations an individual or company has in charging support or distribution fees.

General Purpose Interface Bus (GPIB) Also known as IEEE-488, the GPIB was designed to interconnect computers to lab instruments and other peripherals. The standard was originally defined in IEEE document 488, entitled *Standard Digital Interface for Programmable Instrumentation*, released in 1987. GPIB requires a specific interface, which is not standard on most computers. Therefore, an adapter card must be installed and configured in the host computer. The twenty-four-pin interface makes use of sixteen conductors and transfers data in a parallel configuration. Eight conductors transfer data; three are to transmit and receive handshake signals to keep the devices in synch, and the other five manage various control signals. The remaining eight conductors are ground wires.

Up to fourteen devices can be connected to a single GPIB bus and will share a 200-KB bandwidth. One of these devices will be the actual controller. Only one device other than the controller can be active at a time. While this isn't a blazingly fast throughput, the interface was originally designed for devices that transferred a minimum amount of data. The biggest limitation wasn't its bandwidth, but rather the fact that the cable was limited to approximately 3 meters.

general registers   In the course of processing, it is likely that the same set of data is going to be massaged by a number of different instructions. The general registers are the data storage areas within the CPU where data is being stored as they are processed. The registers consist of a collection of interfaced transistors that store binary values by placing specific transistors in either an ON position or an OFF position. When the transistor is ON, it registers a binary value of 1; it measures a value of 0 when OFF. The number of bits that are used to comprise a register is dictated by the architecture of the CPU. A 64-bit processor has registers that are 64 bits wide. In order to make a processor backwardly compatible with legacy operating systems and applications, registers can be subdivided. When running 16-bit code, the CPU will remap its registers as 16-bit units and process data accordingly. Early processors, such as the 80286, featured a total of sixteen general registers. More recent 64-bit designs, such as the Itanium, have 128 general registers. Table G.4 lists the primary general registers for the x86 processors. Modern processors still use these same registers; they just use a lot more of them. The x64 processors use similar registers.

TABLE G.4
The general registers of an i386-class microprocessor

REGISTER	OPERATIONS
AX	Full word multiplication, full word division, full word I/O
AL	Byte multiplication, byte division, byte I/O, translation, floating point operations
AH	Byte multiplication, byte division
BX	Translation
CX	String variables, loops
CL	Variable shift and rotate
DX	Full word multiplication, full word division, indirect I/O
SP	Stack operations
SI	String variables
DI	String variables

GET request   An FTP command that is used to copy a single file from the remote host to the local machine. The correct syntax for the command is *get filename.ext*. For example, if there is a file on the server called encyclopedia.doc and you wanted to download it via command line FTP, you would type get encyclopedia.doc and press <Enter>.

gigabit   In binary, this is 10^9 bits, or 1,073,741,824 bits. In decimal alliteration it is one billion bits.

gigabyte   In binary, this is 10^9 bytes, or 1,073,741,824 bits. In decimal alliteration it is one billion bytes.

gigaflop   A measurement of CPU performance that defines the number of floating point operations (in billions) the processor can do each second. This is a better measurement of a computer's performance than general clock speed because it actually measures how quickly the processor can perform specific functions. Two processors might both be rated at a clock speed of 3 GHz. However, other factors, including the instruction set, efficiency, and number of floating point units, can result in one of these processors being able to execute instructions or perform calculations faster than the other. Because a floating point calculation involves both execution and calculation, the number of these operations that a processor can perform in a second is a valuable measurement of performance.

GIGO   Garbage In, Garbage Out. This is an old bit of computer-industry jargon that takes the blame of computer errors off the computer and puts it back on the shoulders of the user. The phrase essentially means that the output of a computer is only as reliable as the data provided by the person at the keyboard.

Go-Back-N   A flow control method that requires that all packets arrive in sequence. It is an indigenous feature of the Automatic Repeat Request (ARQ) protocol. In Go-Back-N, a fixed number of packets is transmitted without waiting for an acknowledgment (ACK). The number of frames transmitted is known as the window size. Once all packets are transmitted, the sending device sits back and waits for the ACKs to come streaming in. If one packet is lost along the way or is rejected by the receiving computer, there will be no ACK. The protocol can count backward from the last packet it transmitted and retransmit only the affected packet and all subsequently received packets. There will be no necessity to retransmit successful packets.

H

half duplex A communications method by which a device can either transmit or receive, but cannot do both at the same time. While one device is transmitting, the other can only receive. It must wait for the medium to be dropped by the transmitting device before it can take ownership and begin its own transmission. In order to maintain some degree of control and assure that one device doesn't take over the medium, control mechanisms are in place on most protocols that use half duplex to assure that all communicating devices have an equal opportunity at the medium.

half-height bay A term that describes a disk drive that is 1.75" from top to bottom. The standard 5.25" drive bay on most computers is a half-height bay. Most CD-ROM and DVD drives occupy a half-height bay.

handshake The process two devices go through in order to agree on protocols used, connection speeds, and a number of other issues. Virtually all communications protocols make use of some form of handshaking. The secure socket layer (SSL) is an example. The SSL handshake protocol allows the exchange of data during connection establishment to be transmitted in encrypted form. This information includes user ID, password, along with both public and private encryptions keys (when necessary) in addition to standard agreements, such as connection speed.

hard fault A situation in which data sought by the CPU was neither in memory nor in the paging file. This is also occasionally referenced as a *major page fault*. A hard fault necessitates that a new hard disk search must be initiated. As a result, whatever program initiated the fault comes to an abrupt halt until the new data is loaded into memory.

hardware RAID An implementation of RAID that offloads the processing and memory requirements of RAID from the server hardware and OS to a dedicated controller. While hardware RAID can employ virtually any hard disk technology, the most common implementation is with *SCSI* or *SAS* drives. The chipset of the controller will dictate what forms of RAID are supported. Most advanced RAID controllers allow *nested RAID* configurations as well as the tried and true standards, such as RAID 0, 1, and 5. The RAID controller is equipped with a flash memory chip and a setup program that allows the administrator to set up the RAID configuration. Various parameters under the administrator's control include the RAID level, configuring parity, the size of data blocks used in striping, and the drive mapping configuration (consisting of device ID and logical unit numbers). Once the RAID array is configured and operational, the controller takes over the tasks of data striping, parity calculation, and so forth. Since the computer's processor isn't having to allocate precious resources and system memory for these processes, overall system performance is greatly improved.

harmonics Sound frequencies above the root frequency that are generated by an instrument or voice when a certain note is generated. The harmonics of a stringed instrument differ greatly from those of a brass instrument, which differ greatly from those of a woodwind. It's the harmonics that make a middle C played on a piano sound different than the same note played on a violin. Sound cards for a computer store digital samples of the harmonics of a variety of different sound sources and can apply them to any root frequency that a program generates. These sets of preprogrammed harmonics are called the *voices* of the sound card.

Hayes command set The common commands used to control modems. While there were other command sets in use by proprietary modems in the early days of computing, the Hayes command set was adopted as the industry standard. For many years, even if a modem was configured with a proprietary command set, it could be expected to be compatible with Hayes. This, in fact, is what is meant by a *Hayes compatible* modem. The Hayes extended command set increased the number of available commands by adding an ampersand before the command character. Table H.1 lists the commands typically used.

TABLE H.1
Hayes command set, including the extended set

COMMAND	FUNCTION
AT	Prefix for all commands except for A/ and the escape code. For example, the command DT would be typed ATDT.
A/	Repeat the last command issued (not to be preceded by AT)
A	The modem is set to answer mode and goes off hook immediately. Answer without waiting for ring.
Bn	Bell mode - set 1.200 bps protocol compatibility selects V.22 or Bell 212A in the 1,200 bps mode. n = 0, CCITT V.22 with 2,100-Hz Answer Back Tone. n = 1, Bell 212A with 2,225-Hz Answer Back Tone.
Cn	Where n = carrier state. C1 = carrier state on, C0 = carrier state off.

	Dial number. This command is typically used with a subcommand or trigger. It must be used in conjunction with a telephone number. By itself it accomplishes nothing.
	
	Dial trigger / Function
	  T / **Switch to** Touch Tone dialing
	  P / **Switch to** pulse dialing (rarely used anymore as pulse dial is all but extinct)
	  R / Reverse mode. Puts modem in answer mode immediately after dialing. Uses answer frequencies when originating a call.
	  S = n / Dial a stored number. The numbers are stored in the registers of the microcontroller.

(Continued)

TABLE H.1
(Continued)

COMMAND	FUNCTION
Dn	W / Wait for a continuous tone before dialing the next number. The amount of time to wait is configured in the S7 register @ / Wait for a "quiet answer"—one or more rings followed by 5 seconds of silence—for the length of time defined by register S7. , / (comma) Adds a pause in the dialing sequence equal to the value specified in register S8. The default time is 2 seconds. Adding another comma adds another pause. There is no limit. ! / This character will temporarily put the modem back on hook in order to get a new dial tone. ; / Return to command mode after dialing. This command can only be placed at the end of a dial command.
En	Echo modem command. Determines whether the modem returns data received in command mode to the host. E1 = echo on E2 = echo off
Fn	Full or half duplex operation. F1 = full duplex operation F2 = half duplex operation
Hn	Hook on or off H0 = on hook H1 = off hook
In	Request product code and ROM checksum. Return product ID/checksum. I0 prompts modem to send its three-digit product code. I1 performs and returns numeric checksum of firmware ROM. I2 performs checksum and returns result code. I3 returns ROM part number and revision level.
Ln	Adjusts modem speaker volume L0 = off L1 = low L2 = medium L3 = high
Mn	Speaker control. M0 = speaker is always off M1 = speaker is on when phone is off hook and off when connected to carrier M2 = speaker is always on M3 = speaker ON after dialing until carrier detected, then disables speaker when carrier signal is detected.

(Continued)

TABLE H.1
(Continued)

COMMAND	FUNCTION
On	On-line state. O0 = Online. O1 = Online with equalizer retrain sequence.
Qn	Quiet command for result codes. Result codes ON/OFF. n = 0, codes are sent n = 1, codes are NOT sent
Sn	Displays the contents of the modem's status register, where n = the register number.
Sn = x	Modify the contents of the S-registers n = S-register number x = value to set register to
Vn	Sets format for result codes. V0 = nonverbose. Use only numbers. V1 = verbose. Use text descriptions
Xn	Sets dialing mode and result code format for dial command. Enables extended result code and mode setting. X0 = basic (300 bps). Dial tone and busy signal not recognized. Result: codes 0-4 enabled. X1 = extended. Dial tone and busy signal not recognized. Result: codes 0-5 and 100 enabled. X2 = extended. Detects dial tone but not busy signals. Result: codes 0-6 and 10 enabled. X3 = extended. Does not detect dial tone, but does detect busy signal. Result: codes 0-5, 7, and 10 enabled. X4 = extended. Detects both dial tones and busy signals
Yn	Long Break Disconnect Option Y0 = disabled Y1 = enabled. Disconnects after preconfigured idle time (1.6-second default).
Z	Software modem reset.
&Cn	Data Carrier Detect handling. Enables DCD. &C0 = DCD always on. &C1 = DCD tracks data carrier detected by modem.
&Dn	Data Terminal Ready handling. Enables DTR. &D0 = modem ignores DTR line (RS-232 pin 20) &D1 = switches to command mode when DTR goes off &D2 = ignores DTR. Also hangs up, disables auto answer. &D3 = initializes modem when DTR goes off.

(Continued)

TABLE H.1
(*Continued*)

COMMAND	FUNCTION
&F	Resets modem to factory default &F0 = Hayes default &F1 = Factory default for PC-compatible &F2 = Factory default, MAC with software handshake &F3 = Factory default, MAC with hardware handshake
&Gn	Guard tone selection (used only when in CCITT modes) &G0 = no guard tones &G1 = 550 Hz guard tone &G2 = 1,800 Hz guard tone Used only outside the United States.
&Jn	Telephone jack selection &J0 = RJ-11/RJ-41S/RJ-45S &J1 = RJ-12/RJ-13
&K	Select form of flow control &K0 = disable flow control &K1 = RTS/CTS flow control &K2 = XON/XOFF flow control
&ln	Leased-line or POTS line selection &l0 = POTS operation &l1 = leased-line
&Mn	Asynchronous/Synchronous communication &M0 = asynchronous &M1 = synchronous mode 1 (Dial in asynchronous mode, then switch to synchronous operation) &M2 = synchronous mode 2 - stored number dialing &M3 = synchronous mode 3 - manual dialing
&Pn	Pulse dial make/break pulse length selection &P0 = 39% make, 61% break (United States and Canada standard) &P1 = 33% make, 67% break (European standard)
&Qn	Communications Mode options &Q0 means Idle State is normal, online state is asynchronous &Q1 means Idle State is normal, online state is reserved &Q2 Dial when DTR=1, Hang up when DTR-0, online mode is reserved $Q3 DTR = 0 is task mode, DTR = 1 is data mode, online mode is reserved.

(*Continued*)

TABLE H.1
(Continued)

COMMAND	FUNCTION
&Rn	Request to Send/Clear to Send handling (sync mode only) &R0 = CTS (RS-232 pin 5) tracks RTS (pin4) &R1 = modem ignores RTS and turns CTS on when ready to receive synchronous data
&Sn	Data Set Ready handling. Controls DSR. DRS ON indicates that the modem is connected to a communication channel and is ready. &S0, DSR is always ON. Modem forces DSR ON whenever modem is turned on &S1, DSR (RS-232 pin 6) operates according to EIA specs. DSR turned ON at start of handshaking, off in test mode, idle state, or when carrier is lost
&Tn	Control Test mode (not available in 300 bps mode) &T0 Ends current test and returns to command mode &T1 Initiates local analog loopback test &T3 Initiates local digital loopback test &T4 Prepares modem for a remote digital loopback when requested by another modem &T5 Blocks remote digital loopback &T6 Initiates remote digital loopback with another modem &T7 Initiates remote digital loopback with self-test &T8 Initiates local analog loopback with self-test
&V	Displays active configuration profiles, including S register settings, commands, and stored telephone numbers.
&Wn	Writes an active configuration to memory. Sends and stores acceptable values for certain commands and S registers to nonvolatile RAM. &W0, store active profile in location 0 &W1, store active profile in location 1
&Xn	Select synchronous transmit clock source (sync mode only) &X0 Internal clock, modem generates timing and sends through pin 15 &X1 Reroutes timing signal from pin 24 to pin 15. &X2 Modem obtains timing information from incoming signal and routes it to pin 15
&Yn	Select which stored profile to load on power-up &Y0 Select profile 0 on power up or hard reset &Y1 Select profile 1 on power up or hard reset
&Zn	Reset modem to specified profile, where n = the number of profile to be selected

head crash A critical issue relating to R/W heads is their floating height. In operation, the head does not actually come in contact with the platter. It floats on a cushion of air just a few nanometers above the surface of the platter. That distance is called the *floating height.* To put this in perspective, if the head were the size of an average two-story house that floated above the ground (and just try getting that to happen!), you wouldn't be able to slip a sheet of paper between the house and the ground.

In the event that the head and platter should come in contact with one another, the result is the infamous head crash. Head crashes are disastrous in that not only is the medium damaged, but the head, and therefore the hard drive, will almost certainly be destroyed. There are two things that can cause a head crash. The most common is the irate user kicking a misbehaving computer. The impact of foot against a computer while the disk is spinning can potentially kill the drive. A more uncommon cause is a piece of foreign material that somehow makes its way into the drive. Modern drives are so well sealed that this is an extremely rare event.

head gap The space between the recording and playback heads of a tape recorder and the medium onto which they record. The goal of most designers is to keep this gap as narrow as possible for two reasons. First of all, transcription accuracy is improved. This leads to fewer errors, and in the case of audio recordings, higher fidelity. Secondly, as the gap widens, the recorder's ability to accurately record high-frequency material is degraded.

head parking The entire time that a computer hard disk is operational, the platters are spinning at a fast rate (between 7,200 and 15,000 rpm with modern drives). The R/W heads float on a cushion of air a few nanometers above the spinning surface. When you turn off your PC and the platter stops spinning, that head is going to sit down on the platter no matter what you do. If it does this while the heads are spinning, the drive can easily be destroyed. Manufacturers have accordingly created a head-parking system, designing into the drive platters an area reserved solely for the purpose of providing the head a safe place to sit when the PC is not in operation. This is the *landing zone.* The location of the landing zone is one of the hard disk configuration settings of the BIOS. However, all modern hard drives are designed in such a way that the BIOS can automatically detect the necessary parameters.

In the early days of computer technology, it was up to the user to properly park the heads when the PC was powered down. MS-DOS had a head-parking utility just for that purpose. Fortunately for us, it has been many years since that's been necessary. Hard drives now automatically park themselves as part of their shutdown procedure. This is good, but IBM's approach is better. It uses a process called *load/unload.* When a power-down is in process, the heads are lifted into the air. Instead of dropping the heads onto the surface of the platter, IBM drives slide the actuator arms onto a restraining mechanism, which prevents the heads from ever coming into contact with the platter.

heat sink compound This is a silicone-based grease that you apply to the surface of the CPU before adding the heat sink. Proper use of heat sink compound greatly enhances the ability of the cooling system to dissipate heat. Improper use, or lack of any compound at all, is very likely to lead to CPU overheating. Some heat sink/ fan combinations have a thin layer of compound applied to the heat sink. The heat of the CPU will melt the compound and cause it to form a good seal. With other CPUs, the substance must be applied from a small tube. Figure H.1 shows heat sink compound being applied to a CPU.

FIGURE H.1   Heat sink compound is a necessary addition for most CPUs.

helical scan   With a helical-scan record head, the tape wraps around the head, much the same way video recorders transport tape. Then the data is recorded onto the entire width of tape, treating it as one really wide track. The result is that a significantly larger amount of data can be recorded per square inch of tape. The reason for doing this is that, in order to get sufficient signal density on the medium using conventional recording methods, the tape would have to move past the heads at a very high rate of speed. In order to hold a significant amount of data, tapes would have to be very long. Devices that use helical scan technology include VHS recorders, digital audio tape (DAT), and advanced intelligent tape (AIT).

hexadecimal   Dealing with binary by itself can be a little cumbersome. If you had 8 bytes of data that you wanted to communicate to another technician, you might finding yourself writing something along the lines of 0110 1111, 1100 0000, 0001 1010, 1110 0000, 1011 0001, 0000 0001, 1001 0001, 1111 0000. Now, memorize that, walk down the hall to the next office, and recite it to your coworker.

A byte consists of 8 bits. If you divide a byte into two *nibbles*, there will be two 4-bit chunks to deal with. Hexadecimal provides a single character that represents each possible combination of 4 bits. Two raised to the fourth is 16, so if we want to come up with a character set based on base 16, there must be a total of 16 symbols. The numerical symbols 0 to 9 cover the first 10, and the remainder are represented as the alphabetic symbols A through F. Therefore, in base16 you count 0, 1, 2, 3, 4, 5, 6, 7, 8, 9, A, B, C, D, E, and F.

There are several different places where the computer provides information in hex, so having a good understanding of the concept is important. Table H.2 lists the standard hexadecimal (HEX) values with their appropriate decimal (DEC) notation.

TABLE H.2
Hexadecimal notation

DEC	HEX	DEC	HEX	DEC	HEX	DEC	HEX	DEC	HEX	DEC	HEX	DEC	HEX	DEC	HEX
0	0	32	20	64	40	96	60	128	80	160	a0	192	c0	224	e0
1	1	33	21	65	41	97	61	129	81	161	a1	193	c1	225	e1
2	2	34	22	66	42	98	62	130	82	162	a2	194	c2	226	e2
3	3	35	23	67	43	99	63	131	83	163	a3	195	c3	227	e3
4	4	36	24	68	44	100	64	132	84	164	a4	196	c4	228	e4
5	5	37	25	69	45	101	65	133	85	165	a5	197	c5	229	e5
6	6	38	26	70	46	102	66	134	86	166	a6	198	c6	230	e6
7	7	39	27	71	47	103	67	135	87	167	a7	199	c7	231	e7
8	8	40	28	72	48	104	68	136	88	168	a8	200	c8	232	e8
9	9	41	29	73	49	105	69	137	89	169	a9	201	c9	233	e9
10	a	42	2a	74	4a	106	6a	138	8a	170	aa	202	ca	234	ea
11	b	43	2b	75	4b	107	6b	139	8b	171	ab	203	cb	235	eb
12	c	44	2c	76	4c	108	6c	140	8c	172	ac	204	cc	236	ec
13	d	45	2d	77	4d	109	6d	141	8d	173	ad	205	cd	237	ed
14	e	46	2e	78	4e	110	6e	142	8e	174	ae	206	ce	238	ee
15	f	47	2f	79	4f	111	6f	143	8f	175	af	207	cf	239	ef

(Continued)

TABLE H.2
(Continued)

DEC	HEX	DEC	HEX	DEC	HEX	DEC	HEX	DEC	HEX	DEC	HEX	DEC	HEX	DEC	HEX
16	10	48	30	80	50	112	70	144	90	176	b0	208	d0	240	f0
17	11	49	31	81	51	113	71	145	91	177	b1	209	d1	241	f1
18	12	50	32	82	52	114	72	146	92	178	b2	210	d2	242	f2
19	13	51	33	83	53	115	73	147	93	179	b3	211	d3	243	f3
20	14	52	34	84	54	116	74	148	94	180	b4	212	d4	244	f4
21	15	53	35	85	55	117	75	149	95	181	b5	213	d5	245	f5
22	16	54	36	86	56	118	76	150	96	182	b6	214	d6	246	f6
23	17	55	37	87	57	119	77	151	97	183	b7	215	d7	247	f7
24	18	56	38	88	58	120	78	152	98	184	b8	216	d8	248	f8
25	19	57	39	89	59	121	79	153	99	185	b9	217	d9	249	f9
26	1a	58	3a	90	5a	122	7a	154	9a	186	ba	218	da	250	fa
27	1b	59	3b	91	5b	123	7b	155	9b	187	bb	219	db	251	fb
28	1c	60	3c	92	5c	124	7c	156	9c	188	bc	220	dc	252	fc
29	1d	61	3d	93	5d	125	7d	157	9d	189	bd	221	dd	253	fd
30	1e	62	3e	94	5e	126	7e	158	9e	190	be	222	de	254	fe
31	1f	63	3f	95	5f	127	7f	159	9f	191	bf	223	df	255	ff

hierarchical address model   A method of addressing in which there are multiple levels of addressing. A person's mailing address is hierarchical. At the lowest level is the house number. Going up the levels, you have a street name, the city, and finally the state. Sometimes even the nation in which a person resides is required in the address. Some forms of computer addressing use a hierarchical mode. This addressing scheme would include such items as a network address and a host address. A network device can find the network it's looking for and let that network figure out which host is supposed to get the data.

high memory   In the early days of computing, when MS-DOS was the primary operating system in use, 1 MB of RAM was the maximum amount of memory supported by a PC. System memory was divided into *conventional memory* and *upper memory.* The first 640 K of memory was conventional memory, and that's where applications run. The 384 K above that was upper memory and used for system resources. With the advent of extended and expanded memory, developers needed a way to create a window between the 1 MB of standard DOS memory and the world beyond. To do this, they allocated the first 64 K above the 1 MB of conventional memory and called it *high memory.*

hop   (1) On larger networks or on the Internet, data won't travel directly from one device to the other. It is likely to cross several networks in its path. Each router interface through which the data passes has to process the data to analyze where it is going and figure out where to forward the packets. Each interface is a hop and each hop adds a certain amount of latency to the data transmission. Therefore, the number of hops is used as a factor in calculating the fastest route between end points. (2) A key ingredient of *brew.*

host   Any device connected to a network. This would include computers, servers, printers, network attached storage, and so forth. It does not include users or applications.

host controller   The adapter installed on a system or embedded in the motherboard that manages SCSI (or other) devices. Host controllers contain the firmware and the ports for interconnecting the devices they manage. They can range from very simple devices that control a single device to complex intelligent RAID controllers. Most host controllers have a microprocessor that handles the commands and many have cache memory installed for storing data that is ready for transmission.

   The host controller installs and configures similarly to any other expansion device. Modern SCSI adapters are fully PnP and require little or no help configuring. If you do have to manually configure a SCSI host controller, the standard IRQ and I/O address requirements of any other device apply here as well. In addition, you have to remember that as far as the SCSI chain is concerned, the host controller is just one more device on the chain. Therefore, it must have a device ID, and if it is one of the devices on the end (as it will most often be), it must be terminated. The nice thing about most modern host controllers is that they self-terminate if they are the end device. Performance of the SCSI chain depends on the performance of this device. Therefore, your choice of system bus has a strong impact on performance. Always select the fastest bus available.

hot plug   The ability to add or remove a device on the fly, possibly requiring intervention or reconfiguration by the OS.

hot swap   The ability to replace or remove a device from a computer system without having to shut the system down.

hub   (1) Hubs are devices that interconnect several other devices in a star configuration. Hubs are used in networks to interconnect multiple hosts on the network. Some interfaces, such as USB, use a hub configuration where multiple ports interconnect to a single controller. A network hub generally consists of a rectangular box with several RJ-45 sockets. A USB hub (Figure H.2) is a small box with two or more USB ports. Most computers incorporate a two- or four-port USB hub on the backplane.

Hubs can be either passive or active. The *passive hub* is the most basic hub available. It simply takes a signal coming in from any one of its ports and broadcasts that signal out all ports, including the one from whence it came. An *active hub* doubles as a repeater. Therefore, before rebroadcasting a signal, it cleans it up and amplifies it back to original strength.

While this may superficially seem to be a minor difference, it can have a great impact on the maximum physical dimensions of a network. With a passive RJ-45 hub, two devices can only have 100 meters of wire separating them. Therefore, if one device is 75 meters from the hub and the other device is 50 meters from the hub, the total distance exceeds the capabilities of the medium. They won't see each other. With an active hub, each device can be up to 100 meters from the hub and still communicate.

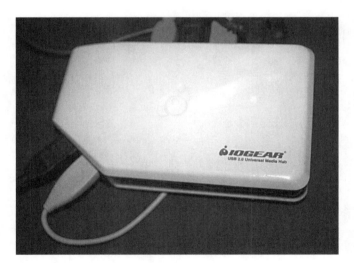

FIGURE H.2   A typical USB hub.

hybrid   Any merger of two forms. Typically in the computer world, the term refers to network infrastructure. Simple networks are *bus networks*, *ring networks*, or *star networks*. As networks get larger and more complex, sometimes maintaining a single topology isn't as easy as it sounds. With many networks that evolved over the years, it's downright impossible. Therefore, many networks are composed of a mixture of different topologies. Some common mixes of the past were to have a few star networks hooked together over a bus. As you might imagine, this was called the *star-bus network*. Another common mix, especially with school districts, was the ring-bus. Individual classrooms were hooked up in a Token Ring network, and then the classrooms were linked over a bus. With FDDI being a ring-structured network, it is likely that we will see a resurgence of this particular hybrid.

hypermedia Any form of communication that allows a dynamic link to another location (be it a Web site, a network location, or another document) qualifies as hypermedia. Any time you include a link to an e-mail address or Web site in the e-mail you send to your boss, you've created hypermedia. All Web pages are hypermedia whether they include additional links or not. They must be accessed from outside sources and they must provide a facility for exiting or going back to the previous location.

hyperthreading A technology used by multicore processors to maximize the efficiency of multithread processing. Each processing core gets its own dedicated L1 and L2 cache, and by providing a high-speed front-side bus, the CPU is fed with data much faster. This differs from single-core processors on which all threads compete for cache space and bus bandwidth. Because of this, dual- and quad-core processors literally perform (within a few tenths of a percentage point) as well as dual processor systems in most situations without the addition overhead required by multi-CPU systems.

hypothesis A fundamental theory as to why a particular situation exists the way it does.

I

i386 instruction set   The basic CPU-level instructions embedded in the 80386 microprocessor. These instructions went on to become the core instructions for subsequent generations of Intel-compatible microprocessors.

IA-32   Intel Architecture, 32-bit. This is the term for the first 32-bit instruction set released by Intel on their 80386 microprocessor. While this instruction set has been described as a 32-bit extension to the x86 instruction set used on previous chips, there was enough completely new code to justify considering it an independent instruction set. IA-32 introduced enhancements such as *virtual 8086* and *virtual memory*. The 32-bit registers handled 32-bit applications and OS code, and register subsets handled the backwardly compatible 8- and 16-bit code. IA-32 has subsequently been a part of all Intel microprocessors up to and including the Pentium 4.

IA-64   Intel Architecture, 64-bit. This is an instruction set written for 64-bit microprocessors. This is the instruction set present on Intel Itanium and Merced processors, to name a couple. Enhancements include long instructions words, branch elimination, and speculative loading. Explicitly Parallel Instruction Computing (EPIC) is integrated into the instruction set.

icon   A small picture linked to an application shortcut.

IFCONFIG Interface configurator   This is a utility that interfaces with TCP-IP in applications such as Unix, Linux, and OS X that allows command line configuration of network interfaces. It is similar to the Microsoft IPCONFIG utility.

incremental backup   A form of data protection that consists of copying only files that have been created or have changed since either the last full backup or the last incremental backup. Once the files are copied, the archive bit is cleared. Incremental backups are generally used as part of a weekly backup rotation that consists of one full backup each week, with a daily incremental backup. This reduces the amount of time required for each daily backup, but in the event that a recovery becomes necessary, it imposes the longest time to restoration. To completely restore a system using incremental backups, first the most recent full backup must be restored to the system. Then each incremental backup must be restored, one tape at a time and in the order that it was created, until all data is copied back to the system.

index hole   A small opening in the covering of a floppy disk that allows the R/W heads to properly align to Track 0, Sector 1.

inductance   A phenomenon that occurs when the electrical properties (specifically, electromotive force) of a circuit are affected by the presence of current in a nearby circuit. This occurs because the current in one circuit creates an electromagnetic field around it. The flow of electrons across another circuit within the proximity of this field is going to be affected.

infection The presence of some form of malignant software, such as a virus, worm or Trojan horse. Antivirus software can detect and neutralize most infections.

infobot An automated email system that analyzes incoming messages to determine the nature of the request, and can automatically respond with the appropriate information or file. Many manufacturers use infobots in their self-service technical support websites.

initialization string When a modem first initiates contact with another modem, there are certain parameters that must be set simply in order to initialize communications. In order to accomplish this, the modem is programmed with the initialization string. This is a series of commands from the *Hayes extended command set* that tells the modem on the other end precisely what the originating modem is capable of doing in terms of compression and speed. Modems ship with a default string that works most of the time. Sometimes fine-tuning the string will do wonders for modem performance. How you go about doing this is determined by the operating system you're running.

Modems ship with one or more sets of commands configured as initialization strings. These sets, or *templates* as they are called, are calculated to accommodate the highest percentage of connection parameters normally encountered. If a unique problem arises that cannot be addressed by changing templates, a configuration utility that ships with the modem allows the user to edit the initialization string, adding or deleting commands.

Some of the many problems that can be solved by editing the initialization string include dropped connections and poor connect speeds. Each brand of modem will have initialization strings specific to that modem; therefore, you will need to be able to access the documentation for your particular model. If you've thrown away or lost the documentation that shipped with your modem you can usually retrieve that information off of the technical support area of the manufacturer's Web page. Also, specific ISPs might suggest initialization strings that are different from the default.

initiator The device in a bus-mastering chain that is to act as the source of the data being transferred.

ink-jet printer Inkjet printers fall under one of two categories. There are thermal and piezoelectric printers. In spite of the diverse sounding nature of their names, they actually work in a very similar manner. Ink flows into a tiny little tube and some force of nature ejects it onto the paper at exactly the right moment. It's the force of nature chosen by the manufacturer that makes the technologies different. Oddly enough, the methods that inkjet printers use to select when and where to place ink is very similar to dot matrix printers. Instead of magnets and pins, they have tubes of ink and the force of nature.

The paper transport mechanism on inkjet printers is very similar to that of the laser printer that will be discussed later in the chapter. Because the exam tests on laser printers in this regard, but not inkjets, I have chosen to defer the discussion of this topic to the section on laser printers.

As you might imagine from the name, the force of nature used by thermal inkjet printers is heat. Heat brings ink up to the boiling point, and forces it through a very small nozzle and onto the paper. In order to assure that the ink can be brought to boiling at precisely the right instant, a thermal inkjet printer keeps the reservoir of ink at a temperature just under the critical point. At the instant a droplet of ink is needed, a heating circuit applies a sudden burst of heat. Poof! Out comes a bubble of ink. This is one of the reasons this type of printer is sometimes called a bubblejet.

The nozzles of a piezoelectric printer are made from a piezoelectric crystal (PEC), which is where it gets its name. A PEC has the unique characteristic that when given a shot of electricity, it changes shape. PECs squeeze inward. A combination of gravity and surface tension keeps a droplet of ink in place inside the nozzle. When the printer needs to eject it onto the paper, it zaps the nozzle with a charge of electricity. The nozzle squeezes inward and the ink is forced out onto the paper.

input   Literally speaking, input is any data entering the system, regardless of source. Input comes from a variety of sources, including human interface devices such as a mouse, keyboard, or a touch screen monitor. Input can also come from any number of devices. Data might be force-fed into your computer without your knowing. Any time your computer is in communication with another device, it is receiving input without waiting for a user prompt. Without data, the system has nothing to do. This information can enter the system in the form of user data, as it would appear in a word processing document or digital image, or it might enter the system as instructions from a program that the user is running from an external source. This data is presented to the system by way of any one of a variety of devices.

instruction cache   A set of registers used for storing instruction code loaded by the prefetch unit until such time as the CPU is ready to use it.

instruction pipelining   In the old days of computers, the CPU could not start one set of instructions until the instructions already in the CPU were completely finished and flushed out of the registers. As a result, when one set of data was nearing completion, many of the CPU registers were sitting idle. Instruction pipelining allows the CPU to start processing the next set of instructions as soon as there are available registers, whether or not the previous set is finished.

insulator   Any substance that tends to resist the flow of electricity.

Int13   Int stands for *interrupt* and 13h is simply the hexadecimal for the number 19. Therefore, you could simply call it *interrupt 19*, and you would be still correct. The Int13h routine provides for a three-dimensional address space used by magnetic media to map data locations. This space allocates a 10-bit address for tracking cylinders, an 8-bit address for heads, and a 6-bit address for sectors per track. As a result, Int13h supports 1,024 cylinders, 256 heads, and 63 sectors per track. All hard drive calls must, in some way, shape, or form, conform to these parameters. The sizes specified in Int13h originated in a day when a 10-*megabyte* hard disk was standard. Therefore, the fact that these numbers add up to a limitation of an 8-GB hard disk received no objections. In that day, the thought that we would need more than 8 GB was unthinkable.

Int13h extensions   Additional instructions added to the BIOS that intercept hard disk I/O operations and provide the drive translation required by hard disks larger than 8 GB. Since Int13h had an inherent limitation of 8 GB, the onset of larger hard disks meant one of two things. Either the interrupt had to be totally abandoned or the industry needed a significant bandage to fix an obvious problem.

So why not just get rid of the Int13h altogether and replace it with something more modern and up to date? The problem there is that it isn't just hardware that addresses this interrupt. Any software that wants to read to the disk, which is any software written in the past thirty years or so, also addresses the Int13h call. If Int13h suddenly disappears, none of that software will work. For some reason people get upset when they find the new computer they just bought won't run several thousand dollars' worth of software they've bought over the past few years.

To make sure this didn't happen, engineers simply added extended instructions that interfaced with the original interrupt. Hardware and software make their calls to the Int13h. The extensions intercept these calls and engage whatever *drive translation* method has been chosen. Newer extensions replace the 24-bit address space of Int13h with a 64-bit space. As a result, drives in the nine and a half trillion-gigabyte range are theoretically possible.

integrated   Two or more devices that are independently designed and/or manufactured, but are intended to work together. For example in IDE hard disks, a separate controller board is manufactured and then installed onto the drive. Another example is when a software manufacturer develops a word processor, a database program, and a spreadsheet, and subsequently stitches them together to form an "office" suite.

Integrated Drive Electronics (IDE)   In the majority of hard disk designs released in the early decades of personal computers, a separate controller card was required to manage hard disk I/O functions. With the release of IDE, the majority of this circuitry was included on a small circuit board embedded in the drive itself. This design released the CPU and the chipset of the motherboard from having to process many of the instructions required for hard disk operation, enhancing computer performance and making systems more affordable.

integrity   The accuracy or validity of information or data. A file loses its integrity if it is edited or appended by mistake or without authorization. Another way data can lose integrity is during a network transfer or an I/O operation between hardware devices. If data bits get altered during the transfer, the file loses integrity.

interactive   Any process or application that provides prompts in order to elicit a response from the user and is capable of multiple responses, depending on the user's input. Most games are interactive. Many websites are interactive.

interactive logon   An interactive logon is one that prompts the user to enter data. An example of this would be the Windows secure attention sequence (SAS). To log on to a Windows NT (or later) machine, the user must first press Ctrl>Alt>Delete to bring up the logon screen. This feature prevents the presence of a program known as a *Trojan horse* from being used to collect user data. The logon screen prompts the user to enter his user name and the correct password.

interlacing   This is a process of drawing alternate lines of an image across an imaging device on one scan and filling in the missed lines on the second scan. CRT monitors use this technique in order to provide faster *vertical refresh rates*. However, interlacing is not as effective a technique as engineers would like. The human eye tends to perceive the overall rate as being only as fast as the total image can be created. Therefore, when comparing monitor specifications, a noninterlaced specification should be compared.

interleave   A method of storing data in a noncontiguous fashion in order to allow the data to be read back in a timed sequence. The technique has been used with hard disks in order to assure that data is streamed from the disk surface to the buffer as smoothly as possible. As disk drives and their controller circuitry got faster, it became unnecessary to interleave data on hard disks. Memory interleaving allows memory from one bank to be read or written to while another bank was being *refreshed*.

interleave ratio   Older hard disks did not have the capacity to read data off the surface of the platters as fast as the platter could spin. Therefore, data was written to the drive in alternating sectors. The heads would write (or read) a sector, skip a preconfigured number of sectors, and then use the next sector. The number of sectors that must pass beneath the R/W heads between the reading of one sector was the interleave ratio; this ratio affected the time the heads would be ready to read the next sector. For example, on a 3:1 ratio, the heads will read or write one sector, two sectors will pass by completely ignored, then the next sector will be written. The unused sectors will be filled in during the next two rotations of the platter.

internal host rate   This is how fast data can move from the R/W head to the drive's buffer in a perfect world when the data is moving downhill with a tailwind. In other words, you're never going to see those speeds. You might see this listed as *burst mode* as well. Essentially, the internal host rate is a theoretical maximum and is not as useful as the external host transfer rate, which measures real-time data transfer to memory.

Internet   A global collection of interconnected computers and networks that provides information services for anyone who has access to a connected computer. Various networks around the world hook together over a high-speed telecommunications link called a backbone. Individual users obtain access by using a computer linked to one of these networks by way of any one of several communications links. These links include dial-up modems, DSL connections, ISDN, or Frame Relay.

Internet Protocol   The standard host/network addressing protocol used by the Internet and most current network operating systems. *See* TCP/IP.

INTERNIC   Inter Network Information Center. The central administration authority for the Internet. INTERNIC is responsible for assigning domain name IP addresses through a subsidiary organization called the Internet Corporation for Assigned Names and Numbers (ICANN). It maintains the global registry for these names and numbers and arbitrates any disputes that may result due to trademark disputes or unauthorized use of domain names.

interrupt   The nature of the microprocessor prevents any device from being able to initiate communication with the CPU. Only the CPU can do that. Therefore, if a device needs to transmit data, it needs a way to get the processor's attention. It has to interrupt the processor from whatever it is doing. On a software level, it is a string of code that is called in order to perform a specific function. The BIOS uses software interrupts to manage hardware. On a hardware level, it is an electrical signal that notifies the CPU that a device needs to open communications (or vice versa). When you have a visitor come to your door, he gets your attention by ringing the doorbell. When a device wants to attract the attention of the CPU, it makes use of its own doorbell, the interrupt request (IRQ).

Interrupts come in two forms—maskable and nonmaskable. A *maskable* interrupt is one that the CPU can essentially ignore until such time as it is ready to deal with it. Most conventional interrupts generated on a software level or through IRQs are maskable. The *nonmaskable* interrupt is one that must be dealt with immediately or the system will be negatively impacted. If the CPU has the resources and data available to deal with the interrupt the system goes "uninterrupted," if I may be permitted a small jest. However, some issues, such as a parity error, are nonmaskable interrupts for which the process has no way to handle. This sort of situation results in a system crash.

intranet   A self-contained private network that dispenses information to authorized users in an environment nearly identical to that of the Internet. An intranet makes use of hypermedia, internal e-mail tools, FTP file access, and all other features that make the Internet so popular. The biggest difference between the Internet and an intranet is that the organization has complete control over content.

intrusion   Any unauthorized access to a network or computers by uninvited guests. While most intrusions are the result of hackers successfully breaking into a system, they can also be less dramatic. A user leaving a logged-on computer unattended can invite intrusions by any curious passersby that happen to see the conveniently running system. Many people who install wireless networks in their home or small business experience intrusions on a regular basis when neighbors or strangers simply passing by find that they are able to log onto the Internet by way of your connection.

invalid file   A file on a disk drive that does not conform to FAT entries that define that file. These problems can include invalid size reporting, generally caused by incorrect reporting of the number of clusters used, a missing entry identifying the parent directory, and others. An invalid file size exists when the file system is recording the file as a particular size, but the clusters add up to a different size. This renders the file unusable, but it is fixable. Another situation that can lead to the invalid file message is when a pointer that provides the location of a parent directory is lost. Files cannot exist without an associated parent directory, even if it is the root directory. If the pointer is missing or points to an invalid directory, the file is unreadable. More critical are problems with the file allocation tables. Because the file tables are the final word in file location, an error there can result in any number of different errors.

It is also possible for a file system to detect an invalid file name or an invalid date. No OS allows the user to create an invalid file name, but data corruption can cause it to happen. If the OS thinks that in invalid character exists, it will mark it as invalid. Invalid dates occur when the date of the file is later than the date the system reports as being current, or there is an invalid date format.

inverter   A device or circuit that converts DC current to AC current.

I/O address   The CPU keeps track of the location of everything on the computer by way of its address bus. Every memory location on the computer, every device on the computer, and every connector must have an associated address. In order to communicate with a particular piece of hardware, the system creates a little drop box in memory at a specific location. This address correlates to the address in memory of the first instruction of a device driver or BIOS instruction. In order to keep track of what device is using what address, an I/O address table is maintained by the CPU. When a device needs to communicate with the CPU, it first lights up its IRQ channel. When the CPU is ready to interface with that device, it looks up the IRQ in the address table and now knows where to go looking for the device driver or BIOS instruction that manages the device.

The number of available I/O addresses is limited. They consist of one or more 8-bit ports. The PC architecture allows for a 64-KB memory bank for I/O addresses. Therefore, there are 216 of these 8-bit ports, or 65,536, available. Any two contiguous 8-bit ports can be combined to form a single 16-bit port, and any four contiguous 8-bit ports can be combined to form a single 32-bit port. Many of these ports are assigned by IBM for specific functions, and others have been claimed by other companies to support their devices.

Most devices are capable of occupying one of several I/O addresses. In addition to the base address, the device will also claim a few bytes of memory as a buffer. This is its I/O range. Depending on the needs of a particular piece of hardware, it may receive an I/O address range of anywhere from an address that is a single byte wide to one as much as 32 bytes wide. In general, I/O addresses are not something that a technician assigns manually. However, for many devices, it is possible to change the I/O address of a particular device, either through a CMOS setting or from the OS. This sometimes becomes necessary when two devices compete for the same address range. An example of this would be a system that was equipped with a second parallel port and a certain brand of network interface card. The default I/O addresses of these devices frequently overlap. Table I.1 lists a few of the most common I/O addresses.

TABLE I.1
A listing of commonly assigned I/O addresses*

I/O ADDRESS	DEVICE
000-00Fh	DMA controller, channels 0 to 3
010-01Fh	(System use)
020-023h	Interrupt controller no. 1 (020-021h)
024-02Fh	(System use)
030-03Fh	(System use)
040-043h	System timer
044-04Fh	(System use)
050-05Fh	(System use)
060-063h	Keyboard & PS/2 mouse (060h), speaker (061h)
064-067h	Keyboard & PS/2 mouse (064h)
068-06Fh	Free to use
070-073h	Real Time Clock/CMOS (nonmaskable interrupt - 070-071h)
074-07Fh	(System use)
080-083h	DMA page register 0-2
084h	DMA page register 3
089-08Bh	DMA page register 4-6
08Fh	DMA page register 7
090-09Fh	(System use)
0A0-0A3h	Interrupt controller no. 2
0A4-0BFh	(System use)

(Continued)

TABLE I.1
(Continued)

I/O ADDRESS	DEVICE
0C0-0CFh	DMA controller, channels 4-7 (0C0-0DFh, bytes 1-16)
0D0-0DFh	DMA controller, channels 4-7 (0C0-0DFh, bytes 17-32)
0E0-0EFh	(System use)
0F0-0FFh	Floating point unit (FPU/NPU/math coprocessor)
100-12Fh	(System use)
130-15Fh	Commonly used for SCSI controllers
160-167h	Free to use
168-16Fh	Quaternary IDE controller, master drive
170-077h	Secondary IDE controller, master drive
178-1E7h	Free to use
1E8-1EFh	Tertiary IDE controller, master drive
1F0-1F7h	Primary IDE controller, master drive
1F8-1FFh	Free to use
200-207h	Joystick controller
208-20Bh	Free to use
20B-20Fh	(System use)
210-21Fh	Free to use
220-22Fh	Sound card
230-23Fh	Some SCSI adapters
240-24Fh	Some sound cards, some SCSI adapters, some NE2000 network cards
250-25Fh	Some NE2000 network cards
260-26Fh	Some NE2000 network cards, some non-NE2000 network cards, some sound cards
270-273h	(System use)
274-278H	Plug and Play system devices
279-27Fh	LPT2
280-28Fh	Some sound cards, some NE2000 network cards
290-29Fh	Some NE2000 network cards
2C0-2E7h	Free to use
2E8-2EFh	COM Port 4
2F0-2F7h	Free to use

TABLE I.1
(Continued)

I/O ADDRESS	DEVICE
2F8-2FFh	COM Port 2
300-301h	MIDI Port
300-30Fh	Some NE2000 network cards
310-31Fh	Some NE2000 network cards
320-323h	Some non-NE2000 network cards
320-32Fh	Some NE2000 network cards
320-327h	PC-XT Hard Disk Controller
330-333h	MIDI Port
330-33Fh	Some NE2000 network cards, some SCSI controllers
340-34Fh	Some SCSI controllers
350-35Fh	Some NE2000 network cards, some SCSI controllers
360-363h	Some tape backup controller cards
360-36Fh	Some NE2000 network cards
370-373h	Some tape backup controller cards
370-37Fh	Some NE2000 network cards
378-37Fh	LPT1 (or LPT2 on monochrome systems)
380-387h	Free to use
388-38Bh	FM synthesizer
38C-3AFh	Free to use
3B0-3BBh	VGA or monochrome video
3BC-3BFh	LPT1 on monochrome systems
3C0-3CFh	VGA or CGA video
3D3-3DFh	VGA or EGO video
3E0-3E3h	Some tape backup controllers
3E8-3Efh	COM Port 3
3EC-3Efh	Tertiary IDE controller
3F0-3F7h	Floppy disk controller
3F8-3FFh	COM Port 1
3f6-3F7h	Primary IDE

*NOTE: While it may appear on this table that some devices overlap in their I/O address range, this in fact is not possible. These overlapping addresses indicate devices that may potentially occupy the range. If one device already possesses that I/O address, no other device may share it.

IP Internet protocol.

IPCONFIG IPCONFIG is undoubtedly the most widely used of the TCP/IP utilities. This utility can return statistics on every connection configured to use TCP/IP. If a device is configured to use DHCP, a user can use IPCONFIG to release an IP address and subsequently renew it.

IPCONFIG displays information for all local TCP/IP connections, whether they are a NIC, a modem, or a virtual connection. As with the other utilities in TCP/IP, there are a number of triggers associated with IPCONFIG. These triggers vary a bit between Windows 98 and the subsequent Microsoft operating systems. Those for Win98 are as follows:

/all Displays detailed report of all adapters on system.
/batch {filename} Writes a report to the file specified by file name.
/renew_all Renews the IP configuration for all adapters on the system.
/release_all Releases the IP configuration for all adapters on the system.
/renew N Renews the IP configuration for only the adapter specified in N.
/release N Releases the IP configuration for only the adapter specified in N.

The command line parameters for Windows 2000 and XP are a bit different and there are more of them as well. They are as follows:

/all Shows complete configuration for all interfaces on system.
/release {adapter} Releases IP configuration for the adapter specified.
/renew {adapter} Renews IP configuration for the adapter specified.
/flushdns Dumps the contents of the current DNS resolver cache.
/registerdns Refreshes all DHCP leases and reregisters DNS names.
/displaydns Displays contents of the DNS resolver cache.
/showclassid Displays the DHCP classes allowed by the adapter.
/setclassid Modifies the DHCP class.

IP spoofing A process by which a target computer is fooled into thinking it is communicating with a device with one IP address, when in fact a completely different entity is at the other end. IP spoofing is used by hackers and spammers to fool data recipients into thinking the source of a file or e-mail is a trusted one. IP spoofing is frequently used in denial of service attacks, where hundred of thousands of service requests are sent to a single server. While all of the requests may originate from a single host, IP spoofing convinces the recipient's device that each message is from a different source.

iterative query A DNS request that must be fulfilled on the local server, providing whatever information it has, if any. An iterative query tells the DNS server to return whatever information it has about a particular DNS entry, along with its list of other servers that the client might be able to query. If the client cannot resolve an address, at least it now has the necessary addresses to continue the search.

J

jabber   When a new device that uses the Local Area Transport protocol first comes alive on a network, it sends out a broadcast packet announcing that it is alive and well and available for other devices. In theory, it only needs to do this once. Occasionally, however, a device fails to recognize the acknowledging packets as they arrive and it continues to broadcast its availability. This redundant bandwidth-intensive traffic is called *jabber*.

jack in   To log on to a bulletin board or a virtual reality session.

jaggies   A slang term for the stair-step effect that results from pixelizing images. The accurate term for this phenomenon is *aliasing*. One of the techniques used by graphics programs and 3D algorithms for graphics adapters is antialiasing, which reduces this effect.

jam   (1) When a signal interferes with another to the extent that the target devices can accurately interpret neither signal, those signals are jamming one another. Jamming is a common wartime maneuver that is used to disrupt enemy communications. (2) On an Ethernet network, when two hosts transmit at the same time, a *collision* event occurs. In order to assure that a second collision doesn't occur when they both broadcast at the same time again, both devices will continue to broadcast for a short duration, thus jamming the signal.

jargon   Technical terminology or slang that is specific to a particular field. When two programmers get together in a conversation that is sixty percent acronyms and one hundred percent gibberish to the average citizen, they are conversing in jargon. It is typically considered in bad form to intentionally use jargon around lay folk simply to either impress or to confound them. Such bad behavior is also very common.

Java   An object-oriented programming language developed by Sun Microsystems that was originally used for programming Web content. The language was particularly useful in this environment because it was platform-independent and has very low processing overhead. As Java applications became more prevalent on the World Wide Web, developers took a greater interest in application development with the language. A vast library of precoded routines allows fast development of new applications without the necessity of writing code for commonly used operations. Because of its popularity, a wide variety of graphical interfaces exist for nearly every available operating system.

Jaz drives   Jaz drives were a removable media offering by Iomega Corporation. The drives used disks that go in and out of the computer with the ease of a floppy disk. Drives were available that could connect internally through an IDE or SCSI connection and externally via a parallel port, USB port, or Firewire connection. The drives supported up to 2-GB disks, and the disks were available in either 1-GB or 2-GB densities. They were much faster that floppy disks and approached the speed of many IDE hard disks. Jaz drives deliver access times in the vicinity of 10 ms, which is comparable to some hard drives (good hard drives hover around 6.5 ms to 10 ms).

jiffy An indeterminate period of time that is intended to be interpreted as a short period of time. When one says she'll be back in a jiffy, she is trying to tell you that she will be back very soon. Depending on the type of person you are dealing with, this can be anywhere from a few seconds to the rest of your natural life.

jitter Most signal timing mechanisms exhibit a measurable amount of inconsistent and generally random variation in the accuracy of their timing. This random inconsistency is jitter. Jitter is never a good thing because it can result in data errors and can slow the system down as those errors are corrected.

Joint Photographic Experts Group (JPEG) An organization of manufacturers involved in imaging devices. This organization oversees the development of file formats used in imaging. They were responsible for one of the most commonly used data compression algorithms used for image files. The JPEG format is named after this group.

journaling A process used by certain operating systems and applications by which any changes made to the basic infrastructure or code are recorded in a log prior to being enforced. Any change that is made to the file system is logged. This would include directory structure changes, file or directory name changes, and changes to security settings. Even an unexpected event such as a fatal shutdown induced by a power failure is recorded. Should the file system become corrupted, the log can be used to restore the file system to a "last known good" state. In all but the most disastrous situations, the repair occurs in the background and the user is blissfully unaware that anything ever happened. Journaling has been a part of the Apple Macintosh OS since the introduction of OS X. The Microsoft world introduced the feature with the NTFS file system.

joystick A device used by gamers to control various functions of a computer game. Typical joysticks have a small lever that can move in any direction and two or more buttons that send signals to the computer. Game programmers can have their production interpret joystick commands in various ways. The lever can move the character around the mazes of the game while the buttons fire the weapons at those grisly aliens. Joysticks are unique in one respect: they are one device that does not require an IRQ. A method called *polling* is used instead. The CPU frequently checks the device's I/O port to see if it has data to send.

jukebox An optical drive that holds a large number of disks. Most jukeboxes can have two or more disks loaded simultaneously and read data from whichever disk is required at the moment. Manufacturers such as JVC and Plasmon offer options that hold as many as 638 DVD disks (as of this writing).

Julian A type of calendar that does not use months and years as temporal increments. A day was selected as the beginning of the calendar that euphemistically identified the "beginning of time." Each day and year has a numerical value associated with it that is based on counting up from the beginning of time. Computers make use of a digital equivalent of the Julian calendar in order to calculate time independent of time zones.

jumper   A pair of pins with a removable cap that, when in place, closes the circuit. This cap (called a *shunt*) is removed to open the circuit. Shunts are typically the same color as your carpet so that when you drop one, it is lost forever. Figure J.1 shows a row of jumpers.

FIGURE J.1   A row of jumpers used to configure settings on a motherboard.

junction   A place where two circuits come together. In transistors, two layers of semiconductor may be joined. This is called a junction as well.

K

Kerberos An authentication system used in several different operating systems that provides advanced control of security for services and applications running on the system. Kerberos was originally developed by the Massachusetts Institute of Technology as an enhancement of the Unix OS. It appeared in Microsoft versions starting with Windows 2000 and has been a part of the Linux OS since the 2.x versions.

Kermit An asynchronous communications protocol used by dial-up modems. It was originally developed at Columbia University as a method of assuring error-free data transfers over a telephone line without the cumbersome overhead associated with synchronous protocols.

kernel As the name implies, the kernel is the core of the OS. It is the kernel that manages all of the central functions of the OS. These central functions include:

- The file system
- Processor control
- Memory management
- Device control
- Security

In the old days of MS-DOS, the kernel consisted of three very small files. Modern operating systems are much more sophisticated. The kernel is broken down into two layers, the executive kernel and the microkernel. The *Executive Kernel* derives its name from the fact that it is the portion of the OS executing commands. When the executive kernel receives a command, it will issue a system call to one or more of several of its subcomponents. Although the names and variety of these subcomponents vary from OS to OS, there will inevitably be components that manage I/O, memory, process and processor control, and security. More sophisticated operating systems add additional components.

The subcomponent processes the requests it receives and passes them on to the *microkernel*. If those requests are requests for more services to be provided on the OS level, they are passed on to the appropriate component. If they are hardware requests, then the appropriate device driver is called on for its services.

In the days of DOS, this amounted to direct access of the hardware by the application. Of course, DOS was not a multitasking OS. However, there were programs written for DOS that emulated multitasking and provided more attractive and (sometimes) more efficient user interfaces. These were referred to as *DOS shells*. If two programs attempted to access the hardware at the same time, there was a complete and total system crash.

Today's operating systems are all multitasking, so that can't be allowed to happen. Therefore, the application isn't permitted to directly access the hardware. Hardware requests are passed onto the *Hardware Abstraction Layer* (HAL). HAL is the only layer of the OS allowed to communicate with the hardware.

Defining HAL is more complex than can be done in a simple one-line description. HAL is a very complex layer of any modern OS. It consists of a collection of virtual device drivers and the *API*s written to support specific hardware types. The virtual device driver is a file native to the OS that is designed to interface with a particular piece of hardware. In Microsoft operating systems, the virtual device drivers are easily recognized by the fact that they end in a .vxd extension.

key   (1) A null space on an edge card connector or memory module that is used for properly aligning the device into its slot. Memory modules, expansion cards, and most connector cables are keyed so that the user cannot inadvertently plug them in backward. (2) A small packet of code that contains information used by an encryption system to decipher encrypted data. Many systems use two keys, one public and one private, to perform this function.

key matrix   The keys on the keyboard are laid out in a series of rows and columns called the *key matrix*. Each key holds a position related to a row and column. When a key is depressed, the keyswitch in that position closes a circuit, sending a signal to the circuit board inside the keyboard. The keyboard controller uses the X and Y coordinates of the matrix position to determine which key was pressed, thereby determining what code is transmitted to the computer by the keyboard.

keyboard   The most commonly used user-input device is the old standard keyboard like the one shown in Figure K.1. Although there is a lot of variation in the cosmetics of keyboard design, it is actually a device that is standardized in most respects. The layout of the keys is based on the old-fashioned typewriter of yesteryear. (Mommy, what's a typewriter?) The seemingly oddball order in which the keys are arranged are based on scientific theory that the keys used the least (such as the letters X and Z) should be positioned on the part of the keyboard that is least easy to get to by a touch typist. The letters most commonly used are then positioned where they are easiest to reach.

Another thing that is tightly controlled is the spacing of keys. Both horizontal and vertical spacing is kept the same on all desktop keyboards so that if you move from one computer to another you don't spend the first 10 minutes figuring out where your fingers have to go. Laptop keyboards are similarly standardized, but are governed by different numbers, which is why your desktop and your laptop computers don't feel quite the same.

The top row of keys on the keyboard holds the *function keys*. These are easily recognized because they all have the letter F in front of a number. Function keys get their name because that is their role. They perform a certain task, either for the computer's operating system or for the application running on the system. Pressing a function key won't add a character to the letter you're writing home to Mom asking for more money.

The largest grouping of keys is the *character set*. These are the keys that type your letters, numbers, and punctuation marks. Each of these keys is capable of generating two different characters. The base character is the one you see on the keycap. On several of the keys, there are two characters displayed on the keycap.

On these keys, the base character is the one on the bottom. Holding the Shift button down while you press a key can create a secondary character. With the letters, the secondary character is the capital version of the letter, while the base character is the lower-case version.

Sound too easy? Okay, let's make it harder. There is another key on the keyboard just above the left Shift key labeled *Caps Lock*. If this button is pressed, a light will start glowing on your keyboard, and holding the Shift key while you type will generate the primary character; the secondary characters will become the default when the Shift key is not used.

To the right of the character keys are eight navigation keys. Navigation keys allow you to move around in a document. The navigation keys include four arrows, Page Up and Page Down, Home and End. and Insert and Delete. Their purposes are somewhat self-explanatory.

Lastly, on the far right-hand side of the keyboard is a section called the number pad. It's laid out like a standard ten-key calculator and can perform two functions. A key labeled *Num Lock* dictates which function the number pad performs. The default function is to work like a desktop calculator. However, if you look at the secondary markings on the keys, you'll see that they are duplicates of the navigations keys I just discussed. With Num Lock pressed, the keypad doubles as a navigation pad. This is very popular with the computer gaming crowd.

Three other keys to discuss are the Control (<Ctrl>) key, the Alternate (<Alt>) key, and the Windows (<WIN>) key. Control and Alternate keys (like the Shift key) are modifier keys. They work with the other keys on the keyboard to allow preprogrammed functions to be performed with the press of a series of keystrokes. These functions are called *shortcuts*. Nearly every application written for the computer has a number of keyboard shortcuts programmed in. For example, pressing the <Ctrl> button along with the letter B in Microsoft Word will tell the application to start typing everything in boldface type. Pressing the sequence a second time turns the function off. The general rule of thumb is that when describing a series of keystrokes, we writers use the plus sign (+) between keys. For example <Ctrl>+F1 means for you to press the control key and the F1 key at the same time. There are <Ctrl> and <Alt> keys on both the right-hand and left-hand side of the grouping of character keys.

FIGURE K.1   *The old-fashioned keyboard is still the most frequently used input device today.*

keycap   The button you push to activate a particular key is called the *keycap*. This is what most people simply call the key. The keycap on modern keyboards is removable, just like the A shown in Figure K.2, allowing you to replace a worn-out keycap. In most cases, they simply pop off with a little prying by a flat-head screwdriver. Most of them are equally easy to get back on. However, that isn't always the case. The <SPACE> key can be particularly difficult. It requires getting the springs and clips properly aligned, holding them in place while simultaneously snapping the keycap into position. On some keyboards, <SHIFT> and <ENTER> are equally entertaining.

    The size of the keys and the spacing of keys are all under strict guidance. The primary character keys on a standard keyboard are spaced .75″ apart, measured center to center. With the exception of the distance between the A-row and the Q-row, the rows are .375″ apart. The A- and Q-rows are separated by a space of .188″.

FIGURE K.2   *Even the lowly keycap on the keyboard is subject to industry standards.*

keycap travel   This is a measurement of the actual distance a user must press a key on a keyboard in order to produce results. Keycap travel can range anywhere from .10″ to as much as .20″. Unless there's a decent amount of travel, they keyboard has a very stiff feel. Too much travel and you feel like your fingers are treading water. What you get accustomed to is what will be better for you. Most touch typists find they work faster on keyboards with a longer travel.

keystroke logging   A method used by hackers to acquire login credentials from unsuspecting users. A small program is introduced into the system (usually as a worm or trojan horse), which launches automatically the next time the computer is booted. As long as the program is running, it records every signal that arrives from the keyboard and stores it in a file. While typically considered a tool of hackers, keystroke logging is also used by law enforcement agencies as a high-tech equivalent of wiretapping, except instead of eavesdropping on telephone conversations, the agency is intercepting computer communications and credentials.

keyswitch   An electromechanical device that informs the keyboard controller circuitry that a key has been pressed. The kind of keyswitch you use will determine if your keyboard is clicky or mushy. The keycap snaps into place over the keyswitch.

Keyswitches have one task: they complete a circuit, sending a signal to the controller that a particular key has been depressed. When released, they send a second signal notifying the controller of that event. The signal that is generated when the key is pressed is called the *make code*. When the key is released, a *break code* is generated. Each key issues a unique code for make and another for break. Having separate codes for connect and release allows the signals of multiple keys to be combined, creating a completely different command set.

kill   To force a process to stop.

kilobit   1,024 bits in binary or 1,000 bits in decimal.

kilobyte   1,024 bytes in binary or 1,000 bytes in decimal.

KVM switch   Short for keyboard, video, and mouse, the KVM switch is a device that allows a user to interconnect two or more computers to a single keyboard, mouse, and monitor (Figure K.3). These are commonly used in server racks where a dozen or more computers are stacked in a single rack. Smaller versions can be useful to individuals as well. A successful KVM installation will make sure the correct terminals are in place. A PS2 mouse and keyboard are common in some brands, while USB is used for others.

FIGURE K.3   *KVM switches range from this inexpensive dual-PC device all the way up to rack-mounted devices that cost thousands of dollars and support many computers.*

L

land   All of the reflective surface of the recording layer in optical media that has not been burned or punched into a pit. On a conventional CD-ROM disk a .002-mm layer of aluminum is deposited on the back surface. The metal coating acts as a mirror onto which billions of little tiny pits, one-sixth of a micron wide, have been stamped. These pits vary in length from slightly under a micron to about 3 microns and are only one-sixth of a micron deep. These pits are put onto the disk in a concentric spiral moving from the center of the disk to the outside. The area of disk surface outside the pits is known as the *land*. While the pits may provide the data, the land areas are equally important. Most CD drives use a technique called *beam splitting*. The CD reader doesn't focus the beam directly onto the disk itself. Instead, it is focused on a diffraction grid, which divides the original laser beam into three different light sources. The beam splitter is designed in such a way that the three outbound beams are passed through to the medium. The reflected light coming back from the CD is bounced 90 degrees to the photoreceptor diode, where the signals are interpreted.

Figure L.1 shows the mechanism of a CD reader at work, and indicates the postion of lands. Of the three beams directed at the CD, the center one is supposed to remain focused on the track containing the data. The two outside beams focus on the land surface on either side of the track. Since there are no pits in this area, the reflections that bounce back from either of these two beams should always be constant. Any flickering of these reflected beams generates electrical signals that cause the servomotor that positions the laser to adjust its focus accordingly.

landing zone   When you turn off your PC and the platter stops spinning, the hard disk head is going to sit down on the platter unless you take steps to prevent that from happening. Manufacturers have accordingly created a head-parking system, designing into the drive platters an area reserved solely for the purpose of providing the head a safe place to sit when the PC is not in operation. This is the *landing zone*. The location of the landing zone is one of the hard disk configuration settings of the BIOS. However, all modern hard drives are designed in such a way that the BIOS can automatically detect the necessary parameters.

laptop   A portable computer system that can easily be carried around and used in any location. The term is derived from the fact that the computer can be operated easily while placed upon one's lap. Today's laptops are every bit as powerful and offer as many options as a desktop machine.

laser printer   A high-quality output device for creating printed pages of documents. The term comes from the fact that a laser beam is used to create an electronic version of the printed page on an imaging drum. The printer then uses differences in electrostatic charge to transfer toner from a cartridge onto the imaging drum and subsequently onto the page.

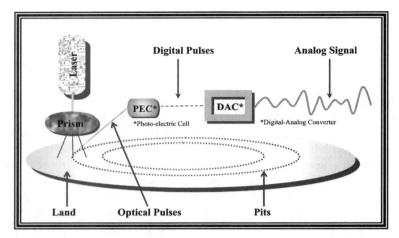

FIGURE L.1   The area between tracks on a standard CD or DVD is called the land.

latency   The delay that occurs from the time a device makes a request for services or data and the time that request is fulfilled. All devices, including memory and hard drives, exhibit latency. Latency is introduced by a number of factors. Among these factors are the time it takes for commands to be executed, physical aspects such as a disk drive's rotational speed, and how many requests are in the queue ahead of a specific request.

launch   To start a program.

layer 3 switch   Most network switches filter packets by MAC address. Since MAC addresses are managed at layer 2 of the OSI networking model, switches are generally considered layer 2 devices. Many advanced switches, however, are also designed to filter by IP address or by protocol. In order to perform these functions, they operate at both layer 2 and layer 3. Such switches are layer 3 switches.

lazy writing   Lazy writing is a disk-caching scheme that allows the OS to perform write operations to a disk at its leisure, when the controller and disk aren't occupied with more important read operations. The bright side to this technique is that it provides significant performance increases for the user. The down side is that if the system is shut down unexpectedly, such as from a power loss or an irate user, all data not yet written to the drive is permanently lost. Therefore, whenever you are running an OS that incorporates lazy writing as part of its bag of tricks, you want to make sure you shut down gracefully. A *UPS* can save you a lot of lost data in the event of a power failure.

lease   The TCP/IP suite includes a protocol called DHCP that dynamically assigns IP addresses to hosts as they log on to the network. DHCP allows the administrator to put all the available IP addresses into a pool and dole them out for a limited time. This time is known as the *DHCP lease*. The default lease is 7 days, but administrators can configure this value to be for as long or as short as the she wishes them to be. By assigning a very short lease, such as 1 hour, to an IP address, that address essentially becomes available again once that person logs off of her machine. It can then be handed out to the next person who wishes to log on. This is useful when there are a limited number of addresses available and you don't want them tied up for any extended period. ISPs frequently use this technique. Longer leases are useful when there are plenty of addresses to go around.

legacy A term that refers to older, outmoded software or hardware that is still in use. The newer computer or OS "inherits" these programs or devices and must learn to manage their legacy. An example of legacy software would be an old MS-DOS game that you refuse to give up and will spend hours tweaking your system until it plays on XP. (Good luck!) An ISA slot on a motherboard is an example of legacy hardware.

level one (L1) cache This is an area of extremely high-speed memory built right into the CPU's die that stores data and external commands until the CPU needs them. It is the CPU's internal memory. Having larger amounts of integrated cache means that more data and commands from the outside world can be moved into the CPU to be ready when needed. The less the CPU is forced to access the rest of the system, the faster it performs. Therefore a 2.4-Ghz CPU that has 2 MB of L1 cache will perform faster than a 2.8-Mhz CPU with 32 KB of cache, assuming that these commands are routinely used by the hardware and programs running on the server.

level triggered A response that is arbitrated by a control circuit and/or device driver that allows the same device to make use of one of several interrupt channels. A level-triggered device contains a control circuit that manages IRQ signals. That circuit, in combination with an intelligent device driver, allows the device to communicate over one of several available channels. This is useful because it allows the OS or the BIOS to dynamically configure the device. The level-triggered interrupt raises the voltage on the appropriate wire and holds it until the expected response is received.

library In programming, a collection of subroutines that is required by several or all applications running on a computer. By storing this code in a single file, it does not need to be duplicated many times over.

line conditioner A device that is able to filter out transient noise, such as EMI, from the current.

linewidth The actual thickness of traces used within the CPU.

Linux Originally developed as a freeware operating system, Linux was originally developed by Linus Torvalds as an offshoot of the Unix OS. The key to Linux is that it is a completely open source, meaning that anyone can download, view, and even modify the source code of the OS. While Linux is essentially a free product, a thriving industry has developed around the packaging and distribution of Linux installation packages. This is done by companies such as Red Hat, Fedora, Mandrake, and many others. Many major manufacturers, including IBM, HP, and Dell offer Linux as an option for OS on their servers and desktop computers.

load balancing A process by which workload is divided among multiple devices. Many devices, including network servers, are capable of being configured for load balancing. Any computer using *symmetric multiprocessing* incorporates a degree of load balancing into basic processing. Some servers allow the administrator to install multiple network cards and divide incoming network traffic between them. This is known as *NIC load balancing* or *NIC teaming*. Server clusters can also be configured to share the load between them.

load point The physical location on a tape where the first byte of data begins to be stored. All tapes require a specific load point, which is the physical location where the actual data begins to be copied. Previous technologies allowed only one load point. If the load point was at the beginning of the tape and a user wanted to restore a specific file, the drive would have to start searching for that file from the very beginning of the tape. This could take several minutes. Some manufacturers sped up the process by using midload points. Midload points placed the load point in the center of the tape so searches could be done in either rewind or fast-forward mode. More recent technologies support multiple load points, which allows the user to preselect a specific point on the tape from which to start a search. This greatly reduces the amount of time required to locate specific files on a long tape.

local bus The local bus is a direct path between a device and the CPU's external data bus. If a peripheral or component is designed to make use of the local bus, then data can move from that component to its destination (which can either be the chipset of the motherboard or L2 cache) at the same speed as the CPU's external clock speed. Data moves along this bus, not only at a higher speed, but also in a more direct route.

local collector ring The network of end users with their different bandwidths that interconnect to a single regional network.

local host The device or computer on which an application or another device resides. It can also be the computer in use at the moment. For example, a network administrator checking the IP address of the local host is checking the address of the machine at which he sits.

local loop carrier Internet services are distributed in an organized fashion. The local loop carrier is a service provider that maintains the circuits that carry the signal between you and your Internet service provider. Depending on your choice of data communications, these options include your local telephone company, cable television company, a satellite dish, or an independent contractor. Your selection here not only has an impact on performance, but security as well. Some carriers are less secure than others.

Some carriers, such as satellites, can be impacted by external conditions such as the weather, solar flares, or other conditions beyond your control. If a constant connection is critical to your organization, you should consider this before investing in the equipment needed.

local procedure call A request for services that can be performed by resources that reside on the machine from which the request was made.

location A process by which data is identified and found on a storage medium. It is also a specific address space where information resides.

logic bomb A piece of code programmed to run at either a specific time or when a specific action is performed. Until then, it sits dormant.

logic gate *See* **gate.**

logical drive Drives can be either physical or logical. A physical drive is just what it sounds like. A floppy disk or a hard disk installed into the system is a physical drive. Drives A: and B: are reserved for floppy disk drives. The first hard drive in the system is drive C:

However, a hard disk can be divided into two or more partitions, and each partition would be seen as a separate logical drive or volume. So if your hard disk is divided into three partitions, you would have drives C:, D:, and E:. Where it gets confusing is when you have two physical disks installed and each disk is divided into multiple partitions. In that case, the first physical disk is drive C: and the second physical disk is drive D:. From that point all the partitions on the first physical drive will be lettered, followed by those on the second physical drive. Figure L.2 shows a diagram of how this works.

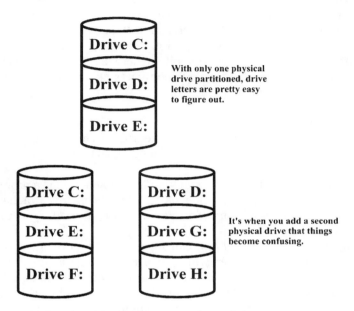

FIGURE L.2   When two or more physical drives exist in a system, the lettering of the logical drives isn't exactly logical.

logical partition   (1) A logical partition is a partition on one drive that is nothing more than a pointer that redirects the file system to a partition on a completely different physical drive. Logical partitions can carry a name other than a simple drive letter. For example, \\DRIVEZERO might point to another physical disk on the system. It might even point to an LUN on a storage area network device (SAN). (2) In the world of mainframe computers, a logical partition is not specific to the file system. Logical partitions look at all system resources—including all available processors, system memory, and hard disk drives—as a single volume and divides that volume into several logical systems. Each of these logical systems is capable of running an independent OS, and each partition is capable of seeing the other partitions on the system.

logon authentication   Modern operating systems require that users "introduce" themselves before gaining access to the computer. This assures that the person signing on has the right to sign on. The process of logging on involves typing in a user name and password. These are the user's *credentials*. The OS can then compare these credentials to a security database and figure out, first of all, if that user name and password is correct, and if so, what rights does this person have on the computer (or network). Each operating system has its own process of managing user logon. However, since there are more similarities than there are differences, the Windows process will be described here.

When the user first logs on to the system (after having pressed <Ctrl><Alt><Delete>, of course), a process called *Winlogon* passes the user ID and password that is provided to LSA. LSA compares the information provided by the user with the information that is stored in SAM. If the data is correct, the user is allowed onto the system. If not, that user is rejected. Across a network, LSA will transmit this information to either a PDC or a BDC.

Once a user is successfully logged on, LSA will generate a security access token that validates the user's session on the network. That token is the key to network resources. If the user logs off and then back on, a new token will be generated. The token includes:

- The user's SID
- The SID for any user groups to which the user has been assigned
- The list of permissions and privileges assigned to that user

Now that the token has been generated, Winlogon opens a new session of EXPLORER.EXE. The access token assigned to the user is attached to this process, and from that point forward, everything the user attempts to do must be validated by the token.

loopback adapter   Testing a serial port can sometimes be more effective if you get that port to talk to itself. By doing this, you are verifying the functionality of the port itself and taking external variables, such as device drivers or cables, out of the equation. In order to do that you'll need a specialized plug called a *loopback adapter* that wraps the signal back to the computer rather than sending it out to a device. This takes the device out of the loop, so to speak, and tells you whether or not it is a bad port rather than a dysfunctional device or cable. Loopback adapters are available for either serial ports or parallel ports. Figure L.3 shows a 25-pin and a 9-pin loopback adapter side by side with a parallel version.

lost cluster *See* **lost file fragment.**

lost file fragment   A file allocation unit on a disk drive that contains data but has lost the pointers that identify the file to which that data belongs. Lost file fragments generally occur when there has been an unexpected system shutdown. If the OS suddenly crashes or if the user turns the machine off without going through the standard shutdown procedures, temporary files are left open, data that has been copied to virtual memory has not been saved, and open files are not properly closed. All of these can result in the file tables finding FAUs on the hard drive that are occupied but have no reference to a specific file. These unclaimed clusters are the ones that are being reported. When a disk verification utility such as ScanDisk finds them, by default they are converted to files in the system root directory with names of file0000.chk, file0001.chk, and so on.

In most cases, these were temporary files the system still had opened at the time of the shutdown. They have little or no impact on the permanent copy of that file still written to the hard drive. Still, from time to time they are user data

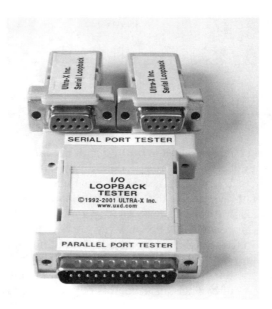

FIGURE L.3   Loopback adapters are devices
that allow you to test the integrity of a serial or
parallel port.

that was never written to file. In many cases, the data is corrupted, but if you can recognize what it is and where it goes, sometimes you can recover it. Most of the time your best bet is to delete the .chk files and free up the space.

LPT port   Short for line printer port, this is a predefined combination of an IRQ and an I/O address configured on a parallel port. The two common LPT ports are LPT1, which is IRQ7 and I/O 378h, and LPT2, which is IRQ5 and I/O 278h. LPT ports should not be confused with parallel ports. While a parallel port is most likely going to have an LPT port assigned to it, the parallel port is a physical port where a cable plugs in and an LPT port is a logical address for that physical port.

MAC address   This is an address that is burned in at the factory and goes with the device wherever it goes. This address is commonly referred to as the *MAC address*, in deference to the sublayer that makes the most use of this address. As the name implies, the MAC sublayer in the data link layer handles this form of addressing.

   The IEEE Registration Authority strictly administers MAC addressing assignments. This is a good thing because having two devices with the same physical address on the network can cause no end of nightmares. While this is theoretically not supposed to happen, manufacturers make mistakes too.

   The MAC address is a 48-bit address, expressed as twelve hexadecimal digits. This address consists of two 24-bits segments of twelve digits each. Figure M.1 shows an example of a MAC address. The first segment is a 24-bit organizational unique identifier (OUI) assigned by IEEE. The manufacturer cannot change this. The remaining 24 bits consist of a manufacturer-assigned interface serial number. Notice that the reference is to an interface serial number and not just a device serial number. Many devices such as routers, switches, and bridges have multiple addressable ports. Each addressable port must have a unique MAC address. Therefore, a router with twenty-four assignable ports will have twenty-four MAC addresses and twenty-four interface serial numbers. The router will only have one device serial number.

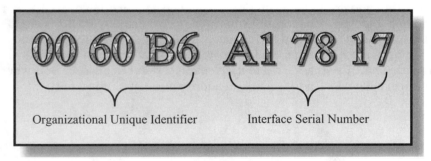

FIGURE M.1   *The MAC address is a 48-bit value hard-coded into a network interface.*

machine language   This is the low-level binary code that provides the instructions that hardware devices use to perform their functions. These instructions are independent of the operating system; therefore, the OS must have a separate set of instructions, known as the hardware abstraction layer, to deal with machine language.

macro   A combination of commands, keystrokes, mouse actions, and text that is programmed into an application to run automatically with the execution of a single command. Most high-level applications support macros on some level. An example of a macro would be a divider line in a Microsoft Word manuscript. By recording the complex series of keystrokes in a macro, the user can change the formatting from left-justified to center, add a hard line return, type a series of characters to use as the divider, add another line return, change back to left-justification and be ready to type the next line. By assigning the macro to the keys <Ctrl> plus 8, by pressing those two keys at the same time, all of that happens. A bit of a time-saver, no?

magnetic storage   Any form of data storage medium that uses the electrical properties of magnetism to encode data. Magnetic storage devices include hard disks, floppy disks, tape drives, ZIP drives, and many others. Typically, the media is composed of some form of substrate, such as a magnesium platter used by hard disks or the plastic film used by tape coated with an emulsion containing particles that can be magnetized. Changing the polarization of the magnetic field creates bit cells that computer hardware recognizes as a bit of information.

mail server   For quite some time now, e-mail has been a way of life for most of us. You don't really think about dedicated mail servers when you're sitting at home sucking down the day's spam and trying to sort the good stuff from the junk. Remember, however, that you are but one of hundreds, or even thousands, of customers that your Internet service provider (ISP) manages. It is their job to handle each and every one of the e-mails that get sent to their clients. Therefore, an ISP will connect you to a mail server when you access your e-mail.

Now imagine the organization with 2,500 users, each one of whom is getting that same amount of mail coming in. Setting up 2,500 free e-mail accounts would be too cumbersome to manage and the security would be a nightmare. Therefore, an organization as large as this would handle its own e-mail functions.

An e-mail server runs a piece of software dedicated to the task of processing incoming and outgoing messages. Each user on the system is assigned an e-mail account, and the server keeps track of what incoming messages are supposed to go where. The advantage of this system is that the administrator has control over several aspects. He can control whether or not attachments are allowed, and if so, what their maximum size can be. Individual users can be limited to the amount of hard disk space they're allowed to eat up. A key point is that prolific sources of spam can be cut off at the source and never make its way into the network to clutter up bandwidth and hard disk space. Specialized antivirus software can be run at the gateway and known viruses blocked before they enter the system.

In order to perform their functions, there are some specific protocols that must be running on both the client and the server. For receiving e-mail and distributing it to the correct user, either the Post Office Protocol (POP) or the Internet Message Access Protocol (IMAP) must be running. For sending messages out to the outside world, you'll need the Simple Mail Transfer Protocol (SMP).

Mail servers require prodigious disk space if there are a lot of users. CPU and memory requirements are not the issue they are with some other types of server. The more users you support, the more work your computer has to do, and the more memory you need to install. Still, even a busy mail server doesn't get hit anywhere near as hard as an applications server. I/O requirements really aren't as rigorous as one might think as it's pretty rare that every single user tries to access e-mail at the same time.

mainframe   Mainframe computers are large, nonmovable computer systems that possess higher than normal processing capabilities, massive storage capacity, and generally are equipped with large amounts of volatile memory. Mainframes typically act as the central computing store for a larger organization or as the main processing facility for a research organization. Using specialized network operating systems, mainframes and desktop computers can be linked together, and the mainframe can be a powerful network server as well.

malware   Any software package that is designed to perform an action that the user will find undesirable. Malware is a general term for various agents such as viruses, worms, trojan horses, adware, and so forth.

make code   A signal generated by a keyswitch when the key is first pressed down. The signal generated by a specific key will continue to be transmitted until the key is released, at which point the keyboard controller will issue a *break code*, indicating that the key is no longer being pressed down. This is why when your cat falls asleep on the keyboard, it starts beeping continuously, waking the cat.

manager   In TCP/IP terminology, this is an application or utility that initiates requests for information to be gathered.

master boot record (MBR)   The first one or two sectors on a hard disk that contains the critical information that the computer needs to go from a dead stop to launching the operating system. The MBR contains information that defines the file system. It holds partition tables that map the hard disk for the system, and it has a pointer that directs the boot process to the first line of the operating system.

medium   The substance or energy wave over which a data signal is transmitted. The plural form of medium is media, and that is the term you will most frequently see. (2) Media also refers to the type of data contained in a file. For example an MP3 file is a media file containing music.

media set   The collections of tapes or other media that represents a complete image of the system.

megabit   1,048,576 bits in binary, or 1,000,000 bits in decimal.

megabyte   Depending on whether you are calculating a value in binary or decimal, a megabyte is either 1 million bytes (decimal) or 1,048,576 bytes (binary). A binary megabyte is 2^{20} bytes, giving it this number. Binary is used in virtually every circumstance except when calculating hard drive capacity. Hard drive manufacturers typically define capacity in decimal values.

memory bank   CPUs have a data bus that is so many bits wide. Memory is the same way. If you have a CPU with a 64-bit bus, then you need to move data in 64-bit chunks. Unless there is a full bank of memory for the CPU to access, the computer will not boot. A bank must contain enough chips to equal the external data bus of the CPU in use. Therefore, if your CPU has a 64-bit data path and you are using 32-bit memory, two memory modules will be needed to fill a bank. This is a virtually obsolete issue in that memory shipping today is practically all 64-bit memory.

memory controller hub   One of the chips in an Intel chipset that controls all system memory. It also has the responsibility for managing the AGP bus.

memory interleaving   A technique accessing multiple memory modules in a series, creating a sort of memory pipeline (Figure M.2). Data and code are stored across the chips in stripes and are accessed accordingly. With multiple memory chips installed, the memory controller starts an I/O operation on one chip, retrieving one stripe of data. While that chip is being accessed, the controller moves on to the next chip to access its stripe of data, and so on.

So when you decide you need a gigabyte of RAM and install a single 1-GB module, that's the only chip that is serviced by the controller. Since some of the more advanced technologies such as DDR-II will allow multiple channel access, these types of memory can take advantage of interleaving as long as the system BIOS supports the technique. If the system supports interleaving, buy your gigabyte of RAM as four 256-MB modules, creating four separate banks of RAM. The downside to this, of course, is that if you decide to upgrade the memory, you must upgrade all four modules at once.

A few rules apply here. For one, all RAM must be of the same density, the same speed, and must use the same number of DRAM modules. Therefore, you can't have two PC-133 modules and two PC-100 modules. Even if you're using all PC-133 RAM, you can't have two 8-chip modules and two 16-chip modules. It just won't work. And lastly, you can't have a mixture of 256-MB, 512-MB, and 1-GB modules either. All must be identical.

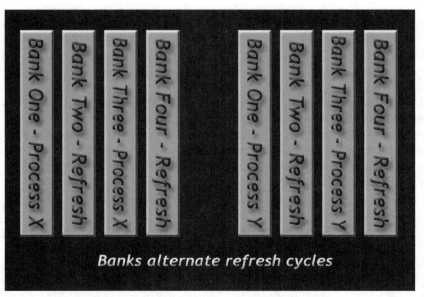

Banks alternate refresh cycles

FIGURE M.2   Memory interleaving is a technique of creating different channels in memory for the CPU to read. This illustration shows just one of several interleaving schemes.

memory leak   All operating systems automatically reserve a block of memory for each application that is opened and for any new user file that is opened. When the application or file is closed, that memory is theoretically released back to the system to be used by the next process that needs it. Some operating systems are notorious for not releasing memory back to the system when the process is closed. This memory is now not being used; but it is still no longer available for use by the system. Therefore, as far as the CPU is concerned it now has less memory available to it than when it started. Some of it "leaked" away.

memory mirroring   Something very much like the equivalent of a RAID 1 implementation in memory. The MCC manages two identical channels of memory. Whatever is stored in the primary channel is duplicated in the secondary channel. If a memory module fails, the server will automatically fail over to the second channel and issue an alert concerning the failure so that the administrator knows to replaced the faulty module. Memory mirroring is OS-dependent. Currently, the operating systems that support memory mirroring are Unix and Linux, and Windows XP and 2003 Server.

memory pool   The total address space, including disk space used by the paging file, available to an OS and the applications running on top of it.

menu   A graphical list of available commands in an application that a user can select from either a pull-down menu, or from a collection of icons on the screen. Use of a menu prevents the user from having to memorize a complex collection of commands to type into the system.

mesh   Logically, the mesh is a network in which every single device directly connects with every other device on the network (Figure M.3). As you might imagine, this architecture is rarely (if ever) implemented throughout the network. The mesh can be either a full mesh or a partial mesh. The full mesh is where everybody talks to everybody. In the partial mesh, there are a few nodes that connect to all others, but the majority of connections interact with only a few. The mesh is used predominately to interconnect the backbone of most networks and not the individual nodes.

message   The format of data, or PDU, processed by the application, presentation, and session layers and sent downward to the transport layer.

message block   Synchronous transmission sends data across the wire in message blocks. A file is broken down into smaller chunks and sent out over the wire. On the receiving end, those pieces are reassembled into the correct order. Each message block consists of several portions.

SYN	*Synchronization character*. This makes sure all the bytes in the frame stick together as they move across the wire and then get reassembled in the right order at the other end. If no data is being transmitted, SYN blocks can be transmitted to keep the session alive.
SOH	*Start of header*. A header is not always used, but is an important part of most protocols.
HEADER	Placed into message block by protocol and can include information such as the sending computer's IP address, the intended recipient's IP address, and so forth.
STX	*Start of text*: Pretty self-explanatory. It tells you that the next series of bits is the data being sent.
TEXT	The data

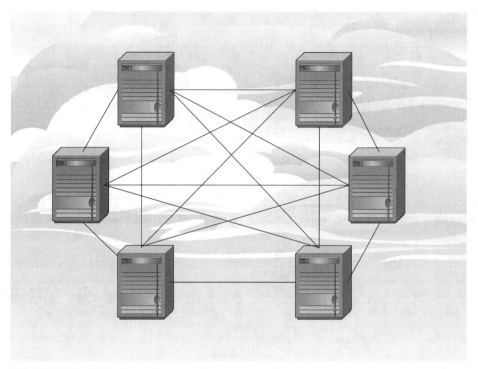

FIGURE M.3   With the mesh network, everything has a direct connection to everything else.

ETX	*End of text*. Okay, I'm done sending text in this block. The next bytes are more control information.
BCC	*The block check character*. Includes error detection and correction data that may include parity (rarely used these days), checksum (on its way out), or cyclical redundancy check (the most common method in use today).
EOT	*End of transmission*. I hope this one is self-explanatory.

All of this additional information is used by the system to make sure data gets where it's going and gets there intact.

metadata file   Hidden information on the hard drive that defines disk structure, file location, and other attributes of the files stored on a drive formatted to NTFS. Table M.1 lists the common files used by NFTS.

metafile   A related string of streaming data that contains the information that is used to implement the file system structure. A metafile is a structured graphical file, also containing streaming data.

metric   A value placed in a routing table that defines the relative cost, in time, of taking that particular hop.

microfarad   The minor measurement of a capacitor's ability to store energy.

TABLE M.1
The metafiles of NTFS

METAFILE	METAFILE FUNCTION
$.	Root directory
$Boot	Boot file
$Mft	Master file table (MFT) table of contents
$AttrDef	Attribute definition table
$Bitmap	Cluster bitmap file indicating the used/free status for each cluster in the file system
$MftMirr	Location of the copy of the metadata files elsewhere on disk
$LogFile	Transaction log (deployed as a circular buffer)
$Volume	Information about file system volume (including its name and NTFS version)
$BadClus	List of bad clusters
$Quota	Reserved for future use for disk quotas (used only in NTFS 5.0)
$Upcase	Unicode lower case-to-upper case conversion table (for translating file names)

microkernel   A single file (or a very small set of files) that provides basic I/O functions and command interpretation within an operating system. In MS-DOS, the microkernel consisted of the files IO.SYS, COMMAND.COM, and MSDOS.SYS.

miniconnector   A smaller four-pin connector coming off a power supply that delivers current to devices such as floppy disk drives.

microprocessor   Any integrated circuit that is hard-coded with a set of commands to perform a specific set of operations. The best example of a microprocessor is the CPU of a computer system. However, a huge number of other microprocessors are used by the computer. The RAMDAC of your video card, the DA/AD converter of a sound card, the BIOS chip, and thousands of others are all microprocessors.

minimize   In a graphical operating system, it is possible to have several applications or documents open at the same time. Each one is displayed in a separately viewable window. Most operating systems have the ability to close a window without closing the document or application. That allows the user to get it out of sight but not lose the data or close the processes. This is the process of minimizing the window.

mirrored volume   A single logical drive that is made of two disks, both of which contain identical data. Mirrored volumes differ from duplexed volumes in that in a mirror, both drives are connected to the same physical controller. In a duplex configuration, each drive will be connected to a separate controller. Figure M.4 illustrates the concept of the mirrored volume.

mirror site   Any location that has an identical collection of computers, routers, applications, and operating systems as the primary location. If disaster strikes

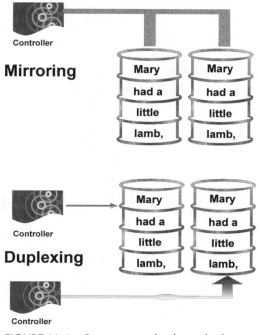

FIGURE M.4   *On a mirrored volume, both disks are hanging off the same controller. As the illustration indicates, with duplexing, a separate controller manages each drive.*

the primary location and that hardware and software are no longer available to the organization, the mirror site becomes a failsafe backup that prevents the organization from becoming completely disabled.

mnemonic   Any word or symbol that is easy to remember that can be used to remind a person of something that is harder to remember. Frequently in an operating system or application, the first letter of a command is used as a mnemonic. P = print, for example. Mnemonics don't have to be letters or words. A physical mnemonic can help you recognize which months of the year have 31 days. Starting with the knuckle on your index finger, tap the knuckle for January, the space between the knuckles of the index finger for February, and so on and so forth, going back to the index finger for August. Every month that is represented by a knuckle has 31 days; every other month has fewer days.

modem   The term *modem* is derived from its original name of modulator/demodulator. It is a device that takes digital data in binary form and sends it over a telephone wire as electrical signals. In order to accomplish this, a modem has two tricks to perform. First of all, it has to be able to convert data from digital form to analog waveforms. Second, since the modem is moving data over the line using serial communications, the data needs to be converted from parallel to serial. A device called the *universal asynchronous receiver transmitter* (UART) handles the serial/parallel conversions. A DAC is responsible for digital/analog and analog/digital conversions.

As a device, the computer treats the modem pretty much like any other I/O device. In the early days, because modems are serial devices, they were assigned a COM port. Therefore, a preset IRQ and I/O allocation was standard for most modems. Over the years that has changed, and it isn't uncommon to see modems grabbing resources not common to the standard COM port settings. Figure M.5 shows an example of an external modem.

In all other respects, it's a typical I/O device, but it's one that has to convert data from serial format to parallel and from digital to analog. Let's say you're chatting with a friend over the Internet. You type a letter and the keyboard turns the action into a series of zeros and ones that are processed and sent to the modem. The UART breaks the bytes down into bits and the DAC converts the bits into the frequencies as previously outlined. From there the data is transmitted over the telephone line.

Modem aficionados have their own collection of buzz words that set them apart from the average person. Unless you know some of the terms they use, figuring out what the guy on the other line is trying to tell you can be pretty challenging. While the following list of terms is by no means all encompassing, it should give you a pretty decent start.

AT/V.25.bis Also known as V90. 56kbs
Bell 103 300 bps U.S. standard
Bell 212A 1,200 bps U.S. standard

FIGURE M.5   *This external modem is a device that still sees a lot of use in certain parts of the world.*

Compression The process of reducing information in data storage or transmission by the elimination of redundant elements. Various compression protocols have evolved over the years. Most current modems use V.90bis as the data-compression method of choice.
Firmware Similar to the computer's BIOS, this is built-in software stored on a ROM chip that controls the operation of a dedicated microprocessor-based device.

Flash ROM A type of memory used for firmware in modems and other digital devices. Unlike conventional ROM (read-only memory), flash ROM can be erased and reprogrammed, making it possible to update a product's firmware without replacing memory chips.

International Telecommunications Union (ITU) The agency in charge of overseeing telecommunications sponsored by the United Nations. The ITU is charged with establishing and coordinating standards for electronic communications worldwide.

ISDN Integrated Services Digital Network, an all-digital replacement for analog telephone service. ISDN provides two 64-Kb/ss channels, which can be combined or used independently for both voice and data.

K56flex A protocol, jointly developed by Lucent Technologies and Rockwell International Corp. to achieve 56 Kb/s modem transmissions over ordinary phone lines. K56flex requires that the host device (at an ISP or online service) be connected to a minimum of an ISDN or preferably a T1 line. K56flex allows downloads at up to 53.3 Kb/s; uploads are limited to the normal V.34 speed of 33.6 Kb/s. *See x2.*

MNP Microcom Networking Protocol (Proprietary)

T1 A digital phone line that provides up to twenty-four channels of data at 64 Kb/s. A fractional T1 is one or several of those channels connected to form a singular link. T1 lines can carry data or digital telephone signals and are commonly used for high-speed WAN connections between offices.

V.32 9,600 bps, 4,800 bps

V.32bis 14.4 Kb/s, 12 Kb/s, 9,600 bps, 7,200 bps, 4,800 bps

V.32terbo Pseudostandard extending V.32bis to 16.8 and 19.2 Kb/s. Never really took off.

V.34 An ITU standard for data transmission at up to 33.6 Kb/s. V.34 is the successor to several earlier ITU standards; modems using this standard are designed to be backwardly compatible with older, slower modems.

V.42 MNP 4 and Link Access Protocol/Modems (LAP/M) modem-to-modem error correction

V.42bis LAP/M and 4-to-1 data compression

V92 56 Kb/s

x2 A technology developed by U.S. Robotics for achieving modem transmissions at close to 56 Kb/s over ordinary phone lines. In most respects, it is similar to K56flex.

Molex   The larger four-pin connector coming off a power supply that delivers current to devices such as CD-ROM drives or hard drives (Figure M.6). Technically speaking, it is the name of the company that invented the plug.

motherboard   A politically incorrect gender-specific reference to the primary system board of a computer. The motherboard is the central hub with which all other devices on the computer must find a way to communicate. The motherboard supports the CPU, the system RAM, the chipset, and sports the connectors for all peripherals.

The motherboard consists of a multilayer sheet of material onto which copper traces are applied (Figure M.7). The traces interconnect all the devices of the motherboard. Motherboards vary greatly regarding which processors they support, how many peripheral devices live on board, and in hundreds of other features.

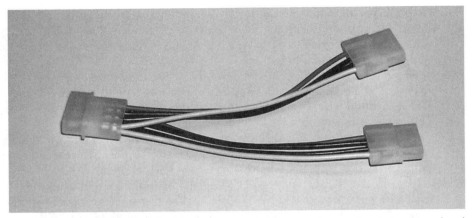

FIGURE M.6   While not technically accurate, the four-conductor plug that powers hard disks and optical drives inside your computer is frequently called a molex. This molex divider allows one molex to power two drives.

mouse   A mechanical or optical/mechanical device that a user moves back and forth over the desktop or a mousepad. The movements are translated into a moving cursor on the computer screen. When the cursor is over a particular spot on the screen, such as an icon, clicking on the buttons of the mouse will initiate a desired action.

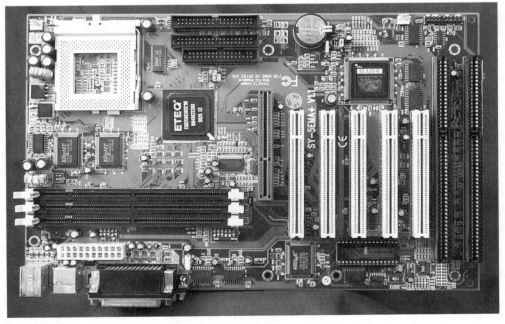

FIGURE M.7   A basic motherboard for a single-processor system.

multicast   A data transmission directed at selected multiple hosts.

multihoming   A technique in which you install two or more NICs into a server. To a certain extent, you server is acting as a router on the network. Each NIC is configured for a separate network, and as such, the same computer is serving both networks. The benefits of doing this are twofold. First, you totally divide the traffic between the two networks. This breaks one larger network down into two smaller ones. This is a process known as *subnetting*. When you subnet your network, you divide it into two or more broadcast domains.

Multihoming a server can serve yet another function. If you have different segments on your network running different NOS platforms, such as a MAC and a PC environment, or different segments running different topologies, a server can be configured with different interfaces to interconnect with each of the segments. In this respect, the server is acting as a bridge. A bridge is a device that interconnects disparate networks such as these.

multimode fiber   Multimode fiber is a single strand of fiber optics that is typically 50 to 100 microns in diameter and is designed to have several different signals traveling over it (Figure M.8). Using different light frequencies for each channel and then bouncing the signal along the fiber at varying angles enables this to happen.

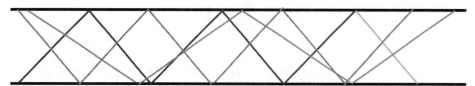

FIGURE M.8   *Multimode fiber is a single strand of fiber optics that sends multiple singles by using different frequencies and angles of reflectance.*

multiplexing   The combining of multiple signals from different sources to be transferred over a single communications link.

multiprocessing   The use of more than one central processing unit by a computer system. In the old days, some computers used asymmetric multiprocessing, in which one processor ran the operating system and applications and the other processor handled user data. This proved to be inefficient, and most systems today use asymmetric multiprocessing. All processors on the system share the load equally.

multipoint   A communications link in which several devices set up a logical connection in order to communicate among themselves.

multisession   The ability to record data onto a CD-R or CD-RW in several stages, without closing out the TOC.

multitasking   The ability of an OS to simultaneously run more than one program at once.

N

Name Binding Protocol (NBP)   A protocol from the AppleTalk suite that takes the alias of any resource on the network and maps the registered name to its internal addressing components. Resources are known as *entities*, and each entity name contains three different fields. The object field identifies the user, the system, or the resource. As its name implies, the type field describes the resource in question. The zone field identifies in which network zone the entity resides. NBP works with dynamic addresses to map resources that have just come online with the network.

naming convention   (1) A predefined logical method for naming the users and the computers on a group. A good naming convention will provide some information that identifies the user or device. You need to have a method of assigning user IDs that identifies the user to the network administrator as well as to the network security files. One of the more common approaches I've seen is to use some combination of the user's last name along with her initials. When a network is small and there are relatively few users, it is easy to simply create users IDs such as mgraves and dearreader. In a larger organization, this quickly breaks down as well. As more and more users are added, the chances of a second mgraves or dearreader coming online increase exponentially. A good naming convention will provide a unique user ID to each account, provide some hint at that user's function without sending the administrator skittering off to the database, and still be easy for the user to remember. (2) The file system's set of rules regarding file names. Typically, a file name must consist of a name followed by an extension. The name identifies the individual file and the extension identifies the type of file. Two commonly used file naming conventions are 8.3 and *long file names* (LFN). The 8.3 file naming convention was a file naming scheme used by earlier file systems that permitted file names of up to eight characters, plus an extension of up to three characters. Because of backward compatibility issues, 8.3 is recognized by most operating systems. LFN allows up to 255 characters, including the extension, and extensions are not limited to three characters. LFN is used in FAT32 and NTFS and is compatible with the Linux and Macintosh operating systems.

native capacity   How much data any given medium can store without benefit of compression. Various compression techniques allow data beyond native capacity to be recorded.

Native File Encryption (NFE)   A built-in encryption algorithm for the NTFS file system. Individual users on a machine can select certain files and directories they don't want others seeing or accessing, and scramble them. If another user is logged onto the machine, that user cannot see the files encrypted by other users that might share the machine. While file encryption existed in previous operating systems and file systems, until NFE, it was an all-or-nothing scenario. You either encrypted the entire drive or none of it. Use of NFE adds a certain amount of overhead to system performance, but for most users it is negligible.

In order to enable EFS, the user right-clicks on the file or folder that is to be encrypted in Windows Explorer and selects Properties. On the General tab, there is a button labeled Advanced. When the user clicks this button, she will get a screen with a checkbox next to the phrase, "Encrypt contents to secure data."

When a user enables EFS, the OS generates a private key. The private key consists of a data set associated with the user's account that determines precisely how data will be scrambled and how to put that scrambled data back into its correct form when needed. The user can be selective about the files or folders that need to be encrypted.

For each file that is encrypted, Windows assigns a randomly generated encryption key that becomes part of that file's attributes. When the user goes to use the file, the user's private key calls up the file's encryption key. The file's encryption key will respond only to the user's private key or to a public key generated by an authorized recovery agent. A recovery agent is any user account that has been given the privilege of being a recovery agent. Having the file's encryption key respond to a recovery agent is the fail-safe that allows the user to recover the data in the event that the private key is lost, or in the event that a rogue employee encrypts all the data on a machine before an unexpected departure.

NBTSTAT NBTSTAT will display statistics for all connections that relate to running NetBIOS over TCP/IP. These connections include computers with current connections to an interface as well as open ports. The utility will also indicate whether a specific connection is unique or part of a group. The NBTSTAT triggers are as follows:

-a {remotehost}	Lists the name table of the remote device named in remotehost
-A {Ipaddress}	Lists the name table of the remote device with that specific IP address
-c	Lists the remote name cache along with IP addresses
-n	Lists local NetBIOS names
-R	Dumps and reloads the remote cache table
-S	Lists open sessions along with destination IP address
-s	Lists open sessions along with destination host name

nested RAID With nested *RAID* you are combining multiple different types of RAID into a single array. All the techniques for nesting RAID involve large numbers of disk drives and either proprietary controllers or specialized software. Some require both. However, extremely high levels of fault tolerance can be achieved with these techniques.

RAID 1+0 involves creating a mirror of a RAID 0 array. You can use as many disks in the RAID 0 array as your system/controller can support. Then, in order to make the system fault-tolerant, that stripe set is duplicated to an identical set of disks. While it is theoretically possible to set up this configuration on a single controller, it actually makes more sense to place each RAID 0 on its own controller, as shown in Figure N.1. In the event that any single disk fails, that entire side of the mirror is broken and the system is dependent on the other side until the defective disk is replaced.

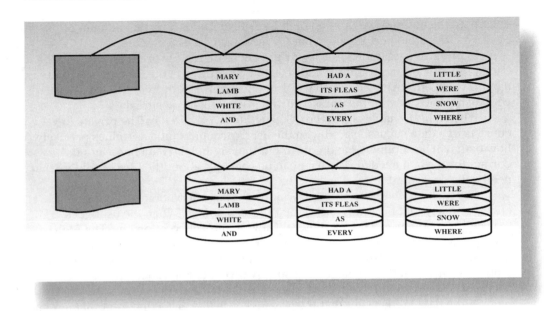

FIGURE N.1   RAID 1+0 is a mirror of a stripe set.

RAID 0+1 (also called *RAID 10*) is stranger yet. RAID 10 requires a minimum of four hard disk drives. Two of these drives will be mirrored. The other pair will be striped in a RAID 0 array for performance. This scheme requires specialized hardware and software support, which adds to the cost of implementation. The advantage is that the machine benefits from a performance standpoint as well as enjoying a certain degree of fault tolerance. The disadvantage to this scheme is that the cost is somewhat high for the limited protection it offers.

RAID 5+1 is one of the most complex arrays you can configure, yet it is by far the most fault-tolerant. First you configure the first RAID 5 array, using anywhere from three to thirty-two disks. Then, on a separate controller, an identical collection of disks duplicates that array (Figure N.2). Because of the expense involved, this strategy would only be employed on critical systems. However, security of data is among the highest that can be obtained. For the system to fail completely, you would have to have four drives fail simultaneously. Failure of one drive in either array would not bring it down. Parity would simply rebuild the array. Failure of two drives in the same array would cause the second array to kick in. Even if two drives in one array fail, failure of a drive in the second array won't kill the computer. Parity rebuilds that array. Therefore, for total failure, two drives in each array would have to go down at the same time.

RAID 0+5 and 5+0 are both used to form very large arrays by combining RAID levels 5 and 0. RAID 05 is created by configuring a RAID 5 array out of several RAID 0 arrays. The number of disks required by this configuration generally precludes it from being used in individual servers. However, it could easily be implemented in *storage area network* devices. The reasoning behind this is that maximum hard disk I/O is achieved while still maximizing fault tolerance.

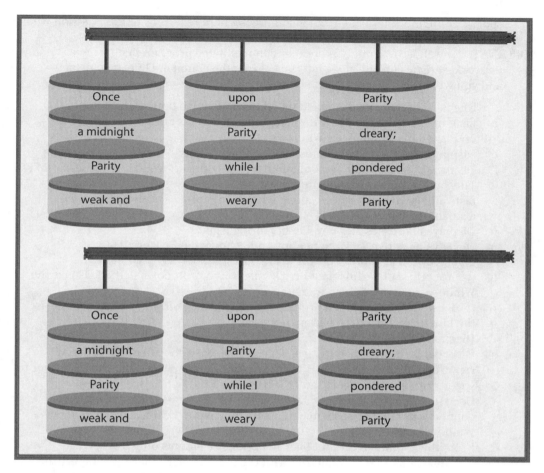

FIGURE N.2   RAID 5+1 is basically a mirror of a RAID 5 array.

RAID 0+5 is far more rare than RAID 5+0. This is where you create a RAID 0 array out of multiple RAID 5s. This provides a higher degree of fault tolerance than 0+5. RAID 50 and 05 both improve the performance of a standard RAID 5 configuration because of the addition of RAID 0. Write operations are particularly enhanced and make these configurations attractive for mission-critical Web servers.

.NET   A software technology developed by Microsoft to integrate Web technology into all aspects of computing. Users who own Windows-based computers with .NET installed see fewer prompts when accessing information from .NET-enabled Web sites. Organizations that employ .NET architecture in their network can interface the network through an Internet-modeled standard. Users will find it easier to browse the network and to access network resources. In order to make it easier to program for .NET, Microsoft created Visual Studio.NET to allow programmers to more rapidly create .NET applications and to bundle applications more efficiently. From an end-user's standpoint, .NET is completely transparent and requires no special configuration (aside from installing it where required) or intervention when .NET services are required.

NETSTAT   The NETSTAT utility is another command-line program that retrieves various network statistics on any given interface. From the command line, type netstat –? and you will receive a report that shows the options. The various triggers include:

-a   Displays information for all connections and active ports

-b   Lists the name of the program that created each port or connection. This option is only available in Windows.

-e   Displays all Ethernet statistics

-f   Displays the fully qualified domain name of connections to outside DNS links. This option is not available in Windows.

-l   Lists all network interfaces, along with their statistics. This option is not available in Windows.

-n   Displays addresses and ports in numeric format

-o   Displays all active TCP connections and shows the Process ID for each connection. This option is only available in Windows XP and later.

-p   {protocol} Displays information specific to the protocol specified. This is the Windows version of the parameter.

-p   {process} Lists all running processes and what socket they are using. This is the Linux version of the parameter.

-r   Displays the routing table

-s   Displays per-protocol statistics. Unless otherwise specified, the protocols reported will include TCP, IP, and UDP. May be combined with the –p trigger to specify other protocols in the TCP/IP suite.

-v   Used in conjunction with -b. Displays the components that created the connections and the sequence in which they were created. Available in Windows only.

-?   From the command prompt lists all options. Windows only.

Interval May be used in conjunction with other triggers listed here to repeat the request at the specified interval. To stop displaying information, press Ctrl>C.

network   Although there have been many books written on the subject of computer networks, the definition is quite simple. A network is any two or more devices connected either directly or indirectly and configured to communicate with one another.

network number   A number used by IPX/SPX and AppleTalk to identify the network on which a device resides. In IPX/SPX protocol it is a 32-bit number; in AppleTalk it is a 16-bit number. The network number is a value assigned by an administrator and bound to a specific network. Only network interfaces bound to that specific network number would be able to communicate without the services of an intermediate device such as a router or a multihomed server.

nibble   Any combination of four zeros or ones. A nibble is one half of a byte of data being transmitted during a single clock cycle.

nibble mode   Sends the 8-bit byte of data to the printer in two cycles, each of which carries four bits, or a nibble of data. This was a primitive form of bidirectional communication in that each 4-bit signal traveled in a different direction. Nibble mode requires software support and more overhead on the part of the host computer. Even slower than compatibility mode, ranging from 50 Kb/s to 65 Kb/s.

Despite the fact that it has long been obsolete, a device must support the communications mode in order to achieve IEEE-1284 compliancy.

node   Any one of several addressable types of allocated space on a hard disk that can contain the data that makes up a file.

node address   In IPX/SPX protocol, the node address is a unique number assigned to an individual host on the network. This number is derived from the 48-bit MAC address of the interface. Since all MAC addresses are unique, this requires no specific configuration by a network administrator. Together, the network number and node address form the station address.

node ID   A number assigned by the AppleTalk protocol that identifies a specific host on the network. The protocol assigns node IDs dynamically so that a single host might have a different ID every time it logs on. Each device on an AppleTalk network needs to have a unique NBP name, sometimes called the *entity name*. The administrator configures the entity name. When NBP assigns a node ID, it binds it to the entity name. This process is performed every time the computer logs on to the network.

noninteractive logon   Typically, when a user initially logs on to the network, she types in a unique user ID and a password. The OS prompts the user to provide this information, and this process is part of the *interactive logon*. Once a user is logged on to the network, subsequent access authentication is done in the background, transparent to the user. The user's credentials are stored in a temporary file in memory. Any time that person tries to access a secured resource, the network security infrastructure will prompt the querying computer to provide the credentials once again. As long as the user's session has not expired, the query will be automatically serviced without user intervention. Therefore, the user does not interact.

nontransitive   Windows domains can communicate with each other through connections called *trusts*. Trusts begin at point A and end at point B. They will not automatically pass through to point C. This means that if an administrator sets up a trust between domain A and domain B, and then another trust between domain B and domain C, a trust between domain A and domain C will not be created by default. In order for that trust to exist, he or she will have to create it separately.

northbridge   Computer chipsets consist of two chips. The faster component of a standard motherboard chipset is called the *northbridge* and it is responsible for memory access, AGP, direct access to the chipset, and other functions requiring maximum bus speed. It handles the high-speed components of the system and sets the pace for the front-side bus. If your CPU is designed with a 133-MHz FSB and you put it on a board that supports only 100 MHz, then 100 MHz will be the speed of the CPU's data bus. In many cases, incorrect setting will prevent the machine from booting properly.

The northbridge also decides how much RAM you're going to be able to use in your machine. Theoretically, all Pentium-based systems should be able to address up to 4 GB of RAM. The address bus of 64-bit CPUs can theoretically address a few million terabytes. Even early processors such as the Pentium II should be able to address 64 GB. The sad truth is that no chipset ever manufactured has taken advantage of more than a fraction of that capability. Current motherboards are designed to support anywhere from as little as 384 MB to 2 GB on boards designed for desktop machines. Those designed for servers are more generous, and there are models available that support up to 16 GB.

object   In reference to the OS, an object is any single resource on the system and/or network, including files, users, or devices.

object counter   Performance Monitor is an application that ships with Microsoft server products that can monitor a huge number of system variables. Variables are broken down into groups called *system objects*. Within these objects are the counters themselves. These counters are the individual properties or variables that are being monitored. Any number of object counters can be added to a Performance Monitor report.

object oriented   A programming schema that involves writing common routines as individual modules. When a specific function is needed, the programmer writes a line calling the module. Each module is called an object and can be used as many times as needed in a program but only has to be written once.

octet   Any collection of 8 bits. In the context of TCP/IP, it represents one of the four sections of an IP address, which will be represented by 1 to 3 decimal characters.

offline   Not currently present and active on the network. A server that is offline cannot be accessed by users.

online content   When you browse the Internet, the material you're searching for generally resides on a Web server. Any material that can be accessed over the Internet qualifies as online content.

open architecture   Any application or hardware specification that is readily available for public scrutiny and modification. Similar to open source.

open source   Any software that is freely available to the public and whose source code can be viewed and/or modified without penalty. Operating systems such as Linux and Beowolfe are open source. In addition, there are a myriad of applications, including entire office suites, that are open source and freely downloadable.

open-ended question   A question formulated in such a way that the answer will leave open further queries. The answer provided by the user has a strong potential of leading to other questions. An example of an open-ended question might be, "What were you doing at the moment the problem first appeared?" The user is less likely to say, "Nothing" in response to this question than if you ask, "What changed?"

operating system (OS)   The OS is an application running on a computer system that makes the computer do what you want it to do. An OS is the program running on the computer that manages all of the services required by applications that are to run on the system and interfaces with the hardware. These services include:

- The file system
- Processor control

- Memory management
- Device control
- Security

An OS differs from a conventional application in several ways. For one thing, the OS provides very few functions that are used directly by the end user. Typical commercial operating systems ship with a number of small applications call *applets* that provide user functions, but these applets in turn rely on the OS to do their work. For example, the user is not directly accessing an OS function when he browses for files in Windows. An applet called *Explorer* provides the interface. In turn, Explorer interfaces with modules within the OS *microkernel* to access the previously mentioned services.

Most operating systems have safeguards that prevent direct user or application access to the hardware as well. In the Microsoft world, a layer of application files and applets known as the *hardware abstraction layer* acts as the OS interface between the device and the application or user interface.

Local security is a function of the OS. When a user fires up a home computer, it may appear as if there is no security involved. In fact, there is more than meets the eye. Clicking on the baseball (or whatever icon you've chosen to represent your account) with the user's name next to it logs that person onto the computer locally, even if there is no network involved. It is possible for an administrator (or parent) to configure permissions in such a way that not everyone can access the color printer or the banking software.

An operating system is directly tied to the CPU installed on a system. An OS written for a PC will not work with a Macintosh without some form of subsidiary application such as Virtual PC running on the host computer. However, some companies ship different versions for different platforms. For example, Unix is the foundation for the Apple OS X operating system, but it is also available for Intel processors. There are literally dozens of options available for operating system selections; however, most computers in use today use one of the following:

- BeOS
- Linux
- Netware
- OS X
- Unix
- Windows

optical stylus   (1) A mechanism consisting of a laser-emitting diode coupled to a beam splitter. This device acts as the read/write head for a CD or DVD player/ recorder. (2) A small, pen-shaped device used with digitizing tablets and personal data assistants. With the digitizing tablet, a user can use the optical stylus to draw pictures or write, or he can use it as an elaborate mouse to select or drag objects on the desktop. With the PDA, it is a substitute for a mouse.

optomechanical mouse   When you use a mouse, you move the device across a surface, usually a mouse pad, and the arrow on the screen follows the direction of your movements. It seems simple enough until you realize what all is going on

FIGURE O.1   As the ball moves across the surface of your mouse pad, these three rollers keep track of the direction that you're moving the mouse.

to make that seemingly simple procedure work right. First of all, the mouse has to be able to detect your motions. The optomechanical mouse uses a small rubber ball protruding from a window on the base of the device. This ball rolls along the surface of your mouse pad.

There are three rollers such as the ones seen in Figure O.1. One is located directly toward the front or back of the mouse and one is located on one side or the other. A third roller is positioned at 45 degrees to the other two.

As the ball rolls along the surface, it moves these rollers. Direction and angle of movement directly affect the speed at which the rollers rotate. As they rotate, they move a wheel attached to one end of the roller. That wheel has a bunch of teeth cut into it. An LED shines a light past the wheel. On the other side of the wheel, a photosensitive receptor picks up the light from the LED. When one of the teeth is in the way, no light hits the receptor. The space between the teeth lets the light through. As a result, the wheel generates a flickering light. In turn, that flickering light causes the receptor to generate a series of electronic pulses, which are sent to the computer. The mouse driver installed in the computer keeps track of the number of pulses generated by each roller and uses the information to move the cursor across the screen.

Orange Book   (1) The US Government standards publication that defines security levels for various operating systems. Levels include A1 as the most secure ranging downward to D, which is the least secure. (2) A publication that lists the standards for hardware development, driver development, and file system standards for recordable CD-ROM devices.

originate modem   For two devices to communicate over a telephone line, each device must be equipped with a *modem*. The device that initiates a call is known as the *originate modem*, while the one on the receiving end is conveniently called the *receive modem*.

Out-of-Order Execution   Computers being what they are, it is pretty easy to assume that data always arrives at the CPU in precisely the order in which it is needed. Instructions always arrive in the right sequence and data is always there when you need it. Right?

The fact of the matter is, data is not always there when the processor needs it and the more complex programs become, the more the CPU starts seeing sets of instructions it is going to eventually need before it gets the ones it needs now. In the old days, the CPU just waited. If you were lucky, instructions waited in cache until the CPU was ready and they would be there when the processor was ready for them. The control unit would then make sure that those instructions ran in the correct order. More often, too many clock cycles would elapse and the instructions would be flushed from cache. The result of that happening was that a new search had to be initiated.

Modern CPUs employ a process known as *out-of-order execution* to keep busy and minimize dead time. A CPU can run certain types of instructions in advance and store the results in the data cache. Then when the data or instructions it was waiting for arrive, it processes those instructions. The results are compiled and moved on to the next step.

output   If users are going to be able to take advantage of the data processed by their computers, those results of that processing somehow must be exported from the computer to the world in which people actually live. It doesn't do a whole lot of good if the CPU simply lets the information it created float to digital heaven when it needs to make room for more data. Output can be printed, transmitted, displayed, stored, or played back. There are literally hundreds of devices on the market that collect the output of your computer and put it into some usable form. Table O.1 shows just a small number of output devices on the market today.

TABLE O.1

Some of the output devices found on a typical system

Floppy diskette	Hard disk drive	Modem
Monitor	Network	Printer
Sound	Tape	Tactile

overclocking   CPU speed is a function of two elements. The first element is the internal bus speed. Secondly, there is a multiplier factor. The multiplier is a factor built into the CPU that determines how many times faster than the internal bus the CPU will run. A CPU with a bus speed of 133 MHz and a multiplier of 8× is rated as a 1,064-MHz (or 1-GHz) processor. Many computer enthusiasts look at this speed as a mere starting point in their efforts to create an even faster system.

There are two ways to increase the actual clock speed of a CPU. You can adjust the multiplier or you can adjust the bus speed. You can't adjust the multiplier on today's Intel-branded CPUs. Some of the AMD chips allow this. However, with nearly all systems, if you tell a 133-MHz bus to run at 266 MHz, it will. This is the process of overclocking. Increasing the bus speed will effectively increase the clock speed of the CPU by the same percentage. If your system components and cooling system aren't up to the task, they might only run for a few seconds before shutting down from thermal overload, but they will run. When you do that, your CPU and your RAM will also run twice as fast (and about 100% hotter). When the CPU overheats, it will shut down. When memory overheats, it is more likely to cause critical memory errors. For a stable system, make sure you set your CPU settings correctly.

However, if you're going to do this, at least pay attention to the basics. First of all, you need a motherboard that allows the adjustments to be made. Not all do. Once you have selected a board that allows overclocking, figure out how the adjustments are made. To adjust either the multiplier (if possible) or the front-side bus speed, you will approach this in one of two ways. Either the motherboard will have a series of jumpers on the board or you will do it in the BIOS Setup. If it is in the BIOS setup, you will be looking for a section called *Advanced Chipset Settings* (or something similar).

Once you have adjusted the multiplier and/or bus speed, you will find out on the next boot if your settings are way off. It won't boot. Sometimes in order to get the CPU to run at its new speed you have to make sure that the core voltage is set correctly. If it is running too high, the CPU runs too hot and the system crashes. If it's set too low, the CPU can't maintain the clock speed and the system crashes. Therefore, to bump clock speed, you might need to bump core voltage—but not too much.

Assuming your system board allows core voltage to be adjusted, you'll find yourself going back into the advanced chipset section once again. The BIOS will show you the available range of settings. Try increasing the core voltage, one increment at a time, rebooting the system with each change.

The benefits of overclocking are obvious. Your system runs faster. However, it only runs marginally faster. The risks may easily outweigh the advantages. If you're lucky, an unsuccessful attempt at overclocking is detected right away. Your system won't boot. If it does make it through the boot process, an unsuccessful overclocking attempt may result in system instability. This may show up as system locks or unpredictable blue screens from the OS. The worst-case scenario is when the result of your experiments is silent data corruption. Errors that neither the user nor the system are able to detect may cause data to be incorrectly processed or incorrectly copied to storage.

A critical component of the CPU subsystem that must not be ignored by the overclocker is its cooling system. This system consists of a set of fans and a large heat sink to draw heat away from the processor(s) and out of the enclosure. A heat sink is a metal device with a large number of fins that dissipate heat. On many high-end systems, a liquid-cooled system similar to the radiator in your car assures that heat is very effectively drawn away.

Another component of the cooling system that doesn't get enough attention as far as I'm concerned is a simple substance known as *heat sink compound*. This is a silicone-based grease that you apply to the surface of the CPU before adding the heat sink. Proper use of heat sink compound greatly enhances the ability of the cooling system to dissipate heat. Improper use, or lack of any compound at all, is very likely to lead to CPU overheating. As I mentioned before, an overheated CPU will shut down abruptly. If it overheats too often, that can lead to premature failure. With Pentium 4 CPUs the heat sink compound is applied to the base of the heat sink as a thin layer of material. As the CPU heats up, the substance fuses to the CPU to form the proper bond, so you don't have to physically apply anything.

P

packet (1) The OSI model for networking breaks the process of networking down into seven layers. Data that is sent over the network is broken down into smaller pieces for transmission. Various layers have different structures for the individual chunks of data that are transmitted from one layer to the other along with the associated control data. The format of data, or protocol data unit (PDU), processed by the network layer and sent downward to the data link layer by the transmitting computer or up to the transport layer by the receiving computer is called a *packet*. The packet includes network addressing information. (2) A generic term for individual pieces of data transmitted over a network that includes the data payload along with all of the control data needed to get that information where it needs to go.

packet switching This is a communications technology for which the switches along the data path will analyze the route for each packet. On any given communications link some packets go by way of Chicago and others by way of Omaha. To complicate matters even further, on any given circuit the packets from hundreds or even thousands of different communications links are all mixed together. You are relying on the different protocols and OSI layers to make sure the right packets get where they belong and that they get put together in the correct order when they arrive. The majority of telecommunication is done by way of packet-switching technologies. In fact, the technology is moving in that direction as far as voice communications are concerned as well. Several different protocols have been developed that provide high-quality voice links over packet-switched networks. These include Cellular Digital Packet Data (CDPD), General Packet Radio Service (GPRS), and Bluetooth, among others. In order to make use of the higher speeds made possible by packet-switching technologies, you need faster carriers as well.

page (1) The amount of data that can be moved on a single memory read/write cycle; usually between 1 and 20 KB. (2) In a word processing document, a page is the amount of data that will fit onto a single sheet of paper, as defined in the formatting of the document.

page description language A programming language used between a computer and a printer that defines precisely how dots of color (or black) will be applied to the page in order to generate printed output. Different manufacturers have produced various page description languages. The most popular are Adobe's Postscript and Hewlett Packard's Printer Control Language (PCL).

page fault When the system does not find the data it needs in RAM, it will search the *paging file*. If it fails to find that data, that is a page fault. This will result in a new search for the required data on the hard disk.

page frame   The 64 KB of high memory that is used for moving data down from addresses above 1 MB into the 640 K used by DOS programs.

page read/write   When physical RAM in a system becomes full, data will be temporarily stored in a file called the *paging file*. A page read is a read operation from this file, while a page write is when data is moved from RAM to the paging file.

pagination   A process by which applications assemble text or graphics output in order to fit correctly onto a page as formatted by the selected printer device. Since different printers use different amounts of space on the page to produce the same output, it is not uncommon for a document to undergo the process of pagination whenever a new printer is selected as an output device.

paging file   The paging file is a chunk of hard disk space that is treated by the system as if it were RAM. Available space on the paging file is reported to the memory manager as being available memory. Data or instructions not actively needed by the CPU at the moment can be moved out of physical RAM to the paging file, and data that is currently needed moved from wherever it happens to be stored to RAM. As a result, total system memory is a function of both physical RAM and the size of the paging file. If you have 2 GB of RAM and a 245-GB swap file, your system thinks you have a total of 247 GB of memory. Figure P.1 illustrates the concept of the paging file.

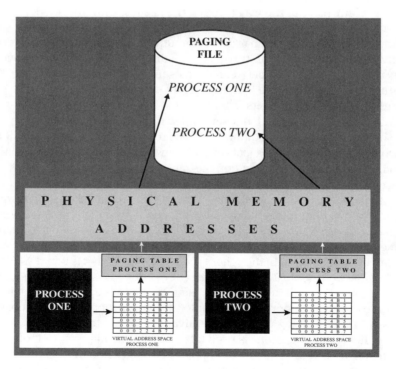

FIGURE P.1   The paging file is simply some acreage on the hard disk that the OS uses as pretend memory.

All operating systems use some form of paging file. The paging file in Microsoft Windows is a good example of how they work. In general, Windows will assign a value equal to the amount of the physical RAM installed in your computer, plus 11 MB. Ideally, you would want the paging file to be 150% of installed RAM. Therefore, if you have 2 GB of memory installed in your computer, you might want to consider kicking the paging file up to 3.5 GB.

The reason for needing a paging file is that moving data back and forth between the hard drive and RAM takes time. While accessing data from the paging file does require a hard disk operation, the data found in the paging file is located in a fixed location and does not require a random search. It is still no replacement for physical RAM. The less physical RAM you have, the more the paging file gets worked and the more your hard drive churns. This is causing your computer to take a noticeable performance hit. Constantly active hard drives on a system are almost always a sign of insufficient RAM and rarely indicate defective drives. The more RAM you install, the less your paging file will be used and the faster your server will perform.

palette   A set of colors that is available to a specific application or device. While 24-bit color is theoretically capable of over 16 million colors, not all applications or devices can manage that many. If a device is only capable of 16-bit color, it may only be able to produce up to 64,000 colors. The 64,000 colors that it selects from the pool of 16 million colors is the palette.

paper jam   An error condition that occurs with a printer when a sheet of paper does not successfully pass all the way through the printer. Until the stuck page is removed, the device is effectively disabled.

parallel communications   With parallel communications a byte is broken down into its individual bits and each bit travels over a different wire. For this to work, the timing and synchronization between devices must be extremely precise. All 8 bits that are part of a single byte must arrive at their destination at the same time (Figure P.2). Otherwise the bits from different bytes may get scrambled together. Eggs may be good scrambled, but scrambled data is destroyed data.

Therefore, for parallel communications to work correctly, there will be eight conductors on the cable just for data flow, and multiple other conductors for clocking signals, synchronization bits, and various other requirements of the specific parallel signal. A number of devices use parallel communications. Conventional hard disks generally use parallel signals. The drives most commonly found in desktop computers make use of a technology called the *Advanced Technology Attachment* (ATA) interface. There are two types of drives that use ATA. The ones that use parallel signaling are called (conveniently enough) parallel ATA or PATA drives. Oddly enough, the other type of ATA hard disk is serial ATA or SATA.

Small computer systems interface (SCSI) drives also come in both serial and parallel format. You will find printers, scanners, and other external devices that hook up to the parallel port on a computer system as well, although most of these devices are rapidly giving way to more advanced technologies.

Parallel communications is used internally on the majority of motherboard components. It used to be the most popular method of hooking up printers, although that has thankfully given way to more advanced technology. And even though it isn't called parallel, your hard drives, for the most part, communicate in parallel.

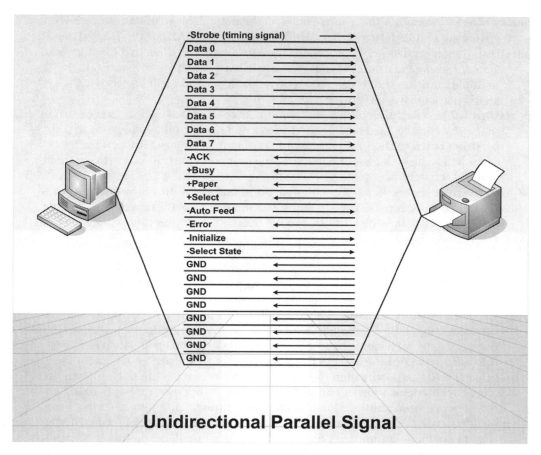

FIGURE P.2   An uncreative artist's rendition of parallel communications at work. This diagram depicts a simple unidirectional printer cable.

parity   (1) With memory technologies, parity is an error-detection method that simply counts the number of 1s in a byte of data. Parity can be implemented either as even parity or odd parity. With either method, each byte of data is accompanied by a ninth bit called a *parity bit*. With odd parity, if there is an odd number of 1s present in a byte, the parity bit is set to 1. An even number of 1s will result in a parity bit of 0. Even parity reverses this approach. (2) In RAID arrays that use parity, such as RAID 3, RAID 5, and some of the nested RAID levels, data is stored in stripes distributed across multiple drives. As each stripe of data is created, a mathematical calculation is performed on that data and the results are stored in a separate block on another drive. This mathematical model of the stored data is known as a *parity block* and can be used to recreate data in the event that one of the disks in the array fails.

parity bit   An extra bit carried by a byte of memory that indicates whether there is an even number or an odd number of 1s in the byte.

parity block   A data set that represents a mathematical image of data stored elsewhere in a RAID array. Parity blocks are used in RAID levels 3, 5, 5+0, and 5+1.

partition   All hard disks contain one or more formatted sections that contain data. One of these logical subdivisions of a single hard disk drive is a partition. If multiple partitions are created on a drive, each partition will be seen by the system as a separate drive, or *volume*.

partition table   Partition tables contain blocks of data that define each partition that exists on the hard drive. A FAT-formatted drive could contain up to four partition entries. The first entry would define the primary partition for that drive while the subsequent entries define extended partitions. Partition tables identify the very first sector on the hard disk where the partition resides as well as the final sector. In addition, the partition table specifies how many sectors the partition occupies. This apparent redundancy provides an error-checking mechanism to allow disk utilities to determine if partition tables have become corrupted.

park   To safely position a hard disk read/write head in a place where it cannot come in contact with the recording surface of the platter. In early systems, a head parking utility was run by the user to park the heads. Modern hard disks automatically park the heads when the system is shut down.

pass-through authentication   The procedure by which one network domain hands off the responsibility for logon authentication to another domain. When multiple domains exist on a single large network, trusts must be established between the domains in order for users from one domain to access resources on the other. The domain on which the user's account resides is the only domain that can provide logon authentication for that user. If that user attempts to log on to the network from another domain, and pass-through authentication has been enabled, when the first domain fails to authenticate the user, before it totally rejects the logon attempt, it passes the request on to all other domains with which it has a trust established. The user's home domain processes the request and then passes the results of authentication back to the domain on which the user is attempting to log in.

Password Authentication Protocol (PAP)   A nonsecure protocol for providing user credentials between hosts on a network. It is considered nonsecure in that passwords are transmitted in plain text.

paste   To insert data that has been copied from one file or location into a selected point of a document or file. For example, when you highlight a paragraph from a letter you wrote home to Mom and then copy that same paragraph into the letter you're writing to Aunt June, you are pasting that paragraph. You are also likely to get caught.

patch   After an operating system or application is released to the general public for use, development does not come to an abrupt stop. As minor improvements are found, flaws are discovered, or new features are added, the manufacturers provide small software updates that allow the users to add these minor changes to their versions of software as needed. An individual fix or addition is considered a *patch* (which sounds much more professional than *bandage*). Periodically the company releases a cumulative collection of individual patches in a major upgrade called a *service pack*.

payload   Packets traversing a network contain a variety of information, including network and host addresses, control data, and the actual data that was the core reason for the communication. The actual information carried in the frame that caused the frame to be transmitted in the first place is called the *payload*. This may include user or application data, or protocol-specific information.

PC card   Any auxiliary device designed to be plugged into a *PCMCIA* slot. PC cards were first released in 1990 as an 8-MHz 16-bit device. They were limited to a 24-bit address space and, as such, could only address 64 MB of memory. They worked with computers that sported, at a minimum, a 386-DX microprocessor. Maximum bandwidth of a PC card was in the vicinity of 16 Mb/s.

For the most part, PC cards were truly Plug 'n Play. In general, they required no intervention on the part of the user as far as installation and configuration of a device other than providing the driver disk when needed during the first installation of a new device. Subsequent insertions of the device require no additional action.

One thing unique to PC cards is the typical structure of the device drivers used. PC cards use a two-tiered device driver. The first level is the socket driver. The socket driver notifies the computer when the device has been either inserted or removed and provides I/O operations. The second level is the card service. The card service interprets the command set for a particular device.

peer entity   According to the *OSI model* of networking, there are seven layers of networking architecture. Hardware devices, application, and OS services communicate with their like counterparts on the other end of the network at the same layer. Any two devices, protocols, or services that operate on the same layer that can communicate with one another over the network are considered peer entities.

peer-to-peer   All network entities are created equal in the peer-to-peer (P2P) networking model. There is no single device that acts as a controller over other devices. All devices act as a client when requesting the services of another device and act as a server when providing services. As such, all devices are "peers" to one another. Security in the P2P model is lax because there is no authentication service to verify a user's rights. Each user sets permissions on the resources they create. Version control is virtually nonexistent. Multiple versions of files can exist in various places on the network, with no clear idea of which might be the correct or most up to date version. However, a P2P network is easy to set up and maintain.

peer-to-peer application server   Peer-to-peer models are the one server model in which there really isn't a dedicated server. While each individual server may perform a separate function, there is no one server that acts as a master controller. The advantage is that it is relatively easy to set up and configure. The disadvantages are numerous. Security is lax, data integrity is almost nonexistent, and anyone who creates a file becomes that file's administrator. Hardware requirements are difficult to specifically define for a server on a P2P network, because you never know what any given computer is going to be doing.

peripheral bus controller   The peripheral bus controller (also known as the *southbridge* in older chipsets) takes care of communication between the CPU and the slower components of the system. The southbridge takes care of things like the

ISA bus, IDE ports, USB ports, and any other devices not specifically handled by the northbridge chip or the memory controller hub. All expansion bus platforms prior to PCI are under the control of this chip as well.

permissions The degrees of access a particular user has been granted to a specific resource on the network. In a simple file system, permissions can include read only, write, change, or full. Read only should be self-explanatory. A user can view the contents of a file but can make no changes. Write permissions allow users to add new files to a directory. Change permissions allow the user to alter the contents of a file or even delete a file. Full permissions allow the user to perform any action to a file or directory.

perpendicular recording Older hard disk recording methods recorded each bit of data as a linear flux line that was applied to the medium as the platter spun beneath a recording head. This required a large number of molecules along the surface of the disk for each bit of data, while trillions of magnetic particles went unused in the layers beneath the surface. Perpendicular recording makes use of a stack of magnetic molecules rather than a long strip. Because of this, a much smaller surface area is used for each bit. Thus, *bit density* is dramatically increased. Hard disks using perpendicular recording technology currently store up to 345 Gb of data per square inch of medium, with industry projections predicting up to 1 Tb per square inch in the near future.

personal computer (PC) A complex computing device that is manufactured in such a way as to be affordable enough for the average person to afford. The first PCs released by IBM cost about six thousand dollars when they appeared on the market, which according to my trusty inflation calculator was worth around $33,600.00 as I write this . . . which brings into question the definition of the word "afford."

phase-change layer Phase change is a fancy way of saying that a substance is changed from one form to another. The phase-change layer is a layer that recordable optical disks use. On the older style CD-recordable (CD-R) drives, this layer contained a type of dye that was easy to burn through when exposed to the heat of a laser beam. This created the *pit* needed by the optical stylus to act as a bit of information. Rewritable CD (CD-RW) drives use a metal alloy that reacts differently to different levels of heat. In place of dyes on which to record data, the CD-RW blank has a layer of a rather exotic material made of silver, antimony, tellurium, and indium. Like all metals, it has a melting point. Unlike most metals, however, this compound also has a crystallization point. Melting point occurs at a moderately low temperature. Intense heat crystallizes it. A crystallized spot becomes a data bit and the disk can be prepared for reformatting by melting the layer.

phase-change printer This is a type of ink-jet printer that uses a radically different technology than standard liquid ink printers. The phase-change ink-jet printer starts with a stick of solid ink. The print head melts the ink and holds the melted ink in a specially designed reservoir. When the print head is called on to apply ink to the paper, it uses a mechanical mechanism to eject the ink. The ink then hardens almost immediately.

These printers have an amazing capability of producing a more photorealistic image for one simple reason. Ink applied by either thermal ink jets or piezoelectric ink jets is going to adhere to the paper in an extremely thin layer. Phase-change printers result in a much thicker coating. So thick, in fact, that Xerox, one of the leading manufacturers of this kind of printer, uses a final process called *cold fusing*. In this process the paper is run through a pressure roller to flatten the droplets of hardened ink. This process has two different but complimentary side effects. The surface of the image takes on a more photographic nature. This is because conventional photographic prints are produced on a gelatin surface that is much thicker than a layer of ink, which gives the image a greater feeling of depth. The thicker coating of the phase-change printer more closely simulates that surface. The second thing that provides a subtle improvement is that the pressure of the fusing roller creates a blending effect between adjacent droplets of ink. There is less pixelization of the image.

phosphor Cathode ray tube (CRT) monitors have layers of phosphorous applied to the inside layer of the viewing tube. A shadow mask is placed against the back surface of the layer. This mask allows only specifically defined areas of phosphorous to be exposed to the electron beams. A single spot of phosphorous exposed to an electron beam is called a *phosphor*. The shadow mask assures that any individual phosphor will always be exposed by the same electron beam and will always glow in one of the three primary colors: red, green, or blue. The intensity at which the electrons strike the phosphor determines how brightly that phosphor glows. In order to produce the myriad of colors that we perceive on our computer screen, it takes three of those phosphors, one of each primary color, working together to produce a hue. These three phosphors working together form a *triad*.

physical address A numerical entry that tells a process or device the actual location of another device. In a network interface card, the hardware address is often referred to as the MAC address, in reference to the Media Access Control layer that manages physical addresses in networking.

physical memory Memory addresses that exist in the installed memory modules of the computers. This contrasts with virtual memory, which is actually hard disk space that is treated by the system as if it were memory.

piezoelectric crystal A substance that changes shape when exposed to electricity. Some types of ink-jet printers use these crystals in place of heat to expel a droplet of ink onto a sheet of paper to create a dot of color. A combination of gravity and surface tension keeps a droplet of ink in place inside the nozzle. When the printer needs to eject it onto the paper, it zaps the nozzle with a charge of electricity. The nozzle squeezes inward and the ink is forced out onto the paper.

Proponents of piezoelectric ink jets claim that this method forms a cleaner image than does the thermal ink jet. Their reasoning is that when the bubble produced by a thermal ink-jet printer strikes the page, it is going to burst, producing a halo effect. According to this theory, the piezoelectric printer is putting a solid droplet of ink onto the page and that won't happen.

PING PING is an acronym for a utility called The Packet Internet Groper. In common use, the term has become a word in itself that can be used as a noun or as a verb. PING works on the basis of the ICMP protocol and can tell you whether or not a particular host on the network is reachable. It works by sending out a series of ECHO packets. The intended host, on receiving the packets, will return an ECHO

REPLY. If the ECHO REPLY returns successfully, ping will calculate the total time elapsed for the round trip. Not only is PING an acronym, it has been universally adopted as a term that can be either a noun or a verb. As a noun it represents the packets sent when pinging another host. As a verb, it represents the process of pinging another host.

The syntax for a ping command is : ping –{trigger} host. Some of the triggers that are useful in ping include:

-t   Sends a continuous ping to the targeted host until stopped by the user. Ctrl>Break will display statistics and then allow you to continue, while Ctrl>C stops the ping.

-a   Resolves a host name to an IP address.

-n   {count} Sends the number of ECHO packets defined in the count. For example, ping –n 16 192.168.0.110 will send a total of 16 ECHO packets to the specified IP address.

-l   {size} Sends a buffer size to the target host.

-f   Sets the Don't Fragment field in the ECHO packet.

-i   (TTL) Sets the time to live for the packet.

-r   {count} Records the route for up to the number of hops specified in the count.

-s   {count} Puts a timestamp on the number of hops specified in the count.

-w   {timeout} Specifies a time out in milliseconds that the sending device will wait for a reply.

In the event that a host is not reachable, ICMP will generate a message that explains the event.

pinned list   This is a section of the Windows Start window (beginning with Windows XP) that allows the user to custom design the start menu. The pinned list can be considered to be similar to the Favorites list in other Windows operating systems and applications such as Internet Explorer. A user can place shortcuts to applications that are used daily in this section. Default shortcuts that appear in the pinned list include the user's Web browser of choice and her e-mail client.

Any program can be added to the pinned list simply by right-clicking on the item. In the pop-up menu that appears, click Pin to Start Menu. Another way an item can be added is by dragging and dropping it to the start button or the start menu. If a user no longer wishes for an item to be a part of the pinned list, it can be removed from this list by right-clicking it and clicking Unpin from start menu or Remove from This List. If a user is not happy with the order in which the items appear on this list, she can rearrange them simply by dragging and dropping items to the preferred position.

pipeline   The path that data takes through the CPU as it is processed. This path consists of the various registers and cache locations at which the data or instruction resides while it waits for other processes to occur as well as the microconductors that carry the data from one stage to the next.

pirate   To make an illegal copy of a piece of software or copyrighted data. Legally, piracy is a form of theft and can be prosecuted accordingly. Any time you make a copy of a program, a digital copy of a song or other intellectual property without express written consent of the owner of that property, you are committing piracy.

pit   A tiny hole embedded in the recording layer of optical media that prevents the laser from reflecting back into the photoelectric sensor. *Also see* **land**.

pixel   A pixel is an individual colored dot that consists of several phosphors or multiple dots of ink. The phosphors or ink dots combine to form a single spot of a particular color. A computer image is built up from thousands or millions of these pixels. One specification of digital cameras consists of how many pixels it can reproduce (in millions). A 10-megapixel camera creates an image composed of 10 million pixels.

pixelize   To convert an analog image into a series of round or square dots in order to generate a digital rendition of the image. All digital image files incorporate pixelization. However the term is almost universally used to describe the effect of block and unsharp images that occur when the dots become large enough for the human eye to perceive.

platen   This is the hard rubber-encased cylinder against which the paper rests in an impact printer. Gears on either end of the platen core engage with a stepper motor that advances or feeds the paper. The stepper motor is user-adjustable so that whoever is using the printer can have it advance the paper in different increments to approximate single spacing and double spacing. Most also provide for space-and-a-half, and some provide even more options.

platter   The disk platters are what give the hard disk its name. The hard disk medium consists of a magnetic coating applied to a metal (or in a few cases, glass) disk. Unlike the once-popular floppy disks, the hard disk platter is a solid and very rigid substrate. Both faces of the platter support a recording surface. Most hard disks contain two or more platters.

Data is encoded onto the surface of the medium with magnetic pulses that change the polarity of a collection of magnetic particles on the surface. The minimum number of magnetic particles required to store a single bit of data is called a *bit cell*. Over the years different techniques have evolved in the manufacturing process to use fewer particles per bit cell and allow smaller spaces between bit cells as a method of increasing bit density. Bit density is simply the number of bit cells that can be crammed onto a single platter. These days, bit density is measured in gigabits per square inch.

Data is stored on the platter using a technology known as *CHS*. This acronym represents cylinders, heads, and sectors per track. The smallest unit of data that can be stored on a hard disk is the sector. A sector is 512 bytes of data that must be read all at once. If you have a really tiny file that is less than 512 bytes, it will still occupy a minimum of one sector. As you will learn later, the file system selected may impose even more restrictions, based on the minimum number of sectors that it can read at a time.

On each platter surface, data is recorded in concentric rings from the center of the disk to the outer edges. Each "ring" of data is called a *track*. Sectors of data are laid down one after another along each track on the platter. The number of sectors that can be laid down in any given track gives us the sectors-per-track variable.

plenum   An architectural term referring to the space between the ceiling of one floor in a building and the floor of the one above it. Network or computer technicians who are called onsite to add a new drop to the network are very likely to be asked to run it through the plenum.

point and click   A process by which an application can be run or a file opened simply by positioning a cursor on the screen over an icon or text string and clicking on the button of the mouse.

Point-to-Point Protocol (PPP)   A protocol that allows virtual connections across a network using dialup or ISDN connections. It is also used with asynchronous transfer mode (ATM). PPP allows direct virtual connections to be made between hosts over the Internet. ATM is a high-speed serial connection protocol used in networking.

PPP replaced an earlier protocol called the *Serial Line IP* (SLIP) as the standard protocol for dial-up connections or ISDN connections. It is a layered protocol that allows the transfer of IP packets over the connection. The three layers are the Link Control Protocol (LCP), the Network Control Protocols (NCP), of which there are several, and the IP control protocol (IPCP).

LCP provides the end-to-end services. It handles the tasks of establishing the connection, exchanging configuration information, and monitoring the connection while it exists. NCP transports the data being sent by specific networking protocol suites, such as TCP/IP or IPX/SPX. IPCP allows for IP packets to be transmitted over a PPP connection.

pointer   A line of code used by UFS to map a cluster used by a specific file.

polarity   The characteristic of an electrical circuit to have one point of relative positive charge (or pole) and another point of relative negative charge (or pole).

popup menu   A series of commands that appears on the screen only when the mouse cursor is either hovered over another menu option or that menu option is clicked on by the user. Popup menus generally consist of related commands.

port   Ports can be confusing concepts to the novice. They exist as both physical and logical entities. In either case, a port is nothing more that a gateway through which data flows in order to get to a specific destination. Physical ports include serial and parallel ports, to which peripheral devices such as printers, scanners, and external storage devices can be attached. Virtually any input/output connection can be considered a port.

Logical ports get a bit more complicated. The *TCP/IP protocol* uses ports as a logical addressing scheme, as do most operating systems. However, the term means something slightly different for TCP/IP than it does for the OS. Hardware can be subject to logical ports as well. COM and LPT ports are preassigned IRQs and I/O addresses that a user can select, making the physical port easier to configure. Serial ports are assigned a COM port and parallel ports are assigned an LPT port. Table P.1 lists the assignments for COM and LPT ports.

TABLE P.1

The standard COM and LPT ports, as defined by IBM

PORT NAME	IRQ	I/O
COM1	4	3F8h
COM2	3	2F8h
COM3	4	3E8h
COM4	3	2E8h
LPT1	7	378h
LPT2	5	278h

Specific protocols from the TCP/IP suite and any applications running on the system are assigned a port as a logical address for the final destination of data as it moves across the network. Ports exist as well-known ports and ephemeral ports. The well-known ports are ports 0 through 1023. Table P.2 lists the well-known ports. These are assigned and administered by an organization called the Internet Assigned Numbers Authority (IANA). Ephemeral ports are addresses used by the client software to establish a connection with a server (or other host). Many ephemeral ports are also assigned ports, but because there are so many and because they are subject to change, they will not be listed here. Ports can also be assigned semirandomly from the pool of available ports for secure transport of data.

TABLE P.2
Commonly used well-known ports

PORT	PROTOCOL
20	FTP, File Transfer Protocol, data
21	FTP, File Transfer Protocol, control
23	Telnet
25	SMTP, Simple Mail Transfer Protocol
80	HTTP, HyperText Transfer Protocol
109	POP, Post Office Protocol, version 2
110	POP, Post Office Protocol, version 3
666	Doom, Id Software

port replicator A port replicator is actually nothing more than a scaled-down docking station. It is used to convert a laptop computer into a desktop workstation of sorts. With most models, the replicator attaches to a docking connector on the back of the laptop computer. A port replicator provides all the I/O ports of a standard desktop computer, but lacks additional PCI slots and/or drive bays. For many portables that lack integrated network support, it is usually possible to get a port replicator with a built-in NIC. As with docking stations, it is possible for the user to create separate profiles for each configuration to speed up the boot process.

port security On a typical network switch, the device does not care what devices is plugged into any given port on the switch. Intelligent switches can be programmed to respond only to a specific *MAC address*. This essentially secures that port from any other device using it to access the network. Once port security is enabled, the switch has to be configured for an IP address/MAC address combination. It doesn't matter if you configure a different device with the same IP address. Once the switch looks at an incoming packet from a specific port and sees a conflict with the MAC address it has recorded for that port, the port is instantly shut down and no device can access it until an administrator turns the port back on.

POST card The POST card is a device used to diagnose problems that occur during the boot process that prevent the computer from starting properly. It mounts into an empty expansion slot and while the computer is booting (or trying to, anyway), it zips off light patterns on an LED readout so fast that you can't possibly read them. Don't worry about that. The ones you can't read are the ones you don't care about. They represent components that passed diagnostics.

At the point that the boot process fails, the readout will display a pattern of lights that represents a specific component. This is the last component to pass POST. The POST card ships with a booklet that itemizes all of those error messages. All you have to do is look up the number displayed and the book tells you what part of the POST process the specific versions of BIOS would have followed, and therefore is the one that failed. JDR Microdevices in Sunnyvale, California, offers four different options. It has standard POST cards in both PCI and (as of this writing) still provides them in ISA form. It also has PCI versions that test the BIOS as well as the POST process.

A more sophisticated version of this card is available from Ultra-X, Inc., in Santa Clara, California. It can go beyond the POST test (which it does rather extensively) and continue to test RAM, drive operation including CD-ROM drives, and much more. The professional kit includes an impressive array of diagnostic software utilities, a collection of loopback plugs, and the PCI card, the card illustrated in Figure P.3. A rather interesting option, offered by pcwiz out of Clearwater, Florida, offers a single card that has an ISA connector on one edge and a PCI connector on other.

P-rating Short for performance rating, this was a labeling method used by earlier competitors of Intel that, instead of designating a CPU by its clock speed, labeled

FIGURE P.3 *The POST card is a hardware device that determines the failure point during the hardware boot process.*

it as the Intel CPU equivalent that it could be compared with, even though the actual clock speed and bus speed were both lower. P-ratings were based on the philosophy that the competing manufacturers had design features that made their processors run faster than anything Intel had running at a similar clock speed. Two things made P-ratings very unpopular with professional hardware technicians. First of all, they weren't really all that accurate. Many of these "advanced features" worked only if the application running on the system was programmed to take advantage of them. Secondly, they made configuring motherboard/CPU combinations much more difficult than it had to be. P-ratings, for the most part, were abandoned after the release of the Pentium CPU.

preemptive multitasking   Early operating systems allowed multiple applications to run on a computer at the same time through a process called *cooperative multitasking*. While this did allow the user to run different applications simultaneously, it wasn't all that efficient. Applications dictated when they would release control of system resources for another application based on break points in the programming code. Sometimes a rogue application would take over the system and all other applications would freeze. Modern operating systems use preemptive multitasking. No longer are the applications in charge of when, where, and how they give up control of the system. A task scheduler runs as an integral part of the OS and makes sure each and every application running on the system has an equal chance at system resources. The task scheduler provides time slices for CPU clock cycle access and other resources needed by the applications running on the system. The scheduler dictates when an application will relinquish control.

prefetch unit   The subcomponent of a microprocessor that is responsible for retrieving data and moving it into the CPU. When the CPU needs additional data or instructions, it sends the prefetch out looking for that data. There is a specific order in the locations where prefetch searches for data. First it looks in the instruction and data cache registers of the CPU to make sure the requested information isn't already there. Next it searches the various levels of onboard cache, starting with L1 and working its way down. If the data is not located in cache, it hands the request off to the chipset for a full system search. The chipset first searches memory, then the paging file, and finally performs a new hard disk search.

pregroove   A spiral track on the CD-R blank is imprinted onto the blank at the factory at the time of manufacture. This is known as the *pregroove* and it is the target area for the *pits* that eventually will be burned by the CD-R drive. The dye is poured over the grooved base in a very thin layer. To simulate the reflectance of the aluminum layer of standard CDs, a microscopically thin layer of metal is placed over the dye. Figure P.4 provides a simplified illustration of the concept.

presentation context   Data moving across the network assumes a completely different form than when stored on a hard disk or even in RAM. This form is considered to be the *transfer syntax*. In addition, more complex transmissions of data, such as a multimedia file, involve multiple file formats. Since a large amount of data transfer involves multiple message types, there will be multiple abstract syntaxes involved. For example, in a multimedia presentation going out over the wire, there will be audio, video, plain text, and protocol data, all of which are

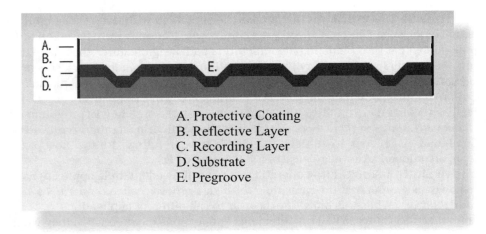

A. Protective Coating
B. Reflective Layer
C. Recording Layer
D. Substrate
E. Pregroove

FIGURE P.4   *Recordable CDs start with a disk already grooved for the tracks, called the pregroove.*

required to reassemble the multimedia presentation properly at the receiving end. Each form of data is considered to be stored in its unique *abstract syntax*. In order to transfer such complex data, the presentation layer of the *OSI model* negotiates a specific transfer syntax for each abstract syntax involved. The complete package is called the *presentation context* and the collection of abstract and transfer syntaxes is the *defined context* set.

preventive maintenance   Regularly scheduled cleaning, checkups, or precautionary work done on a piece of hardware or an application that is intended to keep it functioning properly without requiring emergency repair. Preventive maintenance can include activities such as cleaning dirt from fans or from the rollers of a mechanical device. Running a defragmentation utility on a hard disk is preventive maintenance. Other actions can include updating antivirus files, installing the latest patches to an operating system, or updating the drivers for a device.

primary domain controller   In Microsoft networking, computers, devices, network resources and users are all managed in domains. A domain is any group of those devices or resources that are under the control of a single administrative entity. In early versions of Microsoft network operating systems, there could only be one network server that hosted the prime security database for the domain, and that computer was called the primary domain controller. Other servers, called backup domain controllers, could house copies of that database, but only one server was the master of all. More recent versions treat all domain controllers equally.

primary partition   A primary partition is one that is defined in the master boot record of the hard drive and can be turned into a bootable partition. There can be only four primary partitions on any given physical disk. Primary partitions can be further divided into *extended partitions*. How many extended partitions you can have depends entirely on the file system you select. A key thing to remember here is that extended partitions are not defined in the master boot record. Each primary partition contains a *volume boot record* that defines any extended partitions contained within that primary partition.

print head The mechanism on any impact or ink-jet printer that is responsible for depositing the pigment onto the paper. On the dot matrix printers, there are a few choices in this respect. The most basic printers have a simple nine-pin print head. The pins are aligned vertically, as seen in Figure P.5. In order to achieve higher resolution, manufacturers developed the twenty-four–pin printer. The idea was the same, except that by having a greater number of pins, which were made of a finer wire, a document could be printed that exhibited much finer resolution and detail. The print head squeezed twenty-four wires onto a single print head by arranging them into three rows of eight pins, as shown in Figure P.6. Twenty-four–pin printers were a bit slower, but that was a sacrifice people were willing to make in order to produce "letter-quality" documents.

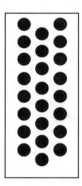

FIGURE P.5   A rough diagram of a nine-pin dot matrix print head.

FIGURE P.6   A rough diagram of a twenty-four–pin dot matrix print head.

The pins are seated into sleeves that are linked to strong springs. The natural position of the spring is such that the pin would be in contact with the paper at all times, if a very strong magnet were not holding it back. An electrical coil is wrapped around one pole of the magnet, which forms an electromagnet. When current is applied to the electromagnet, it neutralizes the energy from the fixed magnet. The spring releases and the pin pops back to its natural position. The dot is pressed into the paper and the electromagnet is turned back off. The fixed magnet pulls the pin back away. Figure P.7 is a rough diagram of the process that takes place.

The print heads on the majority of ink-jet printers are either thermal print heads or piezoelectric heads. As you might imagine from the description, the force of nature used by thermal ink-jet printers is heat. Heat brings the ink up to

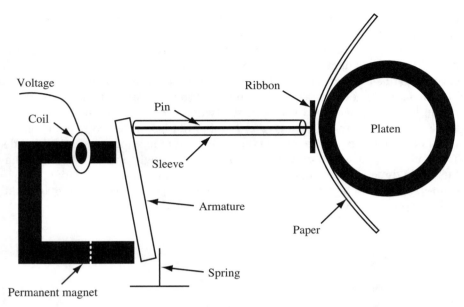

FIGURE P.7 *A diagrammatic representation of the structure of a dot matrix print head.*

the boiling point and forces it through a very small nozzle and onto the paper. In order to assure that the ink can be brought to boiling at precisely the right instant, a thermal ink-jet printer keeps the reservoir of ink at a temperature just under the critical point. At the instant a droplet of ink is needed, a heating circuit applies a sudden burst of heat that ejects a small bubble of ink.

Piezoelectric printers get their name from the fact that the nozzles are made from a piezoelectric crystal (PEC). A PEC has the unique characteristic that, when given a shot of electricity, it changes shape. PECs squeeze inward. A combination of gravity and surface tension keeps a droplet of ink in place inside the nozzle. When the printer needs to eject the ink onto the paper, it zaps the nozzle with a charge of electricity. The nozzle squeezes inward and the ink is forced out onto the paper.

printer   A device that produces hard copy output from digital files. Files that can be printed include graphics files and text files. Most applications output data to the printer in both graphical and text mode. For example, a word processing document that includes fancy fonts outputs the text to the printer, along with graphical renditions of the typefaces used. Other applications, such as a spreadsheet, merge graphics and text as well. In order to perform its job a software routine known as a printer language translates the stream of bits arriving from the computer into the electrical impulses that drive the printing mechanism.

printer access protocol (PAP)   An AppleTalk protocol that manages virtual connections to networked printers and shared printers on the network. PAP manages the mapping of such printers, handles the transfer of data between hosts and printers, and is able to communicate that status of printers to users on the network. PAP is a connection-oriented protocol and can manage multiple simultaneous connections. When a print job is sent from a host to a computer, PAP will engage the services of the *AppleTalk Transaction Protocol* for the transfer of data.

priority boosting   A process by which the privilege level of a thread of code is promoted to a higher level in order to enhance its chances at the CPU. In order to make multitasking computing as efficient as possible, the CPU has to determine the priority of code. Each string of code receives a priority level based on the type of request it represents. Certain requests, by nature, need to be processed more quickly than others. A low-priority request will be the last string of code processed. However, because the processor is constantly bombarded by requests, unless something happens to move that poor little low-priority item along, it may never get processed. Therefore, periodically, the processor "promotes" low-priority threads to a higher level until eventually they make their way to the top. This assures that every string of code has a chance at the CPU.

privilege level   A privilege level basically determines the priority that any given line of code has over another line of code, assuming both want to run at the same time. These privilege levels are called *processor rings*. Processor rings are ordered on the basis of their current privilege level (CPL) and range from CPL-0 to CPL-3. A line of code running in ring 0 (or CPL-0) has priority over ring 1, which has priority over ring 2, which has priority over ring 3. Get the idea?

By having certain functions run in certain rings, the possibility is minimized that a renegade string of code from a poorly designed application might bring the entire system down. Windows specifications call for core system functions, such as the Virtual Machine Manager and the kernel, to run in ring 0, where they enjoy maximum protection. In Windows 3.0, code running in real mode, such as DOS programs and BIOS code, run in ring 3, and all other applications run in ring 1. Starting with Windows 3.1 and in all subsequent 3x releases, all the code running in ring 1 is moved over to run in ring 3. So essentially, rings 1 and 2 are left under the control of the processor.

Microsoft products to this day continue to use this architecture. However, a slightly different vocabulary is used. Processes running in ring 0 are said to be running in *supervisory mode*. These are the processes that require the most protection and the highest processor priority. All other processes, which would be running in ring 3, are running in *user mode*.

privileges   Administrative rights allowed by the system. Individuals' privileges indicate what level of control they have in changing things on the system or network. These can be assigned either directly to a user on an individual basis, or they can be assigned by adding a user to one of the operating system's built-in groups. Most administrators prefer the latter approach.

probabilistic   Any approach that is likely to achieve the desired results, but is not guaranteed to achieve them.

process   Many people get confused when trying to understand the difference between an application, a process, and a thread. It really isn't that difficult. An application is a program you run on a device in order to perform a certain task. As simple as that may sound, performing what appears to you to be a simple task may require the application to be able to perform a number of different functions. These individual functions are called *processes*.

A word processor is an example of an application. It exists solely for me so that I can write this book. However, in the process of writing the book, a large number of different processes come into play. Formatting of characters, page formatting, pagination, and hundreds of other things that users take for granted are accomplished automatically, compliments of the electronic magic of the computer.

When two applications communicate it is not the entire application that talks, but rather the process or processes that require the exchange of information. You can see this concept at work if you run Windows 2000 or XP. Pressing Ctrl>Alt>Delete will bring up the Windows security screen. At the bottom is a button called Task Manager. The middle tab of that screen is the Processes tab. With only one application running, take a look at all the different processes running. Some are specific to the OS and others relate to the application that you're running. Each one represents a string of code currently running on the system that either the OS or the application needs in order to function.

The thread is the most fundamental string of code that the CPU handles when processing data. It is a single line of code or command that is managed by the CPU as it works its way through a single process in the application.

process entity   The protocol or application on a host that is actually requesting or transmitting data during a network session.

processing   This is what occurs whenever data or instructions are executed, manipulated, updated, or altered in any way. Simply through-putting data from an input device, such as a keyboard, to an output device, such as a monitor, constitutes processing. Any manipulation of data that can occur between the time the data has been inputted into the computer and the time that is provided as output constitutes processing. Processing can consist of calculations performed on the data, replication of that data to alternative locations, and the comparison of one data set to another. Not all processing is done by the CPU.

processor ring   Another term for *privilege level*.

product activation   A feature added to recent operating systems and applications that is intended to prevent that product from being installed on more than the number of computers for which it was licensed. The idea is to limit the negative impact of illegal piracy of software. Product activation involves two processes in proving ownership of a license to run the OS. During installation, the user will be prompted to enter a product key. This is a long series of letters and numbers that is virtually impossible to type without mistake. Once the product key in properly inserted, the OS installs.

Product activation is a separate process and is usually run concurrently with product registration. To the beginner, it may appear that these two processes are one in the same, but they are not. Product activation is mandatory and must be done within 30 days of installation or the product will stop functioning (except for the activation feature). Theoretically, product activation collects no personal information at all to be transmitted to the manufacturer's site. During installation a unique number called the *installation ID* is generated. When the user activates the software, the installation ID and the product key are transmitted to Microsoft. This information is stored in a database. Any other attempt to install the OS using the same product key will fail.

profile   Various settings and preferences specific to a particular user or piece of hardware on a system.

promiscuous mode   An operating mode for any network interface in which all incoming packets will be accepted, even if they are not intended for that specific interface.

protected mode   A function of a microprocessor that allows multiple processes to be active in the CPU at the same time without "stepping on" each other. Each thread is protected from the others.

protection ring   A secondary circuit used by SONET to provide a backup path for data in the event the primary ring fails.

protocol   A piece of software that runs on your machine that allows computers of different hardware and OS platforms to exchange data as if they grew up in the same slab of silicone. Protocols work by making sure that the data that moves across the wire follows the same rules, uses the same format, and can perform the same functions regardless of the computer that generated that data or the computer intended to receive it.

proxy server   These servers can actually perform several valuable functions on the network. First, they allow a large number of users to share a single point of access to the Internet. This is far more efficient and less expensive than providing a separate account for each user who needs access. From a security standpoint, proxy servers provide a circuit gateway behind which your actual network IP addresses can be hidden. By caching recently accessed Web pages, they provide a degree of performance enhancement to the end users.

As with *firewalls*, proxy servers can exist as an application running on a server or as a dedicated piece of hardware running a specialized application. In general, proxy servers will provide the gateway services to the Internet for all users. They also will usually incorporate some form of firewall protection.

Unique to the proxy server is its ability to cache recently accessed pages. Once a page has been permitted access and viewed by a user, that page is stored on the proxy server. The next person who accesses that page will see it load much more quickly because it's coming from a local server rather than over the slower Internet connection. When a user makes a request for an Internet resource, that request is forwarded to the proxy server. Proxy checks the request against its filters to make sure the request will be permitted, and if so, does the DNS search, finds the Web page, downloads it, and forwards it to the client. That page is maintained in cache.

phthalocyanine dye   A more stable dye that has been used in recent generations of CD-R that is less sensitive to UV light than cyanine dye. It lasts for up to a 100 years.

Q

quad-pumped   A technique of moving 4 bits of data over each wire on each clock cycle of the frontside bus.

quality control   A process by which the overall excellence of a product is maintained at or above minimum predefined levels. Quality control is something that all manufacturers of hardware and software employ at every level of production.

quantum computing   A method of computing that manipulates the properties of a quantum system to perform calculations and generate data. A quantum system is a collection of atoms or subatomic particles that cluster together. In theory, since these systems can change state (flux) faster than anything created by man, a quantum computer should be faster than any electronic device could ever be. As of this writing quantum computer is still in the theoretical stage, but is rapidly approaching reality.

quarantine   When antivirus software scans a drive and locates malicious software, it does not automatically erase it. Instead, the suspect file is relocated to another folder on the drive and isolated from the applications and operating system. This is the quarantine process. Quarantining allows the user the option of deciding for himself if the file was actually a virus or simply bad code from software he was writing.

query   A request for data. Users make queries of a database when they perform a search. However, even hardware devices perform queries. For example, when the hard disk controller receives a request for data, that request is a query.

queue   A location in memory or on the hard disk where a series of instructions or a data set is stored until actually needed. Hard disk controllers are not only able to queue a long series of commands; they are able to sort the commands into a new order so that the commands can be processed more efficiently. Operating systems make use of a printer queue, in which the data from a streaming print job is stored until the printer is free to process the job.

Quicktime   Apple Computer's application for playing full motion video on a computer.

quorum   A disk or partition on a disk or SAN that acts as an arbitrator between servers in a cluster. Only one device can control the quorum at any given time. When any given computer in a cluster first starts up, the first thing it does is to attempt to take over control of the quorum. If another server already has control, the booting server joins the existing server's cluster. The device that owns the quorum periodically refreshes it ownership. Server states are stored on the quorum and any time one server fails, the other server reads the existing status from the quorum and takes control of the quorum. Failover from one server to another occurs when the primary server (the one that owns the quorum) fails to update its reservation of the quorum. The backup server takes control and becomes the primary server.

quota   Starting with Windows 2000 server, an administrator has the ability to allocate disk storage to individual users based on need. The amount of disk space allocated to any given user is that user's quota. When the user reaches a predefined percentage of their assigned quota, the operating system will generate a warning that the user's quota is close to being reached. The adminstrator has two options when the quota is actually reached. He can either lock the user out of the system or let that person go on as if nothing ever happened.

R

rack Racks provide a far neater and more orderly mechanism for arranging servers than simply piling them up on shelves or stacking them on the floor. Equipment racks are standardized in height, width, and even the distance between bolts. That way, an administrator doesn't get locked into a specific brand of server just because the company invested in a dozen oddball-sized racks. Racks are 19" wide and vary in height by the number of rack units (U) they support. One unit is 1.75". So if a manufacturer tells you they are offering a 42-U rack, you know that rack will be a little over 6 feet in height. It will have the capacity to house 70' worth of rack-mounted equipment (Figure R.1). On top of that, there will be clearance for a base, perhaps some wheels to roll it around on, and some have enclosed tops as well.

Typically, racks will also provide centralized power distribution through *power distribution units* (PDU). Generally, there will be two types of PDU employed. A *front-end PDU* brings in power from the wall. It can be a high voltage (208 V) or a standard 120-V PDU, depending on the requirements of the rack. *Distribution PDUs* (sounds kind of redundant, doesn't it? A distribution power distribution unit?) provide outlets for the individual components to plug into. Many high-end racks also incorporate uninterruptible power supplies (UPS).

rack-mounted server Generally, a low-profile server (Figure R.2) designed specifically to be bolted into industry standard equipment racks. They will be designated according to their size as 1 U, 2 U, or other sizes. (*See the entry for* **rack** *for a description of a unit.*)

RAM disk A virtual disk drive that is actually a contiguous space in physical memory. RAM disks are designed to include virtual sectors and virtual tracks in order to appear as much like a physical disk as possible. RAM disks are used to store data or instructions, or even TSR programs that need to be accessed as quickly as possible.

random access The ability to reach into an ever-changing pool of unrelated data and selectively retrieve only the information that is needed, from any location in the pool, at any time. Most physical memory in a computer system is random access.

range In the computer sense, a range is any subset of data that runs from a defined beginning point to a defined end point. A range can be a minimum/maximum string running from a low value to a high value. It can also be a series of values extracted from specific locations in a table or from a defined set of memory addresses.

RAS/CAS delay One of the bottlenecks in computer memory I/O operations has always been something called the RAS to CAS delay. RAS is an acronym for *row access strobe* and CAS is an acronym for *column access strobe*. These are the circuits involved in locating the specific memory cells where data is located in RAM. RAS/CAS delay is an interval of between two and four clock cycles (up to

FIGURE R.1   Here is a good example of a
rack-mounted server implementation.

seven clock cycles on earlier forms of RAM) between the completion of the RAS
cycle and when CAS can next initiate its cycle. Another term you'll see for this
delay is *CAS latency*. Memory that is advertised as CL2 has a CAS latency of two
clock cycles. Reducing the RAS/CAS delay can have a significant effect on memory
performance.

raster line   Computer monitors create images by combining millions of tiny colored
dots called *pixels*. The image will have a certain number of pixels that make
up a single line moving horizontally across the screen and several hundred (or
thousand) rows moving down the screen. A single row of pixels that make a
horizontal line across an image is called a *raster line*.

raw   Data that has been collected from one or more sources, but not yet processed. An
example of raw data is the stream of 9s and 1s that flow from a word processing
document to a printer. Until the printer has the opportunity to convert the data into
the bursts of energy that create dots on a page, to any person or application, that
data would be meaningless. Many digital cameras store images in raw format.

read power   Rewritable CD burners (CD-RW) perform their job by having a laser beam
that projects at different intensities. The lowest power setting for the beam, which
it uses to extract data from the surface, is the beam's read power.

FIGURE R.2   A single rack-mounted server can take up as little a 1.75" of vertical space in a server room.

read only   A permission setting that allows a user the right to view the contents of a file or directory, but does not allow her to make any changes.

real mode   In the early days of Microsoft computing, MS-DOS programs had to run in the lower 640 K and only one program could run on the machine at a time. This is the proverbial real mode. Real mode means 1 MB of RAM, only one program running on the computer at a time, and the programs have direct access to the hardware. While none of this is a requirement on today's operating systems (or even possible, in some cases), for reasons of backward compatibility, most processors still maintain the capability of running in real mode.

real time clock   A chip within a computer system that keeps track of the actual time of day and date.

real-time OS   An OS designed to be able to perform specific functions at the precise time at which those functions are needed. An example of real-time processing would be a computer program that controls an engraver. The program is capable of turning out incredibly detailed illustrations and designs etched onto metal surfaces. The designs are all computer-rendered. The application that controls the etching process must be able to manipulate the equipment in extremely precise movements. Otherwise the etching will be flawed.

The preceding example is one of many situations where being able to set priorities on specific threads of code becomes essential. Windows NT (and later versions) incorporates a task scheduler, which assigns each thread a priority between 1 and 31. Higher numbers represent higher priorities. Therefore, a thread with a priority of 16 will be run before a thread with a priority of 12. Priority 0 is reserved for the System Idle function, which will cause this thread to run only when no other thread is present on the system. Priorities 16 through 31 are reserved for real-time functions. Priorities can be assigned either by the OS (for system-generated threads) or by the application (as in the example previously related here).

reboot   To restart a computer system. The term boot comes from an old military phrase "to pick up by the bootstraps". Rebooting a system can consist of a cold boot or a warm boot. A cold boot involves turning the computer completely off, waiting a few seconds and turning it back on. A warm boot restarts the OS but does not put the computer though a new POST process.

recognition scan   *Plug and Play* detects hardware on the system during boot up via the recognition scan. A BIOS routine polls each device installed on a computer system to see whether that device is Plug and Play and, if so, what resources it currently claims. It also checks each expansion slot, USB connection, and serial and parallel port, as well as any other available connection, looking for any new PnP devices. This information is stored in a hidden file called the *extended system configuration data* (ESCD) file.

record   (n) Within a database application, each entry is known as a record. The record consists of all data specifically related to the indexed entry (or primary field) of the database file. For example, you might have a database of your antique collection. In the database, you have your grandfather clock listed, and another entry for your silver candelabra. Each one of these entries is a separate record. (v) The process of adding new information or data. When you transfer a music file to a hard disk, you are recording that tune.

Recovery Console   An emergency start mode in Windows operating systems that allows a trained administrator to make changes to the system or to fix problems that are preventing the system from booting properly. Recovery console is one of the options presented when a user presses F8 during the boot process. Recovery console is purely a command prompt environment and requires that the user be well-versed in working with direct-typed commands.

rectifier circuit   A specialized series of components that converts current, AC to DC.

recursive query   A recursive query tells a *DNS server* to check its own resources first and return the information to the client. If the information cannot be found locally, DNS will then look to outside resources for the information. If a server supports recursive queries, the server can forward the request to other DNS servers or to a root server.

redirector   An application process that distinguishes whether a requested resource is local or remote. It then initiates a local procedure call for localized services and a remote procedure call for those services that reside outside the local system.

redundant   Repetitive or duplicated. A mission critical application might exist on two identical servers. One is running all the time, and the other is a redundant backup in case the primary server fails. A mirrored hard disk is a primary disk plus a redundant copy of that disk.

refresh   To recycle an electrical or electrostatic charge. Refresh is a necessary process that standard DRAM must go through. All those little capacitors that activate the transistors are constantly leaking out their charge. Unless something is done to correct this, all the 1s will turn into 0s. In order to prevent this from happening, an additional circuit was added to periodically recharge those little capacitors. That is what is meant by refresh.

Of course, if a cell is supposed to represent a zero you don't want to add a charge to it. This would corrupt data just as surely as losing an existing charge. Therefore, the first phase of the refresh cycle consists of determining the relative charge of a particular cell. Essentially, if the cell is less than half-charged, the MCC assumes it to contain a zero. That cell is not recharged. Any cells containing charges greater than half will receive a fresh charge.

Computer monitors also experience many refresh cycles per second. The phosphor that glows in order to create the image must be exposed to the electron beam in order to keep glowing. Generally, this refresh occurs between 60 and 180 times per second.

refresh rate　(1) CRT monitors work by exciting particles of phosphorous with an electron beam. This causes the phosphorous to glow. However, that effect is extremely brief. Once struck by the electrons, however, that phosphor doesn't glow very long. A few hundredths of a second is all it's good for until it fades away. Therefore, the electron gun has to keep redrawing the screen over and over again to keep a stable image. How frequently it redraws the screen is the monitor's refresh rate. Refresh rates are measured in hertz and range from a low end of around 48 Hz to as high as 200 Hz on some brands. Maximum refresh rate is directly linked to the monitor's selected resolution. The maximum refresh rate advertised by a manufacturer can rarely be used in conjunction with the maximum resolution advertised. To get higher resolutions, a lower refresh rate usually must be used.

(2) The number of columns of memory cells per cycle that the MCC will recharge in a single cycle. This is not based on any specific time interval, but rather how many thousands of columns of bit cells are affected by a single refresh cycle. Early RAM refreshed 1,000 columns in a sweep, and the refresh rate was designated 1 K. Subsequent generations of RAM have included 2 K, 4 K, 8 K, and 16 K.

regional network　The portion of the *SONET* network that provides services to users at varying bandwidths and collates the signals into a single high-speed pipeline.

register　(1, n) A bank of transistors grouped together to perform a specific function. Microprocessors make use of registers to store information as it passes through the processing cycle. Instruction and data cache are divided into registers, and general registers hold data in intermediate forms during the course of processing. (2, v) To record your licensing information with a software manufacturer. Most software developers have some strategy for recording the information about the legal users of their products in a database so when support is requested they can cross check the caller against the database.

registered memory　Registered memory stores a page of data in a buffer (i.e., the registers) and does a comparison of the copy about to be transmitted with the copy in the buffer. This assures a more accurate copy. Registered memory includes the registers themselves in addition to some circuits called *phase lock loops*. The latter makes sure that the integrity of control signals is constantly maintained.

The process of registering does cause the system to take a slight hit. Each bit of data moved across the bus requires an extra clock cycle in order to go through the registering process. This minimal performance loss is easily overshadowed by the performance loss you would have if you were unable to use a sufficient quantity of memory.

registry   In Windows, a relational database that contains all system and application settings and/or parameters. This database contains every setting, parameter, device driver, or file location the system requires for full functionality. The registry consists of a series of six primary registry keys. A key consists of a specific category of setting relevant to a specific area of Windows functionality. Any number of subkeys can exist beneath the primary keys. All of this information is initialized when Windows is first installed and is constantly being updated every time a new piece of hardware or software is installed and every time a user makes a change to the system configuration. It is all stored in two primary files: USER. DAT and SYSTEM.DAT. In Win95, a backup of each of these files existed but carried .DAO extensions. Windows 98 increased the number of backup files from one to three.

   The six primary keys are HKEY_CLASSES_ROOT, HKEY_CURRENT_USER, HKEY_LOCAL_MACHINE, HKEY_USERS, HKEY_CURRENT_CONFIG, and HKEY_DYN_DATA. Each of these primary keys holds specific information critical to the system. Oddly enough, one of these keys does not get stored in the .DAT files mentioned earlier. It is created on the fly as the system boots.

   Beneath the primary key are subkeys. These are frequently referred to as *hives*. Each hive contains sections specific to the properties of a particular function within the OS. For example, one of the subkeys is called *Software*. Beneath this folder are additional folders for each and every brand of software installed on the system, as well as folders for software Microsoft thinks you are likely to install later. The folder that is specific to Microsoft (or any other brand) is called a hive file. The primary key descriptions are as follows:

HKEY_CLASSES ROOT   provides the information that OLE requires in order to work. It also stores the mappings used by different programs when the user takes advantage of the drag-and-drop functionality offered by Windows. Other information, including how different applications deal with different file types based on their extensions, is stored in this key.

HKEY_CURRENT_USER   contains information specific to the preferences of the user logged on to the machine. Win95 is capable of storing the settings for each person who creates an account on a machine. The various settings, preferences, desktop configuration, and application groups for a specific individual make up that user's profile.

HKEY_LOCAL_MACHINE   stores information specific to the hardware and software running on the machine. For most technicians, this key is where the majority of registry changes you'll ever make will take place.

HKEY_USERS   is where the information for all users that have a profile on a specific machine will be stored. If two or more users have created profiles on a machine, this key will be different from that of HKEY_CURRENT_USER. Each profile will point to a specific set of subkeys. When a user logs on, this subkey will form HKEY_CURRENT_USER. If there is only one profile, there will be little or no difference between the two keys.

HKEY_CURRENT_CONFIG   loads a specific hardware profile. As Windows supports multiple user profiles, it also supports more than one hardware configuration on a single machine. For example, you might have a computer with two video cards. When you are running your photo editor, you keep your image on one monitor and the software menus on another. But when you're using your word processor only, you have no use for the second monitor. By creating a separate profile in which the second video card is disabled, when Windows is booting you have the option of selecting the hardware configuration of your choice.

HKEY_DYN_DATA   is the one key that is not permanently stored on a hard drive. It is configured on the fly as the system boots, based on what user has logged on to the system and what specific hardware profile has been selected. It stays RAM-resident until Windows is shut down.

reload   An action that some applications allow that permit the user to start over from a fixed point. Users browsing a web page can reload that page to see if fresh data has been added, or to clear data that they have entered into an interactive page. Most games allow the user to save the game at a certain point and reload every time the monster kills them when they exit the air lock. Unfortunately, there is nothing to teach children that life has no reload and if they go shooting at people like they do in their games, and the people shoot back, they don't get to restart the game.

relational database   Databases keep information in structures called tables. Tables generally contain specific types of information. For example, a car dealership will include a table that contains their inventory of vehicles and another table that contains a list of all of their customers or possible leads for new customers. A relational database allows tables to be linked to one another. When a salesman sees in the inventory table that a new XJ-S has arrived, he can click on a search icon that looks through the customer tables for all the prospects looking for that model.

remote access server   Many organizations allow users to work from their homes. However, in order to do this, there needs to be some way of allowing those users to log on to the network from a computer located in their homes. That is the role of the Remote Access Services (RAS) server. When a RAS server is properly configured to run on the network, users can log on remotely and, as far as they're concerned, the process isn't any different than someone who logs on to the local network. But there are some key differences. A major difference is that the users aren't logging on to the local network. They're logging on over the Internet or over a direct dial-up connection. Once their credentials have been accepted, data moves back and forth over the same fiber optics cables as your e-mail and my football scores. Keeping your company's data secure is probably as important as making sure I get accurate scores.

Data security is a key issue. The RAS server, as well as the client on the user's machine, is configured to use one of the more secure communications protocols that I will discuss in later chapters. Logon authentication will be exchanged in encrypted packets and, once a session is established, all data is encrypted on either end before it is transmitted.

RAS servers have to maintain network security as well. Not just anyone can log on. RAS servers have a few tricks they can play to make sure that people trying to access the network are really who they say they are. In addition to conventional logon authentication, a few other security features can be instituted. One popular method is that a RAS server can be configured to disconnect immediately on authentication and call back to a specific number. The *Callback Control Protocol* (CBCP) makes this feature possible. That way, whoever steals your laptop can't take advantage of the fact that you told Internet Explorer to remember your password. When the thief calls in from a motel room, the server authenticates the user but then it disconnects and dials your number.

For the traveling worker who needs to call in from different numbers each time, the RAS server can employ another security option. The user is equipped with a hardware token that generates a new logon password for each session. This second password must be input after the primary password has been accepted. If a user does not possess the token, she gets no further than the initial logon procedure.

RAS servers can also limit the number of concurrent connections to the server at any given time. While this might not be a particularly useful feature for a work-at-home server, it's a dandy one for a game server where you don't want to tie up bandwidth with too many simultaneous players.

A RAS server needs to be running some form of protocol that provides secure communications over open lines. These protocols include IP Security Protocol (IPSEC), the Point-to-Point Tunneling Protocol (PPTP), and secure socket layers.

remote procedure call   A request for services that can be performed by or resources that reside on, a machine other than that from which the request was made.

removable media   Any data storage mechanism that can be separated from the computer and carried away. Removable storage includes the venerable old floppy disks, CD and DVD disks, flash drives and even removable hard disk drives.

rename   To change the designation or name of a file or directory without altering the contents in any way.

repeater   Network signals move, for the most part, over physical media. The nature of the media dictates that the signal can only go so far before it becomes unusable. Each form of medium has its own distinct characteristics in this respect. Repeaters are relatively inexpensive devices that allow you to work with distances beyond those limitations. Repeaters come in two forms. On the simplest level, you can purchase a box into which a network cable is plugged. You plug a second cable into the output port and keep on moving. The repeater works by taking the incoming signal, cleaning up any noise, interference, or distortion it may have picked up along the way, amplifying the signal to its original strength, and sending it on its way. Active hubs are another form of repeater. The active hub cleans up and amplifies the incoming signal before sending it out through the other ports.

report phase   When performing an upgrade with Windows NT (and later versions), an additional phase is added to the installation procedure to collect data about the existing OS installation. This is the report phase. During this phase, WINNT. EXE (or WINNT32.EXE) will scan the system registry and all .INI files looking for installed components, software, and device drivers. Any inconsistencies that it finds at this time, such as programs that are known not to run on Win2K or incompatible device drivers, are reported to the user. It also generates an installation script based on the information it finds.

After the user has prompted the setup program to continue, it will keep track of all registry settings, user profiles, user accounts and associated security settings, and path locations. All of this will be migrated into the new installation.

reseat   Sometimes components or cables in a device come loose and don't make a good connection with the socket it connects to. To remove the component or cable and plug it back in more firmly is to reseat the device.

reset   To restart a computer without turning it completely off and then back on. Most systems have a reset button that allows this. In the old MS-DOS, pressing <Ctrl> + <Alt> + <Delete> all at the same time would perform the same function. With modern operating systems the latter series of keystrokes brings up a menu that includes the option to restart, which accomplishes the same effect.

resident command   In an OS, any command that is an integral part of the command interpreter and does not require an external executable program. An example of a resident command is DIR. Search as you might, you won't find a DIR.COM, DIR.EXE, or DIR.BAT anywhere on your hard drive. Yet, when you type DIR at the C:\ prompt, your monitor spews out a listing of every file and/or subdirectory contained within. That's because DIR is a function of the command interpreter. The opposite of a resident command is a *transient command*. This is any command that launched an executable file when invoked. For example, when you type FORMAT at the command prompt, FORMAT.COM is launched.

resistance   The tendency for a substance to block the flow of electrons. Resistance tends to degrade the quality of electrical signals. However, it can also be used to advantage when trying to filter a signal or reduce the intensity of current.

resistor   Resistors are devices that resist the flow of electricity. That makes the name conveniently easy to remember. They are measured in ohms. Because they're so tiny, the manufacturers couldn't really expect to be able to print their value on the side. Therefore, a color-coding scheme was adopted by the industry (Table R.1). The manufacturer paints little colored stripes around the outside of the tube, and each color represents a numerical value. The colored stripes allow a technician to calculate the value of any given resistor. The code consists of four stripes. The first two are "significant" digits. The third stripe represents a multiplier, and the fourth indicates tolerance. In more simple terms, the first two are real numbers, 0 through 9. The third will represent a value, starting with 1 and going up in multiples of 10: 1, 10, 100, 1000, and so forth. Tolerance values (or the fourth stripe) will be only red, gold, or silver. You need to be able to determine that it's a 10,000,000 ohm, plus or minus 5% resistor just by looking at four colors.

restore   To resurrect a computer back to a preset condition. This condition can include the data stored on the system, system configuration settings, and any other aspect of system usability. In order to restore a system, there must be a usable backup data set that tells the system how to reconfigure itself.

restore point   Some versions of the Windows operating system feature a utility called *System Restore*. If a system running XP (or later) fails to boot normally or is functioning erratically, the user can "go back in time" to a system configuration that existed before the offending changes were made. It does so by using restore points. A restore point is a copy of critical system files and registry entries that

TABLE R.1
Color coding standards for resistors

COLOR	NUMBER	MULTIPLIER	TOLERANCE VALUE
Black	0	1	Not used
Brown	1	10	Not used
Red	2	100	±2%
Orange	3	1,000	Not used
Yellow	4	10,000	Not used
Green	5	100,000	Not used
Blue	6	1,000,000	Not used
Violet	7	10,000,000	Not used
Gray	8	100,000,000	Not used
White	9	Not used as multiplier	Not used
Gold	Not relevant	Not used as multiplier	±5%
Silver	Not relevant	Not used as multiplier	±10%

were in use at the time a system change occurred (or that a user manually created a restore point). When a restore point is created, copies of critical system files are made and stored in a hidden directory. The restore point directs System Restore to that directory and, when called on, uses those files to copy over the files in the target directory.

retry counter   A value maintained by a RAS server that increments with each attempt to log on. When configured with a specific value, once that value is reached, the account will be locked out.

rights   *See also* **privileges**.

ring network   A topology in which the signal starts at one location, moves around the network, and returns to whence it started. The most widely supported networking standard that made use of it was Token Ring, which went the way of the dinosaur. However, a newer technology, the Fiber-Distributed Data Interface (FDDI), also makes use of the ring topology. The concept of the ring network is more logical than it is physical. Figure R.3 illustrates the logical implementation of a ring network. However, in the real world, the ring is incorporated into the hardware. Physically, the network more strongly resembles the star network.

Were the computers laid out in a physical ring, it would be just like a bus network. Bringing one computer offline would bring down the network. However, in actual implementation, devices called *multistation access units* (MAUs) interconnect the devices. They look, feel, smell, and taste just like a typical hub in most respects. A cable runs from the computer to the MAU, just like it would

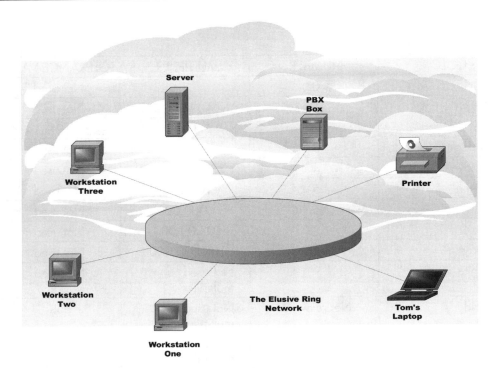

FIGURE R.3   While this diagram shows the logical layout of a ring network, in reality, devices will connect to a multistation access unit, so the physical implementation will appear more like a star network.

to a hub. Internally, however, they are wired in a ring. The circuitry of an MAU can detect when a computer goes offline and redirect the signal around the port that went down. Also, MAUs have two additional ports on the back, a ring in and a ring out. These aren't for hooking up telephones. They are the input and output connectors for interconnecting MAUs. They allow the network to be expanded without losing the logic of the ring.

riser   A specialized expansion card that supports other expansion devices such as PCI or ISA cards horizontally, parallel to the motherboard, in order to save space. Most low-profile form factors incorporate risers into their design. They allow expansion devices to fit into the enclosure without the need to use vertical space.

rollback   The process that some recent operating systems use to restore a computer system to a previous state of configuration. Unlike a complete restore, rollback does not affect the user's data set. A driver rollback simply replaces a newly installed device driver with the older one originally installed.

root directory   On any given hard disk, the root directory is the managing node of any given file system. All else lies beneath the root directory. In the file systems used by most Microsoft operating systems, the root directory is the drive letter followed by a colon and then a back-slash. C:\ is a typical representation of the root directory. In Unix-based file systems, it is simply a forward slash (/). Once the OS has been installed, a directory called *root* will be created. In Microsoft operating systems, there is a maximum directory depth of 21 nested directories. In other words, you can have the documents directory, and in that directory you can have a subdirectory of a subdirectory of a subdirectory, so on, up to 21 levels deep. Attempting to go beyond that limitation will result in an error message. *See also* **subdirectory**.

root frequency The single frequency of any given musical note that makes that note sound the way it does, regardless of what instrument plays it. The overall sound of the instrument is a function of how the root frequency interacts with the *harmonics* created by the instrument when the note is played. Sound cards generate *voices* by calculating a specific set of harmonics, based on the root frequency of a sound.

root server One of several collections of servers scattered around the world that maintains the databases of all domains that reside in any given top-level domain.

round robin algorithm A media access method in which a centralized device, such as an intelligent hub, scans each interface, searching for a device that wants to send data. It skips devices that do not need to transmit. If two or more devices need to transmit on the same cycle, a priority method is used to determine who gets to go first.

route (1) The path that data takes to move from point A to point B. Devices called *routers* maintain tables in memory that tell them the fastest paths between known network addresses. (2) The route command invokes a TCP/IP utility that allows the user to view or add static entries to the local routing table. These entries can include routes to networks or routes to hosts. Entries can also be introduced in numeric fashion or by name, if DNS is available. When inputting a static entry using the route command, the user would need to know the format of the routing tables used by the OS. By typing route print at the command prompt, the existing routing table will be displayed. When generating your own tables, type in your entries using the same format. The route command can be enhanced through the use of several triggers, as follows:

route print   Displays current local routing tables
route add   Adds a static entry to local routing tables
route delete   Deletes an entry from the local routing tables
route change   Modifies an existing route

router Routers are used to interconnect two or more completely different networks to one another. As with switches and hubs, routers will have several different interconnects. Unlike switches and hubs, these interconnects are likely to be of different types. RJ-45 jacks will be required for the internal LAN, but different connections may be required in order to interconnect with telecommunications equipment and/or other routers in the network.

Each port can be configured to a different network address. Internally, the router maintains a list of all network addresses that exist downstream of each port. This list is known as the *routing tables*. When the router receives a packet, it examines the header for the network address and then compares that address to its tables. If it finds the address listed, it simply forwards the packet through the appropriate port. If not, it forwards the packet through the port that the administrator has configured to be the default gateway. The default gateway is the path to the next router downstream. It then becomes the responsibility of the next router to figure out what to do with that packet.

With routers, each port forms the boundary of an independent broadcast domain. Devices on a network are constantly sending out broadcasts to all devices on the network for many different reasons. The larger the network becomes, the more congestion is caused by these broadcasts. Routers (unless configured to do so by the administrator) do not forward broadcasts. Therefore, a very large network can be subnetted into several smaller networks using routers. The broadcasts generated by any given subnet will not interfere with the other subnets.

Routing Table Maintenance Protocol (RTMP)   One of the protocols of the AppleTalk suite. It handles layer 3 routing functions for AppleTalk networks. RTMP routers can exchange all known network numbers and which interfaces have access to those networks, and they can exchange information relating to network conditions along any given route. RTMP supports *split horizon* routing, transferring data related only to directly connected networks. This dramatically reduces bandwidth overhead caused by forcing the protocol to constantly update routing tables that are not relevant to the configuration.

runtime error   Any malfunction that occurs within a program as it is operating on the system. Most runtime errors result in a program crash.

S

Safe Mode   An advanced boot mode of the Windows operating system that allows the user to start the OS without advanced device drivers or device configurations being loaded. This allows corrections to be made to an OS on which a software or hardware installation has gone awry.

sag   A sag in current is when voltage takes a significant drop. This can happen as a result of many things, and in fact happens thousands of times each day. When your refrigerator goes on, voltage drops for a second or so until it stabilizes. Somebody turns on the vacuum cleaner and voltage drops. These sudden drops have a greater negative impact on computer circuits than most other appliances. Loss of current to a memory cell or processor can cause the contents of that chip's *registers* to dump. This can result in crashed applications or even crashed computers. A good *surge suppressor* will usually also protect the devices plugged into it from sags as well as surges. The best solution is an *uninterrupted power supply*.

sampling   A step in the process of converting an analog signal such as a music file or image file into digital format. Such files are chopped up into microcosms of time. Each time slice is converted into a stream of 0s and 1s. The sampling rate, or how often these samples are taken, has a direct result on the accuracy of the conversion.

scalable   A term that defines the ability of a computer or network to support substantial upgrades. A scalable server is one that you can easily upgrade and/or add on to at a later time. Hot-swappable drive bays allow additional drives to be added without bringing the system down. Memory and expansion slots allow growth in those areas as well. A scalable server should provide the options for upgrading any or all of the following:

- Increasing memory
- Adding CPUs
- Adding additional hard drives
- Installing externally accessible drives
- Adding expansion cards as needed
- Upgrading the network interface

Scalable networks allow an administrator to add network switches, routers, and servers as needed in order to keep up with rising demand on system resources.

ScanDisk   A utility that first appeared in Windows 95 and was with Windows users until the release of XP, when a revamped version of Check Disk took over. When ScanDisk is run on a drive, there are two options. A standard check simply checks your files and folders for errors such as invalid names and/or date stamps. A thorough scan finds much more; it scans the surface of the hard disk looking for bad sectors. It can also find other errors such as lost file fragments, cross-linked files, duplicate file names, and errors that occur when Windows converts a long file name to the MS-DOS more primitive naming conventions. Two of these errors are worth examining more closely. These are the lost file fragments and cross-linked files. Many third-party utilities will refer to the lost file fragments as lost clusters.

Lost file fragments generally occur when there has been an unexpected system shutdown. If the OS suddenly crashes or if the user turns the machine off without going through the standard shutdown procedures, temporary files are left open, data that has been copied to virtual memory have not been saved, and open files are not properly closed. All of these can result in the FAT finding file allocation units (FAUs) on the hard drive that are occupied but have no reference in FAT to a specific file. These unclaimed clusters are the ones that are being reported. When ScanDisk finds them, by default, they are converted to files in the system root directory with names of file0000.chk, file0001.chk, and so on. In most cases, these were temporary files the system still had open at the time of the shutdown. They have little or no impact on the permanent copy of that file still written to the hard drive. Still, from time to time, it is user data that was never written to file. In many cases, the data corrupted, but if you can recognize what it is and where it goes, sometimes you can recover it. Most of the time, your best bet is to delete the .chk files and free up the space.

Cross-linked files can be a more serious issue. You may recall when I discussed the formatting of hard drives, I pointed out that every single FAU on the hard drive is mapped, whether it is in use or not. When a file uses the FAU, the entry for that FAU in FAT is marked as occupied and it is claimed. If two or more files mark the same FAU as being a part of that file, there is a problem. None of the files that claim those sectors can access the data on them. This situation can be caused by unexpected shutdowns, failure of a device controller, a glitch that occurred in the application that created the file, or any number of other things.

Some "buzzwords" used with ScanDisk follow:

- **Lost cluster** *See* **lost file fragment**.
- **Lost file fragment** FAU on the hard drive that contains data but that has lost the pointers that identify the file to which it belongs.
- **Cross-linked file** An FAU is claimed by two or more different files and is therefore available to none.

The way ScanDisk "fixes" these files is to compare the creation date in the file entry. The file with the most recent date gets the cluster. Most of the time this will be correct. However, that doesn't mean that the other file didn't, at some time, have data that occupied that file.

Other problems ScanDisk can find are invalid dates and invalid file names. No OS allows the user to create an invalid file name but data corruption can cause it to happen. If the OS thinks that an invalid character exists, it will mark the file name as invalid. Invalid dates occur when the date of the file is later than the date the system reports as being current or as an invalid date format. ScanDisk fixes either of these problems.

scanner A device that uses an optical mechanism connected to an analog to digital converter that allows a user to convert a hard copy document, such as a letter or a photograph, into a digital file. Scanners range from simple hand held devices used to read bar codes from products in a supermarket to large floor standing devices that can automatically feed up to thirty pages per minute through the device and convert them into digital format on the fly.

Scatter-Gather Data Transfer   The ability of a device to execute a command on one set of data and output the results to multiple devices. This technique first appeared in *SCSI-II* and has subsequently been applied to other device I/O interfaces as well.

scope   A database of available addresses maintained by a *DHCP* server. DHCP is a protocol that dynamically assigns TCP/IP configurations on the fly when a device first comes onto the network. An administrator configures the scope to include all available IP addresses. In order to prevent statically assigned IPs from being doled out (creating conflicts), static IP addresses are assigned from a pool of addresses that are maintained in a pool of reserved addresses configured into the scope.

screen buffer   A reserved area of memory that stores the information generated by a video card used to create a single frame of information displayed on a computer monitor.

screen capture   A process by which a single frame displayed on a computer monitor can be stored as a graphics file. Many free utilities exist that accomplish this function. Screen capture is good for creating a record of error messages or proving to a friend that you actually got to level 43 of DOOM 6.

script   A series of commands that can be stored as a separate file, or embedded into a file, that provides a specific sequence of executing a process. Scripts are particularly useful for very complex installations of server operating systems and applications.

scroll lock   A key on a standard keyboard that prevents the system from automatically paging down through a long file without stopping long enough for the user to read the contents.

scroll mouse   A pointing device that includes a small wheel that is used for paging up and down in a long document, image file or web page.

SCSI expander   (*See also* **Small Computer Systems Interface**.) One of the limitations of the SCSI interface has always been the maximum length of cable that could be used to interconnect the device with the host adapter. A device known as a *SCSI expander* allows this distance to be increased. The expander takes the SCSI bus and splits it into up to three different segments. Each segment can support a run of cable equal to that of the bus that it's on. Therefore, if you have a bus of all LVD devices, three segments of 12 meters are possible. Also, if you are not adding any devices to the middle segment, a longer cable than would otherwise be acceptable can be used.

Expanders work by taking the signal, cleaning up the noise that has been picked up along the way, amplifying it back to its original signal strength, and then sending it along its way. The device and the process are completely invisible to the host adapter. In fact, it is not even considered a device, and therefore requires no device ID. Table S.1 shows how much extra distance one can achieve on a SCSI chain using expanders.

Another thing that makes the SCSI expander a very versatile device is that you can mix early SCSI modes with some of the more advanced modes. You can get devices that move a parallel interface across copper wire to a serial fiber-optics interface. There are even devices that move an HVD signal across to an SE interface.

TABLE S.1
Distance extensions using SCSI expanders

BUS TYPE	STANDARD (meters)	FAST (meters)	ULTRA (meters)	ULTRA2 (meters)
Single-Ended SCSI				
No expander	6	3	1.5	N/A
1 Expander	12	6	3	N/A
2 Expanders (populated)	18	9	4.5	N/A
2 Expanders (point to point)	24	12	6	N/A
Low-Voltage Differential				
No expander	12	12	12	12
1 Expander	Not used	Not used	Not used	24
2 Expanders (populated)	Not used	Not used	Not used	36
2 Expanders (point to point)	Not used	Not used	Not used	48
High-Voltage Differential				
No expander	25	25	25	N/A
1 Expander	50	50	50	N/A
2 Expanders (populated)	75	75	75	N/A
2 Expanders (point to point)	100	100	100	N/A

Use of SCSI expanders, on its simplest level, allows someone to stretch a SCSI chain a little farther than he would otherwise be able to. This allows external devices to be installed at a greater distance from the host adapter.

Another use of this device involves using it as a domain divider switch. For example, if you have two separate computers, each with its own array of hard drives in an external storage bank, it is possible to share those devices between the two host computers. By placing a SCSI expander between the two banks of drives, each computer has access to either array when the switch is closed. If for any reason you need to isolate them, you open the switch and they are separated.

search engine   A web-based application that analyzes a request for information based on certain key words or phrases, and then uses a complex indexing system to locate any web sites that contain related information.

sector   The smallest data storage unit recognized by a disk on a hard drive. On magnetic media, the sector is consistently 512 bytes. It can vary for other types of optical media.

Security Descriptor   Windows NT security treats every single resource on the system, including the users, as objects. All of these objects are defined by a specific security descriptor. The security descriptor is a token that defines the security attributes of a specific object. In many cases, by default, this security is minimal unless the administrator chooses to increase it. The security descriptor comprises four components.

   The first two components are the individual security ID (SID) and the group SID. Another component called the discretionary *access control list* (ACL) identifies which users and groups are allowed to access a particular object. The system maintains its own ACL, conveniently named the *system ACL*, which oversees all security descriptors. The system ACL is used by the system for internal security audits when defined by the administrator. It is what allows an administrator to set and enforce security policies over the entire network.

seek time   The amount of time that passes between the time a request for information is made to a specific device and the time it locates the first bit of information on the device related to that request. Seek time is only a fraction of the total time involved in actually retrieving data.

segment   In reference to the transport layer, it is the PDU of that layer. The term can also be used to define a specific length of cable or the network devices that all share a singular collision domain.

segment register cache   Separate cache locations maintained by Pentium II (and later) for keeping 16-bit code running separately from 32-bit code.

Selectively Repeat   A variation on the *Sliding Window* method of flow control. A number of packets are transmitting and the sending computer waits for the replies. Each packet received by the target device is acknowledged. Good packets get an ACK and bad packets get a NACK and then go to that place where all bad packets go. They are discarded into digital oblivion. Unlike sliding window, where all packets since the first failure are retransmitted, only the bad packets are sent again.

self-extracting   File compression utilities are able to take large files and make them smaller, compacting them into files called archives. However, if a person does not have a utility for extracting the compressed information from the archive, then the file is useless. A self-extracting archive is one that contains the mechanism for decompressing the file back to its usable form.

semiconductor   Any substance that conducts electricity well enough to be considered a conductor and resists electrical flow well enough to be considered an insulator. In other words, it's a substance with an identity crisis. But that property makes it an ideal substance for the manufacture of transistors. Any electrical current that reaches a certain strength is allowed to flow. This is the semiconductor's *threshold voltage*. Any current less than threshold voltage is blocked. Therefore, current either flows or it doesn't, depending on how much current there is.

serial communications   When a computer connection makes use of serial communications, it is basically lining all the bits in a row and then sending them over the wire, one right after the other (Figure S.1). It may sound like parallel communications would be faster because the data is moving over eight separate wires, and not just one. It doesn't work that way, however.

   Serial communications can be either synchronous or asynchronous. Synchronous communication is the fastest form of serial hookup. Large amounts

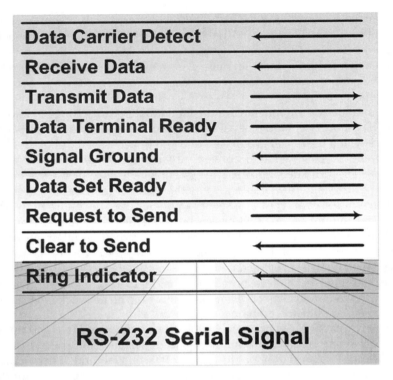

FIGURE S.1   An artist's rendition of serial communications.

of data is collected into chunks called *packets* and sent out that way; therefore, a lot of data moves on a single transfer. A header, which consists of additional control data, is added to the front of the packet, and a trailer, which contains error-correction information, is added to the end. These headers and trailers tell the receiving device where one packet ends and the next one begins. Synchronous communications are used by modems, network controllers, and some forms of hard drive controllers.

Asynchronous communication bundles together the individual bits of a single byte and moves data over the wire a single byte at a time. To separate the bytes, a starting delimiter and an ending delimiter are added to each of the 8 bits. A form of error correction called *parity* may or may not be added, depending on how a particular device is configured.

server   Any device or application that performs a service requested by another device or application.

server cluster   Two or more complete servers configured to appear to the network as a single device, useful either as a fault-tolerant entity or for load balancing.

server farm   A centralized location that houses all of the servers for a larger and more complex network. Basically, it is slang for the IT center.

service   Services are nothing more than applications with fancy, important-sounding names. But as we all know, an application by any other name. . . . In any case, the services need memory. Some services need just a little memory and others are hogs. Any time the service is called, it is going to need to be loaded in RAM. The way a server is configured dictates what type of services are going to run and how many services are required. Web servers and remote access servers have totally different requirements than an authentication server in some respects, and yet will require many of the same services. For example, removable storage is a service that must be running on a server if you want to be able to copy data to any device that makes use of removable media. Turn off that service and devices such as USB drives won't work. One service that must be running on all machines is the service host. Service host is the service that services the services. It has the capability of bundling a number of smaller service applets into a single executable file running in memory.

Service Access Point (SAP)   A predefined address that is used to transfer data between OSI layers. According to OSI, data moving from one layer to another will assume a specific format during the transfer and it will be copied to a specific memory address (the SAP) so the next layer knows where to locate it. In real-world applications, these are applications requesting data and not theoretical entities. So while the application is performing a specific function, such as adding a network address to a packet, it knows that since IP addresses are added at the network layer, and the network layer looks for information at a certain address in memory, it copies that packet to that address so the network layer can find it.

Service access points are added at the data link layer. This layer creates two forms of SAP: Destination Service Access Point (DSAP) and Source Service Access Point (SSAP). Each networking protocol in use needs one of each of these. The DSAP is the receiving station's logical link to the protocol and the SSAP is the transmitting station's link. SAPs are defined in unique headers that identify the logical port assigned to the protocol. These values are defined by OSI and not simply assigned arbitrarily by the programmer.

Why does the network need unique SAPs for each protocol if the SAPs act as the data path between OSI layers? The answer to that is simple. In the event that multiple files are being moved simultaneously, the network needs to keep the data segregated; otherwise, data corruption will occur.

service pack   All of the major NOS manufacturers are constantly updating their different product lines. These updates range from simple patches to full-fledged service packs. There are several reasons for doing this. First, as much as the manufacturers would like to dance around the fact, the first release of just about any product is going to have some "undocumented features." As inconsistencies or flaws in the programming are revealed, the companies provide fixes at no charge. If the problem is severe enough, they may make a public announcement. Usually, however, they simply post the update to their Downloads page on their Web site. Individual fixes are available as patches. A service pack is generally a virtual rebuild of a NOS that includes all patches from the last release date to the release date of the service pack. Because the service pack does rebuild the NOS, be aware of a couple of things. You will have to reboot your server for the service pack to take effect. You might want to do that during a quiet time when there are relatively few, or no, users on the network.

service primitive   The hardware or software that is actually doing some work during a particular networking session is known as the *active element*. During any given session, it is likely that several different active elements will be at work, making the transfer of data between network devices happen. The OSI network model tells us that specific network layers perform specific functions. The active elements at work are performing some sort of service that is necessary to the adjacent layer. The specific function to be performed is known as the *service primitive*. The layer makes use of parameters to define certain data and control information.

setup   The complete process of installing an application or operating system. Since this process can often be more complex than the average user is willing to endure, software developers write an executable file that runs the process automatically. Generally, this file is conveniently named Setup.

shadow mask   A *CRT monitor* creates images by exciting dots of phosphorous with a stream of electrons. A thin metal sheet perforated with tiny holes outlines the individual phosphors in a CRT monitor that make up the primary colors. Frequently, you will hear manufacturers talk about the invar mask that they use in their product. This isn't a type of mask as much as it is the kind of metal from which the mask is made. Invar is a metal that can handle extremely high temperatures without having its shape distorted. Since the steady barrage of electrons hitting the mask does result in the mask getting hot, this is a characteristic that is prized by manufacturers. This mask allows only specifically defined areas of phosphorous to be exposed to the electron beams. There are different layers of phosphorous, each compounded with a different substance to make it glow in a different color. The phosphorous compound is known as a *phosphor*. Each phosphor will always be exposed by the same electron beam and will always glow in one of the three primary colors: red, green, or blue.

share   Any resource on a computer or networked device that has been configured for access by other users. Unless a file or folder has been shared, it won't be visible to other users on the network.

share level security   With share level security, the user places permissions on the file or folder, and those permissions and any passwords the user assigns determine who may or may not access that resource. Share level permissions are attributes that are assigned directly to a specific resource on the network. For any given resource, there will be a specific password that will allow access. Access comes in one of four different forms.

- *Read permission* allows you to access and view the object, but not to modify it in any way. You cannot edit, delete, or rename the object. If changes are made to a file with read permission, that file cannot be saved under the same name.
- *Full control permission* allows you to do what you will with the file. You can edit, delete, or rename the file. You can even change the permissions on it, should you so desire.
- *No access permission* should be fairly self-explanatory. A file with no access assigned to it cannot be opened at all.
- *Depends on password* gives you specific permissions based on what password you supply. There will be one password for full control and another for read.

A problem inherent with share level security is that for every resource, there is a password. If 200 users have all created 10 files, each with a different password, then if you want to be able to access all 2,000 files, you need to know 2,000 passwords. That's handy, isn't it?

shift key   One of the modifier keys on a keyboard. The Shift key is the one that allows the user to select the alternate character or function for any given key by pressing Shift at the same time as pressing the desired key.

shortcut   A link that points to an application or file stored on the system. Shortcuts can be placed anywhere, but generally reside on the user's desktop. When a shortcut is provided, a user does not need to know the complete path to the resource in order to be able to use it.

shuffle   To automatically re-sort tracks or files into a random order.

sideband addressing   The ability of a device to send and receive data in a single memory I/O operation. Sideband addressing is used by AGP video cards to enhance performance.

signal saturation   The strength of signal that tape can accurately record before distortion becomes so great that the recorded version of that signal becomes unusable. What this means to the engineer is that the signal used to record all those tiny little 1s can be much stronger than the signal used to record all the 0s. This allows for higher recording accuracy as well as faster recording speeds.

signal-to-noise ratio   A measurement in decibels (dB) of the difference between the recorded signal and the audible level of random noninformative information picked up when reading back a recorded audio signal. A high signal-to-noise ratio means that the noise is hard to hear. A low signal-to-noise ratio generally indicates that there will be audible hiss in the recording.

signature file   The data file used by antivirus software to compare known viruses to code embedded in your system. The signature is a string of code unique to a specific virus. While antivirus software is scanning the system, it is looking for similar strings of code on your computer system. Without an up-to-date signature file, newer viruses can go unnoticed. Generally, AV software manufacturers will provide a limited *subscription* to their updates when you purchase the software. Once that subscription elapses, you can no longer receive updates until you pay to renew the subscription. Manufacturers emphatically deny any suggestions that they bleed new malicious code onto the Internet periodically in order to maintain subscription rates.

simplex   Devices that use *serial communication* exchange data in one of three ways. Full duplex and half-duplex are methods of bidirectional communications. Simplex is a communications method by which a device can either transmit or receive but cannot do both. Simplex is generally used in devices such as computerized sensors that transmit signals, but would have no way of dealing with incoming signals even if they could receive them. An example of this would be a temperature sensor installed in a remote location that transmits readings to the computer tracking the data.

single-ended signaling   A method by which a single data wire on a parallel cable matches up to a ground wire (Figure S.2). This was the original method of transferring data over a parallel connection. The result of this method was that cable lengths were somewhat limited. The most common method used by most

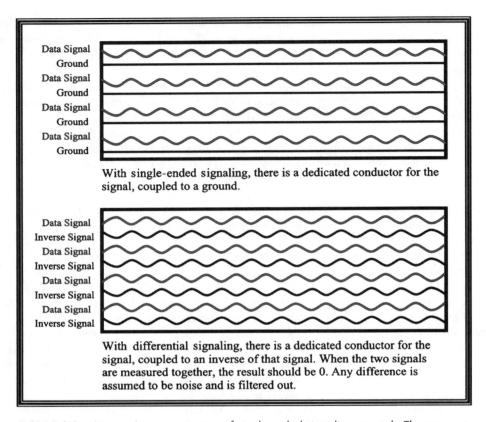

Data Signal
Ground
Data Signal
Ground
Data Signal
Ground
Data Signal
Ground

With single-ended signaling, there is a dedicated conductor for the signal, coupled to a ground.

Data Signal
Inverse Signal
Data Signal
Inverse Signal
Data Signal
Inverse Signal
Data Signal
Inverse Signal

With differential signaling, there is a dedicated conductor for the signal, coupled to an inverse of that signal. When the two signals are measured together, the result should be 0. Any difference is assumed to be noise and is filtered out.

FIGURE S.2 An artist's representation of single-ended signaling at work. The top part of the graphic shows how single-ended signaling works, compared with differential signaling, which is represented in the bottom section.

devices today is *differential signaling,* in which the data signal is matched with a wire carrying a direct inverse of the voltage.

single-mode fiber   A single strand of optical glass encased in a reflective tube and surrounded by a very tough PVC coating. The glass strand is typically between 8 and 10 microns in diameter and carries a single signal in one direction. In order to get bidirectional communications, twin fibers must be run. Single mode fiber comes in different forms. Loose-tube fiber contains a number of different strands of cable, each of which can carry a different signal. Tight-buffered cable houses a single strand. Figure S.3 shows diagrams of each type.

site license   A strategy employed by software manufacturers to reduce costs to large organizations by issuing a license to use a specific piece of software throughout the organization, regardless of the number of users. The cost of site licensing varies with the size of the organization and is based on an estimate of the number of users that will take advantage of the software.

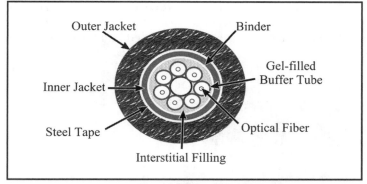

Loose-Tube Fiber-Optic Cable

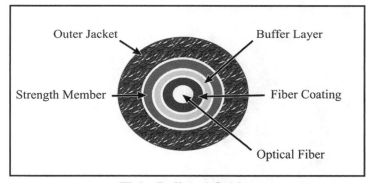

Tight Buffered Cable

FIGURE S.3   This diagram shows the difference between loose-tube and tight-buffered fiber.

skin   The graphical interface of a program that gives it its pretty face. Some applications provide multiple skins and allow the user to pick and choose the one he likes.

slave   Any device on a system that is under the control of another device on the system. A slave drive is one that is secondary to the primary drive and is called on by the device driver only when needed. A slave strobe is a light that automatically fires when it senses the light of the primary strobe.

sleep mode   A mode of operation that a device goes into in order to conserve power when it is not active. In sleep mode only enough energy is consumed to prevent data loss. Unnecessary operations, such as drive motors or display panels are deactivated.

Sliding Window   A method of *flow control* that allows a number of frames to be sent in a burst by the transmitting device. The receiving device will then process those frames and send ACKs or NACKs back for all of the frames at once. The window begins with some mutually acceptable number of frames, usually predetermined by the size of the buffer on the receiving device. If that rate is too fast, the buffer will overflow. The number of NACKs returned to the transmitting computer will suggest how many frames the receiving device is capable of handling. The transmitting device will adjust the window accordingly.

slot   A mounting assembly designed to support edge card-mounted devices (Figure S.4). Also, on a CD-ROM (or similar) drive, it is a form of loading mechanism that engages a CD when it is inserted into the opening and draws the disk into the drive.

FIGURE S.4   This slot is designed to hold an AGP video card.

Small Computer Systems Interface SCSI, pronounced "skuzzy," was a brainchild of a former IBM employee, Al Shugart, who spun off several of his own companies over the years. SCSI was initially released as Shugart Associated System Interface (SASI). It evolved from something called the *OEM bus*, which had been developed by IBM to interconnect peripherals to the 360 mainframe computer. The idea is that multiple unrelated devices can interface together in a single chain.

The American National Standards Institute (ANSI) released the first set of standards in 1986 as ANSI X3.131-1986. ANSI defined an interface that would accept a number of peripheral devices on a single chain, using a parallel bus. *SCSI-1*, as it's now called, supported a total of eight devices, including the host adapter. Each device would carry a unique ID number to prevent conflicts. Unfortunately, very few technical specifications were provided and many of the commands included were considered optional. As a result, many different devices and adapters appeared on the market that were incompatible with one another. The later release of SCSI-II alleviated much of the confusion, and eventually SCSI-III would define a cross-platform interface.

The core of the SCSI chain is the host controller. This can be either a card that plugs into the expansion bus or it can be built right onto the motherboard in many cases. The host controller is the device that is assigned the IRQ and I/O.

A single SCSI chain consists of the host controller and all of the devices connected to it, both internal and external. Many controllers provide an external connection that allows the user to hook up devices like scanners, external SCSI hard drives, and CD-ROMs. Any given controller will be capable of controlling a set number of devices. SCSI-I and II support eight devices, including the controller. SCSI-III supports sixteen devices, including the controller. All internal devices, external devices, and the controller itself count toward this number. However, many adapters are equipped with two or more channels, allowing a separate SCSI chain for each channel.

Devices on the chain are subsequently assigned device ID numbers. Every device on the chain, including the host controller itself, must have a unique ID. The IDs do not need to go in order, and you can skip numbers in the sequence. Typically, the host adapter is assigned ID no. 7. The reason for this is that ID numbers are assigned a priority. The highest priorities are assigned the highest numbers; therefore, with SCSI-I and SCSI-II, ID7 carried the highest priority. In order to maintain compatibility, SCSI-III devices place the order of priority, from highest to lowest, 7 through 0, followed by 14 through 8.

No two devices can share an ID number. To do so will result in one of two things. If the devices are designed to support logical unit numbers (LUN), and each device is assigned a different LUN, then all of those devices will be seen by the controller as a single device. If no LUNs are assigned, then the first device with that ID is recognized and subsequent devices with the same ID are ignored.

Internally, SCSI devices hook up on the same cable. If you have three devices, you need a cable with four connections: one for the host controller and one each for the three devices. It doesn't matter what order they are installed in the system. Device IDs will determine the order in which the system "sees" them. Externally, they hook up a little differently. The back of each external SCSI device has an input port and an output port. A cable goes from the external SCSI port to the device. Another cable goes from that device to the next one, and so on until you reach the end.

Any device that is on the end of the SCSI chain must be terminated. Any electrical signal that reaches the end of a wire will simply turn around and come back home unless there is something on the end of the cable to prevent this from happening. This is referred to as *echo* in computer networks and SCSI chains. Nearly all SCSI devices have been equipped with a termination circuit. This is generally done with resistors, although how those resistors are used varies with the equipment. Sometimes you need to physically plug them into the device; other times they are hardwired into the device and engaged by a switch. With some host adapters, termination can be accomplished through the software, and some older devices have a termination device that must be plugged in. Refer to your manual for the proper procedure for any device you're working with. You can also purchase SCSI cables with terminating resistors installed at one end. Figure S.5 shows some different SCSI connectors and Figure S.6 shows a SCSI controller. Figure S.7 shows a SCSI hard disk.

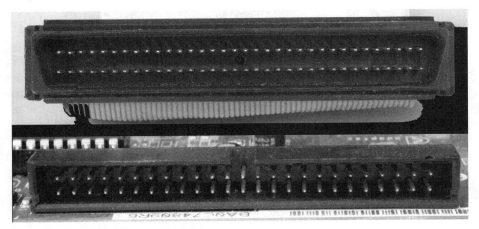

FIGURE S.5   Two different SCSI connectors.

snail mail   Conventional delivery services, such as the United States Postal Service, Federal Express, or United Parcel Service. These services are as slow as a snail when compared to electronic mail or file transfer.

snap-in   A nifty little tool included by Microsoft in some of their recent operating systems is the Microsoft Management Console (MMC). With MMC, Microsoft provided the user with the ability to create his own custom administrative tools. Each one of the Admin Tools either from the start menu or through control panel is available as a snap-in. The snap-in is basically a predefined shortcut to the utility. The user opens MMC, elects to create a new console, and adds whatever snap-ins he desires. Once that console has been saved under a unique name, it will appear in the collection of Admin Tools.

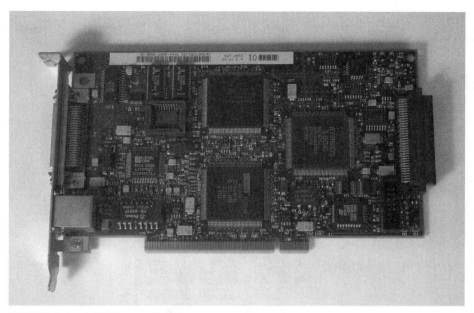

FIGURE S.6   A SCSI controller.

snapshot   In reference to an OS, it is a small binary file that contains information useful in replicating the organization and structure of an application or configuration.

sneakernet   File exchange made possible by running a copy of the file on a floppy disk or other removable medium over to somebody's desk.

sniffer   A device or piece of software that is used to capture data packets off the network for analysis. Microsoft operating systems include a rudimentary packet sniffer in the form of Network Monitor. Once the packet has been captured, the user can view the contents of the packet, broken down into header, payload, and trailer. Packet sniffers can identify the protocol that generated a packet as well as the device that transmitted it along with the intended recipient.

social engineering   A method of accessing information or gaining access to a network by interacting with a person who has the appropriate permissions. It is generally easier to convince that person to either provide the data or provide access to the network than it is to break into the network without attracting attention.

socket   (1) A mounting assembly designed to support pin-mounted devices. Sockets are used with memory modules and expansion cards, as well as most CPUs. Figure S.8 shows an example of a CPU socket. (2) A logical address assigned to an application or process running on the system. Both TCP/IP and IPX/SPX use sockets for logical addressing, although each protocol has a slightly different idea of what a socket is.

socket number   In IPX/SPX the socket number is a logical address consisting of a 16-bit number assigned by the NOS to a process or dialogue operating on a specific node. When a process needs network access, it will request a socket number. Once that number is assigned, any packet containing that socket number will be passed

The back of a SCSI drive is recognizable
by the 50-pin connector and lack of any
master/slave jumpers. There may be some
additional jumpers for setting ID numbers.

An IDE drive will have a 40-pin connector
for the ribbon cable, jumpers labeled M,
S and CS for setting the master/slave
relationships and a power plug.

FIGURE S.7   A SCSI hard disk shown with
an IDE disk for comparison.

on to that process. Certain socket numbers are reserved for NetWare processes. These reserved numbers are shown in Table S.2.

Socket numbers are used with a specific node address. Therefore, IPX/SPX can multiplex the same socket number over several simultaneous communications sessions.

socket services   The PC card bus makes use of a two-layered device driver. The first level is the socket driver. The socket driver notifies the computer when the device has been either inserted or removed and provides I/O operations. These are the *socket services*. The second level is the card service. The card service interprets the command set for a particular device. Because of the socket services, PC cards can be added and removed on the fly as needed. However, before you simply start yanking devices out of your notebook, you might want to check with the manufacturer's instructions. There are some model-specific recommendations in this regard.

soft fault   The data requested by the CPU is in memory, but are not part of the current working set of data. As a result, a new memory search must be initiated. This

FIGURE S.8   This ZIF socket is an example of a CPU socket.

differs from a hard fault in that a hard fault requires a new hard disk I/O operation to be initiated.

software   Encoded instructions that tell a computer how to perform a function or task. All applications and operating systems are software. In addition, some chips installed on a computer or device contain software code.

software RAID   An implementation of RAID that relies of the OS for its command structure and the server for its hardware requirements. The limitations of software RAID are twofold. First, the OS only supports a couple of options. Generally, RAID levels 0, 1, and 5 can be configured in the OS. Anything more sophisticated than that requires a hardware-based RAID controller. Software RAID does *not* support any of the nested RAID levels. Second, software RAID relies on the server's CPU and RAM for all of its processing and memory requirements. This takes away valuable resources that other processes could be using that would be more critical to the users. This can put a noticeable hit on system performance. Therefore, it should come as no surprise that in most networking environments, hardware RAID is the common choice.

sound card   A device that generates the noises and music that a computer plays. Early computers had a single chip on the system that could emit a series of varying beep

TABLE S.2
Reserved IPX socket numbers

SOCKET NUMBER	DESCRIPTION
0001h	Routing Information Packet (RIP)
0002h	Echo Protocol Packet
0003h	Error Handler Packet
0020h–003Fh	Experimental
0001h–0BB8h	(Used by Xerox)
247h	Novell Virtual Terminal Server
451h	NetWare Core Protocol
452h	Service Advertising Protocol
453h	Routing Information Protocol
455h	NetBIOS
456h	Diagnostics
4000h–6000h	Ephemeral sockets; used for interaction with file servers and other network communications
8000h–90B2	Third-party assigned sockets

sounds. That was the extent of their sound capabilities. Modern sound cards can generate sound convincing enough to seem to come from several directions at once. A good sound card coupled with excellent speakers can turn your computer system into an outstanding home music system.

source encoding   A file-compression scheme that introduces compression onto the file itself, regardless of whether or not that file will be transmitted.

source routing   The ability of the host to maintain its own routing tables and make route selections before transmitting data. With source routing, each host on the network maintains a table of routes and constantly updates the condition of those routes. The transmitting device selects the route over which it will transmit. The beauty of this approach is that it takes the responsibility of routing away from being a distributed network issue and makes is a local and centralized issue. In theory, this substantially reduces the overhead of intermediate routers, and hence their inherent latency.

southbridge   Also known as the *peripheral bus controller*, the southbridge handles communication between the CPU and the slower components of the system. The southbridge takes care of things like the ISA bus, IDE ports, USB ports, and any other devices not specifically handled by the northbridge chip (or *memory hub controller*). All expansion bus platforms prior to PCI are under the control of this chip as well. PCI actually spans both the northbridge and the southbridge chips, requiring the services of both, depending of the device installed.

spanned volume   A spanned volume occurs when a user creates a logical single drive that incorporates unallocated space for more than one physical disk. For example, if you have three different hard disks installed in a computer and each disk has some free space on it, most operating systems (or disk controllers) will allow you to merge the free space into a single logical drive. Even though this storage resides on multiple physical disks, it appears to the OS, and therefore to the user, as a single disk drive. All *RAID* configurations are examples of spanned volumes. However, not all spanned volumes are RAID.

spare sectoring   Virtually every hard drive manufactured, even under today's modern methods, has a certain number of sectors that can't be used to store data. Flaws in the surface coating prevent the controller or recording heads to store data there. Hard drive manufacturers use a technique in which extra tracks of recordable space are included with each drive that ships. As bad sectors are discovered on the drive, new sectors are made available from this space to replace the bad ones. This is the process of spare sectoring.

Speculative Execution   An advanced form of branch prediction. The CPU takes a wild guess about which way the code is going and preprocesses the first few lines of code. When it guesses right, it's got a head start in running the subroutine. If it's wrong, it simply dumps the registers and starts over, using the data provided by the prefetch. No harm, no foul. That isn't any slower than it would have been had it not even tried. When it's right, a trip to the hard drive is avoided. And a hard disk I/O operation can cost hundreds, or even thousands, of clock cycles in total processing time.

Speed Mismatch Compatibility   A technology that allows two devices on the same bus to operate at different speeds and still successfully communicate with one another. For this technique to work, both slots and devices must be designed to clock down to the speed of a slower partner. The faster of the two simply throttles down to the speed of the slower device. This occurs transparently and seamlessly with no active intervention or configuration required by the user or technician installing the device. It is part of the integral design of the device.

spike   A sudden transient increase in voltage.

spool   This term started off as an acronym for Simultaneous Peripheral Operations On-Line. Now it is commonly accepted as a word. It is a temporary file created that defines the process involved in transferring data from the computer to a peripheral device. The most commonly recognized spool is the print spool that can store multiple print jobs in a queue and feed them to the printer as it becomes available.

spread spectrum   A form of radio transmission in which the transceiver is programmed with a range of frequencies. Because the broadcast signal is continually bouncing from one frequency to another, intercepting the signal becomes more of a challenge. It isn't impossible. Anybody with the cash can pick up equipment over the Internet that makes it possible. However, it does mean that you're safe from all but the most dedicated of hackers. This security unfortunately does not come without its associated costs. The equipment required for spread spectrum is substantially more expensive and the speeds are abysmally low. How low depends of which of the two primary spread-spectrum technologies you choose to implement. In order to make sure the transmitting station and the intended recipient get all the data that was sent, and receive it intact, some form of synchronization of frequency hopping has to take place. There are basically two choices.

Direct-sequence transmission is the faster of the two methods. Both the sending and the receiving device employ a predefined sequence of radio frequencies along with a predefined timing sequence. They use those sequences to jump from one frequency to the other and never vary from the sequence. As you might imagine, this is the less secure of the two methods. While it will keep out the casual eavesdropper, a dedicated hacker will have no problem cracking the frequencies in use, the hop sequence, or the timing sequence.

Frequency hopping uses a far more complicated timing scheme for switching from frequency to frequency. Also, there can be alternating patterns in the hop sequence. This makes it far more difficult to hack as both the timing and the sequence changes. This is a far more secure method of sending data; however, it comes at the cost of speed. Frequency hopping networks are measured in kilobits per second, not megabits per second.

spyware   Software that is surreptitiously installed on a computer to track the user's activities. Most typically, spyware is used to keep track of a user's Internet usage.

Standard Mode   Standard mode was an operational mode of Windows 3x that took advantage of the protected mode functions of a 286 (or higher) processor. This allowed Windows to address up to 16 MB of RAM and it also allowed multiple applications that were designed for protected mode to run simultaneously (well, sort of, anyway). As you might imagine, this ability caused problems with programs that ran in the MS-DOS *Real Mode*. Also, DOS programs could only run full screen. They could not run in a window.

So if two programs were going to run at the same time on a Windows 3.0 machine, and one of those programs happened to be an MS-DOS program, then Windows had to make sure that the DOS program thought that it was the only ticket holder in the theater. For that to happen, the user needed to be able to run in *enhanced 386 mode*.

standby power supply   A device that uses a generator to provide electrical current to a room or building in the event of a total power failure. If the power is lost, the generator instantly kicks in and provides power to all circuits that are connected to it. As long as the generator is provided with fuel (or doesn't fail), devices attached have the power they need to operate. Standby power supplies are standard equipment wherever computer down time critically impacts an organization. This would include hospitals, financial organizations, Internet service providers, and so forth.

star   Star networks are by far the most commonly implemented topology in today's networking environment. On the simplest level, as shown in Figure S.9, a star can consist of a single hub interconnecting devices. The beauty of the topology is that by using additional devices, such as routers and switches, networks can be as large and complex as necessity dictates. This makes the star topology the most scalable of the network topologies.

Most administrators favor star networks because, regardless of geographic location of workstations and devices, the servers, hubs, routers, and so on can be centrally located. This greatly eases the administrative burden of larger networks. Troubleshooting is made easier as well. One of the easiest ways to tell if a workstation is physically connected when it is having trouble seeing the network is

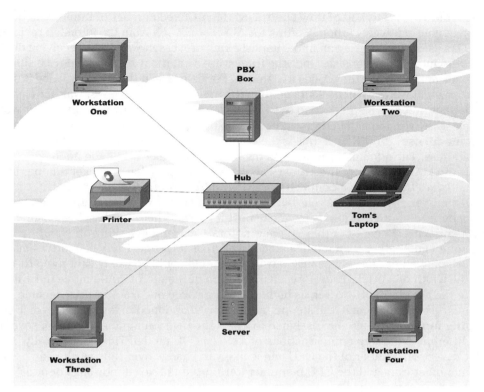

FIGURE S.9   The star network is the topology most commonly seen in larger organizations.

to check for "blinky lights." If both the NIC in the computer and the interface light at the hub are showing a link light, you have connectivity.

    Star networks do require a more complex cabling scheme. Each workstation or other networked device needs to be wired to either a hub or switch. Hubs, switches, routers, and other devices all need to be interconnected. And somehow, you're expected to keep track of it all. A good topology map is a network administrator's best friend.

starting delimiter   A single bit at the beginning of a data byte being transmitted asynchronously that marks the beginning of the byte.

stateful inspection   A process by which a firewall can inspect the contents of a packet to determine whether or not it will be allowed to pass through the interface.

static   Any variable that must be manually configured and/or updated.

static electricity   An electrical charge that exists in an electrically active substance. If another object comes in close proximity with the charged substance a spark will jump between the two objects. This is known as an electrostatic discharge. While generally not harmful to people, this spark can represent extremely high voltage levels and be potentially fatal to electronic components.

static window A method of flow control in which a fixed number of frames will be sent consecutively without waiting for ACKs or NACKs from the intended recipient. This value is set during an initial handshaking process in which the receiving device announces its buffer size. Once the frames are sent, the transmitting device sits back and waits for the replies to come in. For example, if the window value is set to 8, eight frames will be sent and then the transmitting device will wait for eight replies. If it gets six ACKs and two NACKs, or simply six replies of any sort, it will close the session and initiate a new session based on a smaller window size.

station address In IPX/SPX, this is the combination of the network number and node address. The administrator assigns the network number, while the node address is the MAC address of the primary network interface. When a socket number is added to the station, a complete IPX/SPX address is created.

stepper motor A motor that has been designed in such a way that, rather than rotating smoothly, it jumps from one position to another in precisely measured increments. Because of this, stepper motors are useful in ticking off small increments rather than moving smoothly across its range. Early disk drives made use of stepper motors because these increments could be easily calibrated to the width of a track. Therefore, each position of the motor could move the arms to the next track. However, as technology improved and track widths became microscopically small, the stepper motor was abandoned in favor of the voice coil.

stepping number A number assigned to a specific revision number of one of several different evolutionary incarnations of a single CPU model. This is essentially the version number of the CPU and is likely to change over time as chipset manufacturers and the CPU manufacturer finds and fixes minor bugs or adds enhancements.

Stop and Wait Stop and wait is a very simple method of flow control. The transmitting device sends a frame. When the receiving device has received and processed the frame, it will send an ACK and the transmitting device can then send the next frame. This is a very effective, but relatively inefficient, method.

stop bit A single bit of data used in serial communications to designate the end of a transmission.

stop code A number assigned to a particular catastrophic event, along with certain parameters that further define the event. The infamous *blue screen of death* that occurs when Windows crashes nearly always includes a stop code. While there are literally hundreds of different stop codes, there are a few that show up more often than others. Table S.3 lists some commonly seen stop codes.

streaming media Data files, typically music or video, that are sent through to an output device as it is read from the source. An example of streaming media is an MP3 file that is played from a flash drive.

striped volume A logical drive that is created by storing data in chunks that are distributed among multiple physical drives. Several of the RAID levels incorporate striped volume sets. RAID 0 stripes the data across three or more physical disks, but incorporates no error correction. It is used primarily for performance enhancement. RAID levels 3, 5, 7, 1+0, 5+0, and 5+1 all incorporate some form error-correction code, which is stored on the volume set along with the data. Depending on the RAID level, error-correction code may be striped across the volumes along with the data, or it may be stored on a separate disk.

TABLE S.3
Most blue screens result from one of these stop codes

CODE	DESCRIPTION	EXPLANATION
0x19	BAD_POOL_HEADER	Frequently appears as a one-time failure and the machine boots fine afterward. Can be the result of a failed remote procedure call, a corrupted driver, or an invalid application instruction. If it occurs repeatedly, try Last Known Good. If this fails, it's time for the backup/restore procedure.
0x1E	KMODE_EXCEPTION_NOT_HANDLED	A device driver has attempted an illegal CPU function. Either that or an application issued an instruction that could not be decompiled by NT. Unfortunately, you'll probably never know which. The error may or may not repeat itself.
0x35	NO_MORE_IRP_STACK_LOCATIONS	Either someone has attempted to access a shared resource on this computer for the first time and the remote procedure call failed, or you've just installed a new virus scanner. If it is the first situation, rebooting the machine will resolve the issue and you'll probably never see it again. If it's the latter, you may need to check with the software vendor for a patch.
0x51	REGISTRY_ERROR	Oh, oh!! The registry is corrupted. If you're lucky, during the boot process, you can press F8 and select "Last Known Good." As long as there hasn't been a reboot that got as far as the logon screen since the last known good, this will restore that copy of the registry. If there has been, then I hope you have a backup.
0x77	KERNEL_STACK_INPAGE_ERROR	Information requested from the paging file could not be read. This can be the result of the data simply being corrupted or it can be the result of a bad sector on the drive. Worst-case scenario is your controller is failing. Reboot the machine. If it is a bad sector, NT will mark it bad and life will move on. If it's a bad controller, you may or may not get it again.

(Continued)

TABLE S.3 *(Continued)*
Most blue screens result from one of these stop codes

CODE	DESCRIPTION	EXPLANATION
0x7B	INACCESSIBLE_BOOT_DEVICE	BOOT.INI is pointing to a partition that does not exist. If a new drive has just been installed, this simply means that drive letters changed. Edit BOOT.INI to point to the correct drive letter. Unfortunately, it can also mean a failed drive.
0x7F	UNEXPECTED_KERNEL_MODE	See 0x1E
0x80	NMI_HARDWARE_FAILURE	The CPU was just issued a nonmaskable interrupt that it couldn't handle. It's virtually always related to bad memory. A failed parity or ECC memory module will cause this, mixing parity with nonparity or ECC and non-ECC in the same system will also cause it. Replace the offending memory with good memory and reboot.
0xA	IRQL_NOT_LESS_OR_EQUAL	A device driver has attempted an illegal memory access function. Reinstall the device driver.

subdirectory   The root directory is the managing node of any given file system on any given hard disk. Directories can be created within the root directory and additional directories can be created beneath those. Directories within directories are called *subdirectories*. *See* **root directory**.

subharmonics   Sound frequencies below the root frequency that are generated by an instrument or voice when a certain note is played.

subnet   Larger networks are often broken down into smaller segments through a process called *subnetting*. The subnet mask identifies to the OS which part of the IP address represents the network address and which part represents the host address. It does so by placing all the bits of the network address behind a series of 1s and all bits representing the host behind 0s.

A default subnet mask means that you will have only a single network. Subnetting works by stealing bits from the host portion of the address and giving them to the network side. Since the network hides behind 1s and the hosts hide behind 0s, this is a simple matter of turning some of the 0s into 1s. Configuring a custom subnet mask isn't as difficult as it sounds. You can only borrow bits from the host address, and they can only be borrowed from the front end. So effectively, you're changing the first octet in the IP address that represents the host portion of the address from 0 to another number. When you borrow 4 bits from that first octet and give them to the network side, you now have an octet that reads 1111 0000. In decimal, this converts to 240. Therefore, in the IP address configuration screen of your network Applet, you type in a subnet mask of 255.255.240.0 instead of 255.255.0.0.

When you subnet, you have more networks, but you have fewer possible hosts on each network. The formula for calculating either total network or total hosts is $2X - 2 = Y$, where X equals the number of bits you borrowed from the host address and gave to the network address. The reason for subtracting 2 is that neither a host address nor a network address can consist of all 0s or all 1s. Therefore, those are not legitimate addresses and cannot be used. They are not available.

subnet mask   A TCP/IP configuration consists of two parts at a minimum. A 32-bit address identifies the device on the network. The subnet is another value that allows the protocols to distinguish between the network portion of an IP address and the host portion. A subnet will consist of a string of 1s followed by a string of 0s. The network address hides behind the 1s and the host address behind the 0s. However, since the subnet mask is represented as decimal alliterations of four octets, a subnet mask of 11111111 00000000 00000000 00000000 appears as 255.0.0.0. Each administered *class* of IP address has a default subnet mask, as follows:

- Class A address 255.0.0.0
- Class B address 255.255.0.0
- Class C address 255.255.255.0
- Classes D and E cannot be administered directly and do not have subnet masks associated with them.

substrate   The supportive material over which an active substance can be applied. For example, a hard disk platter consists of an aluminum substrate onto which a magnetic coating has been applied. Changing the polarity of the magnetic particles within the coating is the encoding mechanism by which data is stored. The same holds true with magnetic tape. A very thin coating of magnetic material is applied to a thin plastic substrate.

Super I/O   The super I/O is a chip that was included with many early chipsets but that, technically speaking, was not part of the chipset. In many cases, the super I/O didn't even come from the same manufacturer as the chipset. What made this possible was that the super I/O controlled the I/O functions that are typically found in all motherboards. These would include the floppy drive controllers, serial ports, parallel ports, IDE ports, and so on. Some super I/O chips also provide keyboard controller functions and the real-time clock. Since these were all common devices that changed relatively little over time, it was a simple matter to keep the code updated for those devices.

supernetting   A casual term for the use of classless interdomain routing to combine multiple blocks of contiguous IP addresses into a single network. Using supernetting, an organization can take multiple contiguous blocks of class C IP addresses and combine them to form a single network that is larger than a typical class C network is able to support. It works by borrowing bits of the network portion of the subnet mask and using them in the host portion.

Superscalar Architecture   Superscalar architecture was introduced to the world of CPUs with the fifth generation of microprocessors. This technology opens up more than just one path for instructions to follow through the processor. While there is still only a single external data bus bringing data into the CPU, once it's inside there are two different layers of circuitry to process the data. Multiple lines of code can be processed simultaneously. In a way, it is similar to having a second CPU on board. There are some limitations, however. The second execution unit can't handle the full load of commands. Also, programs have to be written specifically to take advantage of this architecture. Otherwise, all that fancy new circuitry goes ignored.

To understand how this benefits most applications, consider the following scenario. If you've ever tried to get into the parking lot at the state fair, you've seen an example of the effect this can have on the speed of throughput. When you first arrive, only a single lane is open and the cars move through very slowly. Then somebody starts showing signs of intelligence and opens a second gate. The parking lot now fills twice as fast. This scenario is doubly accurate because if the CPU requires data or instructions that are at the end of the line, the prefetch moves them ahead of data that has been waiting a while. A good fair attendant won't do that.

supervisor   The administrator account in a Novell network.

supervisory mode   A process by which an OS runs code at the highest possible privilege level.

surge suppressor   These are devices that handle the minor spikes in electrical current that occur on a regular basis (Figure S.10). They work by clamping voltage to a certain level. If a spike hits, a device called a *metal oxide varistor* (MOV) absorbs the differential and sends it to ground. The better ones handle bigger spikes and more of them. Each time the MOV takes a hit, a little more of its life span is used up. It's like the character in the computer games that people play. Every hit takes away some of its health points. When all the health points have been used up,

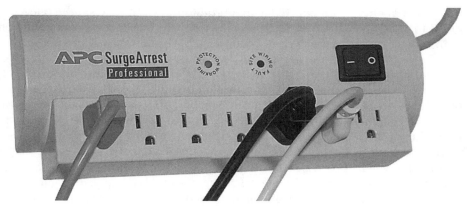

FIGURE S.10   A good surge suppressor should be standard equipment on every computer system.

the surge suppressor is no longer a surge suppressor. It's now an outlet strip that provides no protection.

swap file   *See* **paging file**.

switch   (1) A device that breaks a larger network down into smaller segments, isolating each segment into its own collision domain. A switch accepts a signal through any one of several I/O ports. An IC on the circuit board maintains a table of addresses for all devices hooked up to the switch. The switch examines each incoming packet of data and extracts addressing information from the packet. It then examines the address table, figures out which port hosts the device for which the data is intended, and then transmits that data only through that one port. While the overall behavior of a switch seems similar to that of a hub, it differs in two respects. The hub is indiscriminate in how it transmits traffic. Data that comes in one port goes out all ports, including the one from whence it came. In addition, all ports on a hub must share the overall bandwidth. Twenty-four ports on a 100-Mb hub provide each port with 24/100 Mb. With a switch, each port is dedicated bandwidth. If it is a 100-Mb switch, each port is endowed with 100 Mb/s. (2) In reference to an OS, a switch is an additional parameter added to the end of a command that defines advanced functions for that command to perform. The switch turns a specific function on or off.

symmetric multiprocessing   This term means that an OS is capable of using the services of more than one microprocessor. When a system can do this, it runs faster and responds to user requests more quickly. However, different operating systems over the years have made use of two different forms of multiprocessing. Those two forms are asymmetric and symmetric multiprocessing. *Asymmetric multiprocessing* (ASMP) operating systems typically use the primary microprocessor (processor 1) for the execution of operating system code. The other processors in the system run application code or process user data. Typically, an ASMP-configured machine has more than one processor but the processors do not necessarily have access to the same memory addresses, or even the same amount of memory for that matter.

Most operating systems that support multiprocessing use *symmetric multiprocessing* (SMP). This includes most versions of Windows except for some of the ones targeted at the average home user. SMP allows the operating system code, application code, or user data to run on any free processor. Most hardware configurations share all available memory between all available processors.

SMP is a much more efficient utilization of multiple processors because operating system code has a tendency to hog the processor. Allowing the operating system to run on only one processor frequently resulted in that one processor becoming overloaded, while the others sat back twiddling their virtual thumbs.

synchronization bits   Data included on each sector of a data CD that assure that the information will be processed in the correct sequence.

synchronous communication   The fastest form of serial hookup. Large amounts of data is collected into chunks called *packets* and therefore a lot of data moves on a single transfer. A header, which consists of additional control data, is added to the front of the packet and a trailer, which contains error-correction information, is added to the end. These headers and trailers tell the receiving device where one packet ends and the next begins. Synchronous communications are used by modems, network controllers, and some forms of hard drive controllers.

SYSINIT   In the MS-DOS operating system, SYSINIT was the last subroutine of *IO.SYS* to run. It was, as the name implies, the system initializer. The last task it performed during the boot process was to seek out and run MSDOS.SYS during the MS-DOS boot process. A similar file exists on other operating systems as well. With FreeBSD, SYSINIT allows a certain degree of configuration in how *kernel* processes load during boot. In Linux, a file named SYSINIT defines the system initialization scheme.

system call   A system call is simply a request for a service not directly provided by the application currently running on the system. The OS will then initiate an I/O operation to the specific device or application that can provide the required service.

system controller chip   A chip on Intel chipsets that takes the place of the *northbridge*, handling high-speed functions.

system object   On a system in general, it is any hardware or software entity to which specific properties can be assigned. In Performance Monitor (PM), it is a category of events that can be monitored. For example, in PM, a class of hardware properties specific to the microprocessor exists called (conveniently enough) *processor*. Within this category of objects are various performance measurements that pertain to CPU speed and efficiency. Likewise there are system objects of all other hardware and many OS functions that allow the administrator to track system performance.

system virtual machine   *See* **virtual machine**

T

tab A key on a standard keyboard that moves the cursor a set number of characters across the page. By default the number is five, but most applications allow this to be adjusted by the user.

table A collection of data, arranged in rows and columns, that allows collection and analysis of data to be more efficient and simplified. Spreadsheets and databases all use tables for storing data. Most word processors allow users to create visual tables to make comparing and contrasting information easier.

task A specific action that must be performed by a user or application. Adding a definition to a dictionary is a task. In a word processor, turning a standard typeface into a boldface font is a task. As far as the CPU is concerned any application running on the system is treated as a separate task, regardless of what process may be running.

target Any device that is to be the intended recipient of data. When copying data from one disk drive to another, the drive from which data is being copied is the source drive. The drive onto which it is being copied is the target.

task scheduler A system file that determines how long a particular application can retain control of system resources.

task switching An early form of multitasking that existed within the Windows 3x versions. With task switching there are not two different programs running at once. While one program is running, it has full and complete control of the system. When the user switches over to another program, the first program must be closed.

So if the program was closed, how is it that the user can get back to that program when she's ready to use it once again? Certain information, such as what program threads were running at the time the program was exited, and user data get stored to temporary files. When it is time to return to that application, those files are reopened and read. The information contained puts the computer back into the state in which it was existing when the switch occurred and the user continues where she left off.

There are two problems associated with this approach. First, the time involved in closing one program and opening another was noticeable enough to be annoying. Secondly, this did not permit data to be moved seamlessly from one application to another. True multitasking keeps multiple programs open on the system at once. The CPU simply runs a series of instructions for one program, switches over to another program, and runs a few instructions for it.

telecom or telco A generic term for any provider of telecommunications services.

technical support The help that you're supposed to get when you call a hardware or software manufacturer about a problem you're having with their product. There are rumors that such a service actually exists with some manufacturers in the industry.

telecommunications The interchange of voice or data over long distances, using electronic or optical transmission methods. A telephone call is an example of telecommunication, as is downloading a file over the Internet.

Telnet A terminal emulation software program that allows two devices to communicate directly over a serial connection.

temporary file Any file that is automatically created by an application to store data needed while the program is running. In theory temporary files are closed when the application closes. However, several circumstances can leave temporary files scattered all over your hard disk. An involuntary shutdown of the computer will leave all temporary files written to the drive, never to be accessed again, unless you locate them and open them yourself. Sometimes programs are simply inefficient in closing these files and leave them open even when shut down gracefully.

terabit In binary, a terabit is 10 to the 12th bits. In decimal it is 1,000,000,000,000 bits.

terabyte In binary, this is 10 to the 12th bytes. In decimal it is 1,000,000,000,000 bytes.

teraflop A measurement of CPU performance that defines the number of floating point operations (in trillions) the processor can do each second

terminate To end. With electrical signals, it is necessary to create a dead end for electrical signals traveling down a wire so that they do not echo back the other direction. To do so would destroy the integrity of the data encoded onto the signal.

terminating resistor A small device that absorbs the electrical signal at the end of the conductor to prevent it from rebounding in the opposite direction.

texel Video cards use a process called *texture mapping* to create textures as separate bitmaps, and then store them in memory. These bitmaps consist of very small images, ranging from 32×32 pixels up to 256×256 pixels. These individual bitmaps are called *texels*. As a new screen is drawn, the texture won't have to be redrawn for each new screen. The bitmaps can simply be poured over the corresponding patterns.

texture mapping The only method by which early video cards could retrieve textures was through a technology called *local texturing*. Under this method, the card had to move the information from the computer's memory to local memory on the graphics adapter before the textures could be processed. AGP graphics cards allows for textures to be stored in external memory locations and then imported as needed. This is texture mapping. However, tapping system memory is the slower of the options. If local memory on the graphics card is available, performance is greatly enhanced. This is a primary reason why video cards ship with as much memory as they do.

thermal printer A printer that ejects ink onto a page of paper by heating the fluid. *See* **ink-jet printer.**

thicknet A name commonly given to RG-8 coaxial cable. This cable was used primarily as a backbone cable in older style bus networks. RG-8 would move data between segments on the network and RG-58 moved data between workstations.

thinnet A name commonly given to RG-58U coaxial cable.

third-party DMA Direct memory access is a technology that has been around for a long time. However, the DMA controllers for the computer system are legacy devices that are limited to 16-bit operation and were coupled to ISA, which limited devices attached to system DMA to a 24-bit memory address. Couple this to the fact that there are only a limited number of DMA channels available, and suddenly the limitations of onboard DMA become obvious. Some devices, including IDE hard disks, incorporate their own DMA controller onto their controller circuitry. What this means is that a controlling device separate from that controlling the drive itself is in charge of DMA transfers. The third-party controller dictates system bus, bit depth, and other previously limiting factors.

thrashing   Constant and erratic activity on a hard disk drive. This can be caused by a computer that is equipped with insufficient memory, causing the paging file to be overworked, or it can be caused by a misconfigured paging file.

thread   A single line of code or a small collection of lines that are run as a single process through the CPU. A thread must be run to completion before the CPU or the specific pipeline on the CPU running the thread is free to accept more work.

threshold voltage   The amount of electrical differential required to move a semiconductor from a state of resistance to a state of conductance. If voltage on the circuit is below threshold, no current at all passes. Once this minimal voltage is realized, the circuit opens and current flows freely.

throughput   How quickly raw data can move across the wire. This is typically measured in megabytes or gigabytes per second (MB/s) or megabits per second (Mb/s).

thunking   Microsoft's earliest 32-bit OS was built on the foundation of older 16-bit technology. At the time, it was considered necessary to maintain backward compatibility with older 16-bit applications and devices. As such, the OS was essentially a 16-bit system with other files sewn into the OS to provide 32-bit functionality without losing the ability of the OS to run 16-bit software. In order to accomplish this, Microsoft developed a technique they called *thunking*. Thunking was merely the translation of 32-bit commands into 16-bit format and vice versa. For every 16-bit kernel file, there was a 32-bit file (*see* Figure T.1). The files involved are KERNEL32.DLL, KRNL386.EXE, USER.DLL, USER.EXE, GDI.DLL, and GDI.EXE. The DLLs are all 32-bit components, while the EXE files are 16-bit components. If a 16-bit application or device were communicating with a 32-bit process, it would first communicate with the 16-bit entity, which would translate the request and pass it on to the 32-bit version.

tilde   The character on a keyboard that looks like a horizontal curvy line (~).

time out   Packets on a network and services running on a computer are only given a certain amount of time in which to reach their destination or to complete a process. If the time elapses before the task is completed, it is said to time out. A good example of this is seen when using PING protocol. If the devices being pinged does not respond, the packet times out and the user receives a message informing them of the situation.

token   A small parcel of data that acts as an indicator. In a token ring network, when this piece of data is received by a computer, it indicates that the computer is now free to transmit on the network.

toner   The black or colored powdered pigment used by laser printers or LED printers to imprint data on the page. With a monochrome printer, only black toner is used. A color laser uses black, magenta, cyan, and yellow toners.

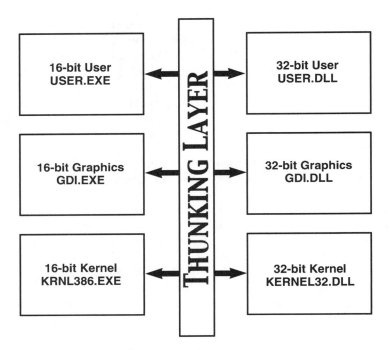

FIGURE T.1   I thunk. Therefore I am.

topology   Physical or logical configuration. For example, the topology of a network shows the pattern in which the computers are interconnected. Common network topologies are the star, bus, and ring.

tower server   The tower server was far and away the most popular configuration for many years. The reasons for this were multiple. For one thing, more expansions slots were available, allowing for a greater degree of future growth. Also, the tower configuration permits a greater number of hard disks to be installed. In the days when the server was the only place for hard disks to reside, this was a critical issue. The fact that there were more externally accessible drive bays meant that the server could host additional drives, such as tape drives, optical drives, Zip and Jazz drives and various other options. In most larger organizations, the tower has given way to the rack or blade in order to optimize space and power utilization.

trace   If you look closely at a motherboard, you'll see fine paths of copper covering both the front and back surface in nice little geometric patterns. (Figure T.2 shows the back surface so the motherboard components won't distract the viewer from seeing the traces.) These patterns are called *traces*. Motherboards are multilayered devices, and the traces aren't just on the front and back surfaces. If you were to peel back the layers, you'd also find them between the layers. These traces provide the path that data takes to move from point A to point B. The path itself is called the *bus*. The term bus can get a little confusing because it's used in so many different ways. To keep things simple, just remember that it is the path data takes.

FIGURE T.2   *The system busses can be seen in all of those little tiny copper paths you see on a motherboard. These are called traces.*

Trace Route   A command-prompt utility that will prompt each intermediate device from source to destination to respond with its IP address and the time to live (TTL) of each hop along the way. Type tracert [host], where host is the IP address or domain name of the device you want to trace, from the command prompt. It works by deliberately exceeding the TTL of any given host.

When you send a trace route request, the utility will send out a packet with an unreasonably high TTL. When the first device receives that packet and the TTL is exceeded, that device responds with its IP address and the amount of time it took for the packet to expire. However, the source computer doesn't discard the packet in this case. It resends it along with way with another TTL that is even higher. Now the first intermediate device will process the packet and send it on its way, but the next device will time out. This process repeats itself until the final destination is reached. The administrator now has a complete path, from source to destination, along with IP addresses and how long each device will take to process a packet.

track   (n) A virtual circle of sectors on a magnetic drive that makes a complete ring around the disk surface. When the drive is formatted, the magnetic medium is mapped out in circular paths. These tracks get subdivided into 512-byte sectors. As the platter rotates beneath the R/W head, the track consists of all the sectors that are read during a single complete rotation of the spindle. Magnetic tapes may also make use of tracks; however, in the case of tape, the tracks are either diagonal slashes across the width of the tape (in *helical scan* recording) or as single stripes that run the entire length of the tape (with *linear scan* technologies). (v) To monitor an object or behavior pattern over a period of time. When editing a document in many word processing packages, it is possible to track the changes that are made by each person who touches the manuscript.

trackball   A trackball is basically a stationary mouse. It performs the same function as a mouse while staying in one place. Many people do not like the repetitive motion involved in using a mouse. In fact, it has caused medical problems with many people. Also, a mouse is rarely where you need it when you need it there. The mouse will be at the top of the mouse pad, but the cursor will be at the bottom of the screen. You're always having to make adjustments.

The trackball is an upside-down mouse. It performs in the same manner except that the ball is positioned at the top of the device and you move it with your thumb and/or fingers. Manufacturers seem unable to agree on how you should move the ball, so when shopping for one of these toys, try them all until you find one that feels right to you.

trackpad   Trackpads, also known as touchpads (Figure T.3), work by sensing the electrostatic energy generated by the user's finger. An array of transistors tracks the movement of the finger as it moves across the surface and relays vector information to the device driver. The driver converts this information into the data needed to display the mouse cursor in the proper position on the screen.

Because of this, the sensitivity of a trackpad is directly proportional to the amount of electrostatic energy emitted by the person using the computer. For example, if you have long fingernails and try to operate the trackpad with the tip of a nail, in most cases it won't work. A technician who has just finished servicing a laptop and is still wearing an antistatic wristband is often surprised to find that the trackpad either responds poorly or not at all.

In general, the trackpad is part of the palmrest. A small ribbon cable that uses an LIF connector similar to the one used by the display connects to the motherboard. With some models, the trackpad can be replaced, if necessary, separately from the palmrest. With other models, it is necessary to replace the entire palmrest.

trackpoint   A trackpoint uses technology similar to trackballs, except that it is a scaled-down version, usually embedded in the keyboard. It is very small, operated by the tip of a single finger, and sports a textured rubber surface. These characteristics earned it the nickname *eraser-point*. The signals generated

FIGURE T.3   *Trackpads are pointing devices that take the place of a mouse on many portable computers.*

by the trackpoint are sent through the ribbon cable that interconnects the keyboard to the motherboard. Should a trackpoint fail, it will be necessary to replace the entire motherboard.

Since many people dislike both trackpads and trackpoints, most manufacturers provide some way of hooking up a standard mouse or trackball to their models of laptop. This can consist of either a USB or a PS2 port. While this does add one more accessory to be carting around in the carrying case, many people find that minor inconvenience far less annoying than the inconvenience of fighting with one of these other devices.

tractor feed   Dot matrix and line feed printers use tractor feed mechanisms to transport paper through the printing path. A geared roller interfaces with holes punched in the edges of the paper. Teeth on the gears interface with these holes. There is a geared belt that keeps the print head moving in synch with the motor. All of this is under the control of commands sent by the printer driver.

traffic   A generic term for all data or voice communications traveling over a specific medium.

transaction-oriented   Any transfer of data that is time-sensitive and requires that data transfer be complete and error-free. An example of transaction-oriented processing is when a user places an order online. If all of the required information isn't supplied then the order is not processed. Another example is when a user attempts to withdraw money from an automatic teller machine and the machine breaks down before the money is issued. In a properly functioning transaction-oriented environment, since the transaction was not completed in its entirety, all references to the transaction are deleted and it never happened.

transceiver   Any device that can both transmit and receive a signal; hence, the name. Media can consist of wire, light beams, or radio waves, or any combination thereof. An example of a typical transceiver is the network interface card in a computer system. However, there are many other examples. The Jetdirect cards and devices are examples of transceivers specific to printers (Figure T.4).

FIGURE T.4   *This HP Jetdirect is an example of a stand-alone transceiver.*

transfer syntax   The form that data will assume as it moves over the wire.

transient   Any signal or current that is very brief and short-lived. A transient spike in current is a brief increase in voltage that is barely detectable by human senses (but that can be damaging to circuits). Most good surge suppressors are able to eliminate all but the most powerful of transient spikes.

transient command   A command that is issued and run from an external source. Transient commands can sometimes be recognized by their extension, which may be .exe or .com. However, applications can issue commands to the OS as well, and these are not easily recognized by a user.

transistor   A semiconductor that acts as a switch, existing in either an on position or an off position. (*See* **semiconductor**.) The transistor is either on or off. Inside the CPU, transistors are grouped together as *registers*. A register is one of a series of transistor banks that will provide a pathway for the processing of data or a storage area for data being processed.

transition cell   On a disk or tape using a magnetic coating, the data is encoded onto the surface of the medium by altering the relative charge of the magnetic particles. As data is written to the drive, it goes down in a series of electrical pulses called *magnetic flux* that creates small groups of magnetized particles. These groups are the transition cells. A transition cell is the minimum number of particles that can be affected by a single magnetic flux. It represents a single bit of data in storage.

transitive   Trust relationships can pass from one domain to another, through a third domain, simply on the basis of trusts that already exist. With a network configured to use transitive trusts, if a trust between domain A is established with domain B, and another trust is created between domain B and domain C, a trust will automatically be generated between domain A and domain C. If the administrator does not wish a trust to exist between A and C, she will have to disable that trust.

transmit   To send data.

transmission rate   The number of bits per second that is being transmitted.

trapdoor   Many times programmers will intentionally provide a way for someone such as themselves or government officials to access a system without being provided proper credentials. This is a trapdoor and is usually something the system administrator is not aware of.

tray   On a CD-ROM (or similar) drive, the tray is a form of loading mechanism that consists of a platform that ejects when the user pushes a button and retracts with the CD in place (Figure T.5).

triad   On a CRT monitor there are different layers of phosphorous, each compounded with a different substance to make it glow in a different color. A single dot of glowing phosphorous is known as a *phosphor*. Each phosphor will always be exposed by the same electron beam and will always glow in one of the three primary colors: red, green, or blue. The intensity at which the electrons strike the phosphor determines how brightly that phosphor glows. In order to produce the myriad of colors that you perceive on your computer screen, it takes three of those phosphors, one of each primary color, working together to produce a hue. These three phosphors working together form a triad.

trigger   (n) Another name for a switch when referenced by an OS command. (v) To initiate an activity or response by providing the correct stimulus. Some software applications monitor events that occur on a computer system. When that event occurs, it triggers

FIGURE T.5   Trays are the most common disk holder used in optical drives.

some other action. For example, a network operating system can be configured to send a message to the administrator when certain things happen. A hard disk getting too full can trigger an e-mail to the administrator, warning of this condition.

Trojan horse   A piece of software that mimics the look and function of another piece of software familiar to users, but in reality it is performing a completely different function altogether.

One of these Trojan horses particularly embarrassing to Microsoft was a program that was designed to look, feel, taste, and smell just like the logon screen for Windows NT 3x. When users typed in their user IDs and passwords, nothing appeared to happen. All too frequently, this resulted in a frustrated user calling the network administrator down to fix the problem. And what was the first thing this person would do? Type in her user ID and password, of course! But the program wasn't sitting there idly watching on. It was collecting all those user IDs and passwords into a file that the attacker could come and collect at leisure.

Trojan horses have appeared on the scene as "free" versions of popular games. While running the game, the user is allowing the program to perform whatever malicious function the designer envisioned.

troubleshooting   The process of identifying and subsequently fixing a problem that exists on a piece of hardware, in an application, or on the network. Good troubleshooting is a process through which the technician follows specific procedures. These procedures include:

- Identify the problem
- Re-create the problem
- Isolate the cause of the problem
- Decide on a possible solution
- Test your idea
- Fix the computer
- Follow up

However, in spite of the mechanical nature this philosophy entails, good troubleshooting is a real talent that requires intuition, clear thinking, and a full understanding of the system being examined. The process is helped along if the technician has a good set of software- and hardware-based troubleshooting tools and a solid understanding of how to use those tools.

True Color   Graphics cards have several settings that allow the user to configure how many colors are displayed. True color makes up two of those settings. Both of them employ 24 bits for creating the hues. Twenty-four–bit true color allows for the maximum number of colors displayed by any of today's graphics adapters. Each phosphor of the triad is allotted 8 bits to determine its intensity. An 8-bit block of data provides for up to 256 combinations. By having three different primary colors working in synch, true color allows for 2,563 colors. That is a total of 16,777,216 colors.

Thirty-two–bit true color is 24-bit true color with an added 8-bit alpha channel. The alpha channel allows programmers to add effects other than raw color to the digital video. These extra 8 bits of data is used for generating the effect of translucency, or how well you can see through the color, to the overall image. It does not, however, increase the number of colors available.

truncate   To intentionally or unintentionally cut off a data file at the end.

trust   A link between two domains over which user authentication is performed on one domain, but the permissions and privileges associated with that user's accounts are honored on another domain. In a trust relationship, there is a trusting domain and a trusted domain. The *trusting* domain is the domain that allows user authentication to occur over there on somebody else's domain. It trusts the authentication to be accurate. The *trusted* domain is the domain that maintains the SAM for the user account that is being verified.

Trusts are only one way. There is no such thing as a two-way trust in the Windows domain structure. For a two-way trust to exist, a separate trust must be established in each direction on an NT network. For that to occur, the administrators of each domain must be actively involved or one or the other of the administrators must know the user name and ID of the other.

trusted domain   A domain that contains the security database that is providing authentication and/or resource access to another domain.

trusting domain   A domain that is requesting authentication services or access to the resources from another domain.

tunnel erasure   Data on audiocassette recorders and most digital tape recorders encode data on tape by streaming electronic pulses onto a magnetic medium. Magnetic energy realigns magnetic particles embedded in the surface of the medium. As information is written to the surface, the erase heads, positioned directly behind the recording head, trim the track cleanly on the medium, eliminating any bleed that might have occurred. This forces the data to reside within its specified track. This helps reduce the possibility of cross-talk between tracks, which could lead to corrupted data. It also provides for a method of organizing data on the diskette.

turnkey solution   Many organizations have very complex requirements that consist of extremely complex hardware configurations loaded with even more complex applications. To purchase the hardware and software separately and then perform the installations frequently requires resources that the organization does not have. So the organization turns to a service provider that builds the hardware, installs the applications, fine-tunes the final configuration, and delivers a working system to the customer. The customer simply "turns a key" and the system starts. Too bad it isn't always that simple.

tweak   To make simple adjustments or configuration changes in order to enhance performance.

twisted pair   Twisted-pair cable is available in two different physical packages, as well as several different categories. Physically, there is unshielded twisted pair (UTP) and shielded twisted pair (STP). UTP is the most commonly used and shows up on the majority of networks. STP has the advantage of being more resistant to outside influences exerted by electromagnetic interference and radio frequency interference. However, its higher cost frequently keeps it from being used in most installations.

Twisted-pair cabling consists of four pairs of 22- to 24-gauge strands of wire. Each pair is twisted together across the length of the cable. Oddly enough, this is where it gets its name. The insulation around each of the strands consists of different colors; some are solid, some are striped. Table T.1 lists the color combinations.

Patch cables are generally terminated with connectors knows as *RJ-45 connectors*. They look very similar to the ends of your telephone wires, only larger. The telephone line uses an RJ-11 connector, which only has four connectors at the most. (Many telephone cables make use of only two of them.) The Electronic Industry Association (EIA) and the Telecommunications Industry Association (TIA) worked together to ratify color-coding standards to assure that uniform wiring was used from installation from installation. There were two different standards adopted for twisted-pair wiring, EIA/TIA 568A and 568B. The most commonly used method follows the color-coding standard in 568B. Both standards are explained in Table T.2.

Twisted-pair cable is designated by its category. In each case but one, the cables are structurally the same but each category is capable of handling different signal speeds. Category Five (Cat5) is the most commonly used, although a newer implementation, Cat5e, is quickly passing it by.

Increased signal speed can be achieved by increasing the number of twists per inch placed onto each twisted pair. Increasing the number of twists acts to reduce cross-talk between cables. Cross-talk occurs any time you lay two runs of cable side-by-side. A portion of the signal carried by each strand will leak

TABLE T.1

Twisted pair cabling consists of eight strands of wire separated into four pairs

PAIR NO.	COLOR COMBINATION
Pair 1	Orange-white/orange striped
Pair 2	Green-white/green striped
Pair 3	Blue-white/blue striped
Pair 4	Brown-white/brown striped

TABLE T.2
Color coding standards for twisted-pair wiring*

PIN NO.	SIGNAL CARRIED	568A	568B
1	Transmit (+)	White/green	White/orange
2	Transmit (-)	Green	Orange
3	Receive (+)	White/orange	White/green
4	Not used	Blue	Blue
5	Not used	White/blue	White/blue
6	Receive (-)	Orange	Green
7	Not used	White/brown	White/brown
8	Not used	Brown	Brown

*Note that the two standards differ only in the colors used for the wire that actually transmits signals.

TABLE T.3
The many different incarnations of twisted pair cabling*

CATEGORY	MAXIMUM FREQUENCY (MHz)	USAGE
1	Voice only, no data	Telephone or modem
2	4	Local talk/ISDN
3	16	Ethernet
4	20	Token ring
5	100	Fast Ethernet
5e	100	Gigabit Ethernet/ATM to 622 MB/s
6	250	Gigabit Ethernet/ATM to 2.4 GB/s
7	600	Not typically used in United States

*Be sure you use the correct wire for the job.

over to the other strand. This affects both the accuracy and the speed of data transmissions. If you can reduce cross-talk, you can increase data throughput. Table T.3 compares the most common twisted-pair cable types.

typeface   The basic shape of the letters and numbers that appear on the page. For example, Times New Roman is a typeface. The term is occasionally confused with font, which refers to a specific size and style (e.g., 12-point italic) of a specific typeface.

U

U-interface   In the United States, an incoming ISDN signal is going to enter the building by way of a U interface. This is the gateway through which the signal enters or leaves the local site from the provider's network. The U interface supports only a single device and that device is the Network Termination-1 (NT1). All the NT1 really does is convert the incoming two-wire circuit to a four-wire S/T interface. The S/T interface provides access to more than one device. It is possible to get S/T interfaces that support up to seven different devices.

universal asynchronous receiver transmitter (UART)   A device that converts serial data to parallel and vice versa. All serial devices requires the services of a UART. Some have a UART chip built in, while others rely on the services of a UART that is part of the chipset of all modern motherboards. There have been a variety of UART chips over the years. Table U.1 lists the most commonly seen UARTs.

TABLE U.1
UART Comparison Chart

UART	BUFFER	DATA TRANSFER SPEED	COMMENTS
8250	None	19.2Kbps	Very buggy and short-lived
8250A	None	19.2Kbps	Fixed some of the bugs, but not all. Slightly faster than the 8250
8250B	None	19.2Kbps	Finally got the 8250 series to work just in time for the 16450 to come out.
16450	None	38.4Kbps	16-bit UART. Buggy and still no buffer.
16550	16 bytes	115.2Kbps	Problems with chip
16550A	16 bytes	115.2Kbps	Fixed bugs from the 16550. Still commonly used today.
16650	32 bytes	460.8Kbps	Programmable flow control and high speed throughput
16750	64 bytes send/56 bytes receive	921.6Kbps	Developed by Texas Instruments
16850	128 bytes	1.5Mbps	Has onboard infrared serial decoder
16950	128 bytes	3Mbps	Found on high-speed devices

Ultra-DMA   A form of direct memory access (DMA) that is used by hard disk controllers for transferring data directly from the hard disk's buffer to system memory without requiring interaction from the CPU. Ultra-DMA is considered to be third-party DMA because it is not hosted by the system board or the chipset but rather resides on the device that uses the services.

ultrawide SCSI   The second generation of the SCSI bus provided support for three different data bit-widths. The original 8-bit SCSI was the default. In addition, SCSI-II provides 16-bit and 32-bit SCSI signals. The later was called *ultrawide SCSI*. It is a bit of a misnomer when used in conjunction with today's 64-bit systems.

unbounded media   Data carrier signal that travels across space (or the airwaves) to get where it's going. This can include radio waves, light waves, microwaves, or any other method that technology may have invented in the meantime. It is the electronic equivalent of telepathy.

Undelete   To reverse the process of erasing a file in order to retrieve the information. UNDELETE was an old MS-DOS utility that first allowed this procedure. The grammatically incorrect term then became a generic term for the process of recovering erased files.

undock   To remove a laptop computer from its docking station.

undocumented   Not mentioned or recorded in any written descriptions of a product or process. Undocumented features can include formatting functions not included in the menu structure of a word processing program, key sequences that perform unusual functions, or Easter eggs. Some operating systems never acknowledge the presence of bugs. Errors in programming are simply undocumented features.

unicast   A data transmission directed at a single host.

uninstall   The process of removing a device or application from a system. With many applications, the process involves not only erasing all related files; it also requires returning registry settings back to their original form and removing hidden directories that were created during the process of installing the program. With hardware devices, uninstalling the device involves removing the device's drivers and registry settings as well as physically removing the device.

uninterruptible power supply (UPS)   A device that takes electricity coming in from the wall and passes it through a rectifier circuit. A rectifier circuit converts the power from AC to DC. This DC charges the batteries in the UPS. The batteries feed power to a circuit called an *inverter*, which turns it back to AC again. This AC powers the computer. It has to revert to AC because that is the current the power supply requires. The power that feeds the computer is now filtered power. All sags and spikes have been filtered out and there is no residual EMI or RFI. Because the UPS is a battery-powered device, if the incoming power from the wall is disrupted, the UPS kicks in and continues to provide power until the batteries are drained. Figure U.1 is an example of a UPS.

Universal Resource Locator (URL)   A user-friendly name that identifies the location of a specific Web page or document on a DNS-powered network. While it may be considered to be user-friendly, a URL can be a complex and very long iteration of a file name. It consists of the *fully qualified domain name* for the server hosting the file, along with the path to that file and its name. Http://www.mwgraves.com/ graves_books.html is one example of a URL.

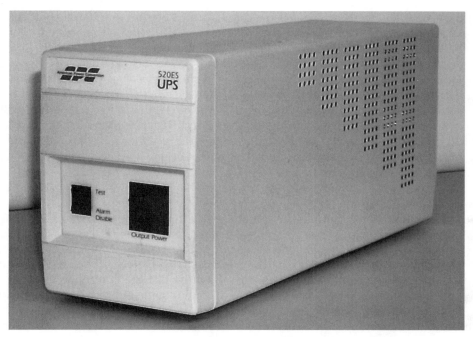

FIGURE U.1   A UPS is a necessary device for any computer system that contains critical data. It prevents a power outage from abruptly shutting down the system.

Universal Serial Bus (USB)   While not the most recent of the technologies to emerge,
the universal serial bus still enjoys immense popularity. The USB interface is 100
percent Plug and Play, and devices are hot-swappable. This means that the user can
add and remove USB devices on the fly without having to shut the computer down. It
also loads drivers only for those devices that are attached. It is theoretically possible
to string together up to 127 devices in a single chain and still tie up only one IRQ.

   The first commercial release of USB, Version 1.0, provided a shared
bandwidth of 12 Mb/s. With one device hooked up, that device enjoyed the entire
12 Mb/s to itself. A second device added to the bus dropped the respective speed of
each by half. A third device caused the bandwidth to be shared three ways, and so
on. A USB 1.0 cable run could be as long as 100M.

   USB 2.0 added a new device class called *high-speed* and upped total
bandwidth to 480 Mb/s. This added speed takes its toll in terms of cable length.
A USB 2.0 cable can only be as long as 15M. USB 2.0 is completely, backwardly
compatible with 1.0. Therefore, all manufacturers are currently shipping nothing
but Version 2.0 product.

   USB requires three different components to be active in order to work. Those
are the host, the hub, and the device. The host would be any computer equipped
with a USB-compatible BIOS, chipset, and controller. This would be practically any
computer built since about 1998. The hub is the actual USB port where the cable
connects. On the back of the computer, the USB hub would be the one or two USB

ports provided by the manufacturer. A hub located on the computer itself is the root hub. Most electronics stores also provide devices that allow additional connections. These are external hubs, such as the one shown in Figure U.2. The device completes the chain. Devices, in USB terminology, are also known as the *function*.

A USB cable consists of two pairs of 28-gauge wire. One pair transfers data between the device and the computer. The second pair provides power to the devices in either low-power or high-power mode. In low-power mode, it will provide up to 100 mA of electricity to the device. High-power mode can provide up to 500 mA. If a device requires more current than either mode provides, it must provide its own power supply. These are self-powered devices. Printers and scanners need a place to be plugged in. Anything that can operate on 500 mA or less is bus-powered and won't need an outlet. Keyboards and modems fall into that category.

unpopulated board   Any printed circuit board that includes empty sockets for future upgrades. In the old days of computing, memory was added with expansion cards. On the card was a collection of sockets into which the user would insert as many chips as needed. The boards could be purchased completely empty, or unpopulated. A more recent example would be a video adapter or a SCSI controller with the option of adding memory. It will generally ship unpopulated, with the expectation that the user will add memory if needed.

unshielded twisted pair   A data transfer cable that consists of four pairs of copper wire, each pair twisted into a single unit. Around all four pairs, a layer of aluminum

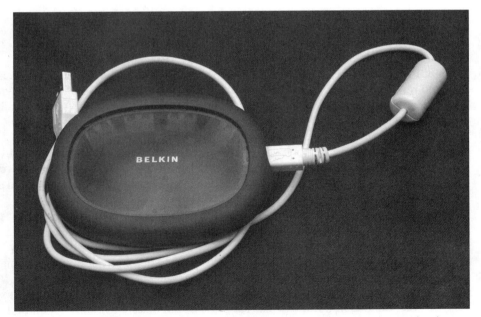

FIGURE U.2   USB hubs are available as simple external devices that let you hook up additional USB devices to your system.

foil or wire mesh protected the conductors from the influence of electromagnetic interference.

unzip   a term for the process of uncompressing a compressed file.

upgrade   The replacement of an older OS with a newer version, migrating as many settings and applications as possible. Generally speaking, there are restrictions on what versions of older OS can be upgraded to what versions of newer OS. For example, it is not possible to upgrade a desktop operating system to a network operating system. The good thing about upgrading an OS or application is that all configuration settings, including resource sharing, personal configurations and so forth are migrated to the new OS. The bad thing is that any incorrect configurations are also migrating. This means that old headaches can easily appear in your new OS.

USB device   Any component designed to operate on the USB bus. *See* **universal serial bus** *for a more detailed explanation.*

USB host   Any computer or other device equipped with USB-compatible BIOS, firmware, and controller. *See* **universal serial bus** *for a more detailed explanation.*

USB hub   A device that manages the I/O for two or more USB device chains. *See* **universal serial bus** *for a more detailed explanation.*

user-level security   With user-level security, the user is assigned a user ID and password. These are the user's credentials. When the user logs on, he types in the credentials and from that point forward, the permissions granted to that user control access to any given resource on the network. As a result, user-level security makes heavy use of file system security.

With file system security, file and folder level permissions are used. But unlike share level security, access is controlled by a centralized security database. This is the SAM I discussed earlier. File system security is much more granular than share level. Any given permission on a resource can be specifically denied to a given user or group. There are also a number of other different permissions that can be assigned:

- **Read**   Similar to the read permission in share level security.
- **Write**   The user can edit the file but cannot delete it or rename it.
- **List contents**   A user with this permission can view a directory listing of a given folder but cannot access the individual files.
- **Read and execute**   Applications can be secured as well as data files. If the administrator denies this permission to a user or group, then that application cannot be run.
- **Modify**   A modify permission allows the user to open, edit, rename, or even delete the file. This is not, however, the same as full permission.
- **Full control**   Full Control grants the user all the abilities granted by modify permission. In addition, the user with full control can change permissions on a resource and take ownership of a resource. In essence, full control is putting the security of that file into the user's hands. By default, the original creator of a file has full control, as does anyone with administrative privileges on the network.

The more astute reader may notice that there is no mention of a no access permission in the preceding list. No access would be the permissions level one might expect to see that blocks a user from knowing that a file or directory even exists. The administrator can accomplish no access simply by denying full control.

user mode   OS functions dealing with the user interface, logons, and services needed to run applications, and network access.

V

valid   A statement that is true or a condition that is legitimate. It is a valid statement to say that computers are complex devices. The installation of an OS is valid once all systems and components are tested and confirmed to be working correctly.

validate   To perform tests to confirm the truth of a statement or the legitimacy of a condition. A network operating system validates users when it checks their credentials against a security database.

value-added   A product that is sold by a source secondary to the original manufacturer who performs some service or adds features to the product in order to increase the apparent worth of the product to the end user. As you might expect, value-added resellers are also cost-adding resellers.

vampire clamp   RG-8 coaxial cable (or thicknet) connects to the network by way of a device called a *vampire clamp*. The rather macabre name of this device comes from the fact that it consists of two halves that are drawn together around the cable by tightening some screws. Sharp teeth sink in through the insulation and make contact with the conductor. On the outside of the clamp, a fifteen-pin D-shell connector, called an AUI connector, hooks up to the patch cable.

vapor deposition   The process of applying a metal coating by the process of evaporation. The substrate on which a coating is to be applied is placed into a chamber. The material to be deposited onto the substrate is heated into a gaseous vapor and the physics of molecular adhesion cause the metal to stick to the substrate. The end result is the thinnest and most uniform coating that, until recently, technology was able to offer.

vaporware   Software that has run significantly past its originally announced release date and still has not seen public distribution.

variable   (1) Any piece of data used by an application that does not have a fixed value. Variables can comprise data input by the end user or information generated by the application as it processes other data. (2) A fixed location in a database or other application that is the designated storage area for a specific piece of information. An application with an interactive screen where a user enters requested information is a variable.

vector font   A typeface that can be increased or decreased in size without the change introducing any degradation in the output quality of the viewed results. Vector fonts use complex mathematical models in order to achieve their results.

verbose   Wordy or detailed. Many command prompt utilities offer the -v (or verbose) option as a trigger. In this mode, the outputted results of the command will provide significantly more detail than the results provided when not using the option.

version   A specific evolutionary stage of a product. Most applications go through several versions before they reach the end of their marketable life. When a product is rereleased with a number of new features, fixes to previous problems or perhaps even simply with a new interface, the product has undergone a version change. Versions generally are identified with two or more numbers separated by dots. MYAPPLICATION 3.3 would indicate that it is the third major release of MYAPPLICATION 3, and the third incremental release of version 3.

VIC 20   A 16-bit computing device of 1981 that employed a 16-bit microprocessor with a 16-bit address space. In a sense, the VIC 20 got around the 16-bit limitation by assigning 16 KB of read only memory on a ROM chip. Of this, 8 K was used for the BASIC programming language and 8 K for the OS kernel. On top of the 16-K ROM, it featured an amazing 5 KB of RAM. Despite this, the little device sold in excess of 20 million units before it was finally discontinued. Much of this was because it was released at a price of $299.00. While this was a much more significant amount of money in 1981 than it is now, it was still a drastic reduction in price from most of its competitors. It got its name from video interface chip (it had a dedicated chip that created a standard TV signal and an interface to hook it up to a television) and the 20 sounded cool. According to Michael Tomcyck, the original project manager for the VIC 20, that is about all the logic there was behind the model number.

video   Any visual output to a display generated by an application. Video can be a still screen showing little more than text against a monochrome background, or it can be as complex as a motion picture played from a DVD.

video card   An expansion card (sometimes called a graphics adapter) that provides graphical output to a computer monitor.

virtual   Pretend.

virtual device driver   A set of files that intercepts hardware calls from applications and redirects them to the device driver. This prevents direct access of hardware by the applications.

virtual IRQ   An interrupt request level assigned by the OS to a device that does not match its physical IRQ. Starting with Windows XP, Microsoft introduced this concept as a way around the physical limitation of fifteen hardware IRQs. The physical IRQ assigned to a device is basically ignored by all applications. The OS interrupts IRQ calls and redirects them to a "pretend" IRQ that might be up in the range of nineteen, twenty-two, or even higher.

virtual machine   With a virtual machine, every component of a computer system is virtualized. A large section of hard disk real estate is isolated and formatted as though it were an independent disk serving the virtual machine. A portion of physical RAM is carved out and dedicated to the virtual box. The VM environment creates a complete hardware abstraction layer that emulates I/O, removable disks, and all other functions of the physical computer.

The concept of virtual machines was first introduced with the Window 3x versions. VMs were used to house MS-DOS applications so they would think they were the only program running on the computer. Over the years, the concept of the virtual machine has evolved to the point that a brisk market exists for third-party VM managers. Many networks feature *virtual machine host* (VMHost) servers, whose sole purpose in life is to emulate the existence of other machines. For example a single VMHost might house multiple web servers in order to load balance access to a web-based application. Entire networks can be virtualized on a VMHost, providing a test environment for administrators. When a new patch or application is to be rolled out onto the network, the VMHost acts as the guinea pig so that the bugs can be worked out before unleashing it on unsuspecting users.

virtual memory   A section of hard disk space that is set aside and used by the OS as though it were memory. Also called a *swap file* or a *paging file,* this is an area of hard disk space that is treated by the OS as if it were memory. If physical RAM fills up and a new process needs to be opened, then processes not currently running on the system will be moved over to the swap file, freeing physical RAM for the new process. When the CPU is ready to resume working on a specific process, all data related to that process is remapped from the paging file to physical RAM.

virtual real mode   With the release of Windows 3x, Microsoft engineers had to overcome a rather complex obstacle. A huge difference between the old MS-DOS applications and the "newer" Windows applications was the ability to multitask. DOS programs couldn't do that. Virtual real mode is a technique of creating separate address spaces and time-slicing CPU time so that legacy applications think they're the only programs running on the machine, even though there may be several running at once. In virtual real mode the OS creates a *virtual machine* for every application that requires this mode of operation. In order to multitask, the OS switches between virtual machines rather than between applications. Naturally, this did not allow data to be exchanged between a program running in virtual real mode and any other application.

virus   The term *virus* is often used incorrectly to describe any malicious software that affects a computer. In fact, a virus is only one of many forms of malicious software you need to protect your systems from. Other forms of malicious software include:

- Worms
- Trojan horses
- Logic bombs
- Trapdoors
- Embedded macros

Each one of these terms defines a slightly different form of software. Their level of malevolence ranges from mischievous to disastrous. Viruses are pieces of code that are inserted into an otherwise legitimate string of code, such as a piece of software or a file. Viruses can be embedded in software programs, image or video files, sound clips, or just about any other file type you want to imagine. Simply opening the host file may activate the virus, or there might be a time/date stamp embedded in the code. The latter is known as a *logic bomb*. When you open the file, the virus is copied to some location in your system. On the specified time and date, it runs as a self-executable.

voice   A collection of sampled frequencies that simulate the sound of a particular instrument. In the real world, sound occurs in waves. These waves are measured in cycles per second, or hertz. The more cycles per second, the higher the perceived pitch. In order to convert sound to a digital computer file, the sound is sampled thousands of times per second. CD-quality sound (audio quality equal to that of a compact audio disk) is generally sampled 44,000 times per second. FM quality, or that of a decent radio broadcast, is considered to be around 11,000 samples per second.

If two instruments play the same note, say a guitar and a trumpet, even though the pitch may be the same, the two instruments still sound dramatically different. This is because, along with the *base frequency*, which is what determines pitch, there is a very complex collection of additional sound frequencies that the instrument produces that are generated along with the root frequency of the note. The root frequency is the single frequency that makes a C sharp a C sharp, regardless of the instrument playing that note.

The additional frequencies generated by specific instruments are called *harmonics* and *subharmonics*. Harmonics are frequencies of sound that are higher than the root frequency of the note being played. Subharmonics are frequencies lower than root.

voice coil   An extremely fast and highly accurate motor that works by applying an electrical current to a tightly wrapped coil of wires surrounding, but not touching, a permanently magnetized cylinder. When current is applied to the coil, the cylinder rotates. Negative voltage rotates the cylinder one direction, positive the other. The amount of voltage determines how far the cylinder moves.

volatile   Unstable or changeable. Volatile memory is completely erased when it loses power. Therefore, it requires a constant source of energy in order to retain the information it holds.

voltage   Voltage refers to a differential charge between two objects. So when you set up a 110-V circuit, the difference between the charge in your television circuit and that of the power box is basically 110 V. The technical term for this is *electromotive force*. This is how much electrical "pressure" you have. You measure air pressure in pounds per square inch; you measure electrical pressure in volts.

There is a common misconception that just because a circuit carries high voltage, it is dangerous. Most of the time, they are. It isn't, however, the voltage that makes them dangerous. People get zapped by charges in excess of 50,000 volts on a regular basis and only jump a bit. That's about how much voltage is in one of those sparks that jumps from your fingers to a brass doorknob after you walk across new carpet.

volume   (1) Any configured contiguous storage space for holding data on a computer system or network. A volume can be a single hard disk if it is formatted with a single partition. However, if that same hard disk is divided into four partitions, then the disk contains four volumes. Conversely, a volume can span multiple hard disks if the OS allows such a configuration. Some OSs, such as Windows 2000 and later, allow a user to select unused space on multiple hard disks and combine all of that space into a single volume, designated by a single drive letter. (2) The apparent loudness of sound output.

volume label   A user-friendly name given to a specific contiguous storage location on a computer or network. For example, Drive C, when shared out on a computer named MYCOMPUTER can't be named C:\ when viewed by another computer. A disk utility such as Microsoft's Disk Manager allows the administrator to name that disk BUBBA. Now, when viewed over the network, MYCOMPUTER Drive C is seen as BUBBA.

volume set   A volume set takes multiple drives and combines them together to appear to the system and the user as a single drive. When you set up a volume set, you are usually doing so with a small collection of hard drives that you are installing into the computer. In this situation, you would decide how many of your drives belong in the set and add each one to the volume. On a unit level, each of the individual drives can be seen as an independent piece of hardware. However, the drives you assigned to that set are now all seen as a single drive by the operating system. RAID arrays are examples of volume sets.

W

wait state   A condition that results when the CPU reaches a point in processing when it cannot proceed further for lack of data or instructions. It will stop processing while the system goes out looking for the data or instructions.

wallpaper   The background image of the desktop on a graphical OS.

warm   (1) The temperature state of an object or device to which a small amount of heat has been applied. (2) A shift in the color of an image toward the yellow or red side. (3) How you feel when you are *this close* to solving a problem, but just can't make that last leap in logic.

warm boot   The process of restarting the computer without turning it completely off and back on again. A warm start can be accomplished by pressing the reset button on some computers or by selecting the reset function from the menu on others. A warm boot does not force another POST by the BIOS.

webinar   More inane slang for an online seminar.

well-known port   In this contexts, a port is a logical address used by common applications and processes through which data specific to that application or process will be sent. The well-known ports are ports 0 through 1023. These are assigned and administered by an organization called the Internet Assigned Numbers Authority (IANA).

wheel mouse   A pointing device that includes a small ribbed disk that, when turned, scrolls up or down on the active screen on the monitor.

white balance   A measurement of how pure the reproduction of white is accomplished in an image. This is based on the source of light illuminating the image. Sunlight has a different white balance than incandescent light bulbs, which are different from fluorescent lamps. Typically, imaging devices need to know the source of light in order to accurately reproduce white.

white box   A generic term for an independently manufactured computer system based on the design factors of an IBM personal computer. White boxes are distributed by some major manufacturers with no brand name, allowing a value-added reseller to make configuration changes and put their own name on the system. Also known as a clone.

white paper   A technical document or sales brochure that provides extensive information about a particular product or subject.

WHOIS   A search process that reveals detailed information about a Web site or domain. WHOIS is available as a TCP/IP command and as a Unix/Linux command. The primary database that provides lookup data is provided by a company called Network Solutions.

wide SCSI   SCSI over a 16-bit bus.

widget   A mini-application represented by a graphical element that remains resident on the user's desktop that provides a simple function. Widgets were made popular with the Apple Macintosh computer and adopted by Linux and Microsoft in some of their later versions. An example of a widget is the graphical clock face in Microsoft Vista that tells you what time it is.

wild card   A character that instructs a command to replace that character with any other character or collection of characters it finds in its place.

window size   The amount of data a given host is capable of absorbing before its buffers overflow.

Wintel   A slang term for the computing platform consisting of the Windows application running on an Intel processor.

wizard   A small application that automates an otherwise complex process. An installation wizard is a program that leads you by the nose through the process of installing an application. Wizards are generally interactive and prompt the user to enter required information by asking detailed questions.

word   The amount of data that can move across the CPU's external data bus in one clock cycle; usually between 2 and 4 bytes.

word wrap   In a word processing program, or other application that involves displaying alpha-numeric information inside of a formatted page, when a sentence reaches the end of a formatted line, it automatically drops to the next line and the user can continue typing. Changing the width of the page changes how many characters can be displayed on a line, and the document automatically increases or decreases the number of words on each line accordingly. This is word wrap.

workgroup   A collection of independently managed users and/or devices on a network that are configured to share files and devices.

worm   An executable program that enters your system through another route and performs mischievous or malignant functions. An example of a worm would be an e-mail that, when you open it, copies a file to a specific location on your hard disk. This file is the source of malicious code.

write power   The highest power setting for the optical stylus of a CD-RW, which it uses to record data onto the surface.

write protect   A process or mechanism that prevents the data on a disk or other medium from being erased or overwritten.

X

Xeon   An Intel processor designed specifically for servers or advanced workstations.

X-on/X-off   A flow control method under the control of the recipient device. As data are moving into this device, their buffers fill. Once the buffers receive as much data as they can hold until it has been processed, the recipient device will issue an X-off command. Once it has cleared its buffers, it issues an X-on command and the flow of data can be resumed.

Xmodem   An early file transfer protocol developed in 1977 designed to allow systems interconnected by serial modems to transfer large files back and forth. Xmodem incorporated an error detection mechanism called checksum that could determine when an error occurred and request that the data affected be sent again. In order to ensure that an entire file didn't have to be retransmitted for each detected error, the file was broken down into 128-byte blocks. Only the block affected by the error had to be resent.

Y

Y2K   The cataclysmic disaster that was supposed to occur when the year 1999 turned into the year 2000 and all the computers of the world stopped working because of a bug in the clock chips. I missed it. What happened?

Yahoo   A popular search engine company that makes billions of dollars per year by flooding your screen with pop-up messages from "sponsored clients" for every search you make.

Ymodem   A serial data transfer mechanism similar to Xmodem. Ymodem differed in that it sent data in 1,024-byte blocks. In addition, it replaced the inefficient checksum error detection with cyclical redundancy checking error correction, and it allowed multiple files to be exchanged simultaneously.

yottabyte   1,208,925,819,614,629,174,706,176 bytes.

yoyo mode   A state of instability in which a computer is alternately up and down, up and down, up and down.

Z

zero configuration   Any application or device that can be configured so that it automatically requires no intervention at all on the part of the user.

zip   To compress or create an archive of a file. Multiple files can be included in a single zip file and occupy far less space on a drive. Until recently, zipping and unzipping files required a third-party utility. However, many operating systems, including Linux and Windows, include zipping functionality within the file system.

Zip drive   A device made by Iomega that held as much as 750 MB of data on a single 3.5" disk. This was a removable disk that the user could easily carry in a shirt pocket. Unlike floppy disks, they are far more resistant to damage when exposed to such treatment.

zombie   (1) Malicious code written whose sole purpose is the type up system resources and processor time in order to negatively impact system performance. (2) A computer that has been commandeered by another user and is being used for some other purpose without the legitimate user's knowledge or permission. Frequently in a Denial of Service attack, the propagators will route their requests through hundreds or even thousands of computers across the Internet that are connected at the time of the attack. All of the computers are the hacker's zombies.

zoom   To move in closer to or away from an image or a page. Many applications have a view mode that allows you to increase or decrease magnification of an image. Limitations of zooming in a computer system are dictated by the resolution of the file. Only so many pixels are used to create an image. As you start magnifying the image, you start viewing the actual pixels and the image become blocks and difficult to interpret.

zone   In an AppleTalk network, this is any logical grouping of devices on the network.

zone bit recording   Early hard drives also were afflicted by the requirement that each track has the same number of sectors, regardless of their position on the platter. The tracks toward the spindle had no fewer sectors than the outermost track. As a result, the tracks toward the outside consisted of wide, sweeping sectors, while the ones toward the inside were all bunched together. Western Digital developed a technology called *zone bit recording* that allowed the sectors to be approximately the same size. Because of this, the outside tracks contain a greater number of sectors than those near the spindle.

Zone Information Protocol   An AppleTalk protocol that manages network numbers and how they associate to different zones in an AppleTalk network.

PART III: Acronyms

A great deal of selectivity was employed for this section of the book. In browsing several dictionaries, textbooks, and Web sites, I concluded that there are approximately 120,000 acronyms in use today in the overlapping fields of computer technology and telecommunications. Some letter combinations have so many meanings that they could fill an entire chapter. Once again, for the sake of brevity, I made an attempt to create a list of "everyday" acronyms a computer professional is likely to encounter.

A/UX   Apple Unix. Version of Unix OS (operating system) used as the basis for Macintosh operating systems.

AAA   Authentication, authorization, and accounting. A method for controlling access to computer resources—enforcing policies, auditing usage—so a company can accurately bill for usage.

AAB   All-to-all broadcast.

AAC   Advanced Audio Coding. The audio compression mechanism used by Apple in their iTunes software. It provides a greater degree of compression, but at the same time retains a higher quality audio output than MP3 files.

AACS   Advanced Access Content System. A standard for distribution of material that includes digital rights management policies.

AAL   ATM adaption layer. Translates the 48-byte content of asynchronous transfer mode (ATM) packets.

AARP   AppleTalk Address Resolution Protocol. Resolves AppleTalk addresses at the physical layer.

ABEL   Advanced Boolean Expression Language. A hardware description language used in early programmable devices.

ABEND   Abnormal end. Fancy word for a computer or application crash.

ABI   Application binary interface. Interface between compiled applications and the OS.

ABIOS   Advanced basic input/output system.

ABM   Asynchronous Balanced Mode. A high-level data link control (HDLC) communications mode in which there is no specific master/slave relationship.

AC   Alternating current. Current that reverses direction many times in a second.

ACE   Access control entity. An individual entry of the access control list (ACL) defining a specific object and its security attributes.

ACIA   Asynchronous Communication Interface Adapter. Transmits or receives 8 bits of data by way of serial communications.

ACK   Acknowledgment. Thank you. It arrived safe and sound.

ACL   Access control list. Contains permissions associated with objects on the network or computer.

ACPI   Advanced Configuration and Power Interface.

ACR   (1) Audio communications riser. A specialized card that takes the concept of the AMR and adds networking functionality as well. (2) Analog Cellular Radio A now-discontinued form of packet-based two-way radio communications over a radio wave. More commonly known as the Advanced Mobile Phone System (AMPS).

AD/DA   Analog digital/digital analog. A microprocessor that is dedicated to converting conventional modulated electrical signals into binary code and vice-versa.

ADB   Apple Desktop Bus. The Apple interface for connecting devices such as keyboards and pointing devices.

ADC   Analog-to-digital converter.

ADP   Automated data processing. This term has been almost universally replaced with IS, or information systems.

ADS   Active Directory service. A Windows 2000 (and later) OS service that integrates active directory with the OS.

ADSI   Active Directory service interface.

ADSP   AppleTalk Data Streaming Protocol. A connection-oriented protocol used by AppleTalk for sending large groups of data. It does not require the maintenance of transactions in order to function.

AEP   AppleTalk Echo Protocol. AppleTalk's answer to Internet control message protocol (ICMP).

AERO   Authentic, Energetic, Reflective and Open. Microsoft's name for the graphical interface used on their Vista operating system. Wonder how long it took them to come up with that?

AES   Advanced Encryption Standard. A block cipher encryption algorithm adopted as the encryption standard of the U.S. government in 2002. It supports up to 256-bit encryption.

AFP   AppleTalk Filing Protocol. A protocol that provided file management services in Apple's OS9 (and earlier) operating systems.

AFS   Automatic File Compression. A technology built into new technology file system (NTFS) that allows files and directories to be compressed and uncompressed on the fly, as needed.

AFTP   Anonymous File Transfer Protocol.

AGP   Advanced Graphics Port. A high-speed bus designed exclusively for graphics.

Ah   Ampere hour. A method of measuring the expected usage of a rechargeable battery on a single charge.

AI   (1) Artificial intelligence. An ability by an inanimate system to make logical conclusions out of processed data. (2) Analog input. Any input to a system that does not enter in binary format. This would include audio, video, and telecommunications signals.

AIFF   Audio Interchange File Format. A music file format used by Apple operating systems.

AIM   AOL Instant Messenger

AIN   Advanced Intelligent Network. A network architecture that allows vendors to incorporate customized services on a selective basis.

AIT   Advanced Intelligent Tape. A tape format that incorporates a linear recording mechanism in conjunction with a memory chip embedded in the tape cartridge to allow for advanced features.

AIX   Advanced Interactive Executive. The IBM version of the Unix OS.

ALB   Advanced load balancing. A form of server or network traffic management that intelligently determines to which ports or hosts data should be routed in order to minimize latency.

ALDC   Adaptive Lossless Data Compression. An advanced data compression algorithm that allows a greater degree of compression without any loss of data.

ALP   Application layer protocol. Any protocol or service that runs at the application layer of the open systems interconnect (OSI) networking model.

ALU   Arithmetic logic unit. The subcomponent of a central processing unit (CPU) that handles rudimentary mathematical functions.

AM   Amplitude modulation. A method of sending signals over an analog medium that encodes data by changing the relative strength of the signal without affecting the frequency.

AMD   Advanced Micro Devices. A North American manufacturer of CPUs and other microchips used in the computer industry.

AMI Alternate Mark Inversion. A modification of return to zero (RTZ).

AMP Asymmetric multiprocessing. A technique of using multiple CPUs in a system in which the OS runs on one processor and applications and user data is processed on others.

AMPS Advanced Mobile Phone Service. A now discontinued cellular phone service that used analog radio waves to send packet based two-way communcations.

AMR Audio modem riser. A specialized card found on certain motherboards that supports either a modem, a sound card, or a device that combines both functions.

ANI Automatic Number Identification. A function of telephony networks that allows a user to capture the number of an incoming call.

ANS (1) Advanced Networking Service or (2) American National Standard.

ANSI American National Standards Institute. This organization is charged with establishing standards for several different industries, including the computer industry. It also refers to an early character set developed by that organization.

AO/DI Always On Dynamic ISDN. A permanent form of Integrated Services Digital Network (ISDN) connection.

AOL American On Line. A large Internet service provider.

AP Access point. A hub in a wireless network that allows networked devices to get onto the network.

APC American Power Conversion. A company that manufactures uninterruptible power supply (UPS) and surge suppressing devices.

APDU Application Protocol Data Unit.

API Application Programming Interface. A collection of files used by Microsoft operating systems that maintains and translates the basic command set required by all devices of a particular type.

APIC Advanced Programmable Interrupt Controller. A device that manages *interrupts* in multiprocessing environments.

APIPA Automatic Private Internet Protocol Addressing. Microsoft's implementation of the IPv4 link-local protocol that assigns temporary Internet protocol (IP) addresses to devices that connect to the Internet.

APM Advanced Power Management.

APM BIOS Advanced Power Management Basic Input/Output Services.

APOP Authenticated Post Office protocol. An implementation of the POP protocol that incorporates encrypted logon functions in place of plain text authentication.

ARC Advanced RISC (reduced instruction set computing).

ARIN American Registry for Internet Numbers. The organization that manages IP addressing (and other Internet functions) for the United States.

ARM Asynchronous Response Mode. An HDLC communications mode that allows the "slave" device to transmit with permission from the "master" under certain circumstances.

ARP Address Resolution Protocol. A protocol that can determine the media access control (MAC) address of any host by sending a query to the IP address.

ARPA Advanced Research Projects Agency. A U.S. government entity that is involved with the advancement of science. They are credited with creating the first continental computer network.

ARQ Automatic Repeat reQuest. An error control mechanism used in serial data transmission.

ASA American Standards Association.

ASCII American Standard Code for Information Interchange. An early character set used by computers.

ASK Amplitude Shift Keying. A method of encoding digital data onto an electrical current by inducing changes in the strength of the signal.

ASMP Asymmetric multiprocessing. The ability of an OS to use more than one processor; the OS code runs on one processor and all other application code and user data is distributed across the remaining processors.

ASP (1) AppleTalk Session Protocol. The AppleTalk protocol that establishes, maintains, and breaks down logical connections between devices. (2) Active server page. A dynamic Web page engine for servers. (3) Advanced signal processing.

ASPI Advanced SCSI Programmer Interface. A two-tied device driver scheme employed by small computer systems interface (SCSI).

AT Advanced Technology. A form factor promoted by IBM in the early days of personal computing.

ATA Advanced Technology Attachment. A form factor for personal computers and accessories.

ATAPI ATA Packet Interface. A device interface that allows data to be transmitted in packets, rather than a byte at a time.

ATC Advanced Transfer Cache. A recent improved design of L2 cache used on certain Intel microprocessors. It features a 256-byte wide memory bus and is totally integrated on the chip die.

ATDM Asynchronous Time Division Multiplexing. A method of sending multiple signals over a single conductor by using "time slices" allocated to each communications session. Simple TDM is based on transmitting over a single wire. ATDM makes use of multiple conductors, and any given slice of data can be sent over the best path.

ATL Automated tape library. A tape backup unit that houses multiple tapes and can automatically shuffle between tapes as needed during backup-and-restore operations.

ATM (1) Asynchronous Transfer Mode. A high-speed telecommunications protocol that breaks down upper-level protocol packets into 53-byte cells and transmits them over a high-speed link. (2) Automatic teller machine. A device that banks charge you extra to use for your banking needs so that they don't have to pay a live teller a salary to perform the same function.

ATP AppleTalk Transaction Protocol. A connection-oriented protocol used by AppleTalk for sending small pieces of data.

ATPS AppleTalk Printing Services.

AT&T American Telephone and Telegraph.

ATX Advanced Technology eXtended. An improvement of the older AT form factor that provided greater accessibility to components and far more efficiency in the use of space.

AUI Attachment Unit Interface. A fifteen-pin female connector used by some early network cards and sound cards.

AUP   Acceptable Use Policy. A document that spells out what is acceptable or unacceptable behavior on a system or network.

AV   (1) Audio/video. A single data stream that contains both sight and sound. (2) Antivirus.

AVATAR   (1) Advanced Video Attribute Terminal Assembler and Re-creator. A series of short commands that allows a user to create text attributes such as boldface, colored text, or other options. (2) One of the useless animated characters you see in certain computer company commercials.

AVI   Audio Video Interleave. A Microsoft file format for streaming data files that contain both audio and video content.

AVR   Automated Voice Recognition.

AWAC   Audio Waveform Amplifier and Converter. An AD/DA converter used on Power Macintosh systems to process audio files.

AWG   American wire gauge. A standard for measuring the thickness of wire.

B   (1) Byte. A unified set of 8 bits used to create a single character. (2) Bold. An HTML attribute assigned to text.

b   Bit. A single 0 or 1 in a binary string.

B2B   Business to business.

BACP   Bandwidth Allocation Control Protocol. A support protocol used by the point-to-point protocol to referee the use of available bandwidth between two communicating devices.

BAT   (1) Baby Advanced Technology. A form factor for personal computer (PC) motherboards that specifies a smaller size. (2) Block Address Translation. A technology used by some memory control circuits that defines multiple address ranges for data and instruction searches.

BBS   Bulletin board system. Before there was the Internet, there were servers set up in many communities that provided resources through dial-up connections. These servers got their name based on the concept of the community bulletin board.

BCC   (1) Block check character. A field in a data packet that includes error detection and correction data, which may include parity (rarely used these days), checksum (on its way out), or cyclical redundancy check (the most common method in use today). (2) Blind carbon copy. A copy of an e-mail message sent that prevents the primary recipient from knowing there are other people receiving the message.

BCP   (1) Base Cryptographic Provider. A Windows service that generates user keys for encrypting data. (2) Best current practice. Procedures that are generally acknowledged as the way to go. (3) Bulk copy program. An application that performs large data duplication tasks automatically.

BCPL   Basic Combined Programming Language. An early programming language that was the basis for CPL.

BCU   (1) BIOS configuration utility. The setup application that allows user configuration of the BIOS. (2) Bus controller unit. A chip that manages the expansion bus on a computer.

BD   Blueray Disk. A video storage mechanism for recording High Definition video content. It stores up to 25 GB of data on a single-layer disk and up to 50 GB on a dual-layer disk.

BeOS   A computer operating system developed by BE, Inc. It is a windowing graphical environment with similarities to Windows and Apple's OS X.

BDC   Backup domain controller. Any server on a network termination (NT) domain that houses a copy of the security database, which is periodically updated by the primary domain controller (PDC).

BDF   Bitmap Description Format. A graphics file format.

BD-ROM   Blue Disk Read Only Memory.

BER   Bit error rate. A measurement of single-bit errors in the transfer of data.

BFF   Binary file format.

BFT   Binary file transfer.

BGA   Ball Grid Array. A chip-mounting socket that uses balls of solder as terminators.

BGP   The Border Gateway Protocol. A routing protocol that takes up where the exterior gateway protocol left off. Advanced algorithms allow for more sophisticated routing decisions.

BIOS   Basic Input/Output System. Basic instruction, usually (but not always) loaded onto a Read Only Memory chip that leads the system through the process of startup and provides instructions as to how to communicate with different forms of hardware.

BIT   Binary digit. The term has been accepted as a word for so long that people forget that it started out as an acronym.

BitBLT   Bit block transfer. The transfer of a section of data in an image file from one location to another.

BMP   (1) Batch message processing. A process by which e-mail or text messages are handled in large groups. (2) Bitmap. A graphics file format specific to the Windows operating system.

BMS   Broadcast Message Server. A communications server used by Hewlett Packard's Visual User Environment (VUE).

BNC   Bayonet Neill-Conselman. Also known as *bayonet nut connector* and *British Naval connector*, a BNC is a barrel-shaped connector that attaches in a simple twist-and-lock motion. Its real name was derived from the two engineers that were the most influential in contributing to the overall design.

BNU   Basic networking utilities.

BOD   Bandwidth on Demand. A telecommunications service that dynamically allocates bandwidth based in immediate need.

BOM   (1) Beginning of Message. (2) Byte Order Mark. A Unicode character that indicates whether the file format is 16-bit or 32-bit. (3) Bill of materials.

BONDING   Bandwidth on Demand Interoperability Group.

BONE   BeOS Networking Environment. The networking infrastructure for the BeOS operating system.

BOOTP   Bootstrap Protocol.

BOT   (1) Beginning of table. (2) Beginning of tape. (3) Short for robot.

BPB   BIOS Pattern Block. A short string of code in a hard disk's Master Boot Record that defines the partition tables.

BPI   Bits per inch. A measurement of recording density for magnetic tape.

BPL   Broadband over Power Lines.

BPS   Bits per second (b/s). A measurement of data transfer.

BRI   Basic Rate ISDN. An ISDN service that provides two 64-K B channels and one 16-K D channel.

BS   (1) Backspace. (2) Base station. (3) Your boss's explanation for why your vacation was cancelled for the year.

BSB Backside bus. The portion of the external data bus (EDB) that moves data back and forth between onboard cache and the CPU.

BSCM Binary Synchronous Communications Mode. A method of serial communications that employs error correction and flow control capabilities.

BSOD Blue screen of death. The last message NT (and later Microsoft operating systems) manages to choke out in its dying breath.

BSV Boot sector virus.

BTAM Basic Telecommunications Access Method. A primitive telecommunications protocol used by early IBM mainframes to communicate across telephone lines.

BTO Build to order. A business model that allows customers to specify the configuration of the server or workstation and have the manufacturer build to their specifications.

BTS Base transceiver station. Used to transmit radio frequency over the air interface.

Btu (1) British thermal unit. A standard measurement of heat. (2) Basic transmission unit. The smallest integrated parcel of data that can be transmitted by a specific device or protocol.

B&W Black and white.

CA Certification Authority. A recognized entity for generating certificates used for security purposes.

CAB Compressed application binary. Also short for cabinet. This is a compressed file that houses a number of smaller files that can be independently extracted as needed.

CAD Computer-aided design. A type of software application that allows engineers and architects to create blueprints and diagrams.

CAL Client access license. A license granting one user permission to access a system or network.

CARP Common Address Redundancy Protocol. This protocol allows a group of devices on the network to share a block of IP addresses.

CAS Column access strobe. A circuit that is part of the memory controller circuit (MCC) responsible for locking onto the first column in a memory module in which the target data is located.

CASE Common Application-Specific Element. An application layer process that is required of most, if not all, transfers of data.

CAT Catalog file. A compressed file format that stores multiple compressed files in a single container.

CATV Cable television.

CAV Constant angular velocity. A data-reading mechanism used by optical drives that allows the rotational velocity of the disk to remain constant, forcing the controller to interpret the data at faster speeds as the optical stylus moves from center to edge.

CBGA Ceramic ball grid array. A socket for mounting microprocessors.

CBR Constant bit rate. A guaranteed data transfer rate defined in ATM.

CBT Computer-based training. Education delivered via software.

CC (n) Carbon copy. (v) To send an e-mail to multiple recipients.

CCD Charge coupled device. A sensor consisting of an array of cells that interpolates a physical image and coverts it into a digital file.

CCDA Cisco Certified Design Associate. Someone who has taken and passed the exams necessary to be certified by Cisco Systems to design networks around Cisco hardware.

CCEA Cisco Certified Enterprise Administrator. Someone who has taken and passed the exams necessary to be certified by Cisco Systems to manage large-scale networks built around Cisco hardware.

CCI Common Client Interface. A definition put forth by Java for a common set of interfaces to be used in Java applications.

CCIE Cisco Certified Internet Expert. Someone who has taken and passed the exams necessary to be certified by Cisco Systems to manage connectivity over Internet connections using Cisco hardware.

CCIP Cisco Certified Internetwork Professional. Someone who has taken and passed the exams necessary to be certified by Cisco Systems to manage multiple networks interconnected with Cisco hardware.

CCNA Cisco Certified Networking Associate. Someone who has taken and passed the exams necessary to be certified by Cisco Systems to work at an entry level on Cisco-based computer networks.

CCNP Cisco Certified Networking Professional. Someone who has taken and passed the exams necessary to be certified by Cisco Systems to perform midlevel functions on Cisco-based computer networks.

CCR (1) Commitment, Concurrency, and Recovery. An application layer process that makes sure that once a transaction begins it is either completed or discarded if not complete. (2) Creedence Clearwater Revival. A kickin' rock band from the sixties and seventies. Rock on!

CCS Common Command Set. Eighteen specific commands that must be included for every device that carries the SCSI-II label.

CCSP Cisco Certified Security Professional. Someone who has taken and passed the exams necessary to be certified by Cisco Systems to design and enforce security policies on a Cisco-based network.

C/D Control data.

CD (1) Compact disk. A optical disk that provides long-term storage for computer or music data. (2) Carrier detect. A conductor in a copper-based circuit that sends a signal to the device when there is an active carrier signal. (3) Collision detect. A function of the Ethernet protocol that determines when two attempts to communicate over the wire occur at the same instant. (4) Change directory. A command-line instruction to switch the target of the file system from one directory node to another.

CDAD Compact Disk, Audio Disk. The file system used by CD-ROMs (read only memory) to store music. (Also known as CD/DA for *compact disk digital audio*).

CDDI Copper Distributed Data Interface. A dual-ring network topology that uses two redundant rings of copper cabling that is capable of sending data in opposite directions.

CDE (1) Common Desktop Environment. A standardized layout and menu set for Unix-based applications. (2) Certified Directory Engineer. An individual who has taken and passed the exams necessary to become certified by Novell to manage Directory Services on Novell servers.

CDF   Comma Delimited Format. A text format for storing database information, using commas to separate information stored in specific fields.

CDFS   Compact Disk File System. The file system used by CD-ROMs to store computer data.

CDL   Computer design language. An earlier programming language used to build dedicated applications.

CDMA   Code Division Multiple Access. A form of digital cellular phone service that is a spread-spectrum technology that assigns a code to all speech bits and sends scrambled transmission of the encoded speech

CDN   Content Delivery Network. A collection of computers distributed across the Internet whose function is to provide access to large data files (specifically multimedia).

CDP   Cisco Discovery Protocol. A protocol used by Cisco routers and layer 3 switches to collect configuration information from directly attached routers so that smaller networks do not require the services of more complex dynamic routing protocols.

CDPD   Cellular Digital Packet Data. A packet-switching technology used to send voice communications.

CD-R   Recordable CD.

CD-ROM   Compact disk/read only memory. An optical data storage disk that cannot be overwritten.

CD-RW   Compact disk rewritable. An optical data storage disk that can be erased and written over after its initial recording.

CERN   Conseil Europen pour la Recherche Nuclaire. A European laboratory that developed the concept of hypermedia. This concept was the foundation for the Internet as we know it.

CERT   Computer Emergency Response Team. An organization charged with the reponsibility of keeping the Internet secure.

CGA   Color Graphics Adapter. An early (now-obsolete) display adapter used on IBM PC and PC-AT computers.

CHAP   Challenge Handshake Authentication Protocol. A password-authentication protocol that makes use of a three-way handshake to provide authentication.

CHS   Cylinders, heads, sectors-per-track. The parameters of hard drive configuration that define total capacity of the drive as well as specific locations on the drive.

CIC   Collect, isolate, and correct. One of the generally accepted troubleshooting models used in the computer industry.

CIDR   Classless Inter-domain Routing. A technology that allows multiple smaller network addresses to be bundled into a single network.

CIFS   Common Internet File System. A protocol developed by Microsoft that allows large numbers of users to share a single file simultaneously.

CIR   Committed Information Rate. The minimum bandwidth guaranteed to a frame relay subscriber. Depending on network conditions, the subscriber may actually enjoy the benefits of even higher bandwidths than those for which he subscribed.

CISC   Complex Instruction Set Computing. A processing method under which instructions vary in length and must be translated into a form the CPU can understand.

CLI   Command line interface.

CLV   Constant linear velocity. A data-reading mechanism used by optical drives in which the rotational velocity of the disk must slow down as the disk is tracked from center to edge, thus assuring that the relative number of tracks per millisecond that passes beneath the optical stylus always remains the same.

CMOS   Complimentary metal oxide semiconductor. The type of chip that houses the user-configurable parameters needed by BIOS.

CMTS   Cable Modem Termination System. A device on the Internet service provider's (ISP) end that combines all incoming cable modem signals into a single channel for transmission over the Internet backbone.

CMYK   Cyan, magenta, yellow and black. Shorthand for the subtractive color system used by printers and other graphical devices or programs. The K is derived from the last letter of the word black and is used instead of B so that it won't be confused with blue, from the primary color system.

CNR   Communications network riser. A specialized card that takes the concept of the AMR and adds networking functionality as well.

COM   Communications.

COMDEX   Computer Dealer Exposition. An annual trade show for businesses in the computer industry.

CPGA   Ceramin Pin Grid Array.

CPL   (1) Current Privilege Level. The level of priority at which code is running on machines. It is the method by which processor rings are defined. (2) Combined Programming Language. An early programming language developed by Cambridge University for their mainframe computers.

CPU   Central processing unit. The primary microprocessor on a modern computer that is responsible for executing programs and processing user data.

CRC   Cyclical Redundancy Check. A form of error correction used by computing systems.

CRT   Cathode ray tube. A video display that uses a device called a *cathode* to fire a beam (or ray) of electrons toward a phosphorus-coated surface.

CSMA/CA   Carrier Sense, Multiple Access/Collision Avoidance. The media access method frequently used by wireless networking.

CSMA/CD   Carrier Sense, Multiple Access/Collision Detection. A technology used by Ethernet to detect and recover from data collisions.

CSS   Cascading Style Sheets. A web designing specification that allows the programmer to define the look and feel of a page once and use it with every other page on the site.

CST   Computer service technician.

CSU/DSU   Channel Service Unit/Data Service Unit. This is the device that interconnects a network to a high-speed wide area network (WAN) connection.

CUI   Common User Interface. A feature of many operating systems that dictates how certain functions related to user interaction with the programs are handled, assuring that all applications have a similar look, feel, and function.

D/A   Digital to analog.

DAB   Digital audio broadcasting. The transmission of audio in binary format.

DAC   (1) Digital-to-analog converter. This is a chip that takes binary information and converts it into an electrical waveform. (2) Discretionary access control. A feature written into the NTFS file system that allows an administrator to apply security on a file or directory level.

DACL   Discretionary Access Control List. A catalog of security settings for all objects under control of the NTFS file system.

DAF   Destination Address Field. A portion of a data packet that contains addressing information for the target host

DAMPS   Digital Advanced Mobile Phone Service. A term for digital cellular radio in North America.

DAP   (1) Directory Access Protocol. An early incarnation of directory access based on the OSI model. (2) Digital Audio Player.

DARPA   Defense Advanced Research Projects Agency. The government agency that first began the research that would eventually lead to the Internet.

DAS   Dual attached station. Any device that is hooked up to both rings in a fiber distributed data interface (FDDI) network.

DAT   (1) Digital audio tape. A tape format that uses an 8-mm metal oxide recording tape and a helical scan-recording mechanism very similar to that used by digital audio recorders. (2) Data. A common file extension used for data files.

dB   Decibel. A measurement of sound amplitude.

DBMS   Database management system.

DBS   Database server.

DC   Direct current. A unidirectional current that flows from the positive side of the circuit to the negative side.

DCD   Data Carrier Detect. One of the control signals used in serial communications.

DCE   Distributed Computing Environment. A technology that allows processing to be performed across multiple computers.

DCS   Digital Cellular System.

DDE   Dynamic Data Exchange. A technology for exchanging data between two autonomous programs running on a single computer.

DDF   Data Decryption Field. A header field that is added to any file encrypted by encrypting file system (EFS) that allows the decryption of that file.

DDK   Device Driver Kit. A package of utilities provided by Microsoft to facilitate the creation of hardware drivers for Microsoft operating systems.

DDNS   Dynamic Domain Naming System.

DDoS   Distributed Denial of Service. An attack on a server or network that focuses a large number of geographically isolated systems onto a single attack.

DDP   Datagram Delivery Protocol. The AppleTalk protocol that provides end-to-end support services.

DDR   Double Data Rate. A technology used by memory and other devices that allows 2 bits of data to move over each wire on every clock cycle. Also known as DDRAM.

DDS   Digital data storage.

DEA   Data Encryption Algorithm. The collection of formulae used to scramble data for security purposes.

DEC   Digital Equipment Corporation.

DECnet   Digital Equipment Corporation networking protocol. A now-obsolete protocol that is still included in some operating systems for backward compatibility.

DEF   Definition.

DEFRAG   Defragment.

DEK   Data encryption key. A small binary token stored on a computer or security device that provides the information required to decrypt data.

DEL   Delete.

DES   Data Encryption Standard. One of the industry standards for encoding data for security reasons.

DEV   Device.

DFS   Distributed File System. A subset of NTFS that allows users to browse to remote resources on a network without requiring the user to know the specific path information.

DHCP   Dynamic Host Configuration Protocol. A transmission control protocol/Internet protocol (TCP/IP) that dynamically assigns host configuration.

DHTML   Dynamic Hypertext Markup Language. A Web site design language.

DICOM   Digital Information and Communications in Medicine. A collection of protocols and applications used in hospital information systems.

DIF   Data Interchange Format.

DIME   Direct Internet Message Encapsulation. A protocol that takes messages from a variety of applications and encodes them into a single message for transmission over the Internet.

DIMM   Dual Inline Memory Module. A 168- or 184-pin memory module that allows the connection on either side of the base to perform disparate functions.

DIN   Deutsches Institut für Normung. A German organization that creates and enforces industry standards.

DIP   (1) Dual Inline Package. Also known as dual inline pin package or DIPP. A form factor for microchips. (2) Dial-up Internet protocol. A protocol used to allow a host to connect to the Internet via a dial-up connection. (3) Digital image processing.

DIR   Directory.

DIX   Digital, Intel, and Xerox.

DL   Download.

DLA   Drive Letter Access. A technology developed by Microsoft that lets a user write to optical drives as though they were hard disks.

DLB   Dynamic Load Balancing. A method of sharing processing or networking traffic across multiple devices.

DLC   Data Link Control. Any networking protocol that operates at layer 2 of the OSI networking model.

DLCI   Data link Communication Identifier. A specific circuit assigned to a frame relay subscriber. It may consist of either a virtual circuit or a permanent virtual circuit, depending on the level of service selected by the subscriber.

DLL   Dynamically Linked Library. A file that contains a collection of subroutines that can be called on the fly by any application running on the system that requires the services it provides, and can be flushed from memory when its task is finished.

DLT   Digital Linear Tape. A tape format that uses metal film tape and a linear transport mechanism that records data in a straight line along the tape, parallel to the edge of the tape.

DMA   Direct Memory Access. A technique by which a large amount of data is moved directly from an application or device to memory without constant intervention from the CPU.

DME   Direct Memory Execution. The ability of an AGP device to process texture maps in video random access memory (RAM) without offloading the work to the processor.

DMS Document Management Server. A computer dedicated to the storage and controlled access of documents.

DMY Day, month, and year.

DMZ Demilitarized Zone. A section of a network that is placed outside of any areas secured from outside access.

DN Distinguished name. The complete network path to any object on a network using directory services.

DNS Domain Name System.

DOA Dead on arrival. Didn't work when you received it.

DOS (1) Disk operating system. Any OS that incorporates a file system targeted for magnetic disk storage. (2) Denial of Service. A malicious attack on a computer or network intended to make it unavailable to legitimate users. This is usually accomplished by hitting the system with more requests that it can service, causing a system crash.

DPI Dots per inch.

DPLL Digital Phase Locked Loop. A clock signal carried in an electrical transmission of data.

DQDB Distributed Queue, Dual Bus. A networking standard that allows multiple-user access over two or more disparate connections. FDDI is a protocol that uses DQDB. It allows a 150-mb/s transfer rate over two separate fiber lines, with a separate queue assigned to each carrier.

DRAM Dynamic Random Access Memory.

DRF Data Recovery Field. A header field that is added to any file encrypted by EFS that allows a recovery agent to decrypt the data in the absence of the original user.

DRM Digital Rights Management. Software technology that prevents copyrighted material from being used without permission.

DSAP Destination Service Access Point. The address to which one layer sends data to the next layer in the flow.

DSIG Digital signature. A small binary token embedded in a file that confirms its authenticity. To be valid, a digital signature must be issued by a trusted authority, such as VeriSign.

DSL Digital Subscriber Line. A broadband high-speed data connection that moves over standard telephone cable.

DSLAM DSL Access Multiplexer. A device on the ISP end that combines all incoming DSL signals into a single channel for transmission over the Internet backbone.

DSLR Digital single lens reflex. A form of digital camera that allows the operator to view the image directly through the lens that will capture the actual photo. This allows for more accurate composition of the image.

DSP Digital signal processor. A chip that performs multiple processing functions on a signal. For example, the DSP on a modem combines the functions of a universal asynchronous receiver/transmitter (UART) and a DAC.

DSSS Direct Sequence Spread Spectrum. One of the frequency-hopping methods used in radio-based wireless networking.

DSU Data Service Unit (or data switching unit). The device that acts as the interface between the local area network and the telecommunications provider.

DTC Desktop conferencing. A service that allows multiple users to meet virtually over a computer connection.

DTCP Digital Transmission Content Protection. A technology that prevents the unauthorized copying of digital material. DTCP is particularly useful in protecting intellectual rights for materials such as music and movies.

DTE Data terminal equipment. The hardware that acts as an interface between the end user and a telecommunications service that converts user data to a transmitted signal and back again.

DTR Data transfer rate. How fast information moves from one device to another.

DUN Dial-up networking. A method for interconnecting a remote user to a network using a modem and a conventional telephone or an ISDN line.

DVD Digital video disk *or* digital versatile disk.

DVD-R Recordable DVD.

DVD-RW Rewritable DVD.

Dword Double word.

E Exa-. Prefix representing 2 to the power of 60 or 10 to the power of 18.

EA Extended attribute. A feature of more advanced operating systems that allows them to apply permissions or other characteristics to a file or directory using *metadata* stored in the file tables.

EAM Enterprise Asset Management. A philosophical approach to an organization's inventory control that allows the organization to maximize and retain values of material inventory.

EAP (1) Extensible Authentication Protocol. A protocol used by wireless networks to verify the identity of users logging on to the network. Since EAP does not define specific authentication mechanisms, a large number of different versions of EAP exist. (2) Enterprise Application Platform. A server application that enables the deployment of scalable applications across an entire organization from a single distribution server or a cluster of servers.

EAPI Extended Application Programming Interface. A collection of applications that provides the building blocks for creating Web-based programs.

EAS Enterprise Access Server. A dedicated computer that provides secure access to a wireless network.

EB Exabyte. A million *terabytes*.

Eb Exabit. A million *terabits*.

EBD Emergency boot disk. A floppy disk or CD-ROM that is used to start a computer system when the OS fails.

EBX Embedded Board eXpandible. One of several form factors whose objective was to keep the system as small as possible.

ECC Error Correction Code. Also *error checking and correction*, ECC is an error-correction method that stored a mathematical image of data being moved on a nibble chip and could correct single-bit errors as they were detected.

ECHS Extended CHS. *See* **CHS**.

ECI Extended Capabilities ID. Information programmed onto a peripheral components interconnect (PCI) card that defines any enhanced functions that device can perform beyond the basic functions defined by its device class.

ECP Extended Compatibility Port. A parallel mode that provides for both data and command cycles, therefore supporting more advanced devices, including scanners, storage devices, and such. Data throughput is similar to that of enhanced parallel port (EPP). However, since DMA is used, there is less delay imposed on the application.

ED   End delimiter. A character or series of characters that acts as the demarcation point between fields in a packet or between bytes in a serial communications stream.

EDB   External data bus. The path that data uses to move from the CPU to an outside circuit or vice versa.

EDC   Error detection code. Code embedded in a file system that allows the system to detect that an error in transmission of that data has occurred and, where possible, alerts the system to take corrective action.

EDO   Extended Data Out. A form of memory that replaced fast page mode (FPM) that allowed the RAS/CAS operations for the next input/output (I/O) operation to be performed at the same time as data from the previous operation is being moved out of the chip.

EEPROM   Electrically Erasable Programmable Read On Memory. A more modern implementation of an integrated circuit (IC) that can be wiped clean and rewritten if necessary.

EFS   Encrypting File System. A subset of NTFS 5.0 that allows individual files to be scrambled on an as-needed basis and subsequently unscrambled only by a user with appropriate permissions.

EFT   Electronic funds transfer. The use of computer systems to facilitate the transfer of money from one account to another. When you use your ATM card, you see AFT at work.

EGA   Enhanced Graphics Array. An early (now-obsolete) display adapter used on IBM PC and PC-AT computers.

EGP   Exterior Gateway Protocol. The first of the border gateway protocols to be released.

EIA   Electronic Industry Association. One of the many governing bodies in the electronic industry.

EIDE   Enhanced IDE (integrated drive electronic).

EIGRP   Enhanced Interior Gateway Routing Protocol. A Cisco protocol for intercommunication between internal routers on a network.

EISA   Enhanced ISA. A 32-bit, 8.33-Mhz bus released by a coalition of manufacturers led by Compaq. Video Electronics Standards Association local bus (VLB) was designed to be backwardly compatible with industry standards architecture (ISA).

EM   Expanded memory. Memory above 1 MB on a conventional system that is used for data storage.

EMB   Extended Memory Block. 64-KB blocks of memory above the first 1MB of conventional memory that is used for data storage.

EMF   (1) Electromagnetic field. An energy layer that surrounds any electrically charged object. In theory, the EMF extends to infinity, while in practice its effect is limited by the strength of the charge. (2) Enhanced metafile. The 32-bit version of a graphics file system introduced in Windows. (3) Extensible message format. A reply message to an e-mail system that reports the status of a transmitted message.

EMI   Electromagnetic interference. Distortion created by a magnetic field generated by an electrical device that can interfere with an electronic signal.

EMM   Extended Memory Management. A method of controlling memory beyond 1 MB of conventional memory that allows for either the storage of data or the execution of code.

EMP Electromagnetic pulse. A burst of energy released by an explosion. Nuclear explosions can generate sufficient EMP to destroy communications systems.

EMS Expanded Memory Specification. An early standard for addressing memory above 1 MB.

ENDEC Encoder/decoder.

ENIAC Electronic Numerical Integrator and Computer. The first fully electronic computer.

EOF End of file.

EOT End of transmission. I hope I don't have to explain that one.

EPIC Explicitly Parallel Instruction Computing. A technology that allows multiple threads to be processed in a CPU at the same time.

EPP Enhanced Parallel Port. Because it provides for different types of signals to be transferred on any given clock cycle, EPP provides for faster and more efficient communication between peripherals. EPP allows continuous data transfer of around 500 KB/s with burst rates of up to 2 MB/s.

EPRML Extended PRML (Partial Response/Maximum Likelihood). A data encoding mechanism used by most hard disk drives that are currently being manufactured.

EPROM Erasable Programmable Read Only Memory. An IC that can be wiped clean and rewritten if necessary.

EPS Encapsulated Postscript. A printer language developed by Adobe (and introduced by Apple) that defines images with text.

ERD Emergency repair diskette. A floppy disk that holds system configuration and account information for a machine running NT (or later) operating systems.

ESC Escape.

ESD (1) Electrostatic discharge. The technical term for static electricity. (2) Emergency startup disk. Similar to an emergency boot disk.

ESDI Enhanced Small Device Interface. An earlier hard disk drive interface that preceded IDE.

ESN (1) Electronic Serial Number. On Pentium III CPUs (and later) this is a number embedded by Intel at the factory that identifies that specific CPU. (2) Electronic serial number. An identity signal that is sent from the mobile to the mobile services switching center (MSC) during a brief registration transmission.

ESO Equipment superior to operator. A technician's tongue-in-cheek method of explaining a user error, without calling it a user error.

ETB End of transmission block. Ending delimiter for a complete data transmission.

E–TDMA Extended TDMA (Time Division Multiple Access). Developed to provide fifteen times the capacity over analog systems by compressing quiet time during conversations.

EULA End User License Agreement. An explicit contract between a software developer and the user that defines what rights the user has with the software.

EXT End of text. Okay, we're done sending text in this block. The next bytes are more control information.

FAQ Frequently asked questions. A list of topics commonly asked by people having difficulty with a specific device or application.

FAT (1) File Allocation Table. The file system originally used by MS-DOS. (2) The table used by file systems to identify the location of each file allocation unit (FAU) used by a file.

FAT16   File Allocation Table, 16-bit.

FAT32   File Allocation Table, 32-bit.

FAU   File allocation unit. The collection of sectors that houses the most basic collective unit of data on a hard drive. A FAU can only hold data from a single file, even if that file doesn't fill it up.

FC-AL   Fibre Channel Arbitrated Loop.

FCC   Federal Communications Commission. The government agency responsible for regulating telecommunications in the United States.

FCCH   Frequency Control Channel.

FCP   Fibre Channel Protocol.

FC-PGA   Flip Chip-Pin Grid Array. A CPU socket designed for easy CPU installation or replacement used in modern machines.

FC-PH   Fibre Channel Physical and Signaling interface.

FDC   Floppy disk controller.

FDD   Floppy disk drive.

FDDI   Fiber Distributed Data Interface. A modern networking technology that makes use of a dual-ring topology and that exchanges tokens. FDDI is capable of sending data in opposite directions.

FDHP   Full Duplexing Handshake Protocol. A protocol that allows two-way communication between modems.

FDMA   Frequency Division Multiple Access. Used to separate multiple transmissions over a finite frequency allocation. Refers to the method of allocating a discrete amount of frequency bandwidth to each user.

FEK   File encryption key. The 128-bit value used by encrypting software to scramble the code.

FHSS   Frequency-Hopping Spread Spectrum. One of the frequency-hopping methods used in radio-based wireless networking.

FIFO   First in, first out.

FIPS   Federal Information Processing Standards. US Government standards for software security and interoperability.

FILO   First in, last out.

FIRST   Forum of Incident Response and Security Teams. An organization charged with maintaining the security of the Internet.

FLOPS   Floating point operations per second. A calculation of CPU performance.

FM   (1) Frequency modulation. A method of sending signals over an analog medium that encodes data by changing the frequency of the signal without affecting the relative strength. (2) A modulation technique in which the carrier frequency is shifted by an amount proportional to the value of the modulating signal.

FNR   Format and restore. Technician slang.

FPM   Fast Page Mode. An early form of memory that eliminated the row access strobe (RAS) cycle from any read operation retrieving data from the same row as the previous operation.

FPS   Frames per second.

FPU   Floating point unit. The subcomponent of the CPU that handles more advanced mathematical functions.

FRA   Fixed Radio Access.

FSB   Frontside bus. The portion of the EDB that moves data in and out of the CPU from external locations.

FTP   File Transfer Protocol. Protocol used for transferring critical data.

FUBAR   Fouled up beyond all recognition. Or something like that.

Gb   Gigabit.

GB   Gigabyte.

GBIC   Gigabit Interface Converter. A networking component that allows any networkable device to interface with several different types of connection at once.

Gbs   Gigabits per second.

GBs   Gigabytes per second.

GDI   Graphical Device Interface. A subset of Microsoft's Windows operating systems that manages imaging devices such as printers, scanners, and graphics cards. Printers that use this interface as their printer language are referred to as *GDI printers*.

GFS   Global File System. A file system that allows flle search and storage functions to span clustered servers.

GFSK   Gaussian Frequency Shift Keying. A scheme for determining shift patterns and frequency in spread-spectrum radio networking.

GID   Group identification. Identifies a group account of which several users might be members.

GPF   General protection fault. A failure of an application (and possibly the CPU) that results from one program invading another program's address space.

GPL   General Public License. A software licensing scheme that allows free use of a product by anyone.

GPRS   General Packet Radio Service. A packet-switching technology used to send voice communications.

GRUB   Grand Unified Boot Loader. An applet used by Unix and Linux to load the operating system.

HAL   Hardware Abstraction Layer. A subset of the Microsoft Windows operating systems that provides a virtual barrier between the computer's hardware and the applications and upper-level OS functions. It was also a really cool computer in *2001: A Space Odyssey* that did exactly what it was told to do. And got in trouble.

HCL   Hardware Compatibility List. A list of hardware published by the manufacturer of an operating system that tells which hardware devices have been tested and verified to work with a specific version of OS.

HD   High Definition. A video standard that specifies 720 or 1080 lines of pixels per screen.

HD-DVD   High-Definition DVD.

HDMI   High-Definition Multi-media Interface.

HDTV   High-Definition Television.

HDB3   High-Density Bipolar Code, level 3. A modification of AMI that prevents more than four 0s from occurring in sequence.

HDLC   High-level Data Link Control. A networking protocol that works at the data link layer.

HFC   Hybrid Fiber Coaxial. A cable specification that calls for copper conductors to carry one signal, while fiber optics carry others.

HFS   Hierarchical File System. Apple's file system for storing data on floppy disks.

HMA   High Memory Area. The first 64KB of address space above 1MB in a Microsoft operating system.

HPFS   High-Performance File System. A file system codeveloped by Microsoft and IBM that was used in the now-defunct OS2.

HPGL   Hewlett Packard Graphics Language. A printer language developed by HP to add complex graphics to the printer's tool set.

HPSF   High Power, Single Frequency. A radio wave-based networking technology using high-powered, assigned radio frequencies.

HR   Horizontal refresh. The speed at which a monitor can draw individual raster lines.

HTML   Hyper Text Markup Language. A programming language used to create Web pages and other media that employs extensive use of links to other documents.

HTTP   Hyper Text Transport Protocol.

HTTPS   Secure HTTP.

HVD   High-Voltage Differential.

Hz   Hertz. A measurement for frequency, or the number of times during any given timing cycle that the measured event occurs.

IANA   The Internet Assigned Numbers Authority. The organization that currently hands out IP address to those that need them.

IC   Integrated circuit. A single microchip onto which the code necessary to provide several different functions has been burned.

ICA   Independent Computing Architecture. Citrix's thin-client protocol.

ICANN   The Internet Corporation for Assigned Names and Numbers. One of several organizations involved in the administration of the Internet.

ICMP   Internet Control Message Protocol.

iComp   Intel Comparative Microprocessor Index. A benchmarking method developed by Intel.

ICS   Internet Connection Sharing. A service that allows multiple computers to simultaneously use a single hookup to the Internet.

IDB   Internal data bus.

IDE   Integrated Drive Electronics. A method of managing hard drives and other devices that takes the controller circuitry off the motherboard or separate controller card and places it on the device itself.

IDR   Intelligent Disaster Recovery. A proprietary backup method developed by Compaq and HP that allows a full system restoration, complete with MBR, FAT, and system files in a single operation.

IEEE   The Institute of Electrical and Electronic Engineers. One of several organizational bodies devoted to the development and ratification of international standards in various industries.

IEPG   The Internet Engineering and Planning Group. An organization involved in overseeing the operational control of the Internet.

IETF   The Internet Engineering Task Force. An organization charged with technological development of the Internet.

IFCA   IEEE Fibre Channel address. A unique address assigned to all FC-AL devices at the factory that allows it to be automatically configured onto the FC-AL loop.

IFS   Installable File System. A feature in Win9x and later operating systems that allows network redirectors and third-party file systems to be installed as needed.

IIS Internet Information Services.

IMAP Internet Message Access Protocol.

IMAP4 Internet Message Access Protocol, version 4.

InterNIC Internet Network Information Center. One of several organizations involved in the administration of the Internet.

I/O Input/output. The process of sending or receiving data between devices.

IOPS I/O operations per second. The maximum number of times a device can receive and then execute either a request for data, or a request to write data to the device, assuming the smallest block of data the device uses.

IP Internet Protocol.

IPCP IP Control Protocol. One of the lower-level protocols of point-to-point protocol (PPP).

IPS Instructions per second. An early measurement of CPU performance that was based solely on how many times in 1 second the device could execute commands.

IPSEC Internet Protocol Security. A security protocol for standard TCP/IP transmissions. Although optional on IPv4 (version 4), it is built into IPv6 (version 6).

IPv6 Internet Protocol, version 6. The latest release of IP that supports 128-bit addresses and several advanced features.

IPX/SPX Internet Packet Exchange/Sequenced Packet Exchange. A networking protocol developed by Novell.

IRC Internet Relay Chat. A protocol that allows real-time text conversations between users across a network or the Internet.

IRQ Interrupt request. An electrical signal used by the CPU or other device on the system to let the opposite end know that there is data to be moved.

ISA Industry Standards Architecture. An 8- or 16-bit expansion bus designed by IBM.

ISDN Integrated Services Digital Network. A telecommunications technology that provides high-speed data transfer over standard telephone lines.

ISO International Organization for Standards. One of several groups that oversees the development and ratification of standards in the computer industry, as well as many other industries.

ISOC The Internet Society. The organization that oversees all the other organizations involved in managing the Internet. (Who oversees them?)

ISP Internet service provider. The end user's gateway to the Internet.

IT Information technology.

ITU The International Telecommunications Union. An organization that deals primarily with communications protocols.

JEDEC Joint Electron Device Engineering Council. An organization that oversees standards for many of the electronic devices we use, including memory modules.

JPEG Joint Photographic Experts Group. A committee that oversees the development of compression algorithms for graphics images. It is also the name of the compression algorithm used for still images.

Kb Kilobits. In binary, this is 1,024 single bits of data in a block. The key to remember is that a small b is bits and a large B is bytes.

KB Kilobytes. In binary, this is 1,024 bytes of data in a block.

KHz Kilohertz. One thousand hertz.

L1   Level 1. A small amount of extremely fast memory used to store data or instructions that the CPU expects it will need within a few clock cycles, or that it uses frequently.

L2   Level 2. A secondary level of slower cache memory. This is usually a larger amount of memory than the L1 and is the second place the CPU looks for needed instructions or data.

L2TP   Layer 2 Tunneling Protocol. A more recent implementation of point-to-point tunneling protocol (PPTP) that works exclusively at the data link layer.

L3   Level 3. A third layer of cache supported by only a select few CPUs.

LAN   Local area network.

LBA   Logical Block Addressing. An extension to a BIOS instruction known as Int13h that numbers each FAU on the hard drive with a unique value.

LCD   Liquid crystal display. An imaging device that consists of transistors suspended in a liquid emulsion.

LCP   Link Control Protocol. One of the subordinate protocols of PPP.

LD   Laser diode. A small electrical device that emits pulses of laser light.

LDAP   Lightweight Directory Access Protocol. A more recent directory access protocol based on TCP/IP.

LED   Light-emitting diode. A small electrical device that emits conventional light waves (usually in the visible spectrum).

LFN   Long File Name. A technology introduced into FAT32 and later operating systems that allows file names up be up to 255 characters long, including the extension.

LIF   Low Insertion Force. One of three forms of CPU socket that requires no special tools to install or remove the CPU.

Li-Ion   Lithium ion. A type of rechargeable battery.

LLC   Logic Link Control. One of the sublayers of the data link layer.

LLC2   Logical Link Control, type 2.

LPSF   Low-Power, Single Frequency. A radio wave-based networking technology using weak, publicly available radio frequencies.

LPX   Low Profile eXtended. One of several form factors whose objective was to keep the system as small as possible.

LSA   Local Security Authority. An NT service that manages the logon process and all subsequent access to system or network resources.

LUN   Logical Unit Number. A setting on SCSI devices that allows multiple devices to be seen by the controller as a single device.

LVD   Low-Voltage Differential.

MAC   Media Access Control. One of the sublayers of data link.

MAPI   Messaging Applications Programming Interface.

MAU   Multistation access unit. A device used on the Token Ring network that interconnects hosts in a physical star, but maintains the logical configuration of a ring.

Mb   Megabit. In binary, this is 1,048,576 single bits of data. The key to watch is that a small b is bits and a large B is bytes.

MB   Megabyte. In binary, this would be 1,048,576 bytes. In decimal, it would be one million bytes.

MBs   Megabytes per second.

Mbs   Megabits per second.

MBR   Master boot record. Information contained on the first one or two sectors of a hard disk that contain code that initializes the file system, defines disks and partitions, and provides a point to the OS.

MBTF   Mean time between failure. An average of the number of hours a particular model of device is expected to operate before it dies.

MCA   Microchannel Architecture. A proprietary 32-bit, 12-Mhz bus released by IBM shortly after Intel's release of the 80386 CPU.

MCC   Memory controller chip *or* memory controller circuit. The chip or circuitry on the chipset that manages memory mapping and refresh functions.

MCSD   Microsoft Certified Systems Developer. A certification given to someone who has proven their ability to write applications in the Microsoft environment through a battery of examiniations.

MCSE   Microsoft Certified Systems Expert. A certification given to someone who has proven their ability to manage a Microsoft-based network through a battery of examiniations.

MDI   The Media Dependent Interface component of the physical layer.

MDRAM   Multibank DRAM. A form of memory that can be accessed in blocks rather than sequentially.

MFM   Modified Frequency Modulation. One of the early data-encoding mechanisms used by hard disk drives.

MFT   Master File Table. The database of information used by NTFS that stores file attributes and information defining their locations on the hard drive.

MFU   Most Frequently Used. The portion of the XP Start Menu that displays applications that have been opened over a predefined period of time and in the order which they were opened. Applications are displayed from most recently used to least recent.

MHz   Megahertz. One million hertz.

MIB   Management information base. A database of objects that are monitored by any one of several network management protocols.

MIC   Memory in Cartridge. The embedded memory chip of an AIT.

MIDI   Musical Instrument Device Interface. A connector for hooking up computerized musical instruments to a computer system.

MIP   Multium in parvo. Latin for "many in one." It is a technique by which several samples of the same texture are created in different sizes.

MIPS   Millions of instructions per second. An early, primitive method of measuring CPU performance.

MJPEG   Motion-picture Joint Photographic Experts Group. An organization that develops and maintains standards for digitizing images. Also a file format used for compressing and storing editable versions of motion pictures developed by that group.

MLP   (1) Multiple load point. A tape drive technology that allows a single tape to be mounted from several different locations on the tape.(2) Mid load point. A tape drive technology that places the load point in the center of the tape. Is that confusing enough for you?

MMC   Microsoft Management Console.

MMX   Multi-Media eXtensions. A set of instructions targeted specifically at multimedia.

MOSFET   Metal oxide semiconductor field effect transistor.

MOV   Metal oxide varistor. An electrical component that can absorb abrupt spikes in current.

MPEG   Motion Picture Experts Group. A shortened variation of MJPEG.

MRH-S   Memory Repeater Hub for SDRAM. A chip in newer Intel chipsets used to arbitrate read/write operations for SDRAM.

MS or MSU   Mobile station or Mobile station unit. Handset carried by the subscriber.

MSC   Mobile-services Switching Center. A switch that provides services and coordination between mobile users in a network and external networks.

MS-DOS   Microsoft Disk Operating System.

MTBF   Mean time between failure. An average of how long a specific device can run before it dies.

MTH   Memory Translator Hub. A chip in newer Intel chipsets that replaces the northbridge chip used by contemporary chipsets.

MTSO   Mobile Telephone Switching Office. The central office for the mobile switch, which houses the field monitoring and relay stations for switching calls from cell sites to wireline central offices.

MTU   Maximum transmission unit. The largest size a packet can be in order to be used by a specific protocol.

MTX   Mobile Telephone eXchange.

NACK   No acknowledgment. It arrived, but there's something wrong. Can you retransmit?

NADC   North American Digital Cellular (also called United States Digital Cellular, or USDC). A Time Division Multiple Access (TDMA) system that provides three to six times the capacity of AMPS.

NAMPS   Narrowband Advanced Mobile Phone Service. NAMPS was introduced as an interim solution to capacity problems. NAMPS provided three times the AMPS capacity to extend the usefulness of analog systems.

NAP   Network access point. The entry point to one of the several large-capacity circuits that transport data across the Internet.

NAS   Network Attached Storage. An array of disks independent of any individual machine that can be used for storage by any user on the network with permissions to access the array.

NAT   Network Address Translation. A technology that hides a private addressing scheme from the public view.

NAU   Network Addressable Unit. Any entity on a SNA network that can be independently addressed.

NBP   Name Binding Protocol. The AppleTalk protocol that handles name resolution.

NCP   Network Control Protocol. One of the lower-level protocols of PPP.

NDIS   Network Device Interface Specification. A Windows device driver that allows several different protocols to access the same piece of hardware simultaneously.

NDS   Novell Directory Services.

NetBEUI   NetBIOS Extended User Interface. An early Microsoft networking protocol.

NetBIOS   Network basic input/output services.

NFS   Network File System.

NIC   Network interface card.

NiCad   Nickel cadmium. A type of rechargeable battery.

Ni-MH Nickel metal hydride. A type of rechargeable battery.

NIS Network Information Service. A Sun Microsystems protocol for distributing network configuration information.

NLA Network Location Awareness. A feature in XP that automatically configures a computer system to network or subnet to the device to which it is attached.

NLB Network Load Balancing.

NLM NetWare Loadable Module.

NLSP NetWare Link Services Protocol.

NLX New Low-profile eXtended. An industry-supported form factor that took the concept of the riser card but established strict standards for development.

NMI Nonmaskable Interrupt. Similar to the IRQs used by devices, an NMI is an interrupt to the CPU indicating that immediate action is required. If the CPU cannot resolve the issue, the NMI will cause it to lock up.

NOS Network operating system. An OS that is beefed up to include services specific to managing networks with large numbers of users.

NT New Technology. The first version of a Windows network operating system that was released in the era of Windows 3.x.

NT1 Network Termination-1. The interface at an incoming ISDN line that converts the incoming two-wire circuit to a four-wire ISDN circuit.

NTFS New Technology File System. A file system introduced by Microsoft that incorporated a greater degree of security and more efficient file management procedures.

NTSC National Television System Committee. This is the technical term for analog television broadcasts in the United States. The name is derived from the committee that defined the specifications used by broadcasters. NTSC is scheduled to be phased out early in the year 2009, to be replaced with all-digital broadcasting signals.

NTWS NT workstation.

OCR Optical character recognition. A technology that reads the characters residing on a scanned image and converts them into characters that are usable by computer software programs.

OCX Optical Carrier Level. A method of defining the different levels of transmission speed over high-speed networks. The X represents the specific level.

OEM Original equipment manufacturer. The term refers to the actual manufacturer of a specific piece of hardware or software used in the assembly of a complex system, such as a computer system. For example, the hard disk in an IBM computer might be manufactured by Seagate, in which case, the OEM is Seagate. Many times, parts or software are distributed specifically for use by manufacturers to build systems. Surplus parts not needed by the systems integrator are frequently sold on the open market. Since they do not include any fancy packaging, instruction manuals, or in many cases do not have the same warranties, the company will refer to the parts or software as OEM. In most cases, OEM parts or software do not include support of any kind from the original manufacturer.

OLE Object Linking and Embedding. A technology that allows an object to be created in one application, imported into a second application, and should the properties of the object ever change in the first, it is automatically updated in the second.

OOP   Object Oriented Programming. A form of programming in which a parcel of data is an object and a variety of command groupings called routines are used to modify the data.

OS   Operating system.

OSA   Open System Architecture. A now-defunct set of protocols for networking multiple platforms onto a singular network.

OSI   Open Systems Interconnect. A seven-layer model of networking defined by the Industry Standards Organization in which the functions of networking are broken down into seven distinct layers.

OSPF   Open Shortest Path First. An interior gateway protocol that uses a link state method of route determination.

OU   Organizational Unit. One of the container objects used in Novell's Directory Services model.

OUI   Organizational Unique Identifier. Half of a MAC address that has been assigned to the manufacturer by the IEEE Registration Authority.

P2P   Peer-to-peer. A network in which all computers act as both clients and servers.

PAE   Physical Address Extension.

PAL   Phase Alternating Line. A color coding system used in analog television broadcasts in parts of Europe.

PAP   (1) Password Authentication Protocol. A nonsecure protocol for providing user credentials between hosts on a network. It is nonsecure in that passwords are transmitted in plain text. (2) Printer Access Protocol.

PATA   Parallel ATA.

PBC   Port Bypass Circuit. A circuit that manages an FC-AL loop and automatically detects when a device has been removed.

PCI   Peripheral Components Interconnect. A 32- or 64-bit expansion bus designed by Intel.

PCI-X   PCI extended. A recently released 133-Mhz version of the PCI bus.

PCL   Printer Control Language. Hewlett Packard's printer language, originally developed for dot matrix printers and later adopted for use with laser printers.

PCM   Pulse Code Modulation. The process of converting electrical current into a digital signal.

PCMCIA   Personal Computer Memory Card International Association.

PCS   Personal Communications Service. A lower-powered, higher-frequency competitive technology that incorporates wireline and wireless networks and provides personalized features.

PDA   Personal digital assistant. Any one of several computing devices designed for maximum portability.

PDC   Primary domain controller. The server in an NT domain that houses the master security database.

PDU   Protocol Data Unit: The format of data as it moves between OSI layers.

PEBKAC   Problem exists between keyboard and chair. A euphemistic way of saying it's a user error.

PEC   Piezoelectric crystal

PGA   Pin grid array. A pin-mounted CPU on which the pins are arranged in perfectly symmetrical patterns of squares.

PGP   Pretty Good Privacy. An early public key encryption algorithm for MS-DOS.

PIF   Program Information File. A small descriptor file that tells Windows how a specific DOS application is going to behave.

PING   Packet InterNet Groper. A TCP/IP utility that sends echo packets and waits for the reply.

PIO   Programmed Input/Output. A transfer of data in which each byte of data must be negotiated and managed by the CPU.

PKE   Public Key Encryption.

PKI   Public Key Infrastructure.

PLS   Physical Layer Signaling. The physical signaling component of the physical layer.

PM   Program Manager. An applet in Win3x that acted as a DOS shell for file and program management functions.

PMA   The Physical Medium Attachment component of the physical layer.

PnP   Plug and Play. An Intel/Microsoft technology that allows the computer system and OS to automatically detect and configure certain settings for PnP-compatible hardware.

POP   (1) Point of presence. The physical connection supplied by an ISP that provides access to the Internet. (2) Post Office Protocol.

POP3   Post Office Protocol, version 3.

POSIX   Portable Operating System Interface. A loosely defined set of standards for interfacing applications with the Unix OS. The X at the end does not stand for anything, but ties the term to the Unix OS.

POST   Power-On Self-Test. A program contained on the BIOS chip of most computers that brings the system from a cold start up to operational condition.

POTS   Plain Old Telephone Service.

PPB   PCI-to-PCI bridge. The circuitry that arbitrates data transfer between two different PCI busses on the same system.

PPP   Point-to-Point Protocol. A networking protocol that works at the data link layer. It is the default protocol of dial-up networking.

PPTP   Point-to-Point Tunneling Protocol. A protocol that allows the encapsulation of encrypted packets for secure transmission over the Internet.

PRI   Primary Rate ISDN. An ISDN service that provides twenty-three 64-K B channels and one 64-K D channel.

PRML   Partial Response/Maximum Likelihood. A data-encoding mechanism used by more recent hard disk drives.

PROM   Programmable Read Only Memory. A chip that contains permanently embedded code. A PROM can be programmed only once. It cannot be erased and written over again.

PSTN   Public Switched Telephone Network. A PSTN is made of local networks, the exchange area networks, and the long-haul network that interconnects telephones and other communication devices on a worldwide basis.

PVC   Permanent Virtual Circuit. A dedicated circuit assigned to a subscriber of frame relay services.

PXE   Preboot eXecution Environment.

QAM   Quadrature Amplitude Modulation. A method of encoding data sent over a modem using a combination of frequency shifting and phase shift keying.

QBE   Query by Example. A database query languaged developed by IBM that was intended to make database searches easier for people who were less than literate when it came to computers.

QDOS   Quick and Dirty Operating System.

QIC   Quarter-Inch Cartridge. A tape format so named because of the size of the tape used (not the size of the cartridge). It uses technology not much different that a standard audiocassette recorder.

QoS   Quality of Service.

RAID   Redundant Array of Inexpensive (or Independent) Disks. Describes several different techniques for storing data across multiple hard disks.

RAM   Random access memory. A device used for short-term storage of data or instructions that are or will soon be required by the CPU in order for it to do its job.

RARP   Reverse Address Resolution Protocol.

RAS   (1) Remote Access Services. A method of authenticating and controlling access to the network by remote users. RAS was originally designed to support dial-up networking. (2) Row access strobe. A circuit that is part of the MCC responsible for locking onto the first row in a memory module in which the target data is located.

RBS   Robbed Bit Signaling. A technology used in voice communications in which a bit is "borrowed" from every eighth byte of data going over the wire for use by the telco.

RDP   Remote Desktop Protocol. A Microsoft protocol that allows remote administration of another computer over the network.

RDRAM   Rambus Dynamic Random Access Memory. A specialized form of memory manufactured by Rambus, Inc.

REQ   Request.

RF   Radio frequency. Electromagnetic waves operating between 10 kHz and 3 MHz propagated without guide (wire or cable) in free space.

RFC   Request for Comment. The method by which TCP/IP protocols and utilities are introduced and subsequently defined.

RFI   Radio frequency interference. Similar to EMI, except that it specifically defines wavelengths in the radio/television area of the electromagnetic spectrum.

RGB   Red, green, and blue. These are the primary colors and are used for many graphics devices such as computer monitors.

RIP   Routing Information Protocol. One of the earlier interior gateway protocols.

RIS   Remote Installation Services.

RISC   Reduced Instruction Set Computing. A processing method under which all instructions are of the same length and can be interpreted directly by the CPU.

RJ-45   Registered Jack number 45. An eight-conductor connector used with twisted-pair cable that looks very similar to a standard telephone jack, only larger.

RLL   Run Length Limited. One of the early data-encoding mechanisms used by hard disk drives.

ROM BIOS   Read Only Memory-Basic Input/Output Services. A chip on the motherboard that contains all the necessary code for jump-starting a computer from a dead off condition to the point where the OS can take over.

RSoP   Resultant Set of Policy. A feature in XP that allows the administrator to test the results of a new policy on a select group of guinea pigs before inflicting it on the entire network.

RST   Reset. Field or packet that initiates a breakdown of a session.

RTC   Real-Time Clock. The chip that keeps actual time, as humans keep track of it, on the systems.

RTMP   Routing Table Maintenance Protocol. The AppleTalk protocol that dynamically maintains routing table information.

RTS/CTS   Ready to Send/Clear to Send. A type of packet that indicates a device using CSMA/CA is about to transmit data.

RTT   Round trip time. The amount of time it takes a packet to go from host to host, and for the resultant ACK or NACK to return.

RTZ   Return to zero. A pulse signaling method used when moving data over copper wire.

SAM   Security Account Manager. An encrypted file stored within the registry of NT that hold the security attributes for all user and group accounts.

SAN   Storage Area Network. A cluster of hard disks connected to a network, usually via a fiber connection, that is used for storing large amounts of data. A SAN is typically used in a corporate environment where a lot of data is stored and a lot of people need to access that data, but security is an issue. Because a SAN is an independent device, it can be separately administered for both access and security.

SAP   Service Access Point. A logical address that moves data between OSI layers on the same machine.

SATA   Serial ATA.

SBCS   Single byte character set.

SCSI   Small Computer Systems Interface. An interface that allows several different types of devices to hook up to the same controller circuit.

SCTS   Security Configuration Tool Set.

SDH   Synchronous Digital Hierarchy. A high-speed telecommunications technology, very similar to Synchronous Optical Network (SONET), that combines multiple signals of different speeds and combines them into a single high-speed signal that moves over a fiber optics backbone.

SDK   Software Development Kit. A collection of utilities and programs provided by an OS manufacturer that makes the development of applications to run on their OS much easier.

SDRAM   Synchronous Dynamic Random Access Memory.

SE   Single-ended.

SECC   Single-Edge Cartridge Connector. A CPU-mounting slot that uses an edge-card design instead of pins.

SFC   System File Checker.

SFP   System File Protection. A Windows utility that prevents critical OS files from being deleted or overwritten; and if they are, the utility can replace them on the fly.

SGRAM   Synchronous Graphics RAM. Memory similar to SDRAM designed specifically for moving large blocks of contiguous data, in contrast to a large number of randomly selected small blocks of data.

SID   Security Identifier. A unique number generated and assigned to an object on the system or network that allows LSA to manage the security for that object.

SIM   Subscriber Identity Module. A smart card that is inserted into a mobile phone to get it going.

SIMD   Single Instruction, Multiple Data. A process by which a CPU can execute an instruction once, but can apply that instruction to several sets of data simultaneously.

SIMM   Single Inline Memory Module. A 30- or 72-pin memory module on which two opposing pins on the base perform the same function.

SIP   SCSI Interlocked Protocol.

SIPP   Single Inline Pin Package. An earlier memory module that put eight or nine DRAM chips on a single IC and was mounted into the system board by way of a single row of pins protruding from the base.

SLIP   Serial Line IP. An early protocol used to transmit IP packets over a serial connection.

SLR   (1) Scalable Linear Recording. A tape drive technology that uses linear recording technology and allows multiple channels of data to be stored across the width of the tape. (2) Single lens reflex. A digital or conventional film camera that has a complex viewing system that allows the user to compose and focus the image through the same lens that creates the image.

SMA   Subminiature assembly. One of several forms of connectors used with fiber optics cabling.

SMART   Self-Monitoring Analysis and Reporting Technology. Commands built into a hard disk interface that allow the drive to do some rather extensive self-diagnostics.

SMP   Symmetric multiprocessing. The ability of an OS to run OS or application code equally distributed across all available CPUs.

SMTP   Simple Mail Transport Protocol.

SNA   Systems Network Architecture. An IBM protocol for networking personal computers to mainframe computers.

SNMP   Simple Network Management Protocol.

SNPP   Simple Network Paging Protocol. A TCP/IP protocol for sending messages to pagers over the Internet.

SNSE   SuperNode Size Enhanced.

SO-DIMM   Small Outline Dual Inline Memory Module. A compact form of memory used primarily in notebook computers, but also seen in some video cards.

SOH   Start of header. A header is not always used but it is an important part of most protocols.

SOHO   Small office, home office.

SOL   (1) Simulation Oriented Language. (2) Simply out of luck.

SONET   Synchronous Optical Network. A high-speed telecommunications technology that combines multiple signals of different speeds and combines them into a single high-speed signal that moves over a fiber optics backbone.

SPC   SCSI Primary Commands.

SPDU   Service Protocol Data Unit. A small package of data used between OSI layers to request a specific service or activity.

SPEC   Standard Performance Evaluation Corporation. A company that specializes in the development of benchmarking applications.

SPGA Staggered Pin Grid Array. A pin-mounted CPU on which the pins are arranged in offsetting rows of pins that results in a pattern of diagonal rows.

SPI SCSI Parallel Interface.

SPS Standby power supply. A device that uses a generator to continue to provide power to an entire room or building after a total loss of electricity.

SQL Sequenced Query Language. An industry standard language for creating relational databases that can be accessed across multiple platforms.

SRAM Static RAM. A form of very high-speed memory typically used for cache.

SRM Security Reference Monitor. An NT service that compares a user's access token to the ACL and either allows or denies access to a specific resource accordingly.

SSA Serial Storage Architecture. A protocol used to connect disk drive arrays to servers via copper cabling.

SSAP Source Service Access point. The address from which a layer will receive data from an adjacent layer.

SSE Streaming SIMD extensions. The set of instructions that supports the execution of a single instruction on several sets of data at once.

SSP Serial Storage Protocol.

SSPI Security Support Provider Interface. A Windows service that handles user authentication transparently after the user's initial logon.

ST Straight tip. A connector used to hook up a fiber optics cable to a device. Also used to describe the Internet streaming protocol.

STP Shielded Twisted Pair.

STX Start of text. Pretty self-explanatory. It tells you that the next series of bits is the data being sent.

SYN Synchronization character. This makes sure all the bytes in the frame stick together as they move across the wire and then get reassembled in the right order at the other end. If no data is being transmitted, SYN blocks can be transmitted to keep the session alive.

T1 Digital trunk line. A circuit that combines up to twenty-four signals into one signal.

TCP Transmission Control Protocol.

TCP/IP Transmission Control Protocol/Internet Protocol. The protocol suite of the Internet.

TDM Time Division Multiplexing. The technology used by SONET and SDH to combine different signals of different speeds into a single high-speed transmission.

TDMA Time Division Multiple Access. Used to separate multiple conversation transmissions over a finite frequency allocation of through-the-air bandwidth; used to allocate a discrete amount of frequency bandwidth.

TDR Time-domain reflectometer. A sophisticated cable-testing device that works by sending a signal down the cable and measuring the amount of time it takes to return.

TFT Thin film transistor. An LCD that uses microscopically thin layers of transistors laid out in a grid pattern in a liquid crystal emulsion.

TFTP Trivial File Transfer Protocol. Protocol used for transferring files that are small or not necessarily critical.

TIA Telecommunications Industry Association.

TIFF Tagged Image File Format. An image file format used for storing digital images that does not result in any loss of quality.

TOC   Table of contents. On a compact disk, this is the part of the file system that lets the OS and device drivers know where specific information is located on a disk.

TSR   Terminate and stay resident. Any program that is launched and performs a task, but then remains in memory in case its services are required again.

TTL   Time to live. The amount of time a packet on a network has to reach its destination before it will be dropped.

U   Unit. Standard computer racks are measured in units. Each U is equal to 1.75 inches.

UART   Universal asynchronous receiver transmitter.

UDF   Universal Disk Format. A file system used on CD-ROM and DVD-ROMs.

UDMA   Ultra Direct Memory Access. A technology that allows an *ATAPI* device to transfer data directly to memory without CPU intervention.

UDP   User Datagram Protocol. Connectionless protocol that simply throws data onto the network and hopes that it gets to its destination.

UFS   Unix File System.

UHF   Ultra high frequency.

UI   User Interface.

UID   User identification. Identifies a specific user's account.

UMB   Upper Memory Block. A segment of memory created by an extended memory manager in the address range between 640 K and 1 MB of conventional memory.

UPNP   Universal Plug and Play. Revised PnP standards that are constantly monitored and updated by the UPNP Forum.

UPS   Uninterruptible power supply. A device that uses a bank of batteries to continue to provide current to the devices plugged in when there has been a total loss of electricity.

URL   Universal Resource Locator. A user-friendly text string that identifies a website.

USB   Universal Serial Bus. A moderate-speed bus that allows 127 devices to share a single chain and a 12-Mb/s bandwidth.

UTP   Unshielded Twisted Pair.

UV   Ultraviolet. Wavelengths of light beyond the upper range of the visible light spectrum.

UVGA   Ultra VGA. High-resolution video graphics array (VGA).

VBR   Volume boot record. Similar to the MBR, this is the descriptor for a specific volume on a portioned disk.

VC-SDRAM   Virtual Channel SDRAM. A newer form of memory that gives each operational application its own address space and path to move data back and forth so they don't compete for bandwidth.

VDD   Virtual device driver. A piece of software running within an OS that emulates a hardware device driver.

VESA   Video Electronics Standards Association. The organization charged with maintaining standards surrounding graphics adapters and monitors.

VFAT   Virtual File Allocation Table. A software driver that emulates the file allocation tables stored on a hard disk and prevents applications from making direct calls to the hardware.

VGA   Video Graphics Array. The most commonly used video display in use today.

VHF   Very high frequency.

VID-VRM   Voltage identifier, voltage regulator module. A device that automatically locks on to the correct voltage of the installed chip and configures the device accordingly.

VLB   VESA Local Bus. A 32-bit, 33-Mhz bus designed by VESA to address issues surrounding the transfer of large amounts of graphics data. VLB was designed to be backwardly compatible with ISA.

VLIF   Very Low Insertion Force. One of three forms of CPU socket that requires no special tools to install or remove the CPU.

VMM   (1) Virtual Machine Manager. A piece of software running within an OS that creates, maintains, and breaks down in memory an environment that emulates an actual computer. (2) Virtual memory manager. A piece of software running within an OS that creates and manages the swap file on a hard drive.

VMS   Virtual Memory System. An OS written by DEC.

VoIP   Voice over IP. A TCP/IP protocol for encapsulating an audio signal over in Internet connection.

VPN   Virtual Private Network. A secure connection between two devices over the Internet.

VR   Vertical refresh. The number of times per second a monitor regenerates the image on the screen.

VRAM   Video RAM. A form of memory designed specifically for video cards that has separate input and output busses so that on any given clock cycle, data can be moving both in and out of the chip.

WAN   Wide area network.

WDM   Windows Driver Model.

WHQL   Windows Hardware Quality Lab.

WINS   Windows Internet Name Service.

WMI   Windows Management Instrumentation.

WORM   Write once, read many. A recording technology that write protects the contents of the medium in order to prevent that data from being erased or overwritten.

WSH   Windows Script Host.

WTX   Workstation Technology eXtended. One of several form factors whose objective was to keep the system as small as possible.

XGA   Extended Graphics Array. A proprietary display created by IBM.

XMS   Extended Memory Specification.

XT   Extended Technology. The PC-XT was the second generation personal computer released by IBM.

Y2K   Year 2000. This was the name given to the so-called calendar bug that was going to send the world back to the ice age at 12:00PM on December 31, 1999.

YB   yottabyte. 1,208,925,819,614,629,174,706,176 bytes.

Yb   yottabit. 1,208,925,819,614,629,174,706,176 bits.

ZIF   Zero Insertion Force. One of three forms of CPU sockets that requires no special tools to install or remove the CPU.